John's Gospel and the formula behind the myth of Jesus

Greg O'Shea

Copyright © 2016 Greg O'Shea

All rights reserved worldwide.

No part of the book may be copied or changed in any format, sold, or used in a way other than what is outlined in this book, under any circumstances, without the prior written permission of the publisher.

Publisher:
Inspiring Publishers
P.O. Box 159, Calwell, ACT Australia 2905
Email: publishaspg@gmail.com
http://www.inspiringpublishers.com

National Library of Australia Cataloguing-in-Publication entry

Author: O'Shea, Greg

Title: **John's Gospel and the Formula Behind the Myth of Jesus**/*Greg O'Shea*.

ISBN: 9781925477122 (paperback)

Notes: Includes bibliographical references and index.

Subjects: Jesus Christ—Divinity.
        Bible. John—Criticism, interpretation etc.
        Christianity—Origin.
        Christianity and culture.

Dewey Number: 226.5

Contents

Foreword 7

PART 1: *The Book of Formation* **and John's Gospel**

    Introduction 12

    Chapter 1 37

    Chapter 2 45

    Chapter 3 48

    Chapter 4 52

    Chapter 5 59

    Chapter 6 63

    Chapter 7 69

    Chapter 8 75

    Chapter 9 82

    Chapter 10 88

Chapter 11 96

Chapter 12 103

Chapter 13 107

Chapter 14 114

Chapter 15 119

Chapter 16 123

Chapter 17 125

Chapter 18 127

Chapter 19 134

Chapter 20 140

Chapter 21 142

PART 2: The Qabalistic Tree of Life and John's Gospel

Introduction 144

'alef 190

Chapter 1 197

Chapter 2 212

Chapter 3 224

Chapter 4 232

Chapter 5 237

Chapter 6 247

Chapter 7 250

Chapter 8 255

Chapter 9 262

Chapter 10 264

Chapter 11 266

Chapter 12 269

Chapter 13 276

Chapter 14 280

Chapter 15 288

Chapter 16 293

Chapter 17 300

Chapter 18 306

Chapter 19 313

Chapter 20 319

Chapter 21 328

PART 3: Genesis and John's Gospel 337

PART 4: A Pictorial Guide to John's Gospel 371

PART 5: *Epilogue* 431

Appendix 1 455

Appendix 2 463

Appendix 3 482

Bibliography 489

Index 500

Foreword

The role played by Scripture and the way it is approached vary greatly across the spectrum of Christian sectarian belief. For most Christians the Bible at least provides a code of ethical conduct upon which to model social relationships. Scripture is also generally seen as a repository of theological truth and revelation about the unseen world and invisible aspects of human nature. Many turn to the Bible for information about the nature of man and the physical world that is normally the ambit of science – we still see battles fought over the age of the universe, whether life arose by direct divine intervention or as the result of natural processes, even whether the earth goes around the sun.

Most importantly, the Christian Scriptures perform the crucial function of providing a record for a religion inextricably tied to a version of history. It is no coincidence that the first book of the Bible, Genesis, gives an account of the world's creation, while the last, Revelation, describes its end. Early theologians like St Augustine and Eusebius declared that Christianity had existed from the dawn of the human race, receiving only its name with the coming of its founder. Yet at its core lies not a set of timeless theological and metaphysical truths and ethical principles, but a belief that certain things took place at definite times and locations on this earth to real people. Since they constitute the sole witness for many of the events central to the Christian faith, Scriptures are absolutely indispensable as historical documents. We are totally reliant upon the Gospels for information about the life story of Jesus, even evidence of his existence.

Some denominations consider the Bible infallible and sufficient for its own interpretation, its meaning self-evident, others lay emphasis on the extrascriptural traditions of their church, or on the ability of their church to interpret the Bible. Nevertheless, the vast majority of Christians approach questions about the historicity of their sacred writings in a similar fashion.

In *De Principis*, Origen, one of the earliest writers to broach the difficulties caused by the Bible's presenting spiritual ideas and mundane facts together, argued that most problems are due to a too literal interpretation of Scripture, which he says has a spirit and a soul as well as a body. Only if self-contradiction and absurdity stand immovably in the way, is a passage to be understood as pure allegory. Yet this is, he says, almost always – an opinion that made him unpopular in some circles. The Holy Spirit, he says, frequently inspired statements that defy all literal interpretation, just in order to indicate that certain passages are purely symbolic. Although it never occurred to Origen to apply his ideas to the New Testament, the Gospels are filled with more allegory and less historical truth than anything ever written.

John's Gospel and the Formula behind the Myth of Jesus is about a set of ideas that largely dictated the form and content of the Gospel According to John, and influenced the Gospels of Matthew, Mark and Luke. While all these are far from what they seem to be at first sight, John's Gospel is especially so, since its author was completely devoted to painting a picture of Jesus as a type of cosmic figure. The way in which John goes about this will surprise and disquiet many, for he employs symbolism drawn from several unlikely quarters: astrology, the yearly cycle of Jewish religious festivals, and Qabalah.

Christians have long viewed astrology as a mixture of idolatry and superstition, quite alien to anything Christian. It is clear, moreover, the Powers in Space or Rulers of the Cosmic Elements that Jesus came to conquer (Matthew xxiv 29; Mark xiii 25; Romans viii 38; 1 Corinthians ii 6-8; Ephesians iii 10, iv 12; Colossians i 16, ii 15, 20; Galatians iv 3, 9) are nothing other than the planets of astrology and the dark spiritual forces behind them. These Ruling Powers of the Present Age are thoroughly inimical to Christianity and its message, which is essentially about ending their dominion. John's reason for turning to astrology is simply that it enables his portrayal of Jesus as a cosmic figure, one who contains within himself the totality of forces and potencies from which the universe is knit.

The intricacies of the Jewish calendar are another subject most Christians are happy to ignore. Many Jewish festivals are not well described in the Jewish Scriptures, some are not mentioned at all, nor does the New Testament does provide any insight into their customs and liturgy. That they should turn out to play a pivotal role in the story of Jesus' ministry is unexpected. Not only that, John is sometimes considered to be the most antisemitic among the Four Evangelists. While the Gospels of Matthew, Mark and Luke have Jesus denounce specific groups, such as Pharisees, teachers of the Law, scribes, Sadducees, in John's Gospel Jesus' harshest attacks are directed at Jews generally, not a particular group, for John's Gospel, it is believed, was written at a time when Jews and Christians were actively distancing themselves from each other. And yet John is obsessed with the Jewish calendar. Again, John's

Gospel offers a sort of replacement theology: Jesus is set in the context of Jewish religious festivals just in order to show that they are being superseded.

Doctrines of the Qabalah, a form of Jewish mysticism and theosophy, also figure very prominently in John's Gospel. The esoteric philosophy and methodology of Qabalah are far removed from everything Christian. Of all the varied streams of thought within Judaism, Qabalah must be least likely to leave its mark on Christian Scriptures. Again, John's employment of qabalistic symbolism is geared to the depiction of Jesus as a cosmic figure, who unites in his own person the fundamental potencies of the universe.

The presentation of Jesus in this way comes at a steep price. First, John's cosmology is set before us in a vivid and detailed way, so that his concept of who Jesus is and what he is about is indissolubly tied to his highly specific view of the cosmos.

In addition, because John is extremely systematic one can perceive a definite formula that underlies the Gospels, the story they tell can be seen to be highly contrived. The proportion devoted to allegory is so high – more than two-thirds of John's Gospel – that it dashes all hope of finding historical truth. John's Gospel looks like the myths that New Testament writers warned against (1 Timothy i 4, iv 7; Titus i 14; 2 Peter i 16).

Anyone interested in the history of Christianity at its inception will find this book offers unique insight into the way the first generation of Christians viewed Jesus, and how the four canonical Gospels were composed. Anyone interested in the history of astrology or history of Qabalah will see state of the art as it existed in the first and second centuries CE. John's astrological ideas are surprisingly similar to those which modern astrologers hold. And although it is commonly thought that Qabalah was largely an innovation of

Jews living in France and Spain during the twelfth and thirteenth centuries, the author of John's Gospel operates with a nearly identical symbolic lexicon and with a high level of sophistication.

Knowledge of these matters has been around for some time, and in fact, there are commentaries on this secret dating from the fifteenth century – it is just that they have not been recognised as such.

While Christianity claims to have no hidden teachings, at one time it did possess arcane doctrines, and these are of a type usually associated with occult belief systems or practices. Modern Christians have, therefore, a vastly different outlook from first and second century Christians, who had a preoccupation with matters more theosophical than theological. It is almost as though were followers of another religion, yet these teachings are not the oral traditions of some heretical sect, but are intrinsic to Christianity's scriptural canon. Nor are they confined to the Fourth Gospel – the Gospels of Matthew, Mark and Luke are littered with details that could only have come from John's metaphysical perspective. If you think you may find it disturbing to see the historical Jesus vanish only to be replaced by a system of doctrines and ideas utterly removed from normative Christian belief, you should be warned that may be happier not to read this book.

Part 1:
The Book of Formation and John's Gospel

Sefer Yezirah or *The Book of Formation* is a short tract of obscure origins, which, although not widely known to Christians, left its mark on the Christian scriptures in a most extraordinary way: it served as a blueprint for the Gospel According to John, and had a profound if less direct influence on the Synoptic Gospels.

Generally considered the earliest example of metaphysical speculation in Hebrew, *Sefer Yezirah* claims a most venerable and ancient source, the biblical patriarch Abraham, as the author of its central teachings, and is therefore sometimes known as *The Midrash of Our Father Abraham*. Several legends portray the populace of Ur, Abraham's birthplace, as given over to worship of the hosts of heaven, with Terah, Abraham's father, the most fanatical idolater of all, so that Abraham's departure from Ur of the Chaldees becomes a metaphor for a shift in his theological outlook. *Sefer Yezirah*, lying at the heart of this tradition, presents itself as a distillation of the wisdom that led Abraham away from an astral polytheism or Sabaism to the monotheistic faith with which he is associated.

Although it appeared at a time when Jewish mystical philosophy was largely hidden from view, *Sefer Yeẓirah* belongs to the same stream of thought that produced twelfth and thirteenth-century classics of the Qabalah like *Sefer ha Bahir* (*The Book of Brilliance*) and *Sefer ha Zohar* (*The Book of Splendour*).

In the past, Western scholarship has dated the composition of *Sefer Yeẓirah* from as early as the second century BCE to as late as the ninth century CE. If doubts arise it is because works of this nature are often orally transmitted for considerable time before being set down in writing. The earliest manuscripts may have been brief notes intended for personal study, or to be shared among small groups of people. Modern scholarship tends to date *Sefer Yeẓirah* in its present form to between the second and sixth centuries CE.[intro.1] We shall conclusively demonstrate, however, the later estimates of *Sefer Yeẓirah*'s composition to be untenable.

One reason for the mystery surrounding its origins is that, although the Talmud and other works speak of a *Sefer Yeẓirah*, we have no certainty that past writers were discussing the same text we possess. Evidently, *Sefer Yeẓirah* was part of a much larger body of allied literature with the general name *Work of Creation* or *Work of the Book of Genesis* (*Ma'aseh Bereshith*) or *Halakah on Creation* (*Bereshith Hilkoth*). It could be that what we now know as *Sefer Yeẓirah* is merely an important commentary on the original, now lost. Hints that our *Sefer Yeẓirah* resembles the tract earlier writers were familiar with began to surface from the fifth century onwards. From passing comments of several witnesses we know, for instance, that a preoccupation with letter-combinations and the employment of a technical term, *sefiroth*, which are distinctive features of our text, were also present in the early manuscripts.

One legend dates the first written version of *Sefer Yezirah* to about 120 CE, ascribing it to the hand of Rabbi Akiba ben Joseph, a famous sage who is sometimes accredited with *The Alphabet of Rab Akiba*, a work dealing with some of same matters *Sefer Yezirah* concerns itself with. The Talmud acclaims him as one of only four learned rabbis of his generation to fathom the depths of the esoteric knowledge hidden within scripture. Of the others, one succumbed to apostasy, one went mad, one lost his life. Akiba alone escaped unscathed. He is said to have been a pupil of Rab Nehunia ben HaQana, to whom authorship of *Sefer ha Bahir*, one of the most important early works in qabalistic literature, is often ascribed.

Whatever its origins, *Sefer Yezirah*, in the form we know it, certainly enjoyed increasingly wide circulation in Jewish circles from the tenth century onwards, until it was published in printed form in the sixteenth century, when the first Latin translations also appeared.

Letters of the alphabet as cosmic powers

Sefer Yezirah is about two and a half thousand words of text, oracular in conciseness in some parts, while needlessly and annoyingly repetitive in others, and full of ambiguity especially in vowelless Hebrew. First and foremost, *Sefer Yezirah* is a book about correspondences of the Hebrew letters of the alphabet, *The Letters of Our Father Abraham* being one of its alternative titles. It is here our interest chiefly lies, for the author of According to John uses these correspondences quite extensively in order to construct and organise his Gospel.

Hebrew occupies a very elevated position in *Sefer Yezirah*, which asserts that God's covenant with Abraham included the stipulation that he and his descendants adopt the language in perpetuity.

TABLE 1: Astrological and calendar month attributions common to all versions of *Sefer Yezirah*

Letter of alphabet	Astrological attribution	Calendar month
'alef	Air	
beth	**planet**	
gimel	**planet**	
daleth	**planet**	
heh	Aries	Nisan
vau	Taurus	Iyar
zayin	Gemini	Sivan
heth	Cancer	Tammuz
teth	Leo	Av
yod	Virgo	Elul
kaf	**planet**	
lamed	Libra	Tishri
mem	Water	
nun	Scorpio	Marheshvan
samekh	Sagittarius	Kislev
'ayin	Capricorn	Tevet
peh	**planet**	
zaddi	Aquarius	Shevat
quf	Pisces	Adar
resh	**planet**	
shin	Fire	
tau	**planet**	

The essential conception behind *Sefer Yezirah* is that the twenty-two letters of the Hebrew alphabet represent fundamental cosmic principles or ultimate realities in creation. It speaks of 'twenty-two foundation letters', since it views the letters of the Hebrew alphabet just as chemistry views the chemical elements, or as physics elementary particles. As Scholem remarks, the idea is found elsewhere: to the Greek philosophers, *stoicheion* meant both 'letter of the alphabet' and 'cosmic element'.[intro.2] *Sefer Yezirah*'s approach is to make the Hebrew alphabet conterminous with an 'astrological alphabet'. Since astrology provides seven planets and twelve zodiacal constellations, in order to make up the complement of twenty-two the author finds it necessary to postulate only a triad of elements: fire, air and water.

Throughout *Sefer Yezirah*, the Hebrew letters are understood to be divided into three groups: three 'mother' letters, seven 'double' letters, and twelve 'simple' letters. It is important to understand that this threefold division of Hebrew letters, which is crucial to *Sefer Yezirah*, is partly nonsense, but not entirely so. The seven double letters (*beth*, *gimel*, *daleth*, *kaf*, *peh*, *resh* and *tau*) anciently had the distinction of being articulated in two ways, the presence or absence of a dot called *daghesh* indicating which pronunciation is in effect in any particular case.[intro.3] This phonetic-orthographic peculiarity of the seven 'double' letters is the only feature of *Sefer Yezirah*'s classification that has objective validity. There is, for example, no real basis for dividing the remaining fifteen letters into three 'mothers' and twelve 'simples'.

For the most part, the author concentrates upon three different scales or levels in which the correspondences operate: the first is the universe or macrocosm, the second is the calendar year, and the third is man, the microcosm.

In the universe, the three mother letters are said to correspond to three primordial elements: air, water and fire. The seven double letters answer to the seven 'planets' known to the ancients: Saturn, Jupiter, Mars, Sun, Venus, Mercury and Moon. The twelve simple letters denote the twelve signs of the zodiac.

In the calendar, the three mother letters correspond to the three seasons of the year: temperate, hot and cold. The seven double letters answer to the seven days of the week. The twelve simple letters denote the twelve months.

In a human being, the three mother letters correspond to the three sections of the body: head, thorax, and abdomen. The seven double letters answer to seven human conditions namely wisdom (and folly), life (and death), fertility (and sterility), wealth (and poverty), peace (and strife), beauty (and ugliness), dominion (and servitude) – the 'double' nature of the letter causing it to manifest as pairs of opposites. The seven double letters additionally manifest as the seven orifices in the human head. The twelve simple letters denote twelve basic activities of the organism: speaking, thinking, walking, seeing, hearing, working, coupling, smelling, sleeping, feeling anger, tasting, laughing, and also manifest as the twelve chief organs of the body.

Qabalistic ideas in *Sefer Yezirah*

As well as dealing the letters of the alphabet, *Sefer Yezirah* also refers to a system of correspondences of the numbers one to ten. Qabalistic numerology, the doctrine of the ten sefiroth or divine emanations, which became a subject of paramount importance in later works, is not well developed. In fact, *Sefer Yezirah* lumps the ten sefiroth and twenty-two letters into a single category, 'thirty-two marvellous paths of Wisdom'. *Sefer Yezirah* does not give away a great deal regarding the sefiroth, not even listing their names, although it hints at some of their common titles. In comparison to other sources it divulges little anything about their attributes, their relationship to one another, or their relationship to the letters of the alphabet. The arrangement of the sefiroth in a Tree, which greatly preoccupied later qabalists, is completely absent. That it does mention the sefiroth, if only passingly, is what marks it as qabalistic. Modern scholarship has even questioned the extent to which its doctrines are in line with those found in works of classical Qabalah that came centuries later. However, we shall show in Part 2 that in the second century CE there already existed a complete system integrating *Sefer Yezirah*'s ideas about astrology and the calendar with the correspondences of sefiroth which are known only from later qabalistic works like *Sefer ha Bahir* (*The Book of Brilliance*) and *Sefer ha Zohar* (*The Book of Splendour*).

Differences in manuscript traditions

In the tenth century, when *Sefer Yezirah* was circulating in manuscript, the textual tradition had already begun to diverge, giving rise to several slightly different recensions. Since *Sefer Yezirah* exists in more manuscript copies than any other work in Hebrew with the exception of the Torah, it is hardly surprising that variations in the written text emerged. Four recensions, which are associated with the names of Saadia Gaon (*Saadia Version of Sefer Yezirah*), Shabtai Donnolo (*Long Version of Sefer Yezirah*), and Donash ibn Tamim (*Short Version of Sefer Yezirah*), an Rabbi Eliahu Gaon of Vilna (*Gra Version of Sefer Yezirah*), eventually became most widely accepted.

All versions agree on which letters are the three mother letters, and also on their attributions on each of the different scales or levels on which they manifest. *'Alef* is always air, *mem* always water, and *shin* always fire, and so on.

All versions agree on which letters are the twelve simple letters, and relate them to the twelve signs of the zodiac and months of the year, twelve basic activities, and twelve chief organs of the human body. However, one version (*Donash Ibn Tamim's Short Version*) does not list the specific sign of the zodiac or month corresponding to a given letter. Later commentators follow the most obvious and natural course: the sequence of signs begins with Aries, and the sequence of months begins with the first month of the religious calendar (which falls when the sun is passing through Aries).

When it comes to the seven double letters, all versions agree that they comprise *beth, gimel, daleth, kaf, peh, resh,* and *tau*, and relate them to the seven heavens, the seven earths, the seven planets, the seven days of the week, and the seven gates of the human body. But the specific attributions are not expressly given by Donash, nor do other versions agree with one another about them. And unfortunately, many versions of the book contain what appear to be internal inconsistencies. For instance, the order of planets given in one place may differ from that given in another place or be incompatible with the order of the seven positive and negative qualities that are given to explain them.

The astrological and calendar attributions are summarised in the table 1 above, which takes into account the differences in the manuscript tradition. As can be seen, these are at variance only in the attribution of the seven double letters to the seven planets. With respect to the other attributions, those of elements and signs of the zodiac, unanimous accord prevails.

(The month Nisan falls more or less when the sun passes through the sign Aries; the month Iyar more or less when the sun passes through Taurus; and so on. See Appendix 1 for the relationship between the Jewish months and the sun's passage through the signs of the zodiac.)

The attributions of the letters to the planets and signs of the zodiac is of key importance, because these come with a ready made set of correspondences thanks to astrology. Each of the planets and signs of the zodiac has a huge network of associations, for astrology tries to provide an all-embracing mirror of the universe, resolving everything in human experience in terms of planets and signs of the zodiac. The other correspondences of the letters that *Sefer Yezirah* lists (such as wisdom-and-folly, life-and-death etc. for the double letters, and speaking, thinking, etc. for the simple letters) do not have the same universal scope as the astrological attributions, from which they may even have been derived, and if so, they are somewhat redundant.

As *Sefer Yezirah* notes, there are 5,040 possible ways of assigning the seven double letters to the planets. Despite the multiplicity of translations and commentaries, however, the seven doubles are commonly attributed to the planets in only a handful of ways in the literature. In his translation of the book, Westcott gives three different schemes, which represent the three important manuscript traditions. He also mentions the existence of yet another variant, which he declines to give, though he was undoubtedly familiar with it. At the time of his writing, this scheme, Westcott says, had not yet been published.[intro.4]

The first way of assigning the planets takes them in their geocentric order as understood by the ancients. It is perhaps the version the most frequently encountered. The *Long Version* (associated with the name Shabtai Donnolo, 10th century) and *Saadia Version* (Saadia Gaon 10th century) both have this order of planets. Mayer

TABLE 2: *Sefer Yezirah's* attributions of the double letters to the planets according to various Western authors as known to Dr. Wynn Westcott (1893).

Letter	Long	Gra	Kircher	Golden Dawn
beth	Saturn	Moon	Sun	Mercury
gimel	Jupiter	Mars	Venus	Moon
daleth	Mars	Sun	Mercury	Venus
kaf	Sun	Venus	Moon	Jupiter
peh	Venus	Mercury	Saturn	Mars
resh	Mercury	Saturn	Jupiter	Sun
tau	Moon	Jupiter	Mars	Saturn

Lambert published a French translation with these attributions in 1891.

The second way of assigning the planets is quite mysterious. It is difficult to understand how this order was arrived at. It is neither the geocentric order of planets, nor can it be derived from the attributions of the planets to the days of the week (Sunday to the Sun, Monday to the Moon, Tuesday to Mars, etc.). This is the order in found the *Gra Version* (associated with Rabbi Eliahu Gaon of Vilna 18th century). Isidore Kalisch published an English translation of this version in 1877.

The third way of assigning the planets has the same cyclical order as the first, but begins with the Sun instead of Saturn. Kircher took these attributions from a particular recension of the *Short Version* to which Donash ibn Tamim provided a commentary. This evidently listed the planets without expressly giving their correspondences;

the order in which the planets are listed was understood to be indicative of the attribution. Kircher's *Oedipus Aegyptiacus* had a huge impact on Western, non-Jewish thought, so that over the next four centuries his attributions were reprinted hundreds of times, though Jewish commentators believe them to be based on a misunderstanding.

The fourth column shows the scheme first published by Aleister Crowley in 1909, though it was doubtlessly known to other members of the Golden Dawn, a semisecret organisation to which Crowley belonged, and of which Wynn Westcott was a founding member. It may have also been known to Eliphaz Levi, a French occultist of the eighteenth century. Crowley certainly did not invent these attributions of the double letters. He received them among other confidential papers upon reaching a certain level within the Golden Dawn, and was bound by oaths of secrecy not to divulge them. It is the scheme to which Westcott was discretely referring when he cryptically noted the existence of another way of assigning the double letters to the planets. It is based not on any manuscript tradition of *Sefer Yezirah*, but another work, which some have taken to be essentially a pictorial version of *Sefer Yezirah*, and to which we shall return later.

Stephen Langton and the twenty-one chapters of According to John

The reason for our interest in *Sefer Yezirah* is that According to John, the fourth book of the New Testament, is based upon it, making extensive use of its system of correspondences in order to create the whole narrative. The table summarises the relationship between According to John and the correspondences of *Sefer Yezirah*. As for the attribution of the seven double letters to the planets, it is seen that the one used in the Fourth Gospel happens to be identical to the one first published by Crowley in *Liber 777*, which he obtained from the Golden Dawn.

The most obvious feature of John's scheme is its simplicity. Each of the twenty-one chapters of According to John is devoted to the correspondences belonging to a single letter of the alphabet; the letters are in their normal alphabetical order. The straightforwardness of the Gospel's chapter by chapter organisation is pleasantly surprising, since According to John, it must be remembered, was not explicitly divided into chapters in its original form. In the early thirteenth century, Stephen Langton, later Archbishop of Canterbury, went through all the books in the New Testament, and divided them into chapters. It is the system universally employed today.

In the case of the Fourth Gospel, Langton merely made use of breaks in the narrative – changes of scenery, of subject, and of characters – and guided by these alone, he divided the Gospel into twenty-one sections or chapters. We have no reason to suspect he was aware that According to John conceals a series of astrological and qabalistic motifs. He merely organised the text in the way any intelligent person would find natural and intuitive. Nevertheless, if we divide the Gospel into sections based on the astrological and qabalistic attributions, we get the same result as Langton. I have therefore not needed to change the chapter divisions as Langton proposed them in any substantial way. John really intended the Gospel be understood in this way.

A conspicuous feature of the scheme is that According to John has only twenty-one chapters, while there are twenty-two letters in the Hebrew alphabet, for the Gospel contains no chapter answering to *'alef*, the first letter of the alphabet. The reasons for this can be deferred, and will be discussed in Part 2 of this book.

TABLE 3:

Letter	Astrological attribution	Calendar month	According to John
'alef	Air		(no chapter)
beth	Mercury		chapter 1
gimel	Moon		chapter 2
daleth	Venus		chapter 3
heh	Aries	Nisan	chapter 4
vau	Taurus	Iyar	chapter 5
zayin	Gemini	Sivan	chapter 6
ḥeth	Cancer	Tammuz	chapter 7
ṭeth	Leo	Av	chapter 8
yod	Virgo	Elul	chapter 9
kaf	Jupiter		chapter 10
lamed	Libra	Tishri	chapter 11
mem	Water		chapter 12
nun	Scorpio	Ḥeshvan	chapter 13
samekh	Sagittarius	Kislev	chapter 14
'ayin	Capricorn	Tevet	chapter 15
peh	Mars		chapter 16
ẓaddi	Aquarius	Shevat	chapter 17
quf	Pisces	Adar	chapter 18
resh	Sun		chapter 19
shin	Fire		chapter 20
tau	Saturn		chapter 21

Style of John

In effect, John takes his readers on a whirlwind tour of his metaphysical universe, a world which is ruled over by the archons, the cosmic powers, among whom the chief are twenty-two in number and denotable by the letters of the Hebrew alphabet. As he progresses chapter by chapter through the Gospel, Jesus, chameleon-like, takes on the colour of his immediate surroundings in order to arrogate every symbolic attribute to himself. In the end, everything has become a symbol of Jesus, who assimilates the full complement of the cosmic powers within his own being. Jesus becomes Lord of Every Jewish Feast in the calendar from Passover to Purim, Lord of the Planetary Spheres and Zodiac. Jesus' theophany becomes all-encompassing.

John's approach to weaving references to *Sefer Yezirah* into his Gospel is easy to follow. Chapters which answer to months of the year contain references to Jewish feasts falling in that month, or else to key features of the zodiacal sign, while chapters answering to planets contain references to key qualities of those planets, or easily recognisable personifications of the planets.

The sixth chapter of the Gospel, for instance, answers to the month of Sivan. The Feast of Loaves is the major religious festival of the month. The chapter, in consequence, abounds in references to bread. The initial section of the chapter describes the miraculous multiplication of the loaves; the remainder is filled with references to bread; most significantly, Jesus identifies himself with bread three times:

> Jesus said to them, 'I am the bread of life...' vi 35
>
> 'I am the bread of life.' vi 48
>
> 'I am the living bread that came down from heaven.' vi 51.

Other minor details subtly point toward the Feast of Loaves. That the festival falls on the anniversary of to the reception of the Torah on Sinai is a major theme of Jewish literature. The terror of the Israelites on hearing God's voice, and their request not to be forced to listen to it (Exodus xx 16) is alluded to in the Gospel in:

> Many of his disciples upon hearing this said, 'This is a hard teaching. Who can listen to it?' vi 60.

A Jewish custom of decorating houses and synagogues with greenery, even grass, during the holiday in order to commemorate that when the Torah was given Sinai suddenly became verdant becomes:

> There was much grass in the place. So the men sat down, about five thousand in number. vi 10.

Pentecost 'Fiftieth', an alternative name the holiday, since it falls fifty days after Passover, is reflected in the number five thousand.

John's use of astrological symbolism is as simple as his use of the calendar of religious holidays. An easy example is seen in the eighth chapter of the Gospel which corresponds to the sign Leo. Since the associated horoscopic mansion is said to rule casual romantic liaisons, premarital and extramarital love affairs, John opens with the moral dilemma of a woman caught in the very act of adultery. The theme appears again later in the chapter when the Pharisees taunt Jesus with references to his supposed illegitimacy,

> 'Where is your father?' viii 19

> 'We are not born out of fornication'. viii 41

prompting Jesus to retort with,

> '... you desire to act out the lusts of your father ...' viii 44.

This horoscopic house is connected with personal liberty and freedom from restraint, an idea which features in:

> 'The truth will set you free'. viii 32

> 'How can you say, "You will be free"?'. viii 33

> 'So then, if the Son sets you free, you will be truly free'. viii 36.

The same house is also connected with children and offspring. In the Gospel this manifests in the argument between the Jews and Jesus about their claim to be children of Abraham:

> 'We are Abraham's offspring and have never been in servitude to anyone'. viii 33

> 'I know you are Abraham's offspring ...' viii 37

> Jesus said to them, 'If you were the children of Abraham, you would do the works of Abraham.' viii 39

> Jesus said, 'If God were your father you would love me, for I proceeded forth from God and came from him.' viii 42.

As for those chapters which contain symbolism related to the planets, John's style is seen in xix, which is devoted to the Sun. The Sun is traditionally connected with leadership and power; the king is one of its commonest personifications. The crown is an important solar emblem in its own right, even apart from its connection with royalty, the Sun being often depicted with a corona or crown of rays. In the Gospel, accordingly:

And having woven a crown of thorns, the soldiers placed it on his head, and they put a purple robe around him, and said, 'Hail, King of the Jews!', and they struck him. xix 2-3.

Then Jesus came out, wearing the crown of thorns and the purple robe. xix 5.

And after that Pilate sought to release him, but the Jews cried out, saying, 'If you release this man, you are not a friend of Caesar. Whoever makes himself a king speaks against Caesar'. xix 12.

And it was the preparation day for Passover, and about the sixth hour. And he says to the Jews, 'Behold your King!'.

But they cried out, 'Take him away, take him away, crucify him'.

Pilate says to them, 'Shall I crucify your King?'.

The chief priests answered, 'We have no king except Caesar'. xix 14-15

And Pilate wrote a sign, and put it on the cross. And it had been written: Jesus of Nazareth the King of the Jews. Many of the Jews read the sign, for the place where Jesus was crucified was near the city, and it was written in Hebrew, Greek, and Latin. Then the chief priests of the Jews said to Pilate, 'Do not write, "the King of the Jews", but rather, "He said, 'I am King of the Jews'".' xix 19-21.

The Sun is connected with fame, and personified in the celebrity, the centre of attention. Crucifixion is, of course, a most public form of execution, the condemned man being stripped naked and held up on display for all to see and jeer at. The idea also appears in:

> 'Behold, I bring him out to you …' xix 4
>
> 'Behold, the man…' xix 5
>
> 'Behold, your king…' xix 14
>
> 'Behold, your son'. xix 26
>
> 'They will look upon him whom they have pierced'. xix 37.

Several features of John's handling of astrological symbolism are noteworthy. When it comes to the signs of the zodiac, John prefers to use symbolism related to the corresponding house or mansion of the heavens. While Aries is not synonymous with the first house, nor Taurus with the second house, and so on, there does nevertheless exist a deep connection between Aries and the first house, Taurus and the second house, and so on. John acts as though zodiacal signs and horoscopic houses were synonymous.

Another minor quirk of John's system is that each of the twelve houses is allotted to a two hour period of the day, beginning at dawn:

> **Aries,** the first two-hour period of the day beginning at dawn, about 6 a.m. to 8 a.m.;
>
> **Taurus,** the second two-hour period of the day, about 8 a.m. to 10 a.m.;
>
> **Gemini,** the third two-hour period of the day, about 10 a.m. to 12 noon;

Cancer, the fourth two-hour period of the day, about 12 noon to 2 p.m.;

Leo, the fifth two-hour period of the day, about 2 p.m. to 4 p.m.;

Virgo, the sixth two-hour period of the day, about 4 p.m. to 6 p.m.;

Libra, the seventh two-hour period of the day, about 6 p.m. to 8 p.m.;

Scorpio, the eighth two-hour period of the day, about 8 p.m. to 10 p.m.;

Sagittarius, the ninth two-hour period of the day, about 10 p.m. to 12 midnight;

Capricorn, the tenth two-hour period of the day, about 12 midnight to 2 a.m.;

Aquarius, eleventh two-hour period of the day, about 2 a.m. to 4 a.m.;

Pisces, the twelfth two-hour period of the day, about 4 a.m. to 6 a.m..

Since astrology came to us through Greek hands, it is not surprising that the planets took over many attributes of the classical gods. This is true in the Fourth Gospel, in which elements of classical myth colour astrological ideas. An example can be seen in the tenth chapter, where the wolf (x 12), an animal having classical mythological associations with the god Zeus-Jupiter, appears because the chapter is under the banner of the planet Jupiter. John differs in this respect from Jewish astrological texts, which tend to keep their ideas about the planets free from associations of classical gods.

At the same time, Johannine astrology possesses certain features that are uniquely Jewish, having no parallel in classical Hellenistic astrology. Astrology was certainly not unknown to the Jews. Rabbinic commentaries do not regard it is as coincidental that Passover, with its slaying of a newborn lamb, falls when the sun passes through the sign of Aries. Nor do they shy away from the fact that the Day of Atonement, when the merits and demerits of the whole world are weighed against each other in a balance, falls when the sun passes through Libra. They can play on the fact that the Feast of Dedication with all its light and fire symbolism falls when the sun passes through the fire sign Sagittarius. Discussing the feast of Purim, which falls when the sun passes through Pisces, the *Midrash* remarks that Haman, villain of the story, forgot that one fish swallows another, and that Moses was born under the sign Pisces. Astrological themes are not doted upon, yet they are not seen as an embarrassment or something that were better swept under the carpet, merely taken for granted. Zodiacal symbolism can therefore be found both in the older cycle of feasts, as well as newer rabbinically instituted ones like Dedication and Purim.

Some of John's astrological symbolism is deeply rooted in the Qabalah, having no counterpart in traditional Western astrology. One way Qabalah tinges John's astrological ideas relates to a specific set of personifications of the planets. In qabalistic writings:

- Jupiter corresponds to the fourth sefirah, H̲esed (Lovingkindness), which is personified in Abraham;

- Mars corresponds to the fifth sefirah, Gevurah (Might), which is personified in Isaac;
- the Sun corresponds to the sixth sefirah, Tif'areth (Beauty), which is personified in Jacob;
- Venus corresponds to the seventh sefirah, Ne<u>z</u>ah (Victory), which is personified in the prophet Samuel in his later years;
- Mercury corresponds to the eighth sefirah, Hod (Glory), which is personified in the prophet Samuel as young boy;
- the Moon corresponds to the ninth sefirah, Yesod (Foundation), which is personified in Joseph.

Sometimes associations of the sefiroth are carried over onto the planets. For instance Hod, the sefirah corresponding to Mercury, is associated in qabalistic writings with *vidui* or *hodaah* ('confession, acknowledgement, admission'). In the Gospel this manifests in:

> He confessed it and did not deny it. He confessed, 'I am not the Christ'. i 20.

Evidently, the planet has picked up an important association of the corresponding sefirah. This is unusual in qabalistic or Jewish astrological writings, but happens routinely in the Fourth Gospel.

It is possible to a limited extent at least to separate astrological symbolism from the symbolism primarily related to the sefiroth, and I have attempted to do so, although this was not John's intention, and much of the Gospel's beauty is lost by doing this. Part 2 of this book is an overview of the symbolism primarily related to the sefiroth.

As well as astrological and calendar attributions, *Sefer Ye<u>z</u>irah* possesses additional series of correspondences, namely twelve bodily activities (speaking, thinking, walking, seeing, and so on) for the twelve simple letters, and seven different conditions (wisdom or folly, wealth or poverty, life or death, beauty or ugliness, peace or strife, dominion or servitude, fertility or infertility) for the seven simple letters.[intro.5] The question naturally arises whether John makes use of these too. Unfortunately, if we depend only upon the internal evidence of the Gospel itself, the matter becomes extremely confusing. This is because some activities – speaking, hearing, walking, working, eating – are described with frequency in the Gospel narrative.

There is enough, I think, within the Gospel to argue John makes use of these correspondences, at least in the case of the simple letters, and his scheme closely resembles that found in the *Gra Version*. However, he does not employ them as intensively as he employs astrological symbolism and images derived from the Jewish calendar, so that one is left to ask why these assignments are handled differently. Perhaps they never came to figure prominently in the Gospel because John did not consider these attributions as important as some of the others. Or this particular set of assignments may have been added late in the proceedings, after much of the Gospel had already crystallised into a definite form. To confine to a single chapter all the speaking, or even all Jesus' speaking, for instance, would then have caused immense problems. John may have found it expedient to allow such unremarkable activities as speaking and walking to occur unrestrictedly.

One might make a case for different assignments for some of the letters, but here is my best guess at the attributions of the twelve simple letters to the twelve basic activities of the human organism as they occur in John's Gospel; it is the same as the assignments

TABLE 4: Twelve simple letters and twelve activities

letter	chapter of John's Gospel	sign (house)	Month	activity
heh	iv	Aries (first house)	Nisan	speaking
vau	v	Taurus (second house)	Iyar	thinking
zayin	vi	Gemini (third house)	Sivan	walking
ḥeth	vii	Cancer (fourth house)	Tammuz	seeing
ṭeth	viii	Leo (fifth house)	Ab	hearing
yod	ix	Virgo (sixth house)	Elul	working
lamed	xi	Libra (seventh house)	Tishri	coupling
nun	xiii	Scorpio (eighth house)	Ḥeshvan	smelling
samekh	xiv	Sagittarius (ninth house)	Kislev	laughing
'ayin	xv	Capricorn (tenth house)	Tevet	raging
ẓaddi	xvii	Aquarius (eleventh house)	Shevat	tasting
quf	xviii	Pisces (twelfth house)	Adar	sleeping

of the *Gra* and *Long Versions of Sefer Yezirah*, but with sleep and laughter interchanged (table 4).

With respect to the attributions of the twelve signs of the zodiac to these twelve activities, the *Gra Version* and the *Long Version of Sefer Yezirah* conform more closely to traditional astrological ideas than the others. Nevertheless, this set of attributions has no real counterpart in traditional Western astrology. It is a distinctive feature of *Sefer Yezirah* and Jewish literature influenced by it. Since these attributions are quite peculiar to *Sefer Yezirah*, with no good parallels in Western astrological lore, John's use of something similar has implications about the antiquity of ideas within the text of *Sefer Yezirah* as we know it. All the more so, if John's attributions are like those of the *Gra* and *Long Versions of Sefer Yezirah*. Were it not for this, it might have been preferable not deal with these attributions at all, since they add another layer of complexity to an already complex work, yet do not greatly further its understanding.

Johannine astrology is therefore heavily coloured with classical myth as well as distinctively Jewish ideas. For the most part, however, John's handling of astrological symbolism is surprisingly modern.

I have appended some notes on Jewish Feasts (Appendix 1) and Planets and Signs in Astrology (Appendix 2).

> intro.1: Gershom Scholem, *Origins of the Kabbalah* p. 25; *Major Trends in Jewish Mysticism* p. 75; *On the Kabbalah and Its Symbolism* p. 167.
>
> intro.2: Gershom Scholem, *On the Kabbalah and its Symbolism* p. 77; *Origins of the Kabbalah*, p. 28 n. 43. Robert Graves, *The White Goddess* p. 150.

intro.3: Aryeh Kaplan, *Sefer Yetzirah, The Book of Creation* p. 159-161.

intro.4: Wynn Westcott, *Introduction to the Study of the Kabalah* p. 105-6.

intro.5: Aryeh Kaplan, *Sefer Yetzirah: The Book of Creation* pp. 178-9, 219.

According to John chapter 1;
beth;
Mercury.

The God of words

The particular version of *Sefer Yezirah* around which John's Gospel is woven assigns the letter *beth*, to which the first chapter answers, to the planet Mercury. John, obedient to the regimen of correspondences, indicates the planetary assignment of the chapter in its opening verse, an example of astrological symbolism remarkable for audacity, yet representative of the Evangelist's style:

> In the beginning was the Word [*Logos*], and the Word was with God, and the Word was God. i 1.

Logos appears again in the same unique and mystical sense later in the chapter:

> And the Word became flesh and dwelt within us (or: amongst us) ... i 14.

John simply uses something with which Mercury has a close and specific affinity in order to indicate the astrological attribution of the chapter. Mercury, or Hermes as the Greeks knew him, was the messenger of the gods, ruler over all forms of communication. Symbols and words, spoken and written, were his special preserve. His name and likeness still appear today in newspaper titles and emblems. As well as 'word', *Logos* means 'thought, reason, intelligence, logic', or 'calculation, computation', senses completely congruous with the character of Mercury as conceived of in astrology. In fact, a second century Christian writer, Justin Martyr, querulously wonders how the Johannine *Logos* could prove difficult to accept since it is so akin to the heathen conception of Hermes as 'the angelic word of God [*logon para theou aggeltikon*]'.[1.1]

The methods by which John invests *Logos* with special prominence in the Gospel's Prologue (i 1-14) illustrate well his approach to signalling symbolic content. First, it occurs at the very beginning of the chapter. Second, he draws the reader's attention by repetition – *Logos* occurs three times in the first verse. Third, the identification of the *Logos* with God underlines its importance further. Finally, it is seen that Jesus is only identified with things that are closely connected to the central theme of the chapter, and in i 1 and i 14 it is tacitly understood that the *Logos* is none other than Jesus. It is also noteworthy that *Logos* does not appear in this elevated mystical sense nor is Jesus referred to as the Word in any other chapter.

In i 38-42 the Evangelist points to Mercury-Hermes with two Greek verbs, *hermēneuein* and *methermēneuein*. The former verb occurs once in this chapter, the latter twice, all in the space of five verses.

> ... they said to him, 'Rabbi,' which translated [*methermēneuomenon*] means 'Teacher', 'where are you staying?' i 38

> He finds his own brother Simon first, and said to him, 'We have found the Messiah', which is translated [*methermēneuomenon*] 'Anointed'. i 41

..…Jesus said to him, 'You are Simon the son of Jonah. You will be called Kephas', which is translated [*hermēneuetai*] 'Stone'. i 42.

Hermēneuein and *methermēneuein*, which are etymologically and semantically related to the god's name, mean 'to interpret or to translate', and are indicative of his primary function as facilitator of communication. *Hermēneutēs*, 'Translator or Interpreter' was actually one of the many cult titles of the god. Justin Martyr calls Hermes 'the interpreting word and teacher of all [*logon hermēneutikon kai pantōn didaskolon*]'.[1.2] Another second century Christian apologist, Aristides, describes him as 'an interpreter of language'.[1.3]

Little doubt can exist that John is employing *hermēneuein* and *methermēneuein* as signal words here, for he takes considerable knowledge of Judaica for granted in his readers. He expects not merely a rudimentary acquaintance with the Hebrew alphabet, but a detailed knowledge of the Jewish calendar of holidays, their customs and liturgical themes. In fact, earlier in this chapter, he plays upon the different senses of a Hebrew or Aramaic word.[1.4] His intended audience did not need to have terms like 'Messiah' and 'Rabbi' translated. Moreover, apart from an instance of *hermēneuein* in ix 7, where its appearance is determined by astrological considerations (it indicates Mercury is ruler of Virgo, the asterism to which ix is assigned), neither of these verbs is to be found elsewhere in the Fourth Gospel.

Personifications

John very often uses the correspondences of a chapter to create comparisons between Jesus and someone else. The astrological or qabalistic correspondences define the particular arena in which the superiority of Jesus is to be demonstrated. In the first chapter of the Gospel it is chiefly the Baptist who is compared with Jesus in this way. On one hand, Jesus is the Word; on the other hand, the Baptist clearly describes himself as a herald, sent ahead to announce the Coming One:

> John testifies concerning him, and has cried out saying, 'He was the one about whom I said, "the one coming after me has come to be ahead of me, because he existed prior to me"'. i 15

> He said, 'I am the voice of one crying in the wilderness, "Make the way of the Lord straight", as the prophet Isaiah said'. i 23

> 'This is the one about whom I said, "After me there comes a man who came to be ahead of me, because he existed prior to me".' i 30.

According to Matthew xi 10 and Luke vii 27 likewise portray the Baptist as a messenger sent in advance to prepare the way. Mercury, god of words, divine messenger and herald, thus provides the contextual framework for setting Jesus and the Baptist side by side. It is normally the part of a herald to go in advance of the one whom he announces, but the Gospel emphasises Jesus' pre-existence as well his pre-eminence.

John refers to a negative aspect of Hermes character in:

> Jesus saw Nathanael coming towards him, and says of him, 'Here is a true Israelite in whom there is no trickery [*dolos*]!' i 47

for *Dolios*, 'Wily, Cunning', *Klepsiphrōn*, 'Deceiver, Dissembler', *Mēchaniōtēs*, 'Trickster', *Poikilometēs* 'Full of Wiles', are among the god's cult titles.

Errant symbolism

Another episode in which Mercury-Hermes takes on human form is ii 14-16, where Jesus enters the Temple to find it has become a market where animals are bought and sold and money-changers conduct their business:

> And in the Temple he found those who were selling cattle, sheep and doves, and money-changers seated. Having made a whip from cords, he threw everyone out of the Temple, along with their sheep and cattle, and he spilled the money-changers' coins and overturned their tables. And to those who were selling doves he said, 'Get them out of here! Do not make my father's house a house of commerce!'. ii 14-16.

The god's patronage of merchants is well-known, his Roman name being etymologically related to 'merchandise', 'mercenary', 'mercantile', 'commerce', and so on, all from the Latin *merx*, 'money'. *Agoraios* ('Of the Marketplace') is an epithet of Hermes. Aristides, the Christian apologist, notes with derision the god's liking for profitable financial transactions.[1.3]

The Gospel is strictly organised, that is to say John for the most part keeps symbolic material confined to the chapter that the regimen of correspondences prescribes for it. It is surprising to see Jesus' encounter with the moneychangers and merchants come in ii, rather than i, where we might have expected it. However, Jesus' violent response actually shows an important principle at work. The fact that the money-changers have come too late, so to speak, is just what makes Jesus overturn their tables and expel them all from the Temple with a whip.

As we read through According to John, we encounter characters who embody zodiacal signs or planets, and from time to time such astrologically cast types show up, not where they might be anticipated, but in the very next chapter. John regularly signals the misplacement by having such characters depart Jesus' presence. For example, in iv 28, the Samaritan woman at the well runs back to the town Sychar, for, as a type of Venus, her proper place is iii, the previous chapter. Again, in vii 10, Jesus' brothers leave him to go to the feast in Jerusalem, for they personify of the house of the heavens connected with siblings, and therefore naturally belong in vi, the previous chapter. And again, the parable of the sheepfold in x 12 describes a hired man who abandons the sheep and runs away, for as the embodiment of the house governing services for a fee, the hired man belongs in ix, the previous chapter.

In this episode we thus have the first instance of a device that is consistently employed with some frequency in the Gospel. It is fortunate that the merchants and money-changers, who are fairly pure, obvious Mercury-types, exit the scene so dramatically, and that Jesus bears such antipathy towards them. These elements render the episode more comprehensible, and make it easier to recognise subtler variations of the trope when it occurs in other places.

The curious relationship between According to John and the Synoptic Gospels

Several episodes from Jesus' ministry are recorded in the Synoptic Gospels as well as According to John. When one examines the Synoptic Evangelists' accounts and compare them with those of John, a curious feature emerges: the Synoptic Evangelists' accounts of these episodes regularly contain material that is not found in According to John, though extremely relevant to the scheme of correspondences around which it is built. The expulsion of the merchants from the temple, which is recounted in all three Synoptic Gospels, provides a clear illustration. As we see from According to Matthew xxi 13, Mark xi 17, and Luke xix 46, John has left out Jesus' accusation that the moneychangers and merchants were turning the temple into 'a den of thieves', a phrase drawn from Jeremiah vii 11. This is puzzling because Mercury was well known as a patron of thieves, as John is no doubt aware, for he uses the god's association with thievery on a number of occasions. John's failure to include the detail may seem a small point, however, such omissions are a conspicuous and regular feature of the Fourth Gospel. Some of the things John excludes are both notable in themselves and have specific importance to the Fourth Gospel's hidden layer of meaning.

In fact, i contains another instance of this. When the Baptist compares himself with Jesus in the Fourth Gospel, he says that he is 'not worthy to undo the straps of his sandals' (i 27), while According to Matthew iii 11 records the Baptist saying rather that he is 'not worthy to lift up his sandals'. The difference appears almost trivial, yet if John had exactly followed Matthew, there would be little doubt that he was alluding to one of the items of Mercury-Hermes' paraphernalia that was most peculiar to him, namely his winged sandals.

In summary

In summary, specific pointers to Mercury occur in i in the form of signal words, *Logos* (Word), and the verbs *methermēneuein* and *hermēneuein* ('to translate'). Mercury is a herald of the gods; John the Baptist is portrayed in the role of herald to Jesus in this chapter. The merchants and money-changers in the next chapter are clear Mercury types; their expulsion from the Temple is a manifestation of their being out of place. The Gospel contains a handful of other instances where a character appears not in the chapter appropriate for them, but in the chapter immediately following, and departure from Jesus' presence regularly serves a pointer that such characters are out of place.

    1.1: Justin Martyr, *First Apology*, chapter xxii.

    1.2: Justin Martyr, *First Apology*, chapter xxi.

    1.3: Aristides, *Apology* x.

    1.4: See Part 2 notes 1.2, 1.3, 1.4.

The Gospel According to John chapter 2;
gimel;
the Moon.

The schedule of correspondences that pervades the Gospel assigns the letter *gimel*, and therefore its second chapter, to the Moon. In natal astrology the Moon often stands for the mother of the native. In fact, the association is found explicitly enough in the Tanakh – when Joseph dreams that the Sun and Moon and eleven constellations bowed down to him, his father's reply, 'What? Shall I and your mother and brothers bow down to you then?' (Genesis xxxvii 10), reveals he understands that the Moon in Joseph's dream represents his mother. The presence of Mary is therefore hardly surprising of this chapter in the opening pericope:

> And on the third day there was a wedding in Cana in Galilee, and the mother of Jesus was there. And Jesus was called to the wedding and his disciples along with him. And as the wine was running out, Jesus' mother says to him, 'They have no wine'.

> Jesus says to her, 'Woman, what is that to you and me? My time has not yet come'.
>
> His mother says to the waiters, 'Do what he tells you'. ii 1-5.

Mary is brought to the foreground by being mentioned before Jesus. It is she who initiates the action by drawing Jesus' attention to the fact that the wine has been exhausted. Her instruction to the wine-stewards to do as Jesus says suggests she fears her son's orders may be ignored while implying her own authority at the wedding. However, just as Jesus is portrayed as superior to John the Baptist in i, so in ii does Jesus assume precedence over Mary. He asks her not to interfere, and after telling the waiters to obey Jesus, she fades from view.

The story continues with more lunar symbolism:

> Six stone water-jars, each holding two or three measures, were sitting there, in accordance with the purification customs of the Jews. Jesus says to them, 'Fill the water-jars with water.' And they filled them up to the very top. And he says to them, 'Draw some off now, and take it to the governor of the feast.' And they took some. When the governor of the feast tasted the water that had become wine, and did not know whence it came, though the waiters who had drawn out the water knew, he calls the bridegroom. ii 5-9.

Since the Moon has a special affinity with water, and presides over occupations involving liquids, such as drink-servers, the waiters of this chapter are personifications based on traditional astrological symbolism. In waxing to full and waning back to new, the Moon was thought to induce an ebb and flow in a universal tide of life-force, as it literally filled and emptied.[2.1] The filling of the empty stone jars to the brim with water in the opening section of ii is therefore also perfectly apt.

2.1: Ptolemy, *Tetrabiblios* book i chap 2.

The Gospel According to John chapter 3;
daleth;
Venus.

In the classical world, Aphrodite-Venus was usually thought of as a goddess of erotic love and sensuality, but she still retained some of her original function as a goddess of fertility. The Romans worshipped Venus as *Genetrix*, while her Greek counterpart, Aphrodite, had *Genetyllis* and *Gennaidas* among her cult titles; all point to the goddess' rulership over the powers of procreation. She is also linked with the birth goddess *Eileithyia*, and sometimes said to be the mother of the three Fates (Moirae or Parcae), who were birth goddesses. Aphrodite represented the fruitfulness of the natural world. Among animals, the hare was sacred to her just because of its extraordinary reproductive prowess. Ptolemy and the Roman astrologer-poet Manilius note signs ruled by Venus are abundantly fertile.[3.1] In natal astrology she may represent the mother of the native. (The Moon is said to be the primary significator of the native's mother, and Venus the secondary or less important significator. Or Venus shows the mother of the native in a diurnal chart, while the Moon shows the mother in a nocturnal horoscope). A brief rabbinical treatise on astrology, *The Beraita of Shmuel Ha Qatan* says Venus influences 'grace, love, lust, children, fruitfulness'.[3.2] The *Gra* and *Long Versions of Sefer Yezirah*, although they do not follow John's scheme of attributions of the double letters to the planets, agree that the letter *daleth* connotes fertility (and sterility), and John may also have this idea.

Venus' association with reproduction partially explains why birth is the dominates the discussion in the opening section of iii, where a Pharisee, Nikodemos, pays Jesus a visit during to be instructed:

> 'Amen, amen, I tell you: unless someone is born from above, he cannot see the kingdom of God'.
> Nikodemos said to him, 'How can a man who is old be born? He can not enter his mother's womb a second time and be born'.
> Jesus replied, 'Amen, amen, I tell you: unless he is born of water and spirit, he can not enter the kingdom of God. What is born of flesh is flesh, and what is born of the spirit is spirit. Do not be amazed because I told you that you must be born from above ...' iii 3-7.

The tension between heavenly and earthly, an important theme in the third chapter of John's Gospel, reflects contrasting aspects of the goddess' nature as revealed in her Greek epithets, *Pandēmos* ('Of All the People') on one hand, and *Ourania* ('Heavenly or Celestial'), on the other.

Nikodemos ('Victor of the People') may seem an unlikely candidate for a personification of Aphrodite-Venus, however, *Victrix* was an epithet of Venus, and *Nikēphoros* 'Bearing Victory' a cult title of the Greek Aphrodite. In fact, Nikodemos' name sounds like a fusion of *Nikēphoros* and *Pandēmos*. To qabalists, moreover, Venus is the planetary correspondence of the seventh sefirah, Nezah (Victory). Qabalists see the particular qualities of Nezah epitomised in the prophet Samuel in his later years.[3.3] Nikodemos is therefore described as 'a leader of the Jews' (iii 1) and 'teacher in Israel' (iii 10).

Nikodemos comes to Jesus by night because the planet Venus belongs to the nocturnal sect in astrological terminology, that is to say, its influence is stronger at night. Aphrodite-Venus is moreover associated with nocturnal activities, as her epithets, *Philopannyx* (Fond of the Whole Night) and *Pannyakhis* (Lasting All Night or Completely Nocturnal), suggest.

Woman from sugartown

The Samaritan woman of the Gospel's fourth chapter is a more obvious personification of Venus. Once again, although the regimen of correspondences strictly determines where symbolic material will go for the most part, we have already seen that personifications can appear one chapter too late. Departure from the scene regularly signals the fact to the reader. The Samaritan woman is another instance: she would naturally belong in iii. After talking to Jesus, she runs back to town immediately upon the arrival of the disciples, whose surprise at her presence (iv 27-28) is another clue to the fact that she is out of place in iv. Her exit is not as dramatic as that of the money-changers in the Temple (ii 14-16), but John implies a suddenness to it in having her abandon her water-jar at the well.

The Samaritan woman qualifies as a type of Venus by having had five husbands and her involvement in a relationship with a sixth person who is not her husband (iv 18), for Venus' life was a series of marriages and love affairs. Honey, confectionery, and sugar are traditional symbolic associations of Venus. After talking to Jesus, accordingly, the Samaritan woman goes back to the town Sychar, that is 'Sugar' in Aramaic.[3.4] Sometimes *Sychar* is understood to mean 'spiritous liquor', but the significance is the same.

- 3.1: Ptolemy, *Tetrabiblios* book i chap. 17; book ii chap. 8; book iii chaps. 4, 5. Manilius, *Astronomicon*.
- 3.2: quoted by Aryeh Kaplan, *Sefer Yetzirah, The Book of Creation* p. 180 t. 35.
- 3.3: *Zohar* 1:21b. Daniel C. Matt *The Zohar: Pritzker Edition* vol. 1 p. 165 n. 459, 460, 461.
- 3.4: *Sekhar* in the Peshitta, the translation of the Gospels into Aramaic.

The Gospel According to John chapter 4;
heh;
Aries, and the first house; the first month, Nisan or Abib.

Isaac

The fourth chapter of John's Gospel corresponds to the letter *heh*, which *Sefer Yezirah* associates with the sign Aries, the Ram, and the month Nisan or Abib. Beginning at the new moon of the spring equinox, Nisan, the first month of the religious calendar, contains the feast of Passover (Hebrew: *Pesaḥ*) in which a lamb was killed and its roasted meat eaten by each family.

The fourth chapter of John's Gospel contains a number of allusions to the biblical patriarch Isaac, which are apposite to the chapter for a handful of reasons. Most importantly, Isaac possesses the ram as his emblem because of the incident related in Genesis xxii. Abraham has a revelation that he should offer up his son, Isaac, as a sacrifice, and together they travel off to a place, Mount Moriah, for the purpose. On their arrival, Abraham binds Isaac, and is about to offer him up as a burnt sacrifice on the altar, when an angel intervenes, saving Isaac at the very last moment. The sacrifice goes on – but now with a ram caught by its horns in a nearby thornbush taking Isaac's place on the altar. In one of the legends that surround the story, the ram sacrificed was a long lost family pet, whom Abraham had named Isaac after his son. In any case, the fact that a ram became his substitute in the sacrifice symbolically identifies Isaac with that animal.

Although the legend of Isaac's Binding has for many centuries been associated with New Year's Day (*Rosh ha Shanah*), which falls in the seventh month, Tishri, it was once just as strongly linked to the month Nisan, in which Passover falls.[4.1] Speculation exists that because Christianity saw Isaac's sacrifice as prefiguring Jesus' death at Passover, there arose a reaction in Judaism to suppress the tradition linking Isaac's Binding and Passover.

In qabalistic literature, *heh*, which serves as a numeral for the number five, can denote the fifth sefirah, Gevurah (Severity), whose personification is Isaac.[4.2] This provides another strong motivation for allusions to Isaac and the story of his binding in this chapter.

The first allusion to Isaac in the Gospel comes when the Samaritan woman asks Jesus, 'Are you greater than Jacob?' (iv 12); the second when she remarks 'I see that you are a prophet' (iv 19). For Isaac is greater than Jacob, since he is Jacob's father; he could even be metaphorically described as the wellspring of Jacob for the same reason. And Isaac is certainly named a prophet in rabbinic and qabalistic literature.

Another allusion to Isaac occurs when the Samaritan woman indirectly brings up the story of Isaac's Binding. Samaritans and Jews have more than a few differences of opinion, and the location of Mount Moriah, where Isaac was bound by Abraham, is one point of sore contention. The Jews hold that Zion, the Temple Mount in Jerusalem, is Mount Moriah, and that the Holy of Holies of the Temple of Solomon marked the very spot where Abraham raised his altar and bound Isaac for sacrifice.[4.3] However, according to

Samaritan beliefs, everything took place on their Mount Gerizim, where their temple stood. The Samaritan Temple is situated near Jacob's Well and the town of Sychar, close to where Jesus and the Samaritan woman meet. Their discussion about the right place to worship is a thinly veiled reference to the dispute between Samaritans and Jews about the true location of Mount Moriah, where Isaac's Binding took place:

> 'Our fathers worshipped on this mountain. You say the place where one should worship is in Jerusalem'.
> Jesus said to her, 'Believe me, woman, the time is coming when you will worship the Father neither on this mountain nor in Jerusalem'. iv 19-21.

The mention of worship in the Samaritan woman's question and Jesus' reply here and in iv 22 is intended to recall Abraham's words in Genesis xxii 5 ('the lad and I shall go yonder and worship').

Isaac's binding also figures in the closing section of iv, where Jesus meets a nobleman and cures his son of the fever that is killing him (iv 52). As will be explained in Part 2, the nobleman is a type of Abraham, who personifies one of the qabalistic correspondences of the letter *daleth*, and for this reason one would therefore expect to find him in iii. His departure from the scene is analogous to the departure of the Samaritan woman in this chapter, and the departure of the merchants and money-changers in ii, and so on.

The nobleman's son, the real focus of the episode, is about to die of a fever because Isaac was to be offered up as a burnt offering. The Passover lamb, moreover, had to be roasted by fire, not boiled nor raw; the uneaten remnants had to be destroyed by fire (Exodus xii 8-10). Fever is also one of the commoner traditional specific associations of Aries, a fiery sign ruled by Mars. *Puroeis* ('Fiery') the usual Greek name for the planet Mars, is etymologically related to *puretos*, the Greek word for 'fever' seen here. The man's son's cure takes place at the seventh hour (iv 52) because Isaac is traditionally credited with having instituted the prayer that is prescribed for this time of day, the Minhah or Afternoon Prayer.[4.4]

The salvific or redemptive nature of Isaac's sacrifice is mentioned in the *Targum PseudoJonathan*, where Abraham prays immediately after the incident that it will merit for Isaac's children the remission of sins and speedy deliverance in time of danger. Moreover, Nisan is called the month of salvation or redemption in Jewish literature, because Passover commemorates the deliverance of the Israelites from Egyptian slavery. In the Gospel, the theme of salvation or redemption manifests in:

> You worship what you do not know, but we worship what we know, because salvation comes from the Jews. iv 22.
>
> And they said to the woman, 'We no longer believe because of your report, but because we have heard him ourselves, and know he is indeed the Anointed, the Saviour of the World'. iv 42.

Unleavened bread

On the second day of Passover, Nisan 16, the Feast of Unleavened Bread, an originally separate holiday, was celebrated. The first of the ripe barley was harvested, roasted, ground and sifted. It was then offered in a Lifted or Wave Offering. The ritual rendered permissible for human consumption all the grain that had taken root during the previous year.

At the time of the Second Temple, the public display of joy during holiday at the actual reaping of the grain, which took place in a field close to Jerusalem, is well recorded. The men who were to cut the barley were accompanied by a mass of spectators who urged them on. The fanfare and extravagance that attended the ceremony was partly due to the settling of a dispute about the precise day the rite was to be performed. One group, followers of Boethus or Baytus, who rejected the Oral Law, performed the rite on the first Sunday after Nisan 15, since the Pentateuch can be literally read thus. Others, like the Pharisees, followed the tradition that fixed Nisan 16 as the day. When those who followed oral traditions won the argument, they wanted to advertise the fact as loudly as they could, and the reaping was done with cheering crowds in attendance. In the Gospel, John alludes to the festival of Unleavened Bread in,

> 'Do you not say, "Still a four-month season, and then comes the harvest"? Look, I tell you, lift up your eyes, and see that the fields are already white for harvest. He who reaps is paid, and gathers in the grain for eternal life, so that he who sows and he who reaps may rejoice together. For in this respect the saying, "One sows and another reaps" is true. I sent you to reap what you have not worked on.' iv 35-38.

The whiteness of the fields suggests Jesus is speaking of barley here – *alphiton* (Greek: 'barley') is cognate with *alphos* (Greek: 'white leprosy'), and the Latin word *albus* ('white'); *Alphitō*, the barley goddess is also known as *Leukotheia*, the White Goddess; wheat in contrast is golden yellow in colour.

Jesus tells the disciples to lift up their eyes (iv 35) because the term used in the Old Testament for the Wave or Lifted Offering, *Tenufah*, is related to the word *nuf*, 'height, elevation'; in modern Hebrew, *tenufah* means 'a lifting up'; in the Septuagint, the Greek translation of the Old Testament, the verb *anapherein*, 'to lift up' often appears where the original Hebrew has *nofef*, 'to wave'.[4,5]

Heh and speaking

In astrological tradition the first house governs the speech of the native, whether he is taciturn or talkative, eloquent or inarticulate. This may be one reason the *Long* and *Gra Versions of Sefer Yezirah*, whose attributions tend toward astrological ideas, associate the letter *heh* with speaking. The fact that Jesus speaks in every chapter of the Gospel makes it difficult to argue strongly that John has any definite ideas on the matter. However, in this fourth chapter we have:

> 'I myself am he, the one speaking to you'. iv 26.

Jesus' 'I am' statements, a peculiar feature of According to John, seem to be very closely correlated with the scheme of correspondences, and his reply here has the characteristic form of one of these, especially in the original Greek, which might be rendered, 'I am the speaking one for you'.

In summary

In summary, the fourth chapter contains references to the sign of the Ram, and to the feast of Passover, a feast of the month Nisan, in the form of allusions to Isaac, especially the legend of his binding on the sacrificial altar, which according to one tradition, took place in the month Nisan. Another important date in Nisan, the Feast of Unleavened Bread, is also alluded to.

4.1: *Exodus Rabbah* xv 11-12. TB *Rosh Ha Shanah* 11a. *Jubilees* xvii 15, xviii 19.

4.2: TB *Berakhoth* 26b. *Bereshith Rabbah* lxviii 9. *Zohar* 1:72a, 132a, 230a; 2:21a-b, 63a; 3:121a. Daniel C. Matt *The Zohar:*

Pritzker Edition vol. 1 p. 162 n. 437; ibid p. 427 n. 645; vol. 2 p. 240 n. 289, 290; ibid 245 n. 328; vol 3. p. 42 n. 306; ibid p. 388 n. 433; vol. 4 p. 341 n. 504.

4.3 Daniel C. Matt *The Zohar: Pritzker Edition* vol. 4 p. 388 nn. 64, 65; vol. 6 p. 219 n. 337.

4.4: See 4.2.

4.5: Exodus xxix 25; Leviticus viii 27, xxiii 11; Numbers v 25.

According to John chapter 5;
vau;
Taurus, and the second house; the second month, Ziv or Iyar.

The fifth chapter of the Gospel begins with a healing miracle:

> Now there is a pool with five porches on the Sheep Gate in Jerusalem, which is called Bethesda in Hebrew. In these a multitude of the infirm, blind, lame, and withered lay, waiting for the agitation of the water. (For an angel sometimes went down into the pool, and agitated the water, and whoever went in first after the agitation of the water was cured of whatever disease he had.) And a certain man was there who had been thirty-eight years in his infirmity. Jesus, on seeing him lying there and knowing that he had been like this for a long time, says to him, 'Do you want to be healthy?'.
> The invalid answered him, 'Master, I have no one to put me into the pool when the water is agitated. While I am coming, another goes down before me.' v 2-7.

Epi tēi probatikēi is normally rendered 'upon the Sheep Gate', but the Greek word *pulēi* (Gate) has been omitted, so that the phrase literally means 'upon the Sheep'. It is understandable as a reference to the position of the sign Taurus, which immediately follows after Aries in the order of the zodiac. The exchange between Jesus and the invalid is not too hard to decipher in light of the relevant astrological data. The sick man complains, 'while I am coming another always gets in before' (v 7), for Taurus is not the first but the second sign of the zodiac, and that 'I have no man', because the second house of the horoscope is shows the nature of any helpers or assistants the native may have.

Taurus is ruled by Venus, and its natives like to keep comfortable. Self-indulgence, laziness and sloth are characteristic vices of the sign. A tendency to stubborn immobility, another Taurean trait, is a consequence of the fixed and earthy nature of the sign. The bed or mattress, on which the infirm man languishes for a large portion of his life, is therefore symbolic. This sector of the horoscope pertains to personal effects and moveable possessions, objects that one would normally carry about on one's person. In the Gospel this manifests in the former invalid's having to carry his mattress around with him.

The constellation of Taurus is connected with the vernal growth of vegetation. The Bull represents the 'life force' in nature, which, having lain dormant in winter, begins to stir when the sun enters Aries, to erupt in midspring when the sun enters Taurus. The less common name for Iyar, the second month of the Jewish calendar is Ziv, meaning 'brightness of flowers' or 'efflorescence'. In the Gospel this idea appears in:

> 'Just as the Father raises the dead and makes alive, likewise does the Son make alive those whom he wants'. v 21.

> 'Amen, amen, I say to you: one who hears my word and believes him who sent me has eternal life and does not

come to judgement but has crossed over from death to life'. v 24.

'Just as the Father has life within himself, so has he given it to the Son likewise to have life within himself'. v 26.

Jesus' words in v 21 and 24 may also have been influenced by the fact that the second house of the horoscope was anciently called the Gate of Hades.

Taurus and its cognate house, like the other two earth signs and their houses, have a certain association with work and enterprise. Of all the animals of the zodiac, the bull is the only one harnessed to perform labour for man. The Bull is credited with more physical endurance and strength and stamina than any other sign. The cognate house, the second, is concerned with unskilled labour, natural abilities and raw talents. In the Gospel:

'...my Father has always been working and I am also working'. v 17

'For the Father loves the Son, and shows him everything he does. He will show him even greater works than these so that you will be amazed'. v 20

'The works that my Father has given me to complete, the works I perform, themselves testify about me that the Father sent me.' v 36.

vau and thinking

With respect to the attributions of the twelve simple letters to the twelve basic activities of the human organism, John often seems to follow the scheme set out in the *Gra* and *Long Versions of Sefer Yeẓirah*. This assigns the letter *vau* to the function of thinking.

That John associates *vau* with thinking is suggested by the repetition of *dokein*, which means 'to think, to suppose, to imagine', in:

> 'You search the scriptures, because you think [*dokeite*] to have eternal life in them, and they are what testifies about me. And yet you are not willing to come to me, in order to have life. I do not accept the opinion [*doxan*] of men.' v 39-41.

> 'How can you believe those who accept one another's opinion [*doxan*] and do not seek the opinion [*doxan*] of God alone? Do not think [*dokeite*] that I shall accuse you to the Father. The one accusing you is Moses, on whom you have hoped.' v 44-45.

It is true that the verb appears on other occasions (xi 13, 31, 56; xiii 29; xvi 2; xx 15), but here it is repeated in the space of a few verses, and with the etymologically related word *doxa* nearby each time. The original sense of *doxa* is 'thought, supposition, fancy or opinion', though in the New Testament it seems almost always to be used in the extended meaning 'good opinion' or 'good reputation'. However, in the context of the passage – Jesus is discussing where beliefs come from, and the role of the scriptures – to render *doxa* as 'opinion or thought' seems quite natural.

The Gospel According to John chapter 6;
zayin;
Gemini, and the third house; the third month, Sivan.

Feast of loaves

The most striking feature of vi is the repeated mention of bread. The chapter commences with the multiplication of loaves and the feeding of the multitude:

> Then Jesus, lifting up his eyes and seeing that a great crowd was coming to him, says to Philip, 'Where are we to buy bread, so these people may eat?'.
> And he said this testing him, for he knew what he would do. Philip answered him, 'Two hundred denarii of bread would not suffice for them, so that every one of them might get a little'.
> One of his disciples, Andrew, Simon Peter's brother, says to him, 'Here is a lad who has five barley loaves and two small fish. But what are they among so many?'.
> And Jesus said, 'Make the men sit down'.
> There was a lot of grass in the place. So the men sat down, about five thousand in number. And Jesus took the loaves

and, after giving thanks, gave them out to the disciples, and the disciples to those who were seated, and likewise as much of the fish as they wanted. When they were filled, he said to his disciples, 'Gather up the remaining pieces, lest anything be lost'. vi 5-12.

Jesus answered them and said, 'Amen, amen, I tell you: you seek me, not because you saw signs, but because you ate the loaves, and were filled'. vi 26

'Our fathers ate manna in the desert, as it is written, "He gave them bread from heaven to eat"'.

Then Jesus said to them, 'Amen, amen, I tell you: Moses did not give you the bread from heaven, but my Father gives you the true bread from heaven, for the bread of God is he who comes down from heaven, and gives life to the world'.

They said to him, 'Master, give us this bread always'. vi 31-34

The Jews then grumbled at him, because he said, 'I am the bread that came down from heaven'. vi 41.

'Your ancestors ate manna in the wilderness, and are dead. This is the bread that comes down from heaven, in order that one may eat it, and not die.' vi 49-50.

This is the bread that came down from heaven. Unlike your ancestors who ate manna and died, he who eats this bread will live forever. vi 58.

Most significantly, Jesus repeatedly identifies himself with bread:

'I am the bread of life'. vi 35

'I am the bread of life'. vi 48

'I am the living bread that came down from heaven'. vi 51.

Jesus' 'I am' statements, which occur sporadically throughout John's Gospel, are usually very easily understood in terms of the correspondences, and Jesus' identification with bread here is no exception. In the third month of the Hebrew religious year, Sivan, when the Sun passes through the sign Gemini, falls one of the major Jewish holidays, the Feast of Loaves or Pentecost (*Shavu'ot*). Every family was required by Mosaic Law to bring two loaves of ordinary leavened bread to the Temple. Thus, bread recalls the feast of which it is the focus, and so indicates the month that contains the feast. John habitually makes such use of major Jewish holidays in this way.

John's remark that there was plenty of green grass in the place (vi 10), a detail which the Synoptics also record (According to Matthew xiv 19, Mark vi 39), is yet another a specific pointer to the holiday, in which greenery is used as a decoration in homes and synagogues. The Feast of Loaves falls on the anniversary of Moses' ascent to receive the Law on Sinai, and Jewish writers explain the custom with an aggadic legend that grass and shrubs had suddenly sprouted everywhere, and that the Israelites were standing on grass when the Torah was received, or else from the warning that flocks not be allowed to graze near the mountain (Exodus xxxiv 3).

When the Decalogue was delivered to the Israelites, they complained they would die from listening to God speaking (Exodus xx 19-20), which is the source of:

Upon hearing this many of his disciples said, 'This is a hard teaching. Who can listen to it?'. vi 60.

Astrological tradition ascribes to Gemini and the third sector of the heavens a rulership of education, communication, news, information and teaching. Teaching and education are mentioned in vi 60 and in:

> 'It is written in the prophets, "And they will all be pupils of God". Everyone hearing and learning from the Father comes to me.' vi 45.

The latter portion of the chapter attempts to symbolically identify teaching or instruction with bread. Initially, people come to Jesus to get the bread of eternal life; by the end of the chapter (vi 68), they come to get the words (*ta rhēmata*) of eternal life. Because the Feast of Loaves falls on the anniversary of the reception of the Decalogue at Sinai, similar ideas appear in qabalistic writings.

If John never quite gets around to spell out the equivalence of bread and teaching, it is given quite explicitly in the Synoptic Gospels. Shortly after the second of the two occasions on which Jesus multiplies a few loaves to feed a multitude, he warns the disciples to avoid the leaven or yeast of the Pharisees and Sadducees. They completely and comically misunderstand, as only the disciples can, thinking Jesus is talking about literal bread, until Jesus, exasperated by their slowness, reminds them of certain numerical details of the two miracles. Somehow this makes everything crystal clear, so that finally:

> Then they understood that he was not telling them to be careful of the yeast of bread but rather of the teaching of the Pharisees and Sadducees. According to Matthew xvi 12 (cf. Mark viii 14-21).

This symbolism may also be implicit elsewhere in the Synoptic Gospels: when the Devil tempts Jesus, who has been fasting for forty days and nights, to turn stones into bread, Jesus confounds him with Deuteronomy viii 3:

> Answering, he said, 'It has been written, "Man shall not live on bread alone, but on every word proceeding from the mouth of God."' According to Matthew iv 4 (Luke iv 4 is parallel).

John's failure to include Matthew's explanation of the symbol is analogous to the other inexplicable omissions from the Fourth Gospel.

Short journeys

Astrology connects Gemini and the third house of the heavens with short journeys. This is probably why *The Long* and *Gra Versions of Sefer Yeẓirah*, which mirror astrological ideas more closely than others, list walking as the activity denoted by the letter *zayin*. In John's Gospel, this results in Jesus' walk across the stormy waters of Lake Tiberias:

> And when evening came his disciples went down to the sea, and after getting into the boat, they went across the sea toward Capernaum. And it had already become dark, and Jesus had not yet come to them. And the sea was roused as a great wind was blowing. So having rowed about twenty-five or thirty stadia, they see Jesus walking on the sea and getting close to the boat, and they were afraid. But he says to them, 'It is I. Do not be afraid'. They wanted to take him into the boat, but immediately the boat touched upon land at the place they were going to. vi 16-21.

Jesus does a lot of walking in According to John, but the miraculous nature of the stroll Jesus takes in vi 16-21 lends it unique significance. The great wind (vi 18) is partly a consequence of the airy nature of the sign Gemini.

Jesus' brothers come late

Gemini and the third mansion of the heavens are also said to chart the native's brothers and sisters; the traditional name for the mansion is Siblings (*Fratres*). Jesus' siblings do not appear anywhere in vi, which is where one would expect to find them on the basis of the correspondences. But in the opening verses of vii, Jesus has a curt exchange with his brothers, who promptly leave for Jerusalem without him. Again we see John's use of a peculiar device: characters who personify one of the astrological correspondences may appear, not in the chapter dictated by the schedule of *Sefer Yezirah*, but in the very next chapter, their being out of place signalled by their departure from Jesus' presence.

Synoptics have twins

The fact that the multiplication of loaves and fishes has a twin, as it were, is altogether omitted by John, though recorded by two of the Synoptic Evangelists. The first miracle occurs in According to Matthew xiv, and in According to Mark vi. The second miracle follows in Matthew xv, and in Mark viii. If their had been such a duplication of the miracle in According to John, it would be an easily recognisable pointer to Gemini.

The Gospel According to John chapter 7;
**_heth_;
Cancer, and the fourth house; the fourth month, Tammuz.**

Cancer is the sign of the summer solstice, where the sun reaches its northernmost declination. The cognate house, the fourth, is situated at the nadir (the point on the celestial sphere that is diametrically opposite the zenith, and lies hidden beneath the earth). This sector rules personal privacy and security, withdrawal, secrecy and seclusion. In the Gospel, seclusion and secrecy become recurring themes of this chapter:

> His brothers said to him, 'Leave here and go up to into Judea, so that your disciples will also see the works you do. For no one who seeks to be before the public eye acts in secret. If you are doing these things, show yourself to the world...'.
> Jesus said to them, 'The right time has not yet come for me, but the time is always suitable for you... You go up to this feast, I am not going up to this feast because my time is not yet full.'

> But when his brothers had gone up to the feast, he also went up, not openly but somewhat secretly. Then the Jews sought him at the feast, and said, 'Where is he?'. vii 3-11
>
> No one spoke in open public through fear of the Jews. vii 13
>
> 'He speaks in open public and no one says anything to him...' vii 26
>
> 'You will seek me, but you will not find me, and you can not come where I am going'.
> Then the Jews said among themselves, 'Where will he go that we shall not find him? Will he go to the Diaspora among the Greeks, and teach the Greeks? What is this that he said to us, "You will seek me, and not find me, and you can not come where I am going"?'. vii 34-36.

An old name for this area of the heavens is Ancestors (*Patres* or *Genitor*). It shows the native's parents, ancestral roots, paternal lineage, family traditions, and the family name. The phrase 'the House of so-and-so' sums up the idea. It also charts the family home, home-life and domestic affairs, as well as one's home town or village. In the Gospel this gives rise to questions about Jesus' point of earthly origin, and his genealogy, and customs inherited from the Patriarchs:

> Because Moses has given you circumcision, although it did not originate with Moses, but the ancestors, you circumcise a man even on the Sabbath. vii 22.
>
> 'But we know where this man is from, and when Christ comes, no one will know where he is from'.

> And Jesus, teaching in the temple, cried out saying, 'Do you know me, and do you also know where I am from?' vii 27-28.
>
> Some said, 'He is the Christ', but others said, 'Will the Christ, come from Galilee? Does the scripture not say that Christ is of the seed of David, and from the town of Bethlehem, where David was?'. vii 41-42.
>
> They answered and said to him, 'Are you too from Galilee? Search and look, because no prophet arises from Galilee'. And everyone went to his own house. vii 52-53.

The Crab possesses claws; this is the basis of the pictographic symbol astrologers use to represent the sign, and why natives of the sign are said to be grasping, and to grab on tenaciously. In John's Gospel this becomes:

> They sought to seize him, but no one laid hands on him, because his time had not yet come. vii 30.
>
> The Pharisees heard the people murmuring such things about him, and the Pharisees and the chief priests sent soldiers to seize him. vii 32.
>
> And some of them wished to seize him, but no one laid hands on him. vii 44.

Like the other water signs of the zodiac, occupations connected with the ocean are associated with the sign of the Crab. In the Gospel this appears in the *hupēretai* (vii 32, 45, 46). The word *hupēretēs* is usually translated as 'soldier' or 'officer', but literally means an 'under-rower or sub-oarsman', a type of sailor or naval officer.

Tabernacles in Tammuz

It has already been seen that John employs references to major religious holidays of Jewish calendar to indicate months of the year, but the second temporal scheme bears no relationship to the external time of the narrative. In v 1, we ae told that Jesus went to Jerusalem to celebrate a Jewish holiday, but the month Iyar contains no holidays. In vi 4 we are told that it is near Passover, while the symbolism consistently points to the Feast of Loaves. In x 22, we are told that it is near the festival of Dedication, which falls in the month Kislev, but the symbolism of the chapter strongly points to New Year's Day, which falls in the month Tishri. In xii 1 John expressly says it is close to Passover, but the events of the chapter very clearly point to the Feast of Tabernacles. No doubt extreme difficulties would have arisen had he attempted to harmonise these two systems, one explicit, one symbolic, because the ye<u>z</u>iratic correspondences bring about a forced marriage between certain chapters of According to John and the months of the year. John would have had no choice but to make most of his narrative move precisely at the rate of one month per chapter, an terrible inconvenience. As things are, in xiii to xviii, John has to telescope into a single night, the night of the Last Supper, the correspondences of five full months of the year (from Mar<u>h</u>eshvan to Adar). Time is of great importance but the dates John expressly supplies may almost always be ignored with advantage, since the explicitly stated time and the time indicated indirectly by liturgical symbolism never agree.

In vii, there is just such a disagreement between the explicitly stated time of events and the internal calendar that forms the basis of the Gospel's symbolic machinery. The Feast of Tabernacles, which is given as the setting of the narrative, falls in the seventh month, while this chapter should have corresponded, if John had consistently followed the attributions given in *Sefer Yezirah*, to fourth month, Tammuz. Because the internal and external calendars regularly disagree, this would not be too disturbing if the feast played only a minor role in vii. However, the feast has a significant influence upon the events of the chapter, as well as comments made by Jesus.

Precisely what allows or persuades John to place the Feast of Tabernacles in vii is something to which I shall return in Part 2. John's reasons emanate from qabalistic considerations, and can be dealt with later. At this point, the important matter to understand is that Feast of Tabernacles is associated with certain themes which are appropriate to vii.

First, the Feast of Tabernacles recalled the forty years of the Israelites' passage through the desert, when they dwelt in makeshift shelters. Its celebration entailed building and living in a temporary dwelling for the week. In the Talmud it is said that Tabernacles actually commemorates how the Divine Glory formed a tent or canopy for the Israelites' protection.[7.1] This is harmonious with the astrological assignment of the chapter, since the fourth house of the horoscope rules over the home or dwelling place.

Second, water is a central theme of Tabernacles, prayers for rain during the coming months making up an significant part of the liturgy. An important rite of the holiday is the drawing of water from Siloam and its pouring on the altar as a libation.[7.2] Jesus' announcement at the climax of the proceedings that 'streams of living water shall come from his belly' (vii 38) reflects the key part played by water in the enactment of the festival. It is also perfectly congenial to Cancer, a water sign.

Lastly, Tabernacles lasts eight days; the last day of the festival (vii 37), which John says is most important, is called the Solemn Assembly of the Eighth Day. The letter *ḥeth*, which is coordinate with this chapter, denotes the number eight in Jewish writings.

7.1: TB *Sukkah* 11b.
7.2: TB *Sukkah* 48a-b.

The Gospel According to John chapter 8;
**_teth_;
Leo, and the fifth house; the fifth month, Av.**

Astrological tradition accords the fifth house a special rulership over love affairs and casual romantic liaisons undertaken just for pleasure, and without the formal partnership of marriage. The opening scene of viii brings the idea dramatically to life:

> The scribes and Pharisees bring a woman who had been caught in adultery, and placing her in the middle, they say to him: 'Teacher, this woman was caught in flagrant adultery.' viii 3-5.

The theme of sexual immorality appears again when Pharisees' snidely question Jesus' legitimacy with,

> 'Where is your father?' viii 19

> 'We are not born in fornication' viii 41.

And in Jesus counteraccusation:

> '... you desire to act out the lusts of your father ...' viii 44.

The fifth mansion of the horoscope charts personal independence, freedom and liberty, and unrestrained self-expression in leisure and recreation. This manifests in the Gospel as references to freedom:

> 'And you will know the truth, and the truth will set you free.' viii 32

> 'How can you say "You will be free"?' viii 33.

John makes a neat quip by alluding to three consecutive celestial mansions, that is three consecutive letters, in a single breath. The fourth sector of the heavens (*ḥeth*) rules the house and home; the fifth (*ṭeth*) is concerned with personal freedom; the sixth mansion (*yod*) is concerned with employees and servants; and thus:

> 'A servant does not remain in the house forever, but a son remains in the house forever. If the son sets you free then you will be truly free.' viii 35-36.

If the reasoning sounds odd, it is because the logic is that of astrology. The example is important because it illustrates that John sometimes strings together the attributions of several letters into a single figure of speech.

Children and offspring are another area over which the fifth house of the horoscope has rulership; medieval astrologers called it the House of Offspring (*Nati* or *Filii*). This determines the topic of conversation in the second half of viii:

> 'We are Abraham's offspring and have never been in servitude to anyone.' viii 33.

> 'I know you are Abraham's offspring ...' viii 37.

> Jesus said to them, 'If you were Abraham's children, you would do the works of Abraham...'. viii 39.

> Jesus said, 'If God were your father you would love me, for I proceeded forth from God and came from him....' viii 42.

The fifth house is concerned with public performances, and lecturing to a crowd falls within its scope. This motivates viii 1.

References to truthfulness in viii 17, 32, 40 are partly due to the fact that the Sun, the ruler of Leo, is a natural symbol of truthfulness, honesty, frankness and openness. Jesus identifies himself with the Sun in:

> Again Jesus spoke to them saying, 'I am the light of the world. Whoever follows me shall not move about in darkness but shall have the light of life.' viii 12.

Month of Av

The month of Av contains the anniversaries of several important dates in Jewish history.

When the Israelites reached the borders of Canaan after two years in the wilderness, they sent spies into the land. On Av 9, the spies returned, and all except Joshua brought back a thoroughly evil report about the place. The Midrash equates this to an act of slander, and immediately appends the parable of a king's son who doubts whether his promised bride is really beautiful and virtuous as he has been told, and thereby angers the king with his scepticism.[8.1] This may have influenced the form of the opening pericope of viii, the Pharisees' accusations against the woman replacing the spies' slander against the land.

On hearing the spies' description of Canaan, the Israelites had a tantrum for which they were punished with having to wander in the desert for an additional thirty-eight years. During this time every member of that generation died. Year after year, death always came on Av 9, the same day that the Israelites had listened to the spies. Legend says that on the eve of the day, people would dig their own graves, and lie down next to them. Rabbinic commentaries say that only men but no women made up the yearly death toll, because only men and no women had maligned the land of Israel when spies were sent to look it over.[8.2] When the deaths finally ceased to occur, the Israelites knew the time had come to cross the Jordan into the Promised Land. In the Gospel, dying off of the older generation of Israelites in the wilderness is becomes:

> They went out one by one, beginning with the oldest. viii 9.
>
> Then Jesus again said to them, 'I am going away, and you will seek me, and you will die in your sins. Where I am going, you cannot come'. viii 21.

The Treasury (viii 20) of the Temple is the background of the conversation because Av 9 was also the anniversary of the destruction of both First and Second Temples (in 586 BCE and 70 CE respectively).

The festival on Av 15 was a happier affair. It was the anniversary of the day the wandering Israelites ceased to die off in the wilderness. Av was a month when unmarried people got engaged, and the fifteenth was celebrated as the anniversary of the rabbinic decree allowing women to freely intermarry across tribal boundaries, Moses having forbidden marriage of an heiress outside her tribe to the first generation of Israelites.[8.3] People from different classes of society, even men and women, freely mingled. The women, dressed in identical white clothing borrowed from their neighbours, went out into the vineyards where they would dance.[8.4] This too has no doubt influenced the episode of the adulterous woman.

teth and hearing

Some versions of *Sefer Yezirah* assign the letter *teth* to hearing, though astrological tradition affords no reason to associate Leo or the cognate house with hearing. The verb 'to hear, to listen' (*akouein*) is of course quite common in the Gospel. The chapters in which it most frequently appears are: v (with six mentions), viii (with seven or eight mentions), ix (with seven mentions), x (with five mentions), xi (with six mentions), xii (five mentions); elsewhere it occurs three times or less.

If we limit ourselves to asking when Jesus, the Father, God or the Holy Spirit hears or listens, or is heard or listened to, and what was heard, the case for viii looks marginally better. I have excluded those chapters which correspond to double letters (iii, x, xvi, xix) or mother letters (xii), from the list, since only the twelve simple letters can possibly correspond to the twelve basic activities the organism:

- iv 42 (the Samaritans heard Jesus);
- v 24 (if someone hears Jesus' word); v 25 (the dead will hear Jesus' voice); v 28 (the dead will hear his voice); v 30 (Jesus judges as he hears); v 37 (the Jews have not heard God's voice);
- vi 45 (some heard and learned from God); vi 60 (hearing Jesus' teaching the disciples ask 'Who can listen to it?');
- vii 40 (the crowd heard Jesus' words);

- viii 6 (Jesus pretends not to hear); viii 9 (Pharisees hear him); viii 26 (Jesus tells what he has heard from God); viii 38 (Pharisees do what they heard from their father); viii 40 (Jesus heard truth in God's presence); viii 43 (the Jews cannot hear Jesus' message); viii 47 (he who is of God hears God's words, but the Jews have not heard them);
- ix 27 (since the Pharisees did not hear the first time, why do they want to hear again?); ix 32 (it has never been heard that a man born blind became seeing); ix 35 (Jesus heard about the man born blind); ix 31 (God does not listen to sinners, he listens to his worshipper); ix 40 (Pharisees heard Jesus' words);
- xi 4 (Jesus heard about Lazarus); xi 6 (Jesus heard about Lazarus); xi 41 (the Father heard Jesus); xi 42 (Jesus knows the Father hears him);
- xiv 24 (the disciples hear the teaching of Jesus and the Father); xiv 28 (the disciples heard Jesus);
- xv 15 (Jesus heard things from the Father);
- xviii 21 (people heard Jesus teaching).

If it is impossible to argue for an outstanding qualitative or quantitative difference between viii and any other chapter, here in any case are the relevant verses in viii in full:

> Hearing this, and being convicted by their own conscience ... viii 9.

> ... and I tell the world what I have heard from him'. viii 26.

> I tell what I have seen at my Father's side, and you do what you have heard at your father's side'. viii 38.

> But now you seek to kill me, a man who has told you the truth that I have heard at God's side... viii 40.

> Why do you not understand my speech? Because you cannot bear to hear my word. viii 43.

> He who is of God hears God's words. You do not hear them, because you are not from God'. viii 47.

Most unusual:

> But Jesus, bending down, wrote on the ground with his finger, pretending not to hear. viii 6.

The verb *akouein* (to hear, to listen) is actually omitted in the Greek in viii 6, the reader having to supply it to make the sentence comprehensible – an elegant way of drawing the reader's attention. (Not included in every version of According to John, the phrase 'pretending not [to hear]' is found in the manuscript tradition followed by *Stephanus 1550, 1551*.)

8.1: *Numbers Rabbah* xvi 6, 7.
8.2: *Numbers Rabbah* xxi 10.
8.3: TB *Ta'anith* 30b.
8.4: TB *Ta'anith* 26b.

The Gospel According to John chapter 9;
yod;
Virgo, and the sixth house; the sixth month, Elul.

Astrological and calendar symbolism of the ninth chapter

The ninth chapter of the Gospel begins with a meeting between Jesus' entourage and a beggar, blind from birth, whom Jesus endows with sight, and ends with a return to the subject of blindness:

> And Jesus said, 'I came into the world for judgement, so that those who do not see might see, and so that those who see might become blind.'
> And some of the Pharisees who were with him heard these words and said, 'We are not blind too, are we?'.
> Jesus said, 'If you were blind no sin would be yours, but since you say, "we see", the sin remains'. ix 39-41.

The significance of sight in ix partly results from the astrological correspondence of the chapter, that is, it intimates an aspect of the Virgo personality: natives of the sign are given to precise and methodical study and meticulous analysis, hair-splitting and pedantry, and obsessive attention to minutiae.

Another reason for the theme of blindness and sightedness that runs through the chapter is connected with the religious calendar. For observant Jews, Elul, the sixth month of the year, is a time of serious preparation, for during the first ten days of the next month, Tishri, the world is judged by the Court of Heaven. It is not possible to avail onself of good works after New Year's Day on Tishri 1, and after the Day of Atonement on Tishri 10, even repentance is of no help. The month of Elul is therefore the last chance to perform meritorious deeds, and also a time of serious introspection. As Jewish literature frequently mentions in this context, *'Elul* means 'Search' in Aramaic.

The theme is dramatically portrayed also in the inquisitorial thoroughness of the Pharisees' investigation into the healing. First the newly-sighted man is himself questioned, then his parents, then the man himself once more. Every aspect of what Jesus did is closely scrutinised: *Teacher, whose sin caused him to be born blind? Was it his own sin or someone else's? Isn't this the man who used to sit and beg? How is it that you can see? Where is he? How could a man who is a sinner perform miracles like these? Is this your son? How is it that he can see? What did he do? How did he cure you?*

A mixture of astrological allusions and ideas related to the religious significance of Elul is seen in:

> Jesus replied, 'Neither he nor his parents sinned, but rather, it was so that the works of God might be shown in him. We must perform the works of the one who sent me while it is still day. Night is coming when no one can work. While I am in the world I am the light of the world...'. ix 3-5.

Virgo and the sixth house of the horoscope are said to chart matters of work and employment. Possibly taking a cue from astrology,

The Gra Version of Sefer Yezirah, like the *Long Version*, lists working as the bodily function associated with the letter *yod*. John apparently follows these attributions. 'Night is coming, when no one can work' recalls Virgo answers to the sixth two-hour period of the day, which ends at sunset (nominally 4 p.m. to 6 p.m.). But it is also reminder that soon it will the seventh month, when it will be too late to perform good deeds.

Jesus claims to be the light of the world is partly due to the fact that Psalm xxvii, which begins 'The Lord is my light and my salvation', is prescribed for daily recitation throughout the month of Elul.

The sixth house is associated with people fallen into miserable or dependent state in life such as beggars. Interestingly, one of the penitential prayers (*selihot*) that characterise the month of Elul, called *L'kha HaShem hazedaka*, begins:

> Like beggars and paupers we knock on your door. O Merciful and Compassionate!

And so, in the Gospel:

> 'Is he not the one who used to sit and beg?' ix 8.

The sixth house is of the horoscope is concerned with the acquisition of expertise, training and refinement of skills, apprenticeship and discipleship, the relationship between master and pupil. In the Gospel this appears as:

> He answered to them, 'I told you before and you did not listen, why are you asking to hear it again? Do you too wish to become his pupils?'.
>
> And they insulted him and said, 'You are his pupil. We are Moses' pupils.' ix 28.

'Wholly conceived in sin as you are, and you are teaching us?'. ix 34.

In ix 7, John obliquely alludes to the zodiacal sign of Virgo as well as its planetary ruler, Mercury:

And Jesus said to him, 'Go wash in the Pool of Siloam', which is translated [*hermēneuetai*] 'One who has been Sent'.

The hidden reference to Virgo hangs on a curious fact, a piece of local knowledge: Siloam is fed from a spring called the Fountain of the Virgin. A tunnel a third of a mile long, acting as a natural siphon, connected Siloam to this underground source. Anyone washing in Siloam necessarily washed in water coming from the Virgin's Fountain. On the pretext of helping out his Hebrew-ignorant reader, John here takes the opportunity to use the verb *hermēneuein*, 'to translate' in order to indicate Mercury under his Greek name, Hermes. 'One who has been Sent' actually indicates the god's primary role as messenger or emissary.

John treats the planets and the sefiroth of the Qabalah as if they are equivalent. Because of this, Mercury can share all the specific attributes of Hod (Glory), the corresponding sefirah. A specific association of the sefirah is confession or acknowledgement (Hebrew: *vidui* or *hodah*). And thus we have the Baptist's confession or acknowledgement in the first chapter of the Gospel:

He acknowledged [*hōmolegēsen*] it and did not deny it.
He acknowledged [*hōmolegēsen*], 'I am not the Christ'. i 20.

And since Mercury is the planetary ruler of Virgo, the idea also occurs here in the ninth chapter of the Gospel:

His parents said this because they feared the Jews, for the Jews had already agreed that if anyone acknowledged [*hōmolegēsen*] that he was Christ, he should be put out of the synagogue. ix 22.

The hired man, another latecomer

Because the sixth house is concerned with paid employment and services performed for a fee, the hired man of x 12-13 aptly personifies this sector of the sky. When a personification appears late, that is, when it appears not in the chapter determined by the scheme of correspondences, but in the chapter immediately following, fleeing from the scene consistently serves as a signal for what is going on. This explains his sudden flight:

> 'But the hired man, who is not the shepherd and does not own the sheep, sees the wolf coming and leaves the sheep, and flees. And the wolf catches the sheep and scatters them. The hired man flees because he is a hired man and does not care about the sheep.' x 12-13.

Mercury-Hermes' connection with thievery is well known; his cult titles include *Pheletēs* (Thief, Robber), and *Archōn Pheletōn* (Chief of Robbers, Prince of Thieves). John in several places shows awareness of this aspect of his character. Mercury, because he is ruler of Virgo, appears in the shape of the thief who 'does not enter through the door but climbs in another way' (x 2). Since the door or gate is itself one of the chief symbols of chapter ten, Jesus himself identifying with the door to the sheepfold, the thief's irregular mode of entry indicates references to Mercury should otherwise have been confined to ix. Cast in the same mould and just as easy is x 8, 'all who came before me are thieves and robbers', which is another way of saying that thieves and robbers are among the symbolic associations proper to the preceding chapter, that is the ninth.

The Gospel According to John chapter 10;
kaf;
Jupiter.

An innovation

In the terminology of *Sefer Yezirah*, *kaf*, the letter corresponding to x, is a 'double letter'; it represents one of the planets, namely Jupiter, and one of the days of the week. The next letter of the alphabet, *lamed*, the letter under whose banner xi falls, is a 'simple letter'; it corresponds accordingly to a month of the year, namely Tishri, and a sign of the zodiac, namely Libra. The following letter, *mem*, the assignment of xii, is a 'mother letter', and corresponds to one of the elements, water, and one of the seasons, namely Winter.

Three holidays fall in the month Tishri: New Year's Day (*Rosh ha Shanah*) is celebrated on the first of the month; ten days later comes the Day of Atonement (*Yom Kippur*); finally, Tabernacles or Feast of Ingathering (*Sukkoth*) begins five days after that. John makes an elegant and innovative change to the calendar scheme that is given in *Sefer Yezirah*. What we end up with is this:

- the letter *kaf*, that is, the tenth chapter of the Gospel, is associated with New Year's Day (*Rosh ha Shanah*), which falls on Tishri 1;

- the letter *lamed*, that is, chapter eleven, with the Day of Atonement (*Yom Kippur*), which falls on Tishri 10;
- the letter *mem*, that is, chapter twelve, to the Feast of Tabernacles (*Sukkoth*), which runs from Tishri 15 to 22.

Thus, John marries the three holidays of Tishri as they fall in chronological order to three consecutive letters, that is to three consecutive chapters of his Gospel. Each of these festivals is important in its own right, and each has its own distinct theme. It would have been quite confusing to have all three celebrated in the eleventh chapter alone.

To allow double and mother letters to pick up symbolism related to Jewish feasts from a neighbouring simple letter constitutes a departure from the original scheme of *Sefer Yezirah*, in which only the twelve simple letters are assigned to calendar months. However, John can get away with it without upsetting the calendar scheme set forth in *Sefer Yezirah*: the letter *yod* still corresponds to the month Elul, the letter *lamed* still corresponds to the month Tishri, the letter *nun* to the month Marḥeshvan, and so on.

Two calendars

The reason for New Year's falling in the seventh month lies in the fact that there is more than one Jewish calendar.[10.1] The annual cycle that begins with the new moon of the vernal equinox, with the month containing Passover (Nisan or Abib), was primarily of religious significance. It loosely coincides with the zodiacal year, which is taken to begin precisely with the vernal equinox. This form of reckoning was not instituted until the departure from Egypt, with the first Passover (Exodus xii 2). It is therefore used throughout the Bible with the notable exception of Genesis. This is the calendar we have been using so far.

Before the Israelites' release from bondage in Egypt, however, only the calendar used for civil or common purposes existed. Because it is used throughout Genesis, and because of a rabbinic tradition that God created Adam on the first day of the civil year, it is sometimes called 'the Creation Calendar'. Since the civil calendar begins at the autumnal equinox, while the calendar of religious feasts begins at the vernal equinox, these ways of reckoning the year are six months out of phase: Tishri, the seventh month of the religious year, is the first month of the civil year. This is why New Year's Day falls in the seventh month.

In rabbinic tradition, New Year's Day was a time of judgement; *Yom ha Din*, Judgement Day is another of its names. Some people were sufficiently evil to be sentenced to die in the following year, while others were virtuous enough to be inscribed in the Book of Life for the coming year, but the sentence of a third group, neither very good nor very evil, was suspended until Day of Atonement (*Yom Kippur*).[10.2] In the 'Days of Awe' between New Year's Day and Day of Atonement, every Jew was supposed to imagine that he fell into that indeterminate category of men, neither extremely wicked nor highly virtuous, whose fate was not sealed on New Year's Day, and who therefore had to wait until the Day of Atonement to receive their verdict. The suspenseful waiting that permeates the days between New Year's Day and the Day of Atonement is hinted at in:

'How long will you take our breath away?' x 24.

The door or gate is a symbol of the New Year drawn from classical paganism: Janus, a Roman god without Greek equivalent, to whom doorways (Latin *januae*) and archways (Latin *jani*) were sacred and whose function was indicated by the set of keys he carried, was also the god of the new year. The beginning of the day, month, season and year were sacred to him; he gave his name to the month of January. The door, accordingly, becomes one of the more important symbols of x, Jesus twice identifying himself with the door or gate of his flock:

> 'One not entering into the sheepfold by the door, but climbing in by some other way is a thief and a robber. The one entering through the door is the shepherd of the sheep. The doorkeeper opens for him.' x 2-3

> 'Amen, amen, I tell you: I am the door for the sheep...' x 7

> 'I am the door. If anyone enter through me he shall be saved, and he shall go in and out, and find pasture'. x 9.

Shepherd of New Year

In x, Jesus is a shepherd whose distinctive features are that he is good, and that he lays down his life for his sheep, and that he is known to his sheep by voice.

One motivation for the identification, but not the only one, comes from the Jewish calendar. The image of God as Shepherd of *Rosh ha Shanah* is quite widespread in rabbinic writings, having its origin in the Talmud, which explains that on New Year's Day everyone in the world passes before God like sheep before a shepherd, that is they pass in single file, so that each creature is scrutinised alone, separate from the rest of flock.[10.3]

The voice of the shepherd is evidently important in its own right:

> 'And his sheep listen to his voice and he calls his sheep by name...' x 3.

> 'And the sheep follow him because they know his voice. They will not follow a stranger but will flee from him, because they do not know the voice of strangers.' x 4-5.

> 'I must lead them, and they will hear my voice...' x 16.

> 'My sheep hear to my voice, and I know them and they follow me...' x 27.

The reason for the prominence given to the Good Shepherd's voice here stems from the fact that the word usually translated 'voice', *phōnē*, also serves for the sound of a musical instrument, and the Biblical name for New Year's Day is *Yom Teruēah*, translated 'Feast of Trumpets', but literally meaning 'Day of Blowing'. The literal sense of *Teruēah*, 'Blowing', explains also the appearance of the word *psychē* ('life') – for the root meaning of *psychē* is 'breath or blowing', seen in *psychein* ('to blow') and *psychos* ('cold' i.e. 'chilled by wind'):

> 'The Good Shepherd lays down his life [*psychēn*] for the sheep.' x 11.

> 'Just as the Father knows me, so do I know the Father. And I lay down my life [*psychēn*] for the sheep.' x 15.

> 'On account of this the Father loves me: I lay down my life [*psychēn*] so that I may take it up again.' x 17-18.

Jesus was walking in Solomon's Portico in the Temple, when the people encircled him and asked, 'How long will you take our breath [*psychēn*] away?' x 23-24.

Zeus-Jupiter

Zeus-Jupiter, according to one myth of the god's origins, was brought up by shepherds on Mount Ida. Dangerous as it was, they were persuaded to conceal him from Kronos-Saturn, his malicious father, by Zeus-Jupiter's promise to protect their flocks from wolves in return. *Zeus Lukaios* (Lupine or Wolfish Zeus) was actually a cult title of the god connected with this worship in rustic Arcadia. One story explains the epithet, telling how he transformed King Lycaon and his sons into wolves for having offered him human flesh to eat.[10.4] Both the Good Shepherd (x 11, 14) and the wolf who chases away the hired man (x 12) are therefore guises of Jupiter.

It is crucial to understand the ambiguity of the motif of the Good Shepherd in x is quite deliberate. It was intended to recall both the astrological attribution (Jupiter, Greater Benefic, Patron of Shepherds), and an image related to the calendar in Jewish religious traditions (God as Shepherd scrutinising his flock on New Year's Day). As will be seen in Part 2 of this work, when we examine the qabalistic side of the Gospel, John has a great predilection for symbols which are simultaneously astrological and qabalistic. Here we see something similar – an image which is astrological on one hand, yet related to the calendar of Jewish holidays on the other.

The generally fortunate or lucky nature of the planet Jupiter, which is known in astrology as the 'Greater Benefic', manifests in that Jesus is not just the Shepherd, but the Good Shepherd:

'I am the Good Shepherd.' x 11.

'I am the Good Shepherd, and know my sheep, and mine know me.' x 14.

Abundance, generosity, expansion, largeness and extravagance are specifically associated with Jupiter and alluded to in the Gospel:

'I came so that they might have life and have it abundantly'. x 10

'My Father, who gives me, is greater than anyone. (or: What my father gives me is greater than anything.)'. x 29.

Several versions of *Sefer Yezirah* attribute life (and death) to the letter *kaf*, and it is likely John does so too.

John makes an allusion to Jupiter by mentioning the Feast of Dedication, *Hanukah*. This begins in the ninth month, which corresponds to Sagittarius, a sign ruled by Jupiter. In addition, *Hanukah* recalls the purification of the Temple after offerings to other gods had desecrated the altar. The first of these was a sacrifice to Olympean Zeus, whose cult became the dominant one.

In summary, allusions to Jupiter, the planetary correspondence of the chapter are found in the shape of the wolf who causes the hired man, a personification of the previous chapter's correspondences, to run away (x 12). The nature of the planet is shown in generosity, extravagance, abundance (x 10, 28-29), and benevolence (x 11, 14). Because the chapter is connected with Jewish New Year, Janus, Roman god of the New Year, and of gates and doors, appears in the shape of the doorkeeper (x 3), and leads to Jesus to identify with the Gate of the Sheep (x 7, 9). It is even possible John has shrewdly guessed Janus is an alterego of Jupiter, as modern mythographers have speculated. Covert references to New Year's Day, the Feast of Trumpets, in the voice of the Good Shepherd (x 3-5, 16, 27), and the word 'breath' (x 11, 15, 17-18, 23-24). The Good Shepherd derives from a Jewish New Year's Day motif, God the shepherd, examining his flock one by one, but also from Jupiter-Zeus' portrayal in classical myth.

10.1: TB *Rosh ha Shanah* 2a, 8a, 27a.

10.2: TB *Rosh Ha Shanah* 16b.

10.3: TB *Rosh ha Shanah* 18a.

10.4: Robert Graves, *The Greek Myths* 38.a-g.

The Gospel According to John chapter 11;
lamed;
Libra, and the seventh house; the seventh month, Ethanim or Tishri.

For John every day and every night of the year consisted of twelve hours by definition, but Jesus' rhetorical question alludes to the fact that Libra is the sign of the autumnal equinox:

> 'Are there not twelve hours in a day?'. xi 9.

Alternatively, it may refer to an apocryphal legend of the twelve hours of Adam's first day on earth. The First Day of creation was Elul 25, so that Adam's creation, on the Sixth Day, took place on Tishri 1. In the first hour, so the story goes, God gathers the dust from the four corners of the world; in the second hour, he makes the dust a shapeless mass; in the third hour, he moulds in into a human form; in the fourth hour, endows it with breath; in the fifth hour, Adam stands erect; in the sixth hour, he gives names to the animals; in the seventh hour, he marries Eve; and so on.[11.1]

Libra is the first of the six 'nocturnal' signs – if the year is scaled down into a day, it corresponds to nightfall, the two hours immediately following sunset (nominally 6 to 8 p.m.), thus explaining the hidden sense of Jesus' words:

> 'If someone walks around in the day he does not stumble, for he sees the light of the world. But if someone walks around in the night he stumbles, because he has no light'. xi 9-10.

The seventh house of the horoscope is accorded rulership over intimate friendships, an important theme of xi:

> 'Master, look, the one you love is sick!' xi 3
>
> And Jesus loved Mary and her sister Martha and Lazarus. xi 5
>
> 'Lazarus our friend has fallen asleep.' xi 11
>
> 'See how much he loved him!' xi 36.

This sector of the heavens, the seventh house or descendant, is connected with relations between equal partners; it shows one's complement or opposite or counterpart. Lazarus is of this type, if he is true to his name, a hellenised form *Eleazar*, 'Whose Helpmate (Hebrew *'azar*) is God (Hebrew *'El*)'; when God makes Eve as 'helpmate' for Adam, the same word *'azer* is used.

Calendar symbolism: Day of Atonement

As already explained, in the calendar system implicit in According to John, the seventh month of the Jewish year, which falls when the sun passes through Libra, and which is represented by the simple letter *lamed*, is especially referable to the Day of Atonement (*Yom Kippur*). The whole first ten days of Tishri, the 'Days of Awe', are concerned with judgement, but there are several important differences between New Year's Day and the Day of Atonement. On the former holiday, the Lower Court of Heaven, a sort of tribunal of angels, held session. Many people lacked sufficient virtue or vice that the court might reach a definitive conclusion about them. By prayer and fasting and repentance, people whose fate were not determined could still do something to save themselves. On the Day of Atonement, however, the Supreme Judge, whose judgement was irrevocable, sits alone. The indeterminate category of men are finally judged, and the sentence that the Lower World Tribunal had already passed on the other two groups was ratified. These are some of the essential features of the day, as described in rabbinic writings, that distinguish it from the preceding nine days.

Another difference is that on New Year's Day, each person was judged as an individual, while the Day of Atonement involved the judgement of the whole world – the merits of all the good people placed on one side of the scales, and weighed against the offences of the wicked on the other side. According to rabbinical tradition, everyone was obliged to consider the world's good and evil perfectly equal, with the fate of the entire universe literally hanging in the balance. The good or evil of a single person could tip the scales and so save or condemn the whole world.[11.2]

The Talmud discusses whether or not it is beneficial to pray after the Day of Atonement, concluding that it cannot do any harm.[11.3] Nevertheless, it was generally felt that no prayer, fasting, self-affliction or repentance could achieve anything at all after that day, when all judgements were finalised. In the Gospel story, when Martha says,

> 'I know that even now God will give you however much you ask him' xi 22

she is hinting that the Supreme Judge has already delivered his irrevocable verdicts, so that it is too late to pray.

It is a custom among some Jewish people to wear a white shroud on the Day of Atonement, called a *qitel*, and which also serves as a burial shroud. It is often said that behaviour on the day – fasting, no sex, no washing, no leather shoes – is modelled on the behaviour of one mourning a dead relative. Apart from this, the image of the death of the old year and its return in the new provides motivation for the death and resurrection of Lazarus in xi. Another lies in the fact that Jewish traditions liken the Day of Atonement to the Day of Resurrection, even though the former is an annually repeated affair and the latter a one-off event at the end of time.[11.4]

It is quite proper to cry on Day of Atonement, in fact, it is almost compulsory in many Jewish communities. The day was not one of rejoicing, but of mourning and fear on which the people were ordered to afflict and humble themselves. A curious passage in the Talmud suggests that it may have been a duty of the High Priest to shed tears on the day.[11.5] In the Gospel this manifests as the weeping of Jesus, the two sisters, and other mourners at the funeral:

> When Jesus saw her weeping, and that the people accompanying her were weeping, he was deeply moved in spirit and was disturbed... Jesus wept... Deeply moved within himself once more, Jesus went to the tomb ... xi 33-38.

The Evangelist closes the chapter with a references to the most important rite connected with the Day of Atonement. Lots were drawn over two he-goats; one was sacrificed to God in the Temple; the other animal, the scapegoat, to whom the High Priest ritually transferred the sins of the people, was driven off into the desert.

In xi, Jesus is clearly cast in the role of scapegoat, killed for the good of the people. Like the scapegoat, he is banished to the wilderness. Kaiaphas, one notes, is said to be speaking, not as an ordinary individual, but as High Priest, who alone could officiate at the chief solemnity of the day:

> One of them, Kaiaphas, being High Priest for that year, said to them, 'You know nothing. Nor do you realise that it is useful to us that one man die on behalf of the people lest the whole nation be destroyed.'
> He said this not on his own authority but, being High Priest for that year, he was prophesying that Jesus was going to die on behalf of the nation, and not only on behalf of the nation, but so that he might gather into one the scattered children of God. From this day, then, they considered [*ebouleusanto*] how to kill him. So Jesus no longer went openly about Judea but went away from there into the country to a town called Ephraim near the wilderness. xi 49-54.

Rabbinic commentators identify the twelve tribes of Israel with the signs of the zodiac, and although some disagreement exists, Ephraim is sometimes given as the tribe corresponding to the zodiacal sign Libra. Aryeh Kaplan, who gives the four different schemes in his invaluable commentary to his translation of *Sefer Yezirah*, says that this particular assignment is drawn from a listing of the tribes of Israel in Numbers, and explains why Ephraim is apparently associated with Libra in the *Gra Version of Sefer Yezirah*, although the assignment is not given explicitly.

The Talmud records that a week before he was to officiate at the Yom Kippur service the High Priest would be secluded in the Chamber of Councillors (*Bouleutai* or *Prohedroi*), so that he could concentrate upon the task ahead, and mentally review the procedures.[11.6] The verb *bouleuein* in xi 53 is most probably intended as a pun on *bouleutēs*, a member of the Sanhedrin. The Talmud says that the Chamber of *Bouleutai* had to have its name changed to the Chamber of *Prohedroi* because the High Priests were replaced on a yearly basis just like 'king's men' (*prohedroi*).[11.7] The Talmud, which was written by Pharisees, and not at all sympathetic to the Sadducean priesthood, explains that the Sadducee High Priests regularly died as a result of divine displeasure because they could not perform the ritual of Atonement competently. John seems to have this in mind, for having noted that Kaiaphas was priest for that year in xi 49, he mentions the fact again in xi 51.

The Talmud relates that on the eve of Yom Kippur measures were taken to prevent sleep from overtaking the High Priest.[11.8] He was allowed to eat only a little since a full belly promotes drowsiness; the junior priests would snap their fingers to keep him awake; he was encouraged to stand and pace up and down; a crowd of people would gather outside his window and converse loudly. This is probably the source of references to sleeping in the opening pericope of this chapter:

> He said this, and then he says to them, 'Our friend Lazarus has fallen asleep, but I am going to awaken him'.
> Then said his disciples, 'Master, if he sleeps, he will be safe'.
> Although Jesus was speaking about his death, they thought that he had spoken about the slumber of sleep. xi 11-13.

11.1 TB *Sanhedrin* 38b. *Leviticus Rabbah* xxix 1. *Pirqe Rabbi Eliezer* chaps. viii, xi. Louis Ginzberg, *Legends of the Jews* chap. ii.

11.2: TB *Rosh Ha Shanah* 17a.
11.3: TB *Rosh Ha Shanah* 18a.
11.4: TB *Rosh Ha Shanah* 16b.
11.5: TB *Yoma* 18b.
11.6: TB *Yoma* 2a.
11.7: TB *Yoma* 8b.
11.8: TB *Yoma* 18a, 19b.

The Gospel According to John chapter 12;
mem;
Water.

In *Sefer Yezirah*, the twelve simple letters correspond to the twelve months of the year, and to the twelve signs of the zodiac. But in John's Gospel, as we have seen, letters which are not simple letters sometimes pick up calendar or zodiacal symbolism from an immediately preceding or following simple letter. This is what allows xii, which corresponds to the mother letter *mem*, to contain references to the third major Jewish holiday in Tishri: the Feast of Tabernacles or Shelters or Tents (*Sukkoth*).

Fasting was not permitted at this time – to eat within the *sukkah*, and to eat well was a religious obligation. One also had to sleep within the *sukkah*, in order to fulfil the command to make it one's actual dwelling for the week.[12.1] The *sukkah* would therefore contain at least a bed and a table. Because of limited space within the structure, it was common to eat at the table while reclining on couches that served for beds at night. Spices and fragrances traditionally play a role in the customs of Tabernacles. This sets the scene for the opening of xii:

> There they held a dinner for him, and Martha served, and Lazarus was one of those who reclined with him at the table. Then Mary took a litra of spikenard ointment, very costly, and anointed the feet of Jesus, and wiped his feet with her hair, and the house was filled with the odour of the ointment. Then one of his disciples, Judas Iscariot, who was going to betray him, says 'Why was this ointment not sold for three hundred denarii, and given to the poor?'. xii 2-5.

Judas' words are entirely apropos: feeding the poor is an important religious duty of the holiday, and a tradition exists that one who shows charity to the unfortunate on this holiday enjoys in his *sukkah* the company of unseen holy guests.[12.2]

Triumphal processions formed a major part in the Feast of Tabernacles, and here we have the Triumphal Entry into Jerusalem:

> The next day the great crowd who had come to the feast, having heard that Jesus was coming to Jerusalem, took branches of palm trees, and went out to meet him, and cried, 'Hosanna! Blessed is the one coming in the name of the Lord, the King of Israel'.
> And Jesus, finding a young ass, sat on it, as it is written [Zechariah ix 9], 'Fear not, O daughter of Zion. Behold, your King comes, sitting on an ass's colt'. xii 12-15.
>
> The Pharisees therefore said among themselves, 'Do you see that nothing profits you? Look, the whole world has gone after him'. xii 19.

The date-palm plays so great a role at Tabernacles that in iconography of synagogues of the first and second centuries CE it could stand alone as a symbol for it.[12.3] The *Hoshana Rabbah*, 'the Great Hosanah', was a part of the celebration, in which the *lulav* (date-palm, citron, myrtle and willow bound together in a certain way) was struck on the ground accompanied by shouts of '*Hoshana!*' ('Please save!').[12.4] The crowd chants "Blessed be he who comes in the name of the Lord", quoting from Psalm cxviii, a processional hymn especially prescribed for Tabernacles.[12.5] This detail is also recorded in the synoptics (According to Matthew xxi 9, Mark xi 1-9).

Tabernacles or the Feast of Ingathering, as it is called, is an agricultural festival, a time for summer crops of fruit and grain to be harvested and stored. This leads to Jesus' comment:

> 'Unless a grain falls to the ground and dies, it remains only one, but if it dies, it brings forth much fruit'. xii 24.

A variation on the idea is seen in According to Matthew xxi 18-20 and Mark xi 12-14, where Jesus, soon after his triumphal entry, vents his anger on a fig tree on finding it bare of fruit. His disappointment stems from the fact that under Jewish Law it is forbidden to clean every last piece of fruit from trees at harvest time – one is supposed to leave some for the poor. Jesus curses the tree just in order to punish its owner for stripping it bare.

Zechariah xiv 16-18 foretells a time when the Gentile nations would receive no rain unless they attended the Feast of Tabernacles in Jerusalem. In the Talmud the prophecy expands into a legend that Gentiles throughout the world would one day seek to convert to Judaism en masse.[12.6] This will take place during the celebration of Tabernacles, and the Gentile nations will be given the injunction to build a *sukkah* to test their sincerity. In the Gospel, the turning of foreign nations to the true religion at a future Feast of Tabernacles in the messianic age becomes:

And there were certain Greeks among those who came up to worship at the feast. They came to Philip, who was from Bethsaida in Galilee, and asked him, saying, 'Master, we want to see Jesus'. xii 20-21.

In summary, Feast of Tabernacles provides the backdrop for the twelfth chapter of John's Gospel, in keeping with his handling of the Jewish calendar. The celebratory dinner, concern for the poor, the triumphal procession, the lopping of palm braches, cries of 'Hoshanah' and 'Blessed be he who comes in the name of the Lord', the wish to see Jesus on the part of certain Greeks, all find their basis in the holiday.

12.1: TB *Sukkah* 2b, 26a-b, 27a, 28a-b, 48b.

12.2: *Zohar* 1:11a; 3:103b, 104a. Daniel C. Matt *The Zohar: Pritzker Edition* vol. 1 p. 72 n. 541. 12.3: Erwin R. Goodenough, *Jewish Symbols in the GraecoRoman Period; edited and abridged by Jacob Neusner,* p. 113.

12.4: TB *Sukkah* 45a-b.

12.5: TB *Sukkah* 37b.

12.6: TB *Avodah Zara* 3a-b.

The Gospel According to John chapter 13;
nun;
Scorpio, and the eighth house; the eighth month, Heshvan, Marheshvan or Bul.

The thirteenth chapter of the Gospel corresponds to the midautumn sign of Scorpio. The sign and its associated house, the eighth in order from the ascendant, rules over shared wealth and common property, especially legacies and bequests from deceased persons. Astrological tradition connects the house with intense feelings, passions, addictions and obsessions; it is concerned with secret drives and motivations, forbidden subjects and clandestine relationships. The eighth house is said to rule death and all matters related to mortality. It is also associated with pollution and uncleanliness, and the need for sanitation or purification. The sign is watery in nature. Its ruler is Mars. These are the ideas to which John has recourse in composing xiii.

Much of the Fourth Gospel involves a demonstration of Jesus' mastery in some sphere of life, and this is determined by the specific correspondences of the chapter. Often a person who embodies some aspect of the astrological correspondences will be set beside Jesus for the sake of comparison. In xiii, it is Judas who serves as a foil for Jesus in this way. On one hand, Jesus' mortality is hinted at in the opening verse of xiii. On the other hand, Judas is clearly branded as a Scorpio-type through his name: *Iscariot* comes from *Sicarii* (Greek *Sikarioi*), a band of dagger-bearing assassins who terrorised Judaea during the Roman occupation.

The emotional intensity that characterises the Scorpio persona is reflected in Jesus in the opening verse of xiii:

> Now before the Feast of Passover, Jesus, knowing that the time had come for him to depart from this world to go to the Father, having loved those who were his own in the world, loved them to the very end. xiii 1.

The sign's particular connection with hidden desires and motivations is seen at work in Judas in the next verse:

> And supper being over, and the Devil having already put it into the heart of Judas, son of Simon Iscariot, to betray Jesus... xiii 2.

That Judas is secretly intending to hand Jesus over to the Jewish elders is a taboo subject, forbidden to mention openly but hinted at, and goes on to become a key theme of the chapter:

> For he knew the one who was betraying him, and therefore he said, 'Not all of you are clean'. xiii 11.

> 'I do not speak about you all: I know whom I have chosen. But it is so in order that the scripture, "he who eats bread with me has lifted up his heel against me", may be fulfilled.' xiii 18.

> 'Having said this, he was troubled in spirit, and testified, and said, 'Amen, amen, I tell you: one of you will betray me'. xiii 21.

In qabalistic texts, the Midrash, in the Targum, the Talmud, *Pirqe Rabbi Eliezer*, the Devil, 'the Evil Impulse' who tempted Eve in the Garden, is said to be none other than the Angel of Death, Samael.[13.1] In both Jewish and Western writings that deal with as angelic rulers of planets, Samael is also listed as the angel over Mars, the planetary ruler of Scorpio.[13.2] The presence of the Devil in xiii is therefore congruous with the astrological assignment of the chapter.

To throw a sop to the Devil to induce him to go away is a common image in qabalistic writings.[13.3] In the Gospel, Jesus hands a morsel or sop to Judas, who is entered by the Devil, and promptly leaves the table:

> Jesus answered, 'It is he to whom I shall give a morsel when I have dipped it'. Then having dipped the morsel, he takes it and gives it to Judas, the son of Simon Iscariot. And along with the morsel Satan entered into him. Then Jesus says to him, 'What you do, do quickly'. xiii 26-27.
>
> Having received the morsel, he immediately went out. It was night. xiii 30.

If the year is scaled down into a day, Scorpio and the eighth house correspond to 8 to 10 p.m., hence when Judas leaves the supper 'it was night' (xiii 30).

Marḥeshvan stands at the beginning of the autumn rains which were prayed for during the Feast of Tabernacles little more than a week earlier. Scorpio is a watery sign, and because of its rulership over the organs of excretion, it is often associated with pollution or dirtiness. At the same time it is associated with purification or sanitation. Such themes constitute the early part of this chapter where Jesus washes the feet of all the disciples in turn:

After this he pours water into a bowl, and began to wash the disciples' feet and dry them with the towel with which he was wrapped. Then he comes to Simon Peter. He says to him, 'Master, are you washing my feet?'
Jesus replied and said to him, 'You do not know now what I am doing, but you will know afterwards'.
Peter says to him, 'Never in all eternity shall you wash my feet'.
Jesus replied to him, 'Unless I wash you, you have no share with me'.
Peter says, 'Master, then not only my feet, but my hands and head too'.
Jesus says to him, 'One who have bathed is completely clean and does not need to wash, except for his feet. And you are clean, but not all of you'. xiii 3-10.

Common property

References to communal or shared wealth occur in xiii. The first is found in Jesus' exchange with Peter when he tells him he can have no share with Jesus unless he washes his feet (xiii 8). The idea appears yet again in xiii 29 where Judas is noted to be holder of the common purse. The disciples thought Judas' motive for leaving the supper was somehow connected his being keeper of the group's wealth, and so it ironically is, since he is going out to surrender Jesus for money. John, who is averse to describing events at which he was not present, fails to include any account of Judas' actual meeting with the authorities. The fact that Judas is in charge of the communal funds also qualifies him to personify the eighth house.

The Last Supper in the Synoptic Gospels

The eighth house of the heavens is connected with the idea of a legacy or bequest. The mansion charts both the abandonment of what is of no further use, so that others may take it up, and the appropriation of what others have similarly discarded; something left behind, like a corpse. The verb *paradidoun*, which appears in xiii 2, 11 and 21, can mean 'to betray' but also has a neutral meaning, that is, one not involving any sense of treachery, but merely 'to give something up, to surrender, to hand over'; 'betray' also had this sense in English not too long ago.

In the Synoptic Gospels Jesus makes a pronouncement at the Last Supper that John leaves out completely, a striking omission, since it is sometimes considered to be the climax of the Last Supper:

> 'This is my body which is given for you. Do this in memory of me... This cup is the new testament [*diathēkē*] in my blood, which is poured out for you. But see, the hand of the one betraying me is with mine on the table. The Son of Man certainly goes in the manner decided, but woe to the man by whom he is betrayed.' According to Luke xxii 19-20 (and Matthew xxvi 21-28, Mark xiv 18-24 are parallel).

If Jesus had made this statement in xiii, its appositeness would be clear. With 'this is my body' Jesus speaks of himself as though he were a corpse. And the Greek *diathēkē* may mean 'a testament' or 'a will', possessing the same connotation as the English phrase 'last will and testament', that is, it pertains directly to the disposal of property of one deceased. This is how the term is understood by the author of Letter to the Hebrews ix 15-17, who remarks that a will only becomes effectual upon the death of the testator. Jesus himself moreover describes it as a testament in his blood.

Summary

In summary, the eighth house's connection with death manifests in allusions to Jesus' mortality on one hand, and in the person of Judas, son of the Iscariot, that is Assassin on the other. The Devil, who puts ideas into Judas' heart, then enters him to receive a sop from Jesus, is Samael, angelic of Mars, ruler of Scorpio, and also Angel of Death. Judas' secret treachery and Jesus' ultimate love also reflect the house specific associations of the house. The eighth house's connection with common property and group finances manifests in mention of sharing in xiii 8 and 18, but is especially embodied in the shape of Judas, who holds the moneybox. The watery nature of Scorpio, the asterism's association with dirtiness and uncleanliness, and the fact that Marḥeshvan is the beginning of the rainy season, contribute to Jesus' washing of the disciples' feet.

13.1: *Zohar* 1:35b, 36a, 52a, 62b, 63a-b, 152b, 153a, 168a, 169b, 178b-179a, 202a. Daniel C. Matt, *The Zohar: Pritzker Edition*, vol. 1 pp. 224, 225 nn. 946, 947, 952; ibid p. 288 n. 1381; ibid p. 364 nn. 164, 167; vol. 2 p. 350 n. 249; vol. 3 p. 15 n. 104; ibid p. 54 n. 387; ibid p. 83 n. 551; ibid p. 238 n. 354. *Exodus Rabbah* xviii 5, xxi 7. *Leviticus Rabbah* xxi 4. *Targum PseudoJonathan Genesis* iii 5. TB *Baba Bathra* 16a. *Pirqe Rabbi Eliezer* chap. xiii, xiv, xxi.

13.2: See various Jewish texts cited by Aryeh Kaplan in *Sefer Yetzirah, Book of Creation* p 168 t. 31. Athanasius Kircher,

Oedipus Aegyptiacus vol. 1 p35-36, 235-236. *The Magic and Philosophy of Johannes Trithemius of Spanheim/The Art of Drawing Spirits into Crystals. Heptameron of Peter de Abano.*

13.3: *Zohar* 2:33a, 39b; 3:101b. Daniel C. Matt, *The Zohar: The Pritzker Edition* vol. 3 p. 55 n. 391; vol. 4 p. 140 n. 13.

The Gospel According to John chapter 14;
samekh;
Sagittarius, and the ninth house of the heavens; the ninth month, Kislev.

The fourteenth chapter of According to John corresponds to the letter *samekh* and thus to the sign Sagittarius. Traditionally pictured as a centaur – half man, half horse – the sign has a natural affinity with horses and equestrian matters. In the Gospel this manifests in the shape of the apostle Philip (Greek: 'Fond of Horses, Horse-loving'), who converses with Jesus here (xiv 8).

Other features of xiv, in particular, Jesus' 'I am' statement of the chapter, stem from the significations of the ninth house of the heavens, the mansion cognate with Sagittarius. This area of the horoscope is said to chart long distance voyages and travel to foreign countries; its traditional name in medieval astrology was the House of Journey (*Iter*). More abstractly, the ninth house denotes the conscience or personal ethical or moral code of the native, one's overall philosophy or attitude, one's way of life. Hence:

> 'If not, would I have told you that I was going to prepare a place for you? But if I do go and prepare a place for you, I shall come

again and take you to myself, so that where I am you too may
be. You know where I am going, and you know the way.'
Thomas says to him, 'Master, we do not know where you are
going, how can we know the way?'.
Jesus says to him, 'I am the Way, the Truth, and the Life.
No one comes to the Father unless it is through me.' xiv 2-6.

Jesus' identification with truth is similarly according to formula, since the ninth sector of the heavens also rules higher knowledge, particularly philosophical or religious knowledge, and matters of higher or advanced education. House of Knowledge or Philosophy (*Sapientia*) is another traditional name of the ninth mansion. In the Gospel this also appears as references to knowledge and Jesus' teachings:

'Had you known me, you would have known my Father too.
But from now on you do know him, and have seen him'. xiv 7

'On that day you will know I am in the Father, and you in me,
and I in you.' xiv 20

Jesus answered and said to him, 'If someone loves me,
he shall observe my teaching, and my Father will love him,
and we shall come to him, and make our dwelling with
him. The one who does not love me does not observe my
teaching. And the teaching which you hear is not mine,
but belongs to the Father, who sent me.' xiv 23-24.

Sagittarians are said to function well as conciliators, referees, and specifically, legal advocates. Accordingly, Jesus mentions the existence of a Paraclete, literally 'one called beside', often rendered as 'Advocate' or 'Intercessor', who is linked with the special gnosis:

> And I shall ask the Father, and he will give you another Paraclete to remain with you forever: the Spirit of Truth, whom the world cannot accept, because it neither sees nor knows him. But you know him, for he dwells with you, and will be within you. xiv 16-17.
>
> 'But the Paraclete, the Holy Spirit, whom the Father will send in my name, will teach you everything, and will remind you of everything I have told you.' xiv 26.

The ninth house is concerned with one's personal morals and ethics, but also the law of the land and legal codification. John introduces the topic into Jesus' discourse, with 'commandment' (*entolē*) and the cognate verb 'command' (*entolasthai*) taking the place of 'law' (*nomos*):

> 'If you love me, observe my commandments.' xiv 15
>
> 'The one who has my commandments and observes them is the one who loves me.' xiv 21
>
> 'But in order that the world may know that I love the Father, I act just as the Father has commanded me.' xiv 31.

The Torah

For a Jew, 'the Way, Truth and Life, the only way to God' must be a nearly perfect definition of the Torah. Many of the ideas in this chapter which have been explained as references the ninth house of the horoscope can be equally well explained as references to the Torah as it is described in Jewish literature. The ninth house, for instance, has been noted to be concerned with morality and ethics and their legal codification; *torah* means 'law, ordinance, decree'.

The ninth house is concerned with higher education; *torah* also means 'teaching or instruction', and in Jewish literature it is particularly connotes 'showing or revelation'.[14.1] This prompts aspects of the dialogue of xiv:

> Philip said 'Master, reveal the Father to us, and that will be enough for us.' Jesus said: 'Have I been with you for so long and yet you not known me, Philip? He who has seen me has seen the Father, so how can you say, "Reveal the Father to us"?' xiv 8-9.

> He who loves me will be loved by my Father, and I shall love him and reveal myself to him'.
> Judas, not Iscariot, said to him, 'How is it that you will reveal yourself to us and not to the world?' xiv 21-22.

Torah can mean 'the course or path of a projectile'; an etymologically related word, *moreh* means 'an archer or shooter'. *Torah* also has the sense of 'a way of life, manner or mode of living' – this is possibly a different word, a homonym, not etymologically related to the root *yarah*, but this meaning is played upon even in the Bible.[14.2] The idea may explain why *Halakah*, from the verb 'to walk' was adopted as a technical term for exegesis of the Mosaic Code.[14.3]

There are several other reasons for the Torah's appropriateness to xiv, but as they pertain either to Qabalah, or to a passage in Genesis which has profoundly influenced John, they are discussed in Parts 2 and 3.

The month Kislev contains the beginning of the Feast of Dedication or Ḥanukah, which commemorates the Jewish revolt against hellenisation imposed by Antiochus Epiphanes. He forbade observance of the Torah, burning all the Torah scrolls he could find and executing those who owned them. A key theme of Dedication is the restoration of the Torah as the national legal code (1 and 2 Maccabees). This is another motivation for reference to the Torah in this chapter.

In summary, John intimates the ninth horoscopic house with mention of journeying, truth and knowledge. At the same time, 'I am the way, the truth, and the life' is an identification with the Torah.

> 14.1: *Zohar* 3:53b. Daniel C. Matt, *The Zohar: Pritzker Edition*, vol. 7 p. 338 n. 27.
>
> 14.2: *Gesenius Hebrew-Chaldee Lexicon to the Old Testament* sv. *tor*.
>
> 14.3: See Part 2 note 5.11.

The Gospel According to John chapter 15;
**'*ayin*;
Capricorn and the tenth house; also the tenth month, Tevet.**

Sefer Yezirah assigns the letter '*ayin* to Capricorn, the sign of the winter solstice. Natives of Capricorn, a sign ruled by Saturn, are said to be controlling and authoritarian, even tyrannical. A traditional name for the tenth house is Rule or Government (*Regnum*), since it charts relationships with superiors and rulers. This area of the sky, situated at the midheaven or zenith, is said to show social status, public honour and recognition, personal ambition, and the height to which one's career takes one in life, and prestige coming from achievement.

In the paenultimate verse of the fourteenth chapter Jesus warns of the Devil's imminent arrival:

> 'From now on I shall not speak much with you, because the Ruler of the World [*ho archōn tou kosmou*] is coming. But he has nothing in me.' xiv 30.

As Ruler of the World, the Devil is well suited to personify the midheaven. His vain ambition, his urge to climb higher, to be in authority, and to receive adulation from others – he is often understood to be the King of Babylon described in Isaiah xiv 13, or the King of Tyre in Ezekiel xviii, figures whose vanity and pride lead them vie with God for worship – make him a perfect representative of this mansion. And of course, the Devil counts the goat as one of his chief emblems in Christian symbolism after the imagery of According to Matthew xxv 32-33.

The use of the future tense or its equivalent – 'is coming' in this instance – at the end of a chapter, that is, in its last or penultimate verse, seems to be a way of indicating that any symbolic material pertains not to the chapter in which at falls but to the next, a device John uses elsewhere.[15.1]

The despotic nature of the Capricorn persona, and the tenth house's concern with social status and with people in positions of absolute power are transformed into references to slaves and masters:

> 'From now on I do not call you slaves, for a slave does not know what his master does. Rather, I have called you friends, for I have informed you of everything that I heard from my Father.' xv 15

> 'Remember the saying that I told you, "The slave is not greater than his master".' xv 20.

The world's hostility toward Christians (xv 18-25) is partly due to the fact that *Sefer Yezirah* associates the letter *'ayin* with rage or anger.

Vine and goat

The fifteenth chapter of According to John opens with Jesus continuing his discourse:

'I am the true vine, my Father is the gardener. He removes every branch in me not bearing fruit, and he prunes every one bearing fruit...' xv 1.

And he quickly repeats the identification, which forms the basis of more than half the chapter:

'I am the vine, you are the branches...' xv 5.

Teveth, the tenth month of the calendar, which corresponds to the time the Sun moves through Capricorn is the time for pruning grape vines. Curiously, there exists a long mythological association between grapevine and goat, which, Graves remarks, was noted even by Plato. Two important classical divinities, Pan and Dionysus, have both vine and goat in their epiphanies, and either may be the False Vine whose existence is implied by Jesus' assuming the title of True Vine.

Aigobolus, 'Goat-slaying' was an epithet of Dionysus, the classical god of the vine, who was offered goats in sacrifice 'because goats gnaw at vines injuring them'.[15.2] Although not commonly depicted in caprine form in art, he could certainly appear in the shape of a goat to his votaries. His nickname, 'Goat-Kid' (*Eriphos, Eiraphiotēs*), recalled that he was born with horns. This particular form of the god, Graves says, was borrowed from another semi-divinity, *Zagreus*, well known in Palestine, with whom he fused. One legend tells that when the gods of Olympus fled from the monster Typhon, and hid in Egypt, Dionysus took the form of a fish-tailed goat; the figure was elevated to the sky as the constellation of Capricorn in commemoration of Dionysus' feat. The story is thought to be a Greek attempt at identification of Dionysus with the Egyptian Goat of Mendes. (Another version of the legend of the gods' flight from Typhon ascribes the assumption of the form of a fish-tailed goat to Aegipan, but Ovid in *Metamorphoses*, among others, puts Dionysus in the story.) The ribald entourage of Dionysus included satyrs – Ampelos ('Vine') was the name of one – and fauns, and Pan was regularly part of his retinue. Priapus, a minor semidivinity connected with gardens, viniculture, and goats, who was often depicted with a pair of pruning shears, is sometimes said to have Dionysus as his father.

Pan, partly because of his goatish form, was used as a basis for the early Christian depiction of the Devil; he is probably nondifferent from Aegipan, Goat-Pan. According to myth his mother was a nymph, Oeneis, 'Of the Vine'. One of his symbols was the thrysus, a staff topped with a cluster of grapes and twined with vines and ivy. The vine that was an important part of his paraphernalia was originally the ivy, but his great fondness for Dionysus' company led to him become associated with the grapevine.

Dedication in Teveth

The verb 'to remain', *menein*, which occurs eight times in the opening passage of xv, is probably meant to recall the fact that Hanukah, which lasts eight days, continues over the change of month from Kislev into Teveth, or it may refer to the behaviour of the sun at the winter solstice.

15.1: For example i 51 (see Part 2) and probably v 47.

15.2: Quoted by Graves *The Greek Myths* 27.2.

The Gospel According to John chapter 16;
peh;
Mars.

The astrological attribution of *peh*, the letter coordinate with xvi, is Mars. The planet's association with bloodshed, noted even in the Talmud[16.1], manifests within the Gospel in:

> Indeed, the time is coming when whoever kills you shall think that he serves God. xvi 2.

In classical mythology, Ares-Mars was primarily god of war, but he was also known as Peace-maker or Pacifier (Latin: *Pacator*), and this probably lies behind:

> I have told you these things, so that you may have peace in me. In the world you will have distress, but take courage: I have been victorious over the world. xvi 33.

In *Sefer Yezirah*, the twelve simple letters answer to the twelve signs of the zodiac and twelve months of the year. But in John's Gospel, as we have seen, there seems to be a general rule that chapters corresponding to double or mother letters may pick up calendar symbolism from an adjacent chapter that corresponds to a simple letter. We have already noted that x (*kaf*, a double letter) and xii (*mem*, a mother letter) are filled with symbolism related to the month Tishri, which should be found in xi (*lamed*, a simple letter). In an analogous fashion, xix (*resh*, a double letter) contains calendar related motifs that would be appropriate in xviii (*quf*, a simple letter), as discussed elsewhere.

Now, xvi corresponds to *peh*, a double letter, while xv and xvii correspond to simple letters, *'ayin* and *zaddi* respectively. Since John seems to follow certain characteristic patterns, we should not be surprised if symbolic motifs appropriate to the months Tevet (*'ayin*) or Shevat (*zaddi*) have made their way into xvi. In fact, the tenth of Tevet was an important day of fasting instituted by the rabbis to mourn the beginning of war with Babylon (2 Kings xxv 1). Building on a comment in the Talmud, homiletic discussions about Tevet 10 often focus on the fact that the Jewish king, Josiah, believed the petitions of the prophetess Hulda would be more successful than those of Jeremiah in averting the looming catastrophe.[16.2] The reason given: being a woman, Hulda would be naturally soft-hearted and therefore more capable of praying with sincere intention. Such ideas may have partly motivated discussion of the efficacy of prayer in xvi 23, 26 and xv 7.

16.1: TB *Shabbat* 156a.

16.2: TB *Megilah* 14b on 2 Kings xxii 12ff., 2 Chronicles xxxiv 21ff.

The Gospel According to John chapter 17;
zaddi;
Aquarius and the eleventh house; the eleventh month, Shevat.

The nocturnal prayer Jesus makes before his arrest occupies the entire seventeenth chapter of John's Gospel. Prayer is itself congenial with the astrological assignment: the eleventh house governs aspirations, hopes and wishes. The content of Jesus' prayer, moreover, is harmonious with matters charted by the eleventh house, which is especially connected with friendship, the tendency to be drawn into fellowships or fraternal associations. It shows altruistic and humanitarian leanings. Friendship (*Benefacta*) is a traditional name. The seventeenth chapter of John's Gospel is chiefly about Jesus' wishes for his friends.

The preoccupation with utopian ideals involving universal human fellowship that characterises natives of Aquarius translates in John's Gospel into unity of believers, an important theme of xvii:

> 'Holy Father, keep in your name those whom you gave me, so that they may be one just as we are'. xvii 11.

'So that they may all be one, just as you, Father, are in me, and I in you, so that they too may be one in us, so that the world may believe that you have sent me. And I have given them the glory which you gave me, so that they may be one, just as we are one. I in them, and you in me, that they may be completed in unity, so that the world may know that you sent me, and loved them, just as you have loved me.' xvii 21-23.

Aquarius and its cognate house are particularly concerned with the mind and mentation, fantasy and the faculty of imagination. Natives of Aquarius are said to be to be idealists, given over to lofty hopes and aspirations; prone to excessive intellectualisation, they may become lost in abstract ideas remote from practical reality. In John's Gospel this aspect of the Aquarian psyche is reflected in:

I have given them your word and the world hated them, because they are not of the world just as I am not of the world. xvii 14.

They are not of the world, just as I am not of the world. xvii 16.

The Gospel According to John chapter 18;
quf; an ear; numerical value 100;
Pisces and the twelfth house; also the twelfth month, Adar.

Pisces and the twelfth equatorial house are said to chart native's contact with the hidden, concealed, dark, mysterious, or secret. It shows work done behind the scenes, out of sight, intrigues, espionage, and hidden enemies. Self-undoing and self-surrender are specific associations. It also charts dangers, both real and imaginary, and the tormenting fears and mental anguish they lead to. The twelfth house is connected with compulsion, confinement and captivity; its traditional name in medieval astrology was House of Imprisonment (*Carcer*). It is also rules over sleep and unconsciousness.

Self-undoing, betrayal and treachery, hidden enemies, subterfuge and secrecy, arrest and confinement: these are the important themes in the narrative xviii sets out before the reader. Jesus enters the garden well aware that an ambush awaits him. Judas, a trusted member of Jesus' inner circle, leads the armed mob (xviii 2-5). Jesus does not attempt to hide, flee, or resist, and they place him under arrest (xviii 12). Peter and John go undercover at the High Priest's house to spy on the proceedings (xviii 15). Peter has to cover his relationship with Jesus by denying him three times (xviii 17, 25, 27). On one hand, Jesus protests that he spoke nothing in secret (xviii 20), on the other, the priest even refuses to tell Pilate the precise nature of the charges (xviii 29-30). Since capital offences are not supposed to be tried at night nor in closed session, the whole trial reeks of intrigue.

Qidron (xviii 1), the name of the valley stream which marked the outer limits of Jerusalem (1 Kings ii 37), means 'turbid, dark'. The valley was a place where various forms of refuse from corpses to idols were thrown. It intimates the baseness, uncleanliness and darkness which are all negative aspects of the twelfth house.

The Sun moves through Pisces in late winter, hence the coldness of the night (xviii 18, 25).

Peter's denial of Jesus takes place, as foretold, before the cock crows (xviii 27), since the twelfth house denotes the two hour period before sunrise (nominally 4 a.m. to 6 a.m.), that is at the time called 'cock-crow'. According to Matthew xxvi 75, Mark xiv 72, and Luke xxii 56-61 also record the detail.

Something fishy about the governor

Several characters who appear in xviii are astrological personifications.

When emphasised in the horoscope, Jupiter is said to lead to philosophical or religious interests, it rules over priestly vocations. In the Gospel, the High Priest is a personification of Jupiter, the planetary ruler of Pisces.

From the appearance of the doorkeeper (*ho thurōros*) in x 3, one might wonder whether John has guessed that Janus is an alter-ego of Jupiter, as some mythographers have proposed.[18.1] If so, the doormaid (*hē thurōros*) in xviii 16-17 may likewise point to Jupiter as ruler of Pisces, despite her gender. Alternatively she may represent one of the qabalistic correspondences of the chapter.

Like the other water signs of the zodiac, the sign of the Fish has a strong traditional affinity with the sea, which led modern astrologers to make Neptune its ruler. Natives of the sign are said to be attracted to occupations connected with water and the ocean. In the Gospel, the *hupēretai* 'under-rowers or sub-oarsmen', a type of naval officer, who appear in xviii 3, 12, 22, 36, embody the watery aspect of the sign.

Of all the astrological personifications in this chapter, Pontius Pilate is the most fascinating. *Pontius* is Latin from the Greek – *Pontios* means 'pertaining to or ruling over the sea (*pontos*), marine, oceanic'. Against Pilate being an astrological personification is the fact that the agnomen *Pontios* is not even mentioned in the Fourth Gospel; only Letter to Titus and some versions of According to Matthew record it. However, John so often leaves it to the reader to supply various details that too much should not be made of this.

The fact that Pilate plays a significant role throughout much of the next chapter also might seem to weigh against his being some sort of Piscean type. If he had been noted to explicitly leave Jesus' presence in xix, it would be otherwise, for characters who leave Jesus' presence often belong in the chapter immediately before the one in which they are found.

Pilate's appearance in both xviii and xix has another explanation: he may embody the correspondences of both xviii and xix. As Roman governor, he is certainly fit to personify the astrological correspondence of xix, which is the Sun. As for a single person's ability to embody the correspondences of two consecutive chapters, this would seem to occur elsewhere. Judas, as has been explained, personifies the astrological attribution of xiii, which is the sign Scorpio; in second part of this work it will be seen that he personifies one of the qabalistic correspondences of xii as well. In a similar way, for reasons that will be given in Part 2 and 3, it appears the Devil and some of his human representatives are able to personify the correspondences of both xv and xvi.

Purim, Feast of Lots

The main religious festival in the month of Adar is the Feast of Lots, Purim, which commemorates events recorded in the Book of Esther.

Many matters associated with the twelfth mansion of the heavens are echoed in the story of Purim's origins. Hidden friends and enemies working behind the scenes are also important themes of Esther. Rabbinic commentaries on Esther note that the name of God is nowhere mentioned; there are no miracles, no divine intervention; the name Esther is related to the verb 'to hide'; the events of book are said to be prophetically spoken of the verse, 'In that day I shall hide my face...' (Deuteronomy xxxi 18).[18.2]

The Purim custom of getting drunk, even to the point of unconsciousness, is hinted at when everyone falls over (xviii 6), and again when Jesus asks:

'Shall I not drink the cup my father gives me?' xviii 11.

The letter of the Hebrew alphabet under whose banner this chapter falls, *quf*, means 'ear'. Since the word does not seem to be used in this sense in the Tanakh, lexica do not often list it. However, reliable sources do give 'ear' as a meaning of *quf*.[18.3] In the Gospel, this becomes Peter's cutting off the right ear of Malchos, the priest's servant (xviii 10). Curiously, a Purim custom of eating 'Haman's Ears' (triangular pastries filled with poppyseed jam) is said to have arisen from the idea that Mordechai 'clipped Haman's ears', that is he wounded his pride. According to Jewish commentators, Haman had to walk home with his head covered (Esther x 7) because he wanted to cover up his earlessness.

The reminder (xviii 14) that Kaiaphas was the one who said it were better one man die on behalf of the people (xi 50) is motivated by traditions comparing Day of Atonement and Purim, reflected in the saying that the Day of Atonement (Yom Kippur) is like the Day of Pur (Yom Ke-Pur).

Only in the synoptics

Allusions to Purim and events told in Esther can also be seen to lie within the synoptic accounts of Jesus trial, which substantially differ from John's version:

> Then the High Priest tore his clothes, saying, 'He blasphemed. Why do we need witnesses anymore? See, just now you heard the blasphemy. What do you think?'.
> Replying they said, 'He deserves death'.
> Then they spat in his face and struck him, and others slapped him, saying, 'Prophesy for us, Christ! Who is it that hit you?'. According to Matthew xxvi 65-68, and Mark xiv 63-65 is parallel.

> And the men who were guarding Jesus mocked him while beating him. After blindfolding him, they struck him in the face and questioned him, saying, 'Prophesy! Who is it that hit you?', and said many other things to insult him. According to Luke xxii 63-64.

The tearing of clothes is a Purim custom associated with the Fast of Esther, sometimes derived from Mordechai's tearing of his clothes in Esther iv 1. 'Striking Haman', punching an object or striking with a stick whenever Haman's name is mentioned during the obligatory public reading of Esther, is another Purim custom. The blindfold is possibly meant to recall Haman's covering his head in shame (Esther vi 12), or 'Scarcely had the king spoken when they covered his face' (Esther vii 8), or 'In that day I shall hide my face from you' (Deuteronomy xxxi 18), which is said in rabbinic commentaries to specifically refer to the events recounted in Esther.

Despondency, fear, anxiety and threatening dangers are charted by the twelfth house, and are important themes in the story of the origin of Purim in Esther. In the Synoptic Gospels (According to Matthew xxvi 36-46, Mark xiv 34-41, Luke xxii 42-46) this manifests in Jesus' anguished prayer and bloody sweat immediately before his arrest. This episode has no analogue in John's Gospel. His mention of a accepting a cup in the Synoptic accounts has the same significance as it does in xviii 11.

Sleeping and laughing

Overall, the attributions of the *Gra* and *Long Version*, which are more harmonious with astrological tradition than the attributions of the other versions of *Sefer Yezirah*, seem to largely agree with ideas found in John's Gospel. Both these versions of *Sefer Yezirah* attribute the letter *quf* to the function of laughing. This makes a sort of astrological sense, since Pisces is ruled by jovial Jupiter, and the revelry at Purim has something of a carnival-like atmosphere. In the Gospel, it may be represented in the form of Jesus' mockery by his captors, which seems to be derived from Purim customs. However, there are several reasons for thinking that laughing and sleeping should swap position. On one hand, Sagittarius, which is also ruled by Jupiter, is often connected with humour and jocularity in astrological tradition. On the other, Pisces and the twelfth house, are connected with sleep and unconsciousness. Moreover, homiletic discussions on Purim, taking a cue from Esther x 1 and the Midrash, often bring up sleep in connection with the festival. for example, it is sometimes said that one should get drunk to the point of falling asleep.[18.4] In addition, the *Short Version* and *Saadia Version of Sefer Yezirah* assign sleep to the letter *quf*.

Most importantly, in the Synoptic accounts, we actually see that immediately prior to his arrest, Jesus repeatedly finds the disciples have been fast asleep while he prayed (According to Matthew xxvi 40-45; Mark xiv 37-41; cf. Luke xxii 45).

18.1 Frazer, *The Golden Bough* p. 164-66; *The Early History of the Kingship* p. 214, 285-6.

18.2: TB *Hullin* 139b.

18.3: Joseph Enthoffer, *Origin of Our Alphabet*. Moses Stuart, *A Grammar of the Hebrew Language*.

18.4: *Esther Rabbah* vii 12.

The Gospel According to John chapter 19;
resh;
the Sun.

Langton

The division of the books of the New Testament into distinct chapters as we know it today was accomplished by Stephen Langton, future Archbishop of Canterbury, in the early thirteenth century. Up to this point I have not had any cause to do more than mention the fact, because the chapter divisions of According to John as Langton gave them work perfectly well. It seems for reasons which will be quite understandable to the reader, however, he made a minor error or two – in particular, the last four verses of the eighteenth chapter should properly be counted as part of the nineteenth. The reasons for this conclusion are deferred to Part 2 of this book, where they are given in the discussion of xviii. In what follows I shall speak as though xviii 37-40 were part of xix.

The Sun is connected in astrological tradition with leadership and power; the fact that Pilate is governor qualifies him as a solar type. The king is one of the commonest personifications of the Sun. This leads to Jesus' being presented as true King of the Jews in this section:

Pilate therefore said to him, 'Are you a king then?'.
Jesus answered, 'You say that I am a king. For this was
I born, and for this did I come into the world: to testify to the
truth. Everyone who is of the truth hears my voice'.
Pilate says to him, 'What is truth?'. And after saying this,
he went out again to the Jews, and says to them, 'I find no
fault in him. But it is your custom that I release someone to
you at Passover. So then, do you want me to release the King
of the Jews to you?'. xviii 37-39

And the soldiers, having woven a crown of thorns, placed
it on his head, and wrapped him in a purple robe, and said,
'Hail, King of the Jews!', and they dealt him blows. xix 2-3

Then Jesus came out, wearing the crown of thorns and the
purple robe. xix 5

And after that Pilate sought to release him, but the Jews
cried out, saying, 'If you let this man go, you are not
Caesar's friend. Everyone making himself a king speaks
against Caesar'. xix 12

And it was the preparation day for Passover and about
the sixth hour, and he says to the Jews, 'Behold your King!'.
But they cried out, 'Take him away, take him away, crucify
him'. Pilate says to them, 'Shall I crucify your King?'.
The chief priests answered, 'We have no king but Caesar'.
xix 14-15

And Pilate wrote a sign, and put it on the cross. And it had
been written: Jesus of Nazareth the King of the Jews.
Many of the Jews read the sign, for the place where
Jesus was crucified was near the city, and it had been written

in Hebrew, Latin and Greek. Then the chief priests of the Jews said to Pilate, 'Do not write, "the King of the Jews", but rather, "He said, 'I am King of the Jews'"'. Pilate answered, 'What I have written, I have written'. xix 19-22.

The crown (xix 2-3, 5) is an important solar emblem in its own right, and the Sun is for this reason often depicted with a corona or crown of rays. Of course, Johannine symbolism is typically multivalent, and Jesus' crown is no exception.

The Sun is connected with fame and celebrity, the idea of being the centre of attention, or being on display. Much of the unpleasantness of crucifixion comes from the fact that it is a most public form of execution. Stripped naked and raised on high, the condemned man is held up on exhibition for all to see and jeer at. The idea manifests in:

'Behold, I bring him out to you ...' xix 4

'Behold the man...' xix 5

'Behold, your king...' xix 14

'Behold, your son.' xix 26

"They will look on him whom they have pierced". xix 37.

The Sun intimates truthfulness, openness, honesty, simplicity; purity, innocence, integrity:

'For this was I born, and for this did I come into the world: to testify to the truth. Everyone who is of the truth hears my voice'. xviii 37

Pilate says to him, 'What is truth?'. xviii 38

'I find no fault in him at all.' xviii 38

'... that you may know I find no fault in him.' xix 4

'You take him and crucify him, for I find no fault in him.' xix 6

... and his record is true, and he knows he speaks true,
in order that you may believe. xix 36.

Only in the synoptics

Jesus' interview with King Herod (According to Luke xxiii 7-11) is left out of the Fourth Gospel. Since xix is aimed at portraying Jesus as the true king of the Jews, it is somewhat strange that John misses an opportunity to have Jesus in a face to face encounter with the impostor. Of course, although John can explain his presence in the High Priest's house, it would have been difficult to explain how he made it into Herod's court. Perhaps this is why he omits the episode – John is averse to describing events for which he was not an eyewitness.

Remarkably, John also omits all mention of the extinction of the sun's light for three hours during the crucifixion:

> And about the sixth hour darkness came upon the whole earth until the ninth hour, the sun having become dark, and the veil of the temple was torn down the middle. According to Luke xxiii 44-45 (cf. According to Matthew xxvii 45; Mark xv 33).

A miraculous portent and perfect given this chapter's astrological correspondence, it screams out to be in the nineteenth chapter of John's Gospel. It is probably one of the most blatant specimens of astrological symbolism in any Gospel. Why John should leave this out is a mystery.

Purim and Passover

As we have seen, John's Gospel has an internal calendar based upon the correspondences of the letters in *Sefer Yezirah*. There is an external calendar as well, consisting of explicit references in the Gospel to holidays like Passover, Tabernacles, and Dedication. The internal and external calendars run independently.

One of the novel features of John's handling of the letter correspondences has been mentioned: John often marries letters other than simple letters to the months of the calendar. In *Sefer Yezirah*, only the twelve simple letters correspond to the twelve months of the year and twelve signs of the zodiac. But in the Gospel, the letters which are not simple letters sometimes pick up calendar symbolism from a preceding or following simple letter. This is what allows John to have symbolism pertaining to the month Tishri in x and xii, as well as xi. Because the mother letters and double letters do not correspond to months, no conflict or inconsistency in the internal calendar arises.

To return to the case at hand, xix corresponds to *resh*, a double letter, while xviii corresponds to *quf*, a simple letter. And as in other analogous cases, xix picks up symbolism which looks as though it would more at home in the previous chapter. In particular, Purim-related motifs occur throughout xix. In the opening verses, Jesus dressed up as a king is presented to the crowd; the scenario recalls the Purim custom of dressing up in costumes, in particular, the account of Haman being forced to dress Mordechai in royal apparel and parade him to the public in order to honour him (Esther vi 8-11). The blows rained upon Jesus (xix 3) derive from the custom of 'striking Haman'. At the foot of the cross, the soldiers cast lots (Purim means 'Lots') for Jesus seamless coat (xix 23-24), a detail which the synoptics also record (According to

Matthew xxvii 35, Mark xv 24, Luke xxiii 28). Jesus' other garments they tear, recalling a Purim custom probably derived from Mordechai's rending of his clothes (Esther iv 1). The more than liberal consumption of wine at Purim is mirrored in Jesus is having a draught of wine during the crucifixion. In the Septuagint (LXX Esther vii 9), Ahasuerus orders that Haman be crucified, using the same verb, *stauroein*, that the New Testament regularly uses for Jesus' mode of execution.

If there seems to be a clash between the symbolism related to Purim, which falls in the month Adar, and other symbolism pointing to Passover, which falls in the month Nisan, it does not seem to worry John greatly. The rules of the game that John follows allow him to put symbolism pertaining to Adar here, and he no qualms about doing so.

The Gospel According to John chapter 20;
**shin; a tooth;
numerical value 300;
Fire.**

As sparks fly up

A reference to the element of fire, which is the yeziratic attribution of the letter *shin*, can be seen in:

> 'Do not touch me [mē mou haptou], for I have not yet ascended to the Father, but go to my brothers and say to them that I ascend to my Father and your Father, to my God and your God'. xx 17.

Mē mou haptou ('do not to cling to me', or 'do not touch me') is a play on the double sense of the Greek verb *haptein*, which in the middle voice means 'to hold fast to, to adhere or cling to', but in the active also means 'to kindle or ignite', and in the passive voice 'to be ignited or kindled, to be set on fire'. Jesus seems to say (taking *haptou* as passive) 'do not be set on fire by me, do not be ignited by me'. The fact that fire goes up while water goes down, a maxim often met with in qabalistic literature, lies behind the second part of the verse.[20.1]

The Holy Spirit, which Jesus expires the onto the disciples in xx 22, is described in Acts ii 3-4 as taking the form of tongues of fire, as foretold in According to Matthew iii 11-12 and Luke iii 16-17.

20.1: Aryeh Kaplan, *Sefer Yetzirah: The Book of Creation*, p. 77.

The Gospel According to John chapter 21;
tau;
Saturn.

Saturn is traditionally the planet of old age and longevity, and ruler of the closing years of life. Astrological literature typically portrays him as a truculent old man. In the Gospel, this aspect of his nature manifests in Jesus' words to Peter, and in the idea that the beloved disciple might not die, merely get older and older:

> 'Amen, amen, I tell you: when you were young you girded [*ezōnnues*] yourself and went where you wished, but when you are old, you will stretch out your hands and another will gird [*zōsei*] you and bear you off to where you do not wish to go.' He said this foretelling the sort of death through which he would glorify God. xxi 18-19.

> Jesus says to him, 'If I want him to remain until I come, what is that to you? Follow me!'. Then the word went out among the brothers that the disciple would not die. But Jesus did not say he would not die, he merely said, 'If I want him to remain until I come, what is that to you?'. xxi 22-23.

In xxi 18-19 he also hints at Saturn's connection with bondage, fatality, compulsion, necessity and death, all part of traditional astrological lore. And in xxi 25 John alludes also to the fact that Saturn moves more slowly than any other planet, taking about twenty-nine years to complete a full circuit of the zodiac, so that he makes for delays and tardiness.

Since Saturn is the outermost of the seven planets, its orbit (*zōnē* is the Greek term) encompasses the orbits of all the others. The ancients understood it to be the outer boundary of the cosmos. For this reason, Saturn intimates limitation, restriction and confinement. This explains the appearances of *zōnnuein* and *diazōnnuein*, both derived from *zōnē*, and meaning 'to gird, to encircle' in xxi 18-19, and in:

> Now when he heard that it was the Master, Simon Peter girded [*ediezōsato*] himself with his coat, for he was naked, and he cast himself into the sea. xxi 7.

Part 2: The Qabalistic Tree of Life and the Fourth Gospel

*S**efer Yezirah* belongs to the literature of the Qabalah, the immense body of mystical teachings that make up the esoteric aspect of Judaism. Although it means 'received tradition', Qabalah was so utterly different in content, style, and philosophical attitudes from what had previously existed that it appears to have sprung from nowhere. Many have been puzzled that an array of doctrines and methods so complex and vast could have come into being in highly developed form with such suddenness. The novel aspect of many qabalistic notions would make them hard to overlook, yet one sees no period in which the core doctrines can be seen to undergo a process of refinement or evolution from some more primitive form. Despite the conservative tendency to regard with suspicion anything of uncertain provenance, for the most part, Qabalah was not rejected as a recent innovation tainted by foreign influences, but accepted as a genuinely ancient Jewish tradition.

Aside from *Sefer Yezirah*, the two most authoritative texts of the Qabalah are *Sefer ha Bahir* (*The Book of Illumination*) and *Sefer ha Zohar* (*The Book of Brilliance*). The former surfaced towards the end of the twelfth century in the Languedoc or in Gerona, while the latter appeared in the last decades of the thirteenth century in Grenada, Castile. Since much of this section's subject matter is drawn from them, it is necessary to make a few comments about these two works, which mark the beginning and end of qabalistic literature's golden age. A wealth of material was produced in the interim, chiefly by writers from the two great centres of qabalistic learning in France and Spain which these two books represent, however, the bulk of the ideas expressed in other works are not directly ascribed to ancient authors. Only the *Bahir* and the *Zohar* and its associated works are framed as genuine teachings of rabbinical authorities living in the first and second centuries CE. Perhaps for this reason they enjoyed greater popularity and wider dissemination than writings of twelfth and thirteenth century qabalists.

The appearance of *Sefer ha Bahir* marks the crucial point in the emergence of Qabalah after a millennium of latency. It is the ultimate source for many qabalistic doctrines, yet the book's beginnings are shrouded in mystery. Possibly originating in Palestine or Babylon, it seems to have tenuous links to a work called *Razza Rabba* (*The Great Mystery*), which was circulating in Jerusalem in the ninth century. Now lost, this was still in the possession of German Hasids in the thirteenth century, who quoted parts of it under its Hebrew title, *Sod Ha Gadol*.

A group of Provence qabalists in the family of Rabbi Isaac the Blind may have had access to all or part of the *Bahir*, having gotten it from German Pietists (Hasids) in the latter half of the twelfth century. Rabbi Isaac's family already had independent sources of qabalistic knowledge that they valued more highly. The book really came out into the open in early thirteenth century Gerona in Catalonia on the other side of the Pyrenees, in a circle of pupils of pupils of the Provence qabalists. It seems to have gone multiple stages of re-editing.

Since he is the first speaker of the book, Rab Nehuniah ben HaQana, a prominent member and possibly the head of a first-century CE mystical school in Palestine, is taken to be the *Bahir*'s author. Elsewhere he is known as the revered teacher of Rabbi Akiba ben Joseph and Rabbi Ishmael ben Elisha the High Priest, authors of important non-qabalistic mystical texts, and of such luminaries of his age as Rabbi Eliezer and Shimon ben Gamaliel.

No qabalistic writing is known for its transparency, and the *Bahir* certainly seems to justify Qabalah's reputation for deliberate obscuritanism and mystification for its own sake. Looking more like a collation of fragments or set of brief notes than something intended for open publication, the reader, Scholem notes, is left feeling like an eavesdropper sitting behind a door, listening to a teacher and pupils, forgotten and ignored. Sometimes it is as if one had just woken up in the middle of the conversation to hear an answer without the context of the question. Enigmatic parables constitute the chief medium through which the book conveys its secrets, presenting a set of recurring motifs that together make up a kind of mystical mythology. The subjects the book discusses are weighty, and include reincarnation, occult powers of the letters, mysteries of the sefiroth, yet the author avoids hyperbole, contenting himself with homely and unassuming imagery. Characters include the king and queen, their sons and daughter; chief symbols include the jewel, the palace, the garden, trees, bread, clothes, and water – not too far from the stuff of Grimm's Fairytales. As

Scholem notes, the author never feels a need to apologise for the system of symbolism, as though taking for granted the reader's acceptance despite its unconventional nature.

What makes the *Bahir* so revolutionary is its doctrine that the Godhead contains or constitutes a sort of world or universe. Scholem terms this the Gnostic element. In addition, in contrast to the somewhat abstruse philosophical treatment of the sefiroth in the writings of the Provence qabalists and their pupils in Gerona, the *Bahir* offers a rich and diverse set of metaphors and images, including sexual symbolism, and embodiment of abstract cosmic principles in human characters. The work, Scholem says, also had a catalytic effect on creativity. Once published, it was soon widely circulated and this led to a change in attitude towards need for secrecy of qabalistic doctrines.

Contrasting with the *Bahir* in many ways, the *Zohar* purports to record of teachings of a mystical group led by Rab Simeon bar Yohai, a pupil of Rabbi Akiba. Unlike the *Bahir*, the *Zohar* has long been held in high esteem among Jews, in some ways ranking with the Talmud, and later counted among the Midrash. Its influence extends to the content of the prayer-book and the customs of daily life. To talk about Qabalah without the *Zohar* is unimaginable.

Borrowing from the writings of the earlier generations of qabalists living in Provence, Gerona and Castile, *Sefer ha Bahir*, *Sefer Yezirah*, as well as conventional sources like the Talmud, Midrash, Targums, common folklore and legend, the *Zohar* is invaluable as an encyclopaedic anthology of Jewish customs, culture and literature. Little wonder the colleagues contradict each other as often as they do, for the *Zohar* is a compendium of qabalistic ideas from different schools that the author seeks to harmonize. And as Scholem observes, in the end there is no such thing as '*the* doctrine of the qabalists' on any matter, only differing schools of thought with diverging views.[intro.1]

Taking the form of a series of homiletic discourses woven around a verse by verse commentary on the Pentateuch, the *Zohar* introduces its doctrines in the order they are required. There is no attempt at systematic organisation of the key elements of knowledge. It commences with an exposition of the first chapter of Genesis, one of the most perplexing sections of the book, so that the reader is thrown in the deep end from the start.

Difficulties for the reader arise because the methods with which qabalists convey their sense are the same as those they employ to decode the Bible. Chief among these is the development of extended chains and networks of associations. One person or thing is linked with another, which is then linked to a third, and so on. The problem for the reader is that a hundred pages of text may separate one link in the chain from the next, and to miss a single one is to be lost. It is often impossible to determine the direction of an argument; one cannot tell whether a general principle is being invoked to make a deduction about a particular event, or whether a general principle is being derived by a process of induction. All sorts of florid and extravagant metaphor abound, the author well aware that he is creating a literary work for publication. On top of this, qabalists often understand the terms 'metaphorical' and 'real' in an inverted sense, arguing that the higher levels are more real than the lower, material levels of creation, the reflections of their counterparts in the archetypal worlds. Passages which the most die-hard literalist would take to be allegorical are to a qabalist plain descriptions of events on a spiritual level of reality. The notion that an analogy can be taken too far seems almost unknown. Despite their allegorical interpretation of scripture, qabalists are in a sense the greatest literalists of all.

To a 'true believer', the book is just what it seems to be: the teachings of a second-century mystical school headed by Rabbi Simeon Bar Yoḥai. A more sceptical viewpoint regards the *Zohar* as entirely the work of a school of thirteenth-century qabalists centred around Moses ben Shem Tob de Leon, of Guadalajara in Castile. In *Major Trends in Jewish Mysticism*, Scholem marshalled powerful internal evidence that the *Zohar* is a late invention.[intro.2] The author of the *Zohar*, he says, betrays a profound ignorance of Aramaic, the language of Simeon bar Yoḥai. Syntax is modelled on thirteenth century Hebrew and a formal type of Aramaic that developed late; vocabulary is limited and anachronistic; a want of genuine etymological knowledge and a tendency to extrapolate from Hebrew lead to an abundance of false derivations; pronominal inflections, tense and modal forms are incorrectly modelled on the author's faulty knowledge of the Babylonian Talmud and the Targums (translations of portions of the Old Testament into Aramaic). The author, in fact, practically invents a synthetic language. Biographical and geographical errors that would be inconceivable for someone living in Palestine in the first or second century are common. Not only is the language anachronistic, but one finds second century rabbis expounding tenth and eleventh century doctrines.

Another view is that it consists of layer upon layer of material added by different authors over the centuries. A fraction of the work was truly ancient, but the older strata of the book were not always correctly interpreted, so that original material accreted a mass of frequently erroneous explanations. However, some sort of middle or compromise position seems untenable, Scholem says, because a single style is apparent throughout the work, the same errors being reproduced in every section. The intricately cross-referenced nature of the work points to a single author or a small circle of authors working closely.

It remains plausible, however, that Moses de Leon and his colleagues, residing in a centre of qabalistic learning, had access to genuine first- and second-century material lost to us, which they set down in a peculiar linguistic form, and adorned with generous elaborations of their own fancy, yet all the while remaining faithful to the original conceptions of more ancient and primary sources. Evidently, they had the requisite ability, mystical or intellectual, to reconstruct certain trains of thought. This would explain why the work seems written by someone who has found a key and is busily trying it in every lock that presents itself, so that one gets the feeling the writer is learning along with the reader.

To elucidate According to John by means of works that appeared in the thirteenth century poses its own set of problems. It is, however, no exaggeration to say that just as According to John provides ample evidence that *Sefer Yezirah* existed in the second century CE, so too does it provide excellent witness to the fact that the symbolic language of the *Bahir* and *Zohar* was alive and well at the time John composed his Gospel.

Subject matter

The subject matter of the Qabalah comprises such diverse matters as:

- God and his nature, i.e. theology and theosophy;
- man's physical makeup and nature, occult anatomy, e.g. cheiromancy and physiognomy;

- the pre-existence of the soul; its destination after death, including reincarnation;
- pneumatology: i.e. the different 'souls' or subtle sheaths of man;
- the history of the human race and its final destiny, the future of the Jewish race, the coming of the Messiah;
- the natures, hierarchies, names and specific offices of angels and demons, and other intelligent quasihuman life;
- creation and form of the universe, i.e. cosmogony and cosmology; cosmic cycles of time;
- mysticism of Hebrew letters, numerological analysis of words (*gematria*), understanding words as anagrams (*notariqon*), creation of substitution ciphers (*temurah*), permutations of the letters of a word (*ziruf*);
- esoteric bases for ethical conduct, Jewish ceremonial observances and forms of prayer;
- esoteric explanations for events related in the Bible, legend and folklore.

Qabalists saw the Torah as the blueprint of creation, the totality of God's thoughts, which God repeatedly turns to for advice during creation. It contains the ideal prototypes or archetypes of everything. It is the law of the universe. The sections into which it is divided are compared to organs and limbs, for it is a living organism, like the universe. Because they were always explaining the scriptures of Judaism, the images and metaphors have a different character than those of astrology or other systems of natural philosophy or metaphysics.

Qabalistic doctrines seek refuge in scripture, whose every word becomes a symbol for something else, a code term in a system of double meanings. A most surprising feature of qabalists' understanding of language is the very large number of perfectly commonplace words that are invested with symbolic value: 'I', 'you', 'he', 'who?', 'what?', 'this', 'there', 'thus', 'all', 'very', 'in', the accusative particle (*'eth*), 'call', 'make'. Much of the Qabalah depends upon the assumption that the Tanakh (Jewish Scriptures) was written in this coded language, all its words imbued with technical meanings. Qabalists saw themselves as possessors of the secret lexicon. Although an elevated respect for the Torah was not unusual for Jews, particularly of the time, the qabalists' assertion that the scriptures could be interpreted on a multiplicity of levels, the qabalistic interpretation of course being the highest or innermost, went against the current of orthodoxy.

Sefiroth and the qabalistic Tree of Life

One hallmark feature of the Qabalah is the great importance it attaches to the doctrine of the ten sefiroth (singular: *sefirah*). The precise definition of *sefirah* is not completely clear, but since the Hebrew root *sfr*, from which it is derived means 'to number, or count', or 'to write or record', or 'to tell or relate', it is probably fair to render *sefirah* in English as 'enumeration' or 'counting', or perhaps even 'number', though later writers could pun on like-sounding Greek words, *sapphiros* (sapphire) and *sphairos* (sphere). While *Sefer Yezirah* provides scant information about the sefiroth, failing even to provide their names, later qabalistic works like the *Bahir* and *Zohar* not only list the common and uncommon titles of the sefiroth, they describe their natures and multitude of their attributes and associations. The *Bahir* largely avoids the term sefirah,

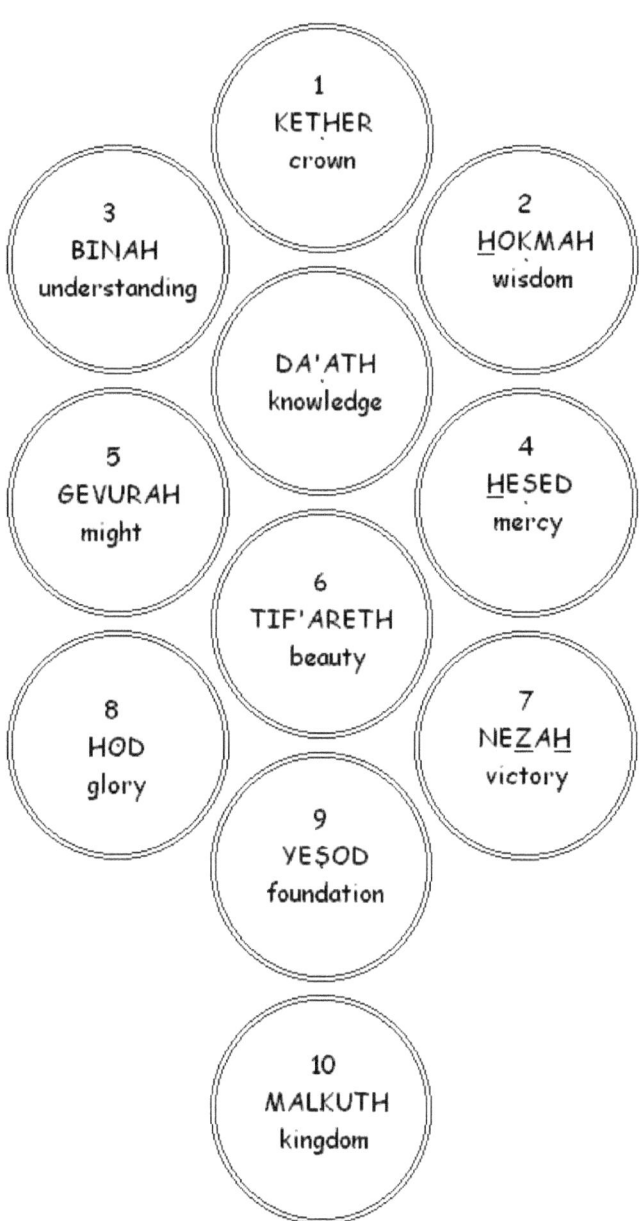

DIAGRAM 1 *(tree of life with sefiroth named but without paths)*

calling them *ma'amroth*, 'utterances'; the *Zohar* calls them 'grades' or 'rungs'. Just as astrology builds a system of correspondences around the planets and signs of the zodiac, so the Qabalah builds its extensive and complex web of correspondences around the sefiroth. Later texts describe a special arrangement of the sefiroth, a schematic diagram that summarises much about the dynamic of their interrelationships with one another. This is called the Tree of Life. In it, the ten sefiroth are laid out in three columns or pillars, on seven different levels, each level containing either one sefirah on the central pillar or else a pair of sefiroth symmetrically disposed on the side pillars.

For qabalists the Tree of Life is the key to everything. Whether the question involves man's physical, psychic or spiritual structure, or the form of the universe, recourse to the Tree never fails to provide an answer. The Tree of Life constitutes a true mirror of the universe, like astrology in that its scope is all-encompassing. It represents both the structure and economy of the universe as it exists in present, 'finished' form, and the process of its unfolding. It is also man, the microcosm. It is truly protean in adaptability in that anything at all can be analysed through its perspective.

Not only did it reveal the mysteries of Creation, it also provided a set of metaphors for understanding and talking about the Creator. It is particularly concerned with divine attributes, their interrelationships and mutual interactions, speaking as if God were invested with a vibrant organic life. It was nothing less than detailed knowledge of the divine anatomy and physiology that qabalists were seeking after. This caused a lot of trouble to early qabalists, who were often required to defend themselves against accusations of polytheism. Their tendency to carry metaphors a long way led to the charge of idolatry. Their description of interactions between the sefiroth suggested to some that they thought God was mutable.

The sefiroth of the qabalistic Tree of Life

Qabalists[intro.3] find some of the commoner names of several sefiroth listed in 1 Chronicles xxix 11-13:

> Thine, O Lord, is the Greatness (Gedulah),
> and the Might (Gevurah),
> and the Beauty (Tif'areth),
> and the Victory (Nezah),
> and the Glory (Hod),
> For All (Kol) that is in Heaven and Earth is Thine.
> Thine is the Kingdom (Mamlakah).
> Thou art the Exalted Head over all.

One form of the doxology to the Lord's Prayer, 'For thine is the kingdom, and the power, and the glory, forever and ever (*sou estin hē basilea kai hē dunamis kai hē doxa eis tous aiōnas*)', which is thought to be an echo of 1 Chronicles xxix, and which is found in some but not all versions of According to Matthew and elsewhere, has been understood by non-Jewish commentators to contain the names of the last four sefiroth in reverse order.

Much about the nature of an individual sefirah follows directly from the meaning ascribed to up and down, and to right and left in the context of the Tree.

The descent from Kether (Crown) to Malkuth (Kingdom) is a development from a subtle or spiritual level down into gross matter; things get progressively denser as one descends into the physical. The sefiroth are conceived as though coming into being in numerical order beginning with Kether (Crown) and ending with Malkuth (Kingdom), so that Kether is the root of the Tree of Life, Malkuth is the fruit, not vice versa.

The sefiroth are disposed in three vertical columns, right, left and middle. In a manner of speaking, the central pillar, which extends all the way from the highest sefirah to the lowest, is the most important of the three. It is called the Pillar of Tenderness or Compassion (*Raḥamim*), or the Pillar of Mildness, since it is the neutral point of equilibrium of the extremes denoted by the side pillars, which it unites and harmonises. The right-hand pillar is termed the Pillar of Mercy; it is active, energetic, male, expansive and giving. The three sefiroth on the left side of the Tree comprise the Pillar of Severity or Rigour; it is passive, female, receptive and constricting. The left side of the Tree is intimately concerned with the mystery of the existence of evil. For example, Binah (Understanding) is said to permit choice between alternatives; Gevurah (Strength) is often directly associated with moral wickedness; Hod (Splendour) is associated with a permissive tolerance of wickedness.[intro.4] Sometimes the left side pertains to God's power to limit, punish and destroy evil.

First triad

Kether (Crown), Ḥokmah (Wisdom) and Binah (Understanding) make up the highest triad of sefiroth. They are called 'Mentalities' (*Moḥin*), because they comprise the intellectual world (*'Olam Muskal* or *'Olam ha Sekel*). In man, these first three sefiroth are the point of contact with the divine, the highest, most purely spiritual parts of the soul.

Kether

The chief attribute of the first sefirah, Kether (Crown), is absolute sublimity and transcendence. The verb 'to crown' also means 'to surround' and secondarily 'to be outside of or beyond', as in the rabbinic dictum, 'God is in the world and surrounds it', which means God is both immanent and supraordinate. Kether is in a way inaccessible to and disconnected from the other nine sefiroth, constituting by itself a World of Solitude (*'Olam Mithboded*). It is really the most subtle form of being, without any attributes except simplicity and unity. *'Ain* (Nothingness) is commonly used in qabalistic writings to denote Kether, since it is not perceptible in any way, nor can anything be predicated of it. Its titles include 'Concealed of Concealed' or 'Most Mysterious'. Sometimes it is not counted among the sefiroth.

Hokmah

Since Kether (Crown) is too recondite to be recognised, Ḥokmah (Wisdom) is counted as the first, and *Reshith* (First or Beginning) is one of its common alternative names in qabalistic writings. It is the energy that provides the initial impetus. Ḥokmah is therefore associated with spontaneity and causelessness, and qabalists are wont to render Job xxviii 12 as 'Wisdom was completed from *'Ain* (Nothing)'.

Ḥokmah is playfully analysed as *koaḥ mah*, ('a certain power' or 'what power?'), as it is implies unrealised possibility, undifferentiated potentiality, indefiniteness.[intro.5]

In the mind, Ḥokmah is the subjective aspect of truth or knowledge. It relates to innate or axiomatic knowledge, as well as creative imagination, genius, inspiration and revelation. It is connected with ideas that have not been, or cannot be, formulated in words. Hokmah is often equated with Thought in the *Zohar*.^{intro.6}

Hokmah is linked to the concept of sameness and similarity, since it reflects the mind's nature to liken one thing to something else, to perceive analogies and parallels so that a multiplicity of diverse things are reduced to single case. Qabalists speak of the sefirah as the place of archetypes, primordial patterns, rather like the Ideal Forms of Platonic philosophy.

Water is one of the chief symbols of the second sefirah because it is amorphous or homogenous.[intro.7]

Binah

Binah (Understanding) can also be rendered Intelligence. While Hokmah is connected with subjectivity, Binah, complementary in every way, represents the objective side of knowledge. Binah is often related to the verbal mind; it represents logical analysis, and formal processes of reasoning rather than intuition. Key ideas associated with Binah (Understanding) are separation, division; it relates to the ability of the mind to discern differences and contrasts. The giving of a name to a thing tokens its identity as a discrete and separate being, it individuates and differentiates, and so Binah is connected with verbal thinking. For every word there exists an antonym, for the mind's nature is to perceive things in terms of diametric opposites.[intro.8]

In qabalistic literature, when Hokmah is likened to water, which has no shape of its own, Binah (Understanding) is likened to a container, or a vessel, or system of pipes or channels through which the water flows. Binah gives outward form or definition, its nature is to restrict and channel the formless inchoate energy of Hokmah.[intro.9]

Da'ath

Some qabalistic works speak asthough the first three sefiroth were Hokmah, Binah and Da'ath (Knowledge), leaving Kether off the list. Such verses as Proverbs iii 19 ('By wisdom the earth is founded, by understanding the heavens are established, by knowledge are the deeps broken up') and Proverbs xxiv 3 ('By wisdom the house is built, by understanding is it established, by knowledge are its chambers filled') are expounded in such a way that Hokmah, Binah, and Da'ath naturally constitute a triad. Conversely, when Kether is counted as a sefirah, then Da'ath is not, so that there are always ten sefiroth. Even when Da'ath is not included amongst the ten, the term nevertheless appears to denote the conjunction of Hokmah, as knower, and Binah, as known.[intro.10] This is consistent with the sexual connotation of 'knowledge' in Hebrew, and with the fact that Hokmah and Binah are called 'Father' and 'Mother'. The *Zohar* says that among the books of the Bible ascribed to Solomon, the Song of Songs reflects the nature of Hokmah, Ecclesiastes of Binah, and Proverbs of Da'ath, 'because its verses are twofold and can be read either way'.[intro.11]

Da'ath is called Peace in the *Bahir* since it unites the polar opposites, Hokmah and Binah.[intro.12] Da'ath descends to become Tif'areth, or is sometimes thought of as an extension of Tif'areth.[intro.13]

Kether, Hokmah, and Binah are spoken of as though they were so far above the following seven that their separate influence is never apparent. Da'ath, their synthesis, is all that can be discovered of them.

Second triad

The triangle formed by Ḥesed (Mercy), Gevurah (Strength) and Tif'areth (Beauty) is called the ethical or moral triad. It relates to distinctively human aspects of consciousness with its awareness of beauty and ethics. It is called the Emotional World (*'Olam Murgash*).

Ḥesed

Ḥesed (Mercy) is the first sefirah in the ethical or moral triad. The Hebrew word means Love, Kindness, Lovingkindness, Benevolence or Piety. In the human psyche, it is represents tenderness, charity, tolerance, generosity, magnanimity, grace, and simple goodness. Being situated on the right side of the Tree, it is associated with enthusiasm and energy. Ḥesed manifests in expansion, increase, largeness, growth; another of its titles is Gedulah (Greatness).

Gevurah

Gevurah (Strength, Might or Power) is complementary to Ḥesed. Alternative titles include Din (Justice), and Peḥad (Fear). Its key attributes are ruthlessness, severity, rigour, strictness and harshness. In man it symbolises emotional restraint and reserve, and more generally economy and parsimony, contraction, decrease and destruction. In the psyche it is connected with focus, concentration, narrowing of attention, scepticism.

Like Binah, which sits above it, Gevurah is associated with division and separation; sometimes it manifests as strife and dissension and animosity.

Tif'areth

Tif'areth (Beauty, Ornament), the sixth sefirah, is halfway between Kether and Malkuth. Lying on the middle pillar, it unites the Pillar of Mercy on the right side of the Tree with the Pillar of Severity on the left; its key associations are balance, harmony, mildness and compromise. Peace (*Shalom*) is a common designation of the sefirah in the *Bahir*, as it reconciles the opposing tendencies in Ḥesed and Gevurah. When the fourth and fifth sefiroth are represented by water and fire, Tif'areth may be represented by air, or be referred to as Heavens (*Shamayim*), the word being taken to indicate the combination of fire (*'esh*) and water (*mayim*). All the sefiroth from Ḥesed to Yesod are heavens, that is, celestial spheres, and Tif'areth, in the middle and in contact with all, can represent their totality. Since paths link Tif'areth to every other sefirah except Malkuth, it is associated with synthesis, integrity and wholeness.

In man it corresponds to the heart as the focus of consciousness and emotion. Compassion or Love (*Raḥamim*) is another title. Since it represents the seat of morality and conscience, Judgement (*Mishpaṯ*) is another designation of the sixth sefirah in the *Bahir*.[intro.14] It is not the stern, harsh justice of Gevurah, which demands strict and rigorously exact retribution; rather, the sense is that behind *Sefer Yeẓirah*'s image of two opposing forces in equilibrium, and a third which makes the final tie-breaking decision. The *Zohar* uses a very similar image, describing how the sefiroth on the right side of the Tree give life, those on the left bring death, but the central pillar wields the final verdict by casting the decisive vote in a court of three.[intro.15]

Truth (*'Emeth*) is another commonly used in the *Bahir*.

Third triad

The triangle consisting of Nezah (Victory), Hod (Splendour), and Yesod (Foundation) forms the *'Olam ha Nefesh*, World of the Animal Soul. In man it corresponds to feelings and instincts, and semiautomatic functions of the mind, the ability to calculate and remember. This triad is concerned with practical efficiency in action.

Nezah

Nezah means Victory, Domination, Success, Triumph, and Superiority, but also Eternity, Survival, Persistence, Endurance, Firmness and Constancy. As the lowest sefirah on the right column of the Tree, in man, it corresponds to feelings and sentiment, desires, wishes and wants that act as motivating forces and drives within the psyche. An alternate meaning of Nezah is 'a goal or object, what leads one on, or that towards which one moves', hence, it is said to denote primary purpose, namely pleasure and happiness, the *Zohar* adducing 'Bliss in thy right hand is for eternity [Nezah]' (Psalm xvi 11) to clarify its nature.[intro.16]

Hod

Hod (Splendour) is often translated as Majesty, Grandeur, Renown, Fame or Reputation. At the base of the left sided pillar, it is essentially passive. Its qualities include adaptability, elasticity, flexibility. Qabalists relate it also to *hodah, hoda'ah* and *hodayah*, 'submission, weakness, acknowledgement, or obedience', although these words derive from an unrelated root.[intro.17] *Hodhod* and *hed*, near homonyms but also etymologically unrelated, mean 'echo, reverberation', and indicate the nature of the sefirah is reactive rather than active, that is responsive rather than initiating.

Yesod

Yesod means Foundation or Basis. Western, that is non-Jewish writers often relate Yesod to subtle or etheric matter, partly psychic, partly physical, the shadowy world of mental eidola or images of physical objects, but also images of things that exist only in the higher worlds and could not properly attain solidity.

'All' is one of its commoner designations in early qabalistic literature, since it brings together the forces of the other sefiroth above it for transmission to Malkuth below it.

In the human body it corresponds to the reproductive organs. One of the commonest signal words in qabalistic literature is 'seed' or 'semen'. Another keyword is 'covenant', which is almost always understood to be the covenant of circumcision, but in addition relates to the idea of agreement between contending opposites because Yesod lies on the central pillar.

Malkuth

Malkuth (Kingdom, Dominion) is the end result, fruit of the Tree. Texts portray the sefirah as a passive receptacle, 'the sea into which all rivers flow'. It is called 'Poor' because it has no light of its own, and shines only by reflecting the light of the sefiroth above it.

It commonly symbolises the tangible, material universe, and in man it represents the physical body. Metaphors for the sefirah involve the mineral world in which life and consciousness are apparently absent; the land, the earth, or a field are an important symbols. Malkuth serves as a barrier insulating the higher sefiroth from the demonic world of shells that lie immediately below it.

Correspondences of the sefiroth

Qabalists were constantly trying to understand the Tanakh through the Qabalah, and the Qabalah through the Tanakh. Some books – the Pentateuch, Proverbs, Ecclesiastes, Song of Solomon, Psalms, Job, Ezekiel, Isaiah, Jeremiah – were of far greater interest to them than others. Qabalists had to find a symbolic vocabulary that could adequately deal with the contents of the Jewish scriptures, but not necessarily with anything outside them. This profoundly influenced their imaginative speculations about the natural world.

The Tree of Life forms the basis of a system of correspondences like those of astrology. The most important correspondences:

- planets;
- Biblical characters;
- orders of angels;
- individual angels;
- parts of the body;
- faculties of the psyche or soul;
- divine names;
- commandments.

Each sefirah has an enormous number of miscellaneous associations that are not amenable to classification or tabulation.

Planets

Although not obvious at first sight, the Tree of Life is closely related to the same cosmological scheme that was generally believed in throughout the ancient world: the earth sits motionless at the centre of the universe, while the sun, moon, and planets revolve around it. Though the arrangement of the sefiroth in three pillars and seven levels obscures the Tree of Life's connection to the cosmos of planetary spheres, it remains intrinsic to the numbering of the sefiroth, which corresponds to the geocentric order (Fixed Stars, Saturn, Jupiter, Mars, Sun, Venus, Mercury, Moon) known to Hipparchus (second century BCE) and Ptolemy (second century CE). The second sefirah is zone of fixed stars; sefiroth three to nine are planetary spheres from Saturn to Moon; the tenth and lowest sefirah is Earth. When we look at the qualities of the sefiroth and those of the planets, the harmony between the two systems is quite clear; the qualities of Hesed and those of Jupiter, for instance, are similar.

As well as pointing to parallels between qabalistic cosmology and the Ptolemaic traditions, the correspondence of the planets to the sefiroth is significant because much astrological symbolism thereby became available to qabalists.

Kether: the supracelestial sphere or empyrean (*Gilgal*).

Hokmah: the sphere of the fixed stars (*Mazloth*).

Binah: Saturn (*Shabtai*).

Hesed: Jupiter (*Zedek*).

Gevurah: Mars (*Madim* or *'Adom*).

Tif'areth: Sun (*Hamah* or *Shemesh*).

Nezah: Venus (*Nogah*).

Hod: Mercury (*Kokhab*).

Yesod: Moon (*Levanah*).

Malkuth: Earth (*'Erez*).

Along with various points of agreement, certain differences between Qabalah and astrology are easy to spot. A parallel exists in that the 'greater and lesser benefics' of astrological parlance, Jupiter and Venus, correspond to sefiroth on the right side of the Tree, whereas Saturn and Mars, the 'greater and lesser malefics', answer to sefiroth on the left side. However, if qabalistic ideas were taken over into astrology, the zone of constellations would become 'lucky' like Jupiter and Venus, while Mercury would become 'unlucky' like Saturn and Mars.

In passing, one notes that Kircher gives three different assignments in his *Oedipus Aegyptiacus* (17th century). John uses the one in which the natures of the sefiroth matches those of the planets most closely.[intro.18] In an earlier section, Kircher attributes Saturn to Hesed, Jupiter to Gevurah, Mars to Tif'areth, Sun to Nezah, Venus to Hod, Mercury to Yesod, and Moon to Malkuth[intro.19]. Here Kircher was probably influenced by the fact that qabalists have always stressed that the first three sefiroth form a special group, and the lower seven sefiroth form another distinct group. Moreover, the author of the *Zohar* habitually likens the tenth sefirah, Malkuth (Kingdom) to the Moon, 'because it has no light of its own, and must shine by borrowed light'. And in places the author of the *Zohar* seems to associate Binah with the starry firmament.

In a later section, Kircher assigns Saturn to Hesed, Jupiter to Gevurah, Sun to Tif'areth, Mars to Nezah, Venus to Hod, Mercury to Yesod, and Moon to Malkuth[intro.20]. Here Kircher was swayed by the fact that astrologers often pair the planets on the basis of complementary qualities. Saturn ('the greater malefic') and Jupiter ('the greater benefic') form one such pair, while Mars ('the lesser malefic') and Venus ('the lesser benefic') form another; Sun and Moon comprise yet another; Mercury is 'supplementary'.

Numbers and letters

The letters of the Hebrew alphabet commonly served as numerals in Jewish writings. This is the basis of *gematria*. Since the sefiroth also have a sequential order, which gives them specific numerical associations, it is hardly surprising that the each of the letters may also connote a single sefirah.

Kether (Crown): the number one, the letter *'alef*;

Hokmah (Wisdom): the number two, the letter *beth*;

Binah (Understanding): the number three, the letter *gimel*;

Hesed (Mercy): the number four, the letter *daleth*;

Gevurah (Strength): the number five, the letter *heh*;

Tif'areth (Beauty): the number six, the letter *vau*;

Nezah (Victory): the number seven, the letter *zayin*;

Hod (Splendour): the number eight, the letter *heth*;

Yesod (Foundation): the number nine, the letter *teth*;

Malkuth (Kingdom): the number ten, the letter *yod*.

Parts of body

Kether (Crown) denotes the area above the head.

Hokmah (Wisdom) and Binah (Understanding) are the right and left sides of the head or of the brain.

Da'ath (Knowledge or Gnosis) is the neck, or the cerebellum, or tongue.

Hesed (Mercy) is the right arm; Gevurah (Severity) is the left arm.

Tif'areth (Beauty) is the heart.

Nezah (Victory) is the right leg; Hod (Splendour) is the left leg.

Yesod (Foundation) is the reproductive organs.

Malkuth (Kingdom) is the feet.

Psyche

Kether (Crown): the will (*razon*);

Hokmah (Wisdom): selflessness, self-abnegation, or self-nullification (*bitul*);

Binah (Understanding): intelligence (*tebunah*), or joy or happiness (*simhah*);

Da'ath (Knowledge): union (*yihud*);

Hesed (Mercy): love (*ahavah*);

Gevurah (Severity): fear or awe (*yirah* or *tirah*);

Tif'areth (Beauty): compassion (*rahamim*);

Nezah (Victory): confidence, trust, security (*bitahon*);

Hod (Splendour): acknowledgement, confession (*vidui* or *hodah*), or sincerity, completeness (*tehimuth*);

Yesod (Foundation): truth (*'emeth*);

Malkuth (Kingdom): humility (*shifluth*), prayer (*tefillah*), or praise (*tehillah*).

People

There are occupational associations of a general nature:

Hesed (Mercy): a priest;

Gevurah (Strength): a warrior or soldier; a Levite;

Tif'areth (Beauty): a king, a judge;

Neẓaḥ (Victory): a musician or singer; a prophet;

Hod (Splendour): a scribe; a prophet.

More important are biblical personages who exemplify the specific virtues of a sefirah:

Ḥesed (Mercy): Abraham, because of his extraordinary hospitality and magnanimous generosity, characterises the sefirah's nature. Aaron, because he was high priest.

Gevurah (Strength): Isaac epitomises the sefirah because of his obedience to his father, displayed in his willingness to be offered as a sacrifice, thus perfectly fulfilling the fifth commandment. *Peḥad*, Fear or Awe, is an alternate name for Gevurah, and because Isaac embodies the sefirah, Jacob swears by 'the Fear of his father, Isaac'. Moses, because Levites in general personify Gevurah.[intro.21]

Tif'areth (Beauty): Jacob-Israel because he has a double nature, being honest with the honest, but cunning with the cunning. Also Moses, because he received the Torah, an important symbol of Tif'areth, by unique personal revelation.

Neẓaḥ (Eternity): the prophet Samuel in his later years, because he achieved the corresponding level of prophetic ability, and because he calls God 'the Eternal One of Israel' (Neẓaḥ Israel), a name uniquely found in 1 Samuel xv 29.

Hod (Splendour): the prophet Samuel while he was a young boy, because he operated on the corresponding level of prophecy.

Yesod (Foundation): Joseph, because he rose only to the level of interpreting dreams (a lower level of prophetic ability) than the foregoing.

Malkuth (Kingdom): King David. When Binah is represented by Leah, Malkuth is represented by Rachel.

Commandments

Kether (Crown): I am the Lord your God; do not worship other Gods;

Ḥokmah (Wisdom): do not form images;

Binah (Understanding): do not take the Name in vain;

Ḥesed (Mercy): work six days and rest on the Sabbath;

Gevurah (Strength): honour parents;

Tif'areth (Beauty): do not kill;

Neẓah (Victory): do not commit adultery;

Hod (Splendour): do not steal;

Yesod (Foundation): do not bear false witness;

Malkuth (Kingdom): do not covet what belongs to another.

Divine names

Kether: *'Ehyeh* (I am), *'Ehyeh 'Asher 'Ehyeh* (I am Who am), *'Elyon* (Most High);

Ḥokmah: *Yah* (a shortened form of the Tetragrammaton);

Binah: *'Elohim* (God), *'Elohim Ḥayyim* (Living God);

Ḥesed: *'El* (God), *'El Gadol* (Great God);

Gevurah: *'Elohim* (God), *'El Gibor* (Mighty God);

Tif'areth: *YHVH* (Lord), *Ha Qodesh* (the Holy One);

Neẓah: *YHVH Ẓabaoth* (Lord of Hosts);

Hod: *'Elohim Ẓabaoth* (God of Hosts);

Yesod: *Shadai* (Almighty), *'El Hai* (Living God);

Malkuth: *Adonai Melekh* (Lord King).

Days of the week

Ḥesed: First Day, creation of light, separation of light and darkness;

Gevurah: Second Day, creation of a firmament, separation of upper and lower waters;

Tif'areth: Third Day, separation of dry land from sea, and creation of vegetable life;

Neẓaḥ: Fourth Day, creation of sun, moon, planets, stars;

Hod: Fifth Day, creation of aquatic and aerial life;

Yesod: Sixth Day, creation of terrestrial animals, creation of man;

Malkuth: Seventh Day, rest from work.

Thus, light becomes a symbol of Ḥesed, division of Gevurah, trees of Tif'areth, celestial bodies of Neẓaḥ, fish and fowl of Hod, humanity of Yesod.

Angels

Much disagreement about these attributions exists, along with some confusion as to whether angels are actually those of the sefiroth or the planets.

Kether (or the supracelestial sphere or empyrean): Metatron ('Near to the Throne');

Ḥokmah (or the sphere of the fixed stars): Raziel ('Secrets or Mysteries of God');

Binah (or Saturn): Zafqiel ('Contemplation of God'), or Kapziel;

Hesed (or Jupiter): Zedekiel ('Righteousness or Charity of God'), Hasdiel ('Lovingkindness of God'), or Michael;

Gevurah (or Mars): Samael 'Poison or Medicine of God', Kamael, Gabriel ('Strength of God');

Tif'areth (or Sun): Uriel ('Light of God'), or Michael (because he said, 'Who is like God?');

Nezah (or Venus): Nuriel ('Light of God'), Anathiel, or Hanael ('Graciousness of God');

Hod (or Mercury): Raphael ('Healing of God');

Yesod (or Moon): Gabriel ('Strength of God'), or Anael;

Malkuth (Kingdom) or Earth: Sandalphon 'Sound of Sandals'.

Angelic ranks

Kether (Crown): *Hayoth HaKodesh* (Holy Living Creatures); *Serafim*.

Hokmah (Wisdom): *'Ofanim* (Wheels); *Kerubim*.

Binah (Understanding): *'Erelim* (Thrones); *'Ofanim*.

Hesed (Mercy): *Hashmalim* (Shining, Brilliant Ones).

Gevurah (Strength): *Serafim* (Burning).

Tif'areth (Beauty): *Malakim* (Messengers, Angels).

Nezah (Victory): *'Elohim* (Gods).

Hod (Splendour): *Benei 'Elohim* (Sons of God).

Yesod (Foundation): *Kerubim, Tarshishim*.

Malkuth (Kingdom): *'Ishim* (Men or Flames).

Again, considerable variation exists with respect to these attributions. Another scheme, probably of more relevance to the Fourth Gospel, assigns the Serafim to the World of Creation, the Holy Living Creatures to the World of Formation, the Wheels to the World of Action.[intro.22]

Four worlds

Qabalistic texts describe a spiritual hierarchy consisting of five levels of existence:

– Primordial Adam (*Adam Qadmon*);
– the World of Emanation (*'Olam ha 'Aziluth*);
– the World of Creation (*'Olam ha Bri'ah*);
– the World of Formation (*'Olam ha Yezirah*);
– the World of Action (*'Olam ha 'Assiyah*).

Very little is said about the highest level, Primordial Adam, except that it is inseparable from and merges into the Infinite Light (*'Ain Sof 'Aur*).

The sefiroth in the World of Emanation are divine attributes. In order to have anything to do with a creation, God has to take on various roles and assume specific qualities; he has to become wise, intelligent, merciful, just, powerful, and so on. This sphere consists of the different names that God adopts. It is the first stage of descent or limitation.

The World of Creation is the realm of the highest rank of angels, Seraphim.

The World of Formation is the realm of Holy Living Creatures, also known as Cherubs.

The World of Action is the realm of *'Ofanim* (Wheels).

A human being is said to have five different souls, one corresponding to each level. They are: *yehidah* (uniqueness or unity), *hayah* (life), *neshmah* (intellect or mind), *ruah* (breath or spirit), *nefesh* (animal soul or vitality).

The relationship between these four worlds and the Tree of sefiroth is described differently by different authors. The most important scheme identifies Kether with Adam Qadmon, the World of Emanation with Hokmah, the World of Creation with Binah, the World of Formation with the six sefiroth from Hesed to Yesod inclusive, and the World of Action with Malkuth.

Parzufim

One qabalistic doctrine which initially met with great resistance from some conservative circles concerns the existence of *parzufim* or faces or visages or personifications within God. Since Christians were speaking of a divine trinity of persons in their God, it is understandable that Jewish writers should eschew 'person' as a translation of *parzuf*, but the term derives from the Greek *prosōpos*, which means 'a character in a drama', and is equivalent to the Latin *persona*. Five *parzufim* are described in qabalistic texts[intro.23]:

- Ancient of Days (*'Atiq Yomin*) or Long Suffering (*'Arikh 'Anpin*, literally 'Long in Nose') or corresponds to Kether (Crown);
- Father (*'Abba*) is the visage of Hokmah (Wisdom);
- Mother (*'Imma*) is the visage of Binah (Understanding); she is referred to as the Superior Shekhinah; she is also sometimes known as the Spirit of God, identified with the Spirit of God mentioned in *Genesis* i 2, the Breath of Life which God

breathed into Adam's nostrils, animating him, and the holy 'over-soul' the righteous receive.[intro.24]

- Son or Bridegroom is the *Parzuf* of Tif'areth (Beauty), or more precisely of the six sefiroth from Hesed to Yesod; he is also called *Ze'ir 'Anpin*, Short Tempered (literally 'Short of Nose'), or Microprosopus;
- Daughter or Bride corresponds to Malkuth (Kingdom); she is called the Lower Shekhinah or Holy Spirit. The Shekhinah is the Presence or Immanence of God in all things, the personified Omnipresence of God. Portrayed as being in exile from the rest of the Godhead, sometimes she is thought of as dwelling within the souls of the elect, as the Holy Spirit, at other times she is spoken of as if she were their aggregate, the Community of Israel.[intro.25]

The last four *Parzufim* are commonly discussed together, since they are likened to members of a family. They are often related to the four worlds, and to the four letters of the Tetragrammaton. One significance of the *Parzufim* is simply that the letters of the Tetragrammaton have an additional set of correspondences: *yod* is associated with Hokmah, *heh* with Binah or Malkuth, *vau* with the six sefiroth from Hesed to Yesod centred on Tif'areth.

It would be remarkable if the parallels between the Christian doctrine of the Trinity and the qabalistic doctrine of *Parzufim* were coincidental. Christianity, as it exists now, describes three Persons. There is no sign of the Great Face, the Ancient of Ancients. There is a Father. There is a Son, who is also known as the Bridegroom. There is a Holy Spirit, but no Mother within the Godhead. As

Waite notes, a late credal statement affirms that it is the Holy Spirit who proceeds from the Father and Son, not the Son who proceeds from Father and Holy Sprit. This seems to settle the issue. There is no Daughter, though there is a Bride. She is not part of the Godhead, merely the church personified, not the Holy Spirit within the souls of the elect. Yet traces of the original doctrine are still to be seen in,

> 'Whoever speaks against the Holy Spirit can be forgiven neither in this world, nor in the world to come'. According to Matthew xii 32

and,

> The Spirit and the Bride say, "Come!' Revelation xxii 17.

Letters as paths between sefiroth

The notion that the letters of the Hebrew alphabet denote paths connecting one sefirah to another on the qabalistic Tree seems to have arisen quite early, though precisely when is not certain. In any case, none of the early manuscript versions of *Sefer Yeẓirah* we possess actually gives the scheme didactically. The Ari (Rabbi Isaac Luria sixteenth century) and the Gra (Rabbi Elijah Gaon of Vilna, eighteenth century) suggested two slightly different schemes; they are alike in assigning the three mother letters to the three horizontal paths, the seven double letters to the seven vertical paths, and the twelve simple letters to the twelve sloping paths. This may be inspired by the fact that the twelve simple letters are referred to in *Sefer Yeẓirah* as obliquities, and by the fact that Wisdom is said to have a house built with seven pillars in Proverbs ix 1.

TABLE 1: Attributions of the Hebrew Letters to paths on the Tree of sefiroth, listed by Athanasius Kircher in *Oedipus Aegyptiacus* vol. 2 pp. 305-307:

letter	from sefirah	to sefirah
'alef	1 Kether	2 Hokmah
beth	1 Kether	3 Binah
gimel	1 Kether	6 Tif'areth
daleth	2 Hokmah	3 Binah
heh	2 Hokmah	6 Tif'areth
vau	2 Hokmah	4 Hesed
zayin	3 Binah	6 Tif'areth
heth	3 Binah	5 Gevurah
teth	4 Hesed	5 Gevurah
yod	4 Hesed	6 Tif'areth
kaf	4 Hesed	7 Nezah
lamed	5 Gevurah	6 Tif'areth
mem	5 Gevurah	8 Hod
nun	6 Tif'areth	7 Nezah
samekh	6 Tif'areth	9 Yesod
'ayin	6 Tif'areth	8 Hod
peh	7 Nezah	8 Hod
zaddi	7 Nezah	9 Yesod
quf	7 Nezah	10 Malkuth
resh	8 Hod	9 Yesod
shin	8 Hod	10 Malkuth
tau	9 Yesod	10 Malkuth

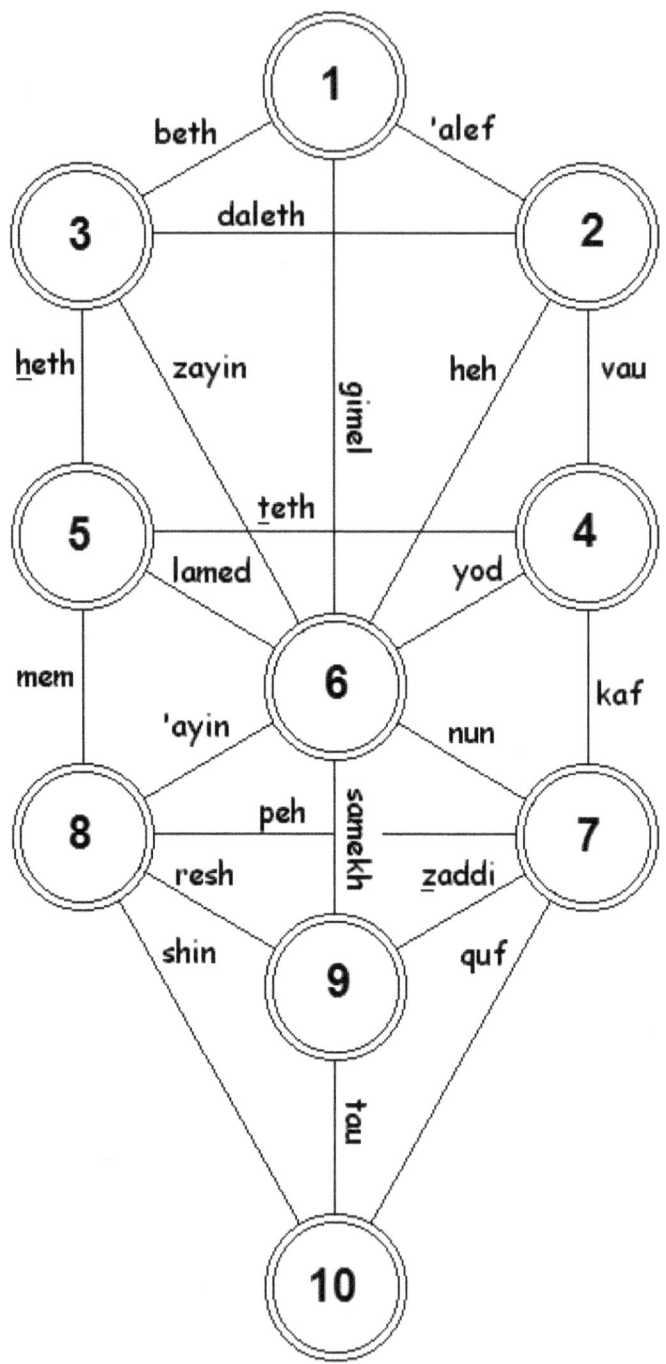

DIAGRAM 2: *Attribution of letters to paths on the Tree of Life*

In Rome in 1628, Athanasius Kircher, a Jesuit scholar of formidable erudition, published *Oedipus Aegyptiacus*, in which he describes, among other things, his own ideas about the relationship between the Tree of sefiroth and the letter-mysticism of *Sefer Yezirah*. *Oedipus Aegyptiacus* was his examination of great pagan religions and philosophies, including astrological and magical beliefs of the ancients. Kircher possessed encyclopaedic knowledge of a long list of subjects: mathematics, science, oriental and classical languages, and had travelled widely. It is clear from *Oedipus Aegyptiacus* that Kircher was acquainted with *Sefer Yezirah*, parts of the *Zohar*, and another well known qabalistic text, *Pardesh Rimmonim* (*Orchard of Pomegranates*). Most of the correspondences of the letters that Kircher gives come out of *The Short* or *Donash Version of Sefer Yezirah*, but the origin of some of his ideas remains a mystery. He gives the impression that it is just standard Qabalah.

If the disposition of the paths on the qabalistic Tree that Kircher uses is taken as given, is not hard to understand the algorithm underlying the way he allocates letters to the paths. It is perhaps easier to see by looking at the table than the diagram.

The first sefirah, Kether (Crown), has three paths diverging from it, and the first three letters of the alphabet (*'alef, beth, gimel*) are assigned to them. The second sefirah, Hokmah (Wisdom), has four paths diverging from it; one of these links it to the first sefirah (*'alef*) and has already been counted, the remaining three paths are assigned the next three letters of the alphabet (*daleth, heh, vau*). The next sefirah, Binah (Understanding), has four paths connecting it to the rest of the Tree; two have already been counted, namely those which lead to Kether and Hokmah (*beth, daleth*); the remaining two are assigned the next two letters of the alphabet (*zayin, heth*). The process is continued all the way through to the end.

Kircher could not have gotten this scheme from the *Donash Version of Sefer Yezirah*, on which he depended for some of his knowledge, nor indeed from any version of *Sefer Yezirah* that we possess. A likely explanation is that he had acquaintance with a version of *Sefer Yezirah* that included the attribution of the letters to the paths that he gives. He may have had a Jewish teacher. In any case, *Oedipus Aegyptiacus* profoundly influenced Western thinking for many centuries. Kircher's version of the Tree of Life was reproduced hundreds of times over.

The Fourth Gospel

As well as the letter correspondences of *Sefer Yezirah*, the author of According to John has the qabalistic Tree of Life in front of him, with the same system of paths and the same attribution of letters to them as Kircher gives. Every chapter of the Gospel answers to a path, and thus contains references to the two sefiroth joined by that path.

John has an additional set of attributions of the chapters. Based upon the numerical values of the letters, it is part of a widespread tradition, and Kircher records it in *Oedipus Aegyptiacus*.[intro.26]

The scheme extends to letters after *yod* in an obvious way. That is, the tenth chapter of the Gospel, which answers to *kaf* (numeral for 20), and the nineteenth chapter, which answers to *resh* (numeral for 200), correspond to Hokmah like the first chapter, which answers to *beth* (numeral for 2).

In the end, every chapter may therefore contain references to three different sefiroth: two are drawn from table 2; one drawn from table 3. The fact that John uses these two different sets of attributions concurrently may sound inconsistent, but it is no more

Table 2: Attributions of the chapters of *According to John* to Hebrew letters and paths on the Tree of Life

letter	chapter	from sefirah	to sefirah
'alef	<no chapter>	1 Kether	2 Ḥokmah
beth	chapter i	1 Kether	3 Binah
gimel	chapter ii	1 Kether	6 Tif'areth
daleth	chapter iii	2 Ḥokmah	3 Binah
heh	chapter iv	2 Ḥokmah	6 Tif'areth
vau	chapter v	2 Ḥokmah	4 Ḥesed
zayin	chapter vi	3 Binah	6 Tif'areth
ḥeth	chapter vii	3 Binah	5 Gevurah
ṭeth	chapter viii	4 Ḥesed	5 Gevurah
yod	chapter ix	4 Ḥesed	6 Tif'areth
kaf	chapter x	4 Ḥesed	7 Neẓah
lamed	chapter xi	5 Gevurah	6 Tif'areth
mem	chapter xii	5 Gevurah	8 Hod
nun	chapter xiii	6 Tif'areth	7 Neẓah
samekh	chapter xiv	6 Tif'areth	9 Yesod
'ayin	chapter xv	6 Tif'areth	8 Hod
peh	chapter xvi	7 Neẓah	8 Hod
ẓaddi	chapter xvii	7 Neẓah	9 Yesod
quf	chapter xviii	7 Neẓah	10 Malkuth
resh	chapter xix	8 Hod	9 Yesod
shin	chapter xx	8 Hod	10 Malkuth
tau	chapter xxi	9 Yesod	10 Malkuth

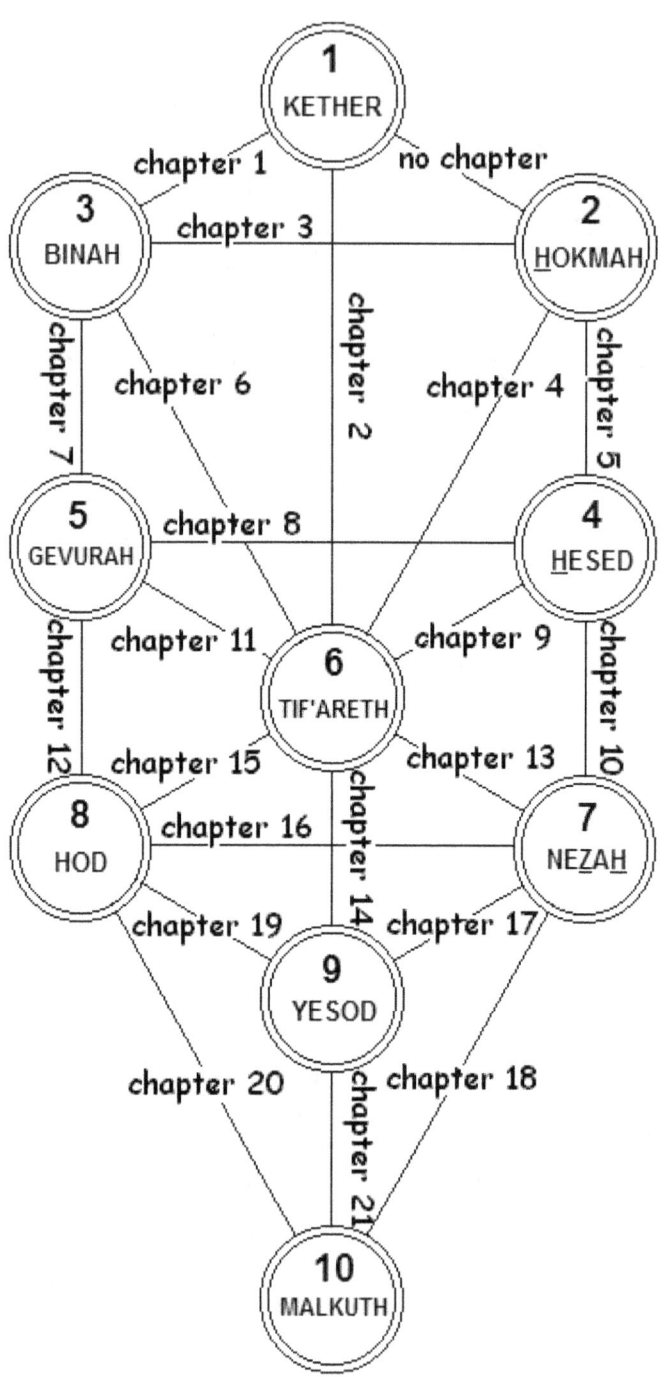

DIAGRAM 3: *Chapters of John's Gospel and paths on the Tree of Life*

TABLE 3: Attribution of the first ten chapters of *According to John* to the sefiroth, through the numerical values of Hebrew letters

According to John	letter	letter as numeral	sefirah
<no chapter>	*'alef*	1	1 Kether
chapter i	*beth*	2	2 Hokmah
chapter ii	*gimel*	3	3 Binah
chapter iii	*daleth*	4	4 Hesed
chapter iv	*heh*	5	5 Gevurah
chapter v	*vau*	6	6 Tif'areth
chapter v	*zayin*	7	7 Nezah
chapter vii	*heth*	8	8 Hod
chapter viii	*teth*	9	9 Yesod
chapter ix	*yod*	10	10 Malkuth

confusing than the fact that the chapters have both astrological and qabalistic correspondences.

On a few occasions, John indicates a sefirah by its one of its common designations. Sometimes he puns with a near homonym. An example is xvii 24, where the Jesus uses the phrase 'foundation of the world', which is the full title of the ninth sefirah, Yesod (Foundation). In xviii, Peter cuts off the ear of a slave called Malchos, a pun on the tenth sefirah, Malkuth (Kingdom). In the fifth chapter, which answers to that path between Hokmah and Hesed, Jesus performs a miraculous healing at a pool called

Bethesda, which most standard lexica interpret as *beth ḥesidah*; the Peshitta, a translation of the New Testament into Aramaic, also has *beth ḥesidah* here. Since *ḥesidah* is just the feminine correlate of Ḥesed, while *beth* represents the second sefirah, Ḥokmah, *beth ḥesidah* very neatly indicates both sefiroth joined by the path.

Sometimes John uses other titles well known to us from the *Zohar*. For instance, the second chapter, which answers to a path leading to Tif'areth, begins with 'On the third day...', 'the Third Day' being a standard title for Tif'areth (Beauty).

Sometimes John creates scenarios to illustrate the qualities inherent in the sefiroth. The eighth chapter of his Gospel, which answers to the path from Ḥesed (Mercy) to Din (Justice), opens with the Pharisees dragging an adulteress before Jesus, who is asked whether she should be stoned in the way they say the Law requires. Jesus allows them to stone her, but with the proviso that one sinless should cast the first stone, so that she escapes without punishment. The scene is a dramatic illustration: Ḥesed meets Din, softhearted Mercy versus rigorously strict Justice.

John sometimes uses commandments to point to sefiroth. The fourth commandment, the prohibition against working on the Sabbath, signals Ḥesed, the fourth sefirah, in v and ix, chapters corresponding to paths leading to and from that sefirah. Likewise, the eighth commandment, the prohibition against stealing, gives rise to mention of thievery which signals the eighth sefirah in xii, xix and xx, chapters corresponding to paths leading to and from that sefirah. And again, the ninth commandment, the prohibition against falsehood, leads to mention of truthfulness in viii and xix.

Often John uses human characters to represent the sefiroth. Mary, Jesus' mother, represents Binah, whom qabalists associate with the Parzuf called 'Mother'. Sometimes a character from the Jewish scriptures will stand for a sefirah. They may be mentioned by name, as in viii, where Abraham, the most important personification of Hesed, enters the conversation because of the chapter's connection with that sefirah. Sometimes they barely veiled, like Joseph of Arimathea, who appears in xix because he is Joseph the Patriarch, the foremost representative of the ninth sefirah.

Unusual features of John's qabalistic symbolism

Scholem felt that certain aspects of qabalistic terminology were still in a state of flux at the time of the *Bahir*'s writing. In the century that separates the *Bahir*'s appearance from the *Zohar*'s, major clarifications in several key areas took place: the primary designations of several sefiroth changed, and even the arrangement and numbering of the last four sefiroth were revised. Yet in *According to John* we see what eventually became the most widely accepted scheme. While John's brand of symbolism is uncannily like that of the *Zohar*, significant differences exist.

One noteworthy feature of John's treatment is that certain chapters are brought into intimate relationship with one another because of the way they are allocated to paths on the Tree of sefiroth. For instance, v and x, which answer to paths making up the right-sided Pillar of Mercy, are evidently allowed to share certain symbolic material; similarly vii and xii, which answer to the paths making up the left hand Pillar of Severity. Likewise, ii, xiv and xxi, which correspond to paths which together constitute the central pillar of the Tree.

Again, iii, viii and xvi, which correspond to the three horizontal paths on the Tree, are advantageously considered together because of the common threads of symbolism they share. For instance iii, viii and xvi all have references to birth (iii 3-8; viii 41; xvi 21), and a preoccupation with the relationship between what is above and what is below.

Another unusual feature of John's handling of qabalistic symbolism is the fact that he treats the sefiroth as though they were more or less interchangeable with the planets of astrology. Qabalistic literature does not greatly preoccupy itself with the planetary attributions of the sefiroth. When it does, it is always understood that the sefiroth occupy a higher place in the ontological order. The planets are among the innumerable correspondences belonging to the sefiroth, and not the other way around. Yet in the Fourth Gospel not only do we have instances where the planets absorb qabalistic symbolism proper to the sefiroth, there are one or two cases where the sefiroth have absorbed astrological symbolism pertaining to the planets.

Another difference between the shadow language of the Fourth Gospel and that of the *Zohar* is that there seems to have been a transference of certain symbolic attributes among the *Parzufim*, from Son and Daughter to Father and Mother. For example, in the *Zohar*, Voice almost always represents Tif'areth, the Son or Bridegroom, while Speech denotes Malkuth, the Daughter, his Bride. However, discussing Voice and Speech as they appear as technical terms in *Sefer Yezirah*, Aryeh Kaplan explains, because Hokmah and Binah are connected with non-verbal and verbal aspects of thought, Hokmah may be denoted by Voice, that is inarticulate sound, and Binah by Speech or Utterance, that is fully differentiated pronouncement built up of definite letters organised into a sentence.[intro.27] John seems to follow the usage Aryeh Kaplan describes in connection with *Sefer Yezirah*, rather than that found in the *Zohar*; that is, he represents Hokmah and Binah as silent, inner 'Voice' and 'Speech' respectively.

Fortunately, John largely sticks to what might be called run-of-the-mill symbolism. The *Zohar* and *Bahir*, which are written after the style of midrash, prepare the reader for John's Gospel, which was meant to be approached just as a midrashist would approach the Tanakh. Like the *Zohar* and *Bahir*, According to John is about sefirothic Qabalah. Like the *Zohar* and *Bahir*, John prefers images and symbols drawn from the Tanakh, often turning to the same verses qabalists turn to. His innovations are few and not hard to deduce.

> intro.1: Gershom Scholem, *On the Kabbalah and Its Symbolism*, p. 89.
>
> intro.2: Gershom Scholem, *Major Trends in Jewish Mysticism* p. 156ff.
>
> intro.3: *Zohar* 1:31a, 235b; 2:42b, 43a. Daniel C. Matt, *The Zohar: Pritzker Edition*, vol. 3 p. 426 n. 606. Aryeh Kaplan, *The Bahir* pp. 101.
>
> intro.4: Aryeh Kaplan, *The Bahir*, pp. 107, 115, 178.
>
> intro.5: Aryeh Kaplan, *The Bahir*, p. 162; *Meditation and Kabbalah* p. 136.
>
> intro.6: *Zohar* 1:21a, 65a; 2:220b, 226a, 234b. Daniel C. Matt, *The Zohar: Pritzker Edition*, vol. 1 p. 379 n. 275, 276, 278; vol. 4 p. 297 n. 100.
>
> intro.7: Aryeh Kaplan, *Sefer Yetzirah: The Book of Creation* p. 77; *The Bahir* para. 119; p. 125.
>
> intro.8: Aryeh Kaplan *The Bahir*, pp. 97, 107, 132, 139, 173. Gershom Scholem, *Major Trends in Jewish Mysticism* p. 219.

intro.9: *Zohar* 2:42b, 43a. Aryeh Kaplan, *Sefer Yetzirah: The Book of Creation* pp. 12.

intro.10: Aryeh Kaplan, *The Bahir* pp. 119, 126-127, 139-141. Gershom Scholem, *Major Trends in Jewish Mysticism* p. 235.

intro.11: *Zohar* 3:64a. Daniel C. Matt, *The Zohar: Pritzker Edition*, vol. 7 p. 421 n. 195.

intro.12: Aryeh Kaplan, *The Bahir* pp. 130, 140.

intro.13: See note 2.20.

intro.14: Aryeh Kaplan, *The Bahir* pp. 126, 130, 132. Daniel C. Matt, *The Zohar: Pritzker Edition*, vol. 3 p. 406 n. 514; vol. 7 p. 494 n. 446.

intro.15: *Zohar* 1:22b.

intro.16: Aryeh Kaplan, *The Bahir* p. 115. *Zohar* 1:21b. Daniel C. Matt, *The Zohar: Pritzker Edition*, vol. 5 p. 482 n. 830.

intro.17: Aryeh Kaplan, *The Bahir* p. 115.

intro.18: Athanasius Kircher, *Oedipus Aegyptiacus* vol. 2 pp. 292-294.

intro.19: Athanasius Kircher, *Oedipus Aegyptiacus* vol. 2, p. 214.

intro.20: Athanasius Kircher, *Oedipus Aegyptiacus* vol. 2, p. 356.

intro.21: *Zohar* 1:21b. Daniel C. Matt, *The Zohar: Pritzker Edition*, vol. 1 p. 129 n. 159; ibid p. 165 n. 458.

intro.22: Aryeh Kaplan, *Sefer Yetzirah: The Book of Creation* p. 79, table 11; *The Bahir* p. 120.

intro.23: Aryeh Kaplan, *The Bahir* pp. 93, 120, 122, 127, 131.

intro.24: Aryeh Kaplan, *The Bahir* pp. 120-121, 173.

intro.25: A.E. Waite, *The Holy Qabalah* p. 362.

intro.26: Athanasius Kircher, *Oedipus Aegyptiacus* vol 2. pp. 225-226.

intro.27: Aryeh Kaplan, *Sefer Yetzirah: The Book of Creation* pp. 11-13, 39, 45, 70-71; *The Bahir* p. 118. *Zohar* 1:16b, 234b; 2:25b, 137a. Daniel C. Matt, *The Zohar: Pritzker Edition*, vol. 1 pp. 122-3 nn. 109, 110; vol. 3 p. 420 n. 584; vol. 4 p. 93 n. 84; vol. 5 p. 263 n. 207; vol 7 p. 171 n. 7. *'Idra Rabbah Qadisha (The Greater Holy Assembly)* vv. 351-356.

The Gospel According to John has no chapter corresponding to 'alef;

'alef, an ox; numerical value 1; the first sefirah, Kether (Crown);
the path from the first sefirah, Kether (Crown), to the second sefirah, H̲okmah (Wisdom).

Twenty-one or twenty-two?

The familiar division of According to John into chapters, accomplished by Stephen Langton in the 13th century, was an essential part of John's original conception. This is because the key to the Fourth Gospel, its fundamental organising principle, is the implicit pairing of its chapters with the letters of the alphabet, which causes every chapter to inherit all the qabalistic and astrological symbolism attendant upon the letter under whose banner it falls. But the Hebrew alphabet consists of twenty-two letters, while According to John has only twenty-one chapters, because there is no chapter answering to *'alef,* the first letter of the alphabet. The rest is straightforward: *beth*, the second letter of the alphabet, is assigned to the first chapter of the Gospel, and the twenty remaining letters are assigned, one by one in normal alphabetical order to the twenty remaining, consecutively numbered chapters. Since the Gospel's relationship to the alphabet is paramount, it is necessary to explain why John did not follow the simpler course of giving it twenty-two chapters, one for each letter. We need to understand why the number of chapters in the Gospel falls one short of the number of letters in the Hebrew alphabet, and why it is *'alef*, and not any other letter, that is omitted from the system of correspondences upon which the Evangelist bases his work.

In the beginning

A clue to this puzzling feature lies in the fact that the words 'In the beginning', with which John opens his Gospel, and which he repeats in the next verse (i 2), are also the opening words of the book of Genesis. Of course, the Jewish Scriptures were composed in Hebrew, while According to John was composed in a dialect of Greek, but the Gospel commences with the same words as the standard Greek translation of the Bible, the Septuagint: *En archēi*. The remainder of the Fourth Gospel's Prologue is modelled after the initial verses of Genesis i. This section of Genesis deals with the world's creation; the Prologue (i 1-4) of Fourth Gospel nods towards cosmogonic themes with: 'Everything came into being through it, and not one thing which has come into being came into being without it' (i 3). The light and darkness mentioned in the Gospel's Prologue (i 4-9) hark back to the light and darkness in the opening verses of Genesis i. As we shall see in Part 3, Genesis provides an extremely important key to Johannine symbolism.

The *Zohar* elaborates a qabalistic tradition pertaining to Genesis i 1 into a fanciful tale that commences the work. It tells how immediately prior to the creation of the world the twenty-two letters assemble before the divine throne, aware that God is about to choose one of them for the purpose of initiating creation. Starting with *tau*, which normally comes last, God works through the alphabet in reverse order, allowing each letter to present its case for deserving the especial honour. As one by one each is rejected, the naive reader is led to expect that *'alef* will ultimately be chosen for the purpose. It seems only natural to begin creation with the first letter. However, in a surprise turn to the story, God finally settles upon *beth*, the second letter of the alphabet, to begin the work of creation. *'Alef* is to be set aside as an emblem of divine unity.[0.1]

Qabalistic texts attach enormous significance to the fact that the Torah commences with the letter *beth* – the first word of the Bible in Hebrew being *Bereshith*, 'In the beginning'.[0.2] Since the writing of the Torah and the creation of the universe are equivalent to the qabalist, only *beth* can be 'the letter that begins creation'. It is safe to say that apart from the letters of the Tetragrammaton (the Four Lettered Name of God) more has been written about the first two letters of the alphabet than has been written about all the others together, and most of it in the context of Genesis i 1, and why *beth* rather than *'alef* is the first letter of the Torah. Although to view the Torah as a mirror of the universe and the letters as agents in cosmic creation is often considered a distinctive feature of Qabalah, why the world was created as it were through *beth* instead of *'alef* is a matter of discussion even in texts which are not overtly qabalistic.[0.3]

The first reason for the absence of a chapter corresponding to *'alef* is John's acquaintance with the tradition that regards *beth* as the letter that begins the world's creation. If the Evangelist, writing in a Greek dialect, cannot literally commence his Gospel with the Hebrew letter *beth*, yet he can still make it the first letter of the Gospel in a figurative manner: the opening words of the Gospel are intended to recall the opening words of Genesis. *Beth* is the first letter of the alphabet to have a chapter of the Gospel assigned to it.

Like nothing

John has more than one reason not to include a chapter devoted to *'alef* and its correspondences. Among the more important is the fact that the letter *'alef*, being the first of the alphabet, and serving as the numeral one, is routinely used in the literature to denote the first sefirah, Kether (Crown).[0.4]

Kether possesses no positive attributes except existence, and its sublime transcendence is more akin to nonexistence. The sefirah is associated with nonbeing, nonmanifestation, and imperceptibility; it is often said nothing at all can be predicated of it. Qabalistic writings advise that the first sefirah is so utterly recondite that one should not even attempt to think about it, sometimes citing 'Do not inquire into what is beyond your intellect ...' (Ben Sirah/Ecclesiasticus iii 21-23).[0.5] This is why 'Most Concealed' (*Temira de Temirin*) and 'Most Secret' (*Sitre de Sitrin*) are among its common designations. *'Alef* (*'alef-lamed-peh*) is itself explained as an anagram of *pela'* (*peh-lamed-'alef*), which means 'hidden, concealed, mysterious'.[0.6]

'Ain (Nothing) is commonly used in qabalistic writings to denote the first sefirah.[0.7] Qabalists even find instances where *'Ain* is used in the Tanakh in this sense. Appearing in Exodus xvii 7 ('Is the Lord with us or not [*'ain*]?') and Numbers xiii 20 ('whether there is a tree in it or not [*'ain*]'), where one would normally expect the commoner negative particle, *lo'* ('not'), hints that the real question is whether the divine *parzuf* of Kether was present with them, or merely the *parzuf* of Tif'areth.[0.8] In a similar vein, noting that *'ain* may also mean 'where', qabalists are fond of rendering 'Whence [*me'ain*] is

Wisdom completed?' (Job xxviii 12) as 'Wisdom [Hokmah] was completed from Nothing [*me'ain*]'.[0.9] And again, 'There [*me 'ain*] is no one like you' (Jeremiah x 6-7) is read as 'Who is Nothing like you?', and taken to indicate that God is absolutely concealed and unknowable.[0.10]

The essence of a sefirah is often revealed in the human characters who are taken as its representative types. Kether does not have a human personification, but Enoch is sometimes connected with it, since he is said in qabalistic legends not to have died, but to have undergone ethereal transformation to become the archangel of the sefirah (Metatron). In qabalistic and rabbinic writings Enoch is linked with the first sefirah because he 'was not [*ainenu*] for God took him' (Genesis v 24).[0.11]

Similar ideas are derivable from the essential nature of air or breath, the yeziratic assignment of the letter *'alef*. It is the most insubstantial and tenuous and the least perceptible of the elements, 'next to nothing'. *Sefer Yezirah* speaks of 'air which cannot be grasped' (Kaplan), 'intangible air' (Kalisch), or 'immaterial ether' (Scholem).

Certain phonetic peculiarities of the letter *'alef* are also relevant even if coincidental. The letter is an unvoiced aspirate, that is, a 'silent breathing', which transparently carries whatever vowel is combined with it. In contrast to the other twenty-one consonants, it does not have any intrinsic sound, being analogous to the 'smooth breathing' in Greek or silent 'h' in French and some English words, except that *'alef* can occur in the middle or at the end of a Hebrew word. Commentators often remark on its silent or inaudible character.[0.12] In his *Explanation of the Letters*, Rabbi Jacob ben Jacob ha Kohen, a medieval qabalist of Castile, relates this to God's utterly hidden nature.[0.13]

Summary

The absence of a chapter devoted to the letter *'alef* and its correspondences is not at all difficult to explain. The letter has, for a more than one reason, something like imperceptibility, or even nonexistence, as one of its chief 'attributes': it is an emblem of Kether (Crown); it is a symbol of air, the most imperceptible or immaterial element; it is intrinsically silent. In addition, behind an apparently trivial detail, that the Torah begins with the second letter of the alphabet, *beth*, lies a qabalistic tradition of no mean importance. Although the Evangelist, writing in Greek, cannot literally commence his Gospel with the Hebrew letter *beth*, yet he does make it the first letter of the Gospel in a figurative manner: *beth* is the first letter of the alphabet to have a chapter of the Gospel assigned to it.

0.1: *Zohar* 1:3b. Daniel C. Matt, *The Zohar: Pritzker Edition*, vol. 1 p. 16 n. 110.

0.2: Aryeh Kaplan, *The Bahir* para. 3-5, 17-18, 55. *Zohar* 1:2b, 30a, 205b; 2:234b. Daniel C. Matt, *The Zohar: Pritzker Edition*, vol. 1 p. 180 nn. 594-596; vol. 3 p. 259 n. 8.

0.3: *Genesis Rabbah* i 10.

0.4: *Zohar* 1:120b. Daniel C. Matt, *The Zohar: Pritzker Edition*, vol. 1 p. 216 n. 892; vol. 2 p. 200 nn. 649, 650; vol. 6 p. 297 n. 102; vol. 7 p. 492 n. 436. Aryeh Kaplan, *Sefer Yetzirah: The Book of Creation* pp. 11, 133; *The Bahir*, pp. 99-100.

0.5: *Zohar* 1:65a; 2:42b. Aryeh Kaplan, *The Bahir* para. 49; ibid pp. 96, 100, 118, 120.

0.6: Aryeh Kaplan, *The Bahir*, para. 70; ibid pp. 133-4. *Zohar* 2:239a. Daniel C. Matt, *The Zohar: Pritzker Edition*, vol. 6 p. 384 n. 356.

0.7: Aryeh Kaplan, *Sefer Yetzirah: The Book of Creation* pp. 11, 89. *Zohar* (*'Idra Zuta Qadisha*) 3:288a-b (*The Lesser Holy Assembly* vv. 63-65. See translations by Mathers, Michael Berg, Work of the Chariot, and by Dale and Sassoon.). *Zohar* 1:30a; 2:43b; 2:90a. Daniel C. Matt, *The Zohar: Pritzker Edition*, vol. 1 p. 179 n. 585; vol. 4 p. 510 n. 525; vol. 6 p. 297 n. 102.

0.8: *Zohar* (*'Idra Rabbah Qadisha*) 3:129a (*The Greater Holy Assembly* vv. 83, 84. See translations by Mathers, Michael Berg, Work of the Chariot, and by Dale and Sassoon.) *Zohar* 2:64b; 3:158b.

Daniel C. Matt, *The Zohar: Pritzker Edition*, vol. 4 p. 351 n. 539; ibid p. 457 n. 328; ibid p. 169 n. 106.

0.9: *Zohar* (*'Idra Zuta Qadisha*) 3:209a (*The Lesser Holy Assembly* v. 209).

0.10: *Zohar* 1:10a. Daniel C. Matt, *The Zohar: Pritzker Edition*, vol. 1 p. 67 nn. 506, 507.

0.11: *Zohar* 1:37b, 223b; (*Sifra Dezeni'utha*) 2:179a (*Book of the Mystery* v 35). Daniel C. Matt, *The Zohar: Pritzker Edition*, vol. 1 p. 238 nn. 1044, 1045; vol. 3 p. 342 n. 222; vol. 5 p. 582 nn. 87, 88. *Targum PseudoJonathan* Genesis v 24.

0.12: Aryeh Kaplan, *Sefer Yetzirah: The Book of Creation* p. 99, 133. Gershom Scholem, *On the Kabbalah and its Symbolism* p. 30.

0.13: *The Early Kabbalah*, edited Dan p. 153.

According to John chapter 1;
beth, a house; numerical value 2; the second sefirah, Hokmah (Wisdom);
the path from the first sefirah, Kether (Crown), to the third sefirah, Binah (Understanding).

First sefirah

The first chapter of According to John corresponds to the path from the first sefirah, Kether (Crown), to the third sefirah, Binah (Understanding). Allusions to these two sefiroth, some taking the form of single words, can be found scattered through the text of i.

In qabalistic texts, terms pertaining to the number one, like 'unity', 'oneness', 'unique', 'solitary', and so on, are naturally associated with the first sefirah. *Yehidah*, 'one and only, solitary, unique' is used, for instance, to describe the highest human soul, whose nature is that of Kether (Crown). In the first chapter of the Gospel, the Greek word *monogenēs*, which may be rendered as 'only', 'sole', 'unique', or 'only-begotten', hints at this aspect of Kether:

> And we saw his glory, glory he possesses as the Father's only son [*monogenous*]... i 14.

> No one has ever seen God, but the only son [*monogenēs*], who is in the Father's bosom, has explained him. i 18.

Kether (Crown) manifests in the soul as *razon*, 'will, will-power, free will', the supreme faculty in the human psyche, the ultimate and uncaused cause of everything else, standing above and beyond both the intuitive powers of Hokmah (Wisdom) and the rational powers of Binah (Understanding).[1.1] Among other senses of the word *razon* are 'desire, consent, grace, graciousness, goodwill, acceptance; an acceptor or receiver'. In the *Greater* and *Lesser Holy Assemblies*, qabalistic texts associated with the *Zohar*[1.2], these different meanings of the word played upon in a way reminiscent of i 11-16, where a handful of Greek synonyms of *razon* lie clustered together.[1.3, 1.4] No semantic or etymological connection exists between the Greek words, *lambanein* and *paralambanein* ('to accept'), *thelēma* ('will or desire'), and *charis* ('grace'), for the connection exists not in the Greek language but in the Hebrew word *razon*, which John has in mind:

> He came to his own, and his own did not accept [*parelabon*] him. But he gave he power to become the sons of God to all who did accept [*elabon*] him, who believe in his name, who were born neither from blood, nor the will [*ek thelēmatos*] of the flesh, nor the will [*ek thelēmatos*] of man, but of God. And the Word became flesh and dwelt within us (or: amongst us). And we saw his glory, glory he possesses as a father's only son, full of grace [*charitos*] and truth. i 11-14.
>
> And from his fullness we have all accepted [*elabomen*], and grace upon grace [*charin anti charitos*]. i 16.

Third sefirah

The Gospel's Prologue has a simple pun on Binah (Understanding) in:

> The light shines in the darkness but the darkness did not understand it. i 5.

Another pointer to the third sefirah lies in the term *Logos* (i 1, 2, 14), which has already been looked at from an astrological perspective. In *Sefer Yezirah* at least, Voice indicates Hokmah, while Speech or Utterance, Binah. Even in the *Zohar*, the verb *'amar* (Hebrew 'to say, to name, to say to oneself, to intend') implies silent speech or verbal thought that characterises Binah. The metaphor is related to the fact that Hokmah is the formless and inchoate aspects of thought, while Binah implies the differentiation and structured order of logic and verbal reasoning.[1.5] The fact that *Logos* can connote the third sefirah as well as the planet Mercury shows John's penchant for symbolism that is simultaneously qabalistic and astrological. Much of the beauty of the Gospel emanates from John's mastery of equivocation.

The Baptist's description of himself as 'a voice in the wilderness' (i 23), drawn from Isaiah xl 3, is a pun based on the fact that the Hebrew word for 'wilderness' (*midbar*) is a homonym of one word for 'speech' (*midbar*).[1.6] Since Voice denotes Hokmah (Wisdom), while Word or Utterance denotes Binah, this verse alludes to both of these sefiroth.

Qabalistic texts associate Binah with the *Parzuf* or aspect of the godhead called the Superior Shekhinah.[1.7] The term means 'Indwelling (Presence)', and comes from the Hebrew verb *shakan*, 'to dwell, to reside, to remain, to abide'. The Shekhinah is referred to as the Spirit of God in qabalistic texts.[1.8] This motivates the mention of the Spirit in i 32-33. It also partially explains the fivefold appearance of the Greek verbs *menein* ('to dwell') in i 32-39 and *skēnoein* ('to dwell') in i 14, though John can play on the fact that *beth* means 'house':

> And the Word was made flesh, and dwelt [*eskēnōsen*] within us (or: amongst us) ... i 14

> And John testified, saying, 'I have seen the Spirit coming down from heaven like a dove, and it remained [*emeinen*] upon him. And I did not know him, but he who sent me to baptise with water said to me, "The one upon whom you see the Spirit descending and remaining [*menon*] is the one baptising with the Holy Spirit."' i 32-33.

> Then Jesus, on turning around [*strapheis*] and seeing them following, says to them, 'What are you looking for?'.
> 'Rabbi', which is translated 'Teacher', they said to him, 'where are you staying [*meneis*]?'.
> He says to them, 'Come and see'. They went and saw where he stays [*menei*], and they stayed [*emeinan*] with him that day, for it was about the tenth hour. i 38-39.

A dove is sometimes a symbol of Binah. 'Turning around, turning back' (Hebrew: *teshuvah*) is also an association of Binah in qabalistic texts.[1.9]

The Coming World, or World to Come (Hebrew *'Olam ha Ba*), is a term used to intimate Binah in qabalistic writings.[1.10] In John's Gospel, the participle 'coming' (*erchomenos*), which is applied to Jesus only in a handful of chapters – i, iii, vi, xi and xii, all of which have some connection with Binah[1.11] – has a similar connotation:

It was the true light, which illumines every man, that was coming into the world [*erchomenon eis ton kosmon*]. i 9.

John testifies about him, and has cried out, saying, 'He was the one about whom I said, "The one coming after me [*ho opisō mou erchomenos*] has come to be ahead of me, because he existed prior to me"'. i 15.

'There stands among you one whom you do not know: the one coming after me [*ho opisō mou erchomenos*], whose sandal-strap I am not worthy to unloose'. i 27.

The next day John sees Jesus coming [*ton Iesoun erchomenon*] towards him, and says, 'Look! The Lamb of God, the one taking away the sin of the world'. i 29.

The one coming from above [*ho anōthen erchomenos*] is above all. The one who comes from the earth is of the earth, and speaks of the earth. The one coming from heaven [*ho ek tou ouranou erchomenos*] is above all. iii 31.

Then the people, on seeing the miracle Jesus did, said, 'He truly is that prophet who was coming into the world [*ho erchomenos eis ton kosmon*]'. vi 14.

She says to him, 'Yes, Master, I believe that you are the Anointed, the Son of God, who was coming into the world [*ho eis ton kosmon erchomenos*]'. xi 27.

They took branches of palm trees, and went out to meet him, and cried, 'Hosanna! Blessed is the one coming in the name of the Lord [*ho erchomenos en onomati kuriou*], the King of Israel!'. xii 13.

Ḥokmah (Wisdom) in i

References to Kether and Binah occur in i because these are the sefiroth joined by the path indicated by the letter *beth*. Every chapter of the Gospel corresponds to one path on the Tree, and therefore contains references to two sefiroth. John's scheme is that first published by Kircher. But as noted, an additional set of correspondences exists, which is based upon the numerical values of the letters. Since *beth* serves as a numeral for the number two, it can denote the second sefirah, Ḥokmah (Wisdom).[1.12]

The idea is presented in various ways. 'She opens her mouth with wisdom' (Proverbs xxxi 26) is understood to refer to the Torah, which begins with the *beth* of *Bereshith* in Genesis i 1. Qabalists, moreover, are fond of suggesting a connection between Ḥokmah and *beth* ('a house'), sometimes citing Proverbs xxiv 3 ('With Wisdom the house is built ...') or Proverbs ix 1 ('Wisdom has built her house ...'), the house being understood as Binah or Malkuth or both.[1.13]

The word 'beginning' (Hebrew, *reshith*) is a code term for Ḥokmah, qabalistic texts appealing to 'The beginning is wisdom ...' (Psalm cxi 10), 'The beginning is wisdom' (Proverbs iv 7) and 'the Lord procured me, the beginning of his way ...' (Proverbs viii 22) for support.[1.14] In fact, an Aramaic translation of the Old Testament, existing only in fragmentary form, *The Jerusalem (Fragment) Targum*, a work held in high esteem by qabalists, renders Genesis i 1: 'In Wisdom [*be-ḥukmetha*] God created the heaven and earth'. This explains the appearance of the word 'beginning' in i 1-2.

Qabalists saw Ḥokmah as the divine Sophia or Primordial Torah, the personification of Wisdom who speaks in Proverbs (and the extracanonical Ben Ṣirah and Wisdom).[1.15] Turning to the Gospel, we see a subtle reference to the identification in the Gospel's Prologue,

> Everything came into being through it, and nothing that has come into being came into being without it. In it was life, and life was the light of men. i 2-4,

which has been influenced by Proverbs viii 22-31, where Wisdom personified speaks. Even early Christian authors, Athenagoras, Justin Martyr, Theophilus, Origen and Eusebius, when discussing i 1, equated the Johannine *Logos* with this personification of Wisdom.[1.16] Every one of these Christian apologists quotes Proverbs viii 22ff., identifying Jesus as *Logos* with the speaker of that passage; Origen cites also Psalm civ 24 ('In Wisdom you have made them all'). The feminine nature of Wisdom, which everyone takes for granted, is no impediment to her identification with Jesus as *Logos*. The Jewish exegetical text, *Genesis Rabbah*, also turns to these verses from Proverbs in its exposition of Genesis i 1.[1.17]

Hokmah is strongly associated with water in qabalistic traditions.[1.18] It is likely, moreover, that since it is concerned with beginnings it has developed for John a specific association with baptism, which marks the entry into Christian faith, for if we examine those chapters of the Fourth Gospel which correspond to paths leading to and from Hokmah, we see references to water (e.g. iii 5, 22-23; iv 1-2, 14; v 4-7), some in the context of baptism:

> 'Unless a man is born of water and spirit...' iii 5.

> ... and after this Jesus and his disciples came into the land of Judaea and he passed some time with them there and

baptised. And John also used to baptise at Aenon near Salim. iii 22-23.

When Jesus knew the Pharisees had heard that he made more disciples and baptised more than John – though it was not Jesus himself who baptised but his disciples... iv 1-2.

Hokmah's association with water generally but especially with baptism explains why the Baptist is mentioned in i, iii, iv and v, and why Jesus' own baptism at his hands is figures prominently in this chapter:

And they questioned him, and said to him, 'Why do you baptise then, if you are neither Christ, nor Elijah, nor the prophet?'.

John answered them, saying, 'I baptise with water, ... '.

These things happened in Bethabara beyond Jordan, where John used to baptise. i 25-28.

'And I did not know him, but it was so that he might be revealed to Israel. On account of this I came baptising with water.. And I did not know him, but he that sent me to baptise with water said to me, "The one ... the one baptising with the Holy Spirit"'. i 31-33.

Beth

Remarking on the mystical implications of the shapes of the Hebrew letters, the *Bahir* and the *Zohar* both comment on the fact that the letter *beth* is open in front.[1.19] Although the womb is a common symbol of Binah, it is just as likely that the shape of the letter *beth* motivates the statement that Jesus is 'in the hollow [*en tōi kolpōi*] of the Father' (i 18).

The *Zohar* says that because *beth* consists of two horizontal parallel strokes, one lying above the other, it represents the upper and lower worlds, one above the other, the latter a copy of the former.[1.20] The unusual phrase, *charin anti charitos*, 'grace upon grace' or 'grace opposite grace' (i 16), may also allude to the form of the letter *beth*.

Bethabara (i 28) plays upon the Hebrew of Genesis i 1: *bētha* puns on the Hebrew letter *beth* and its Greek equivalent *bēta*, while *bar'a* ('he created') is the second Hebrew word of the verse.[1.21]

In summary

In summary, John alludes not only to Kether and Binah, but also the second sefirah Hokmah in this chapter. He can do this because he has two sets of attributions to the letters, that is the chapters. The first set of attributions come from identifying the letters with paths on the Tree. The second set of attributions come from the fact that Hebrew letters function also as numerals.

References to the first sefirah appear in 'only, unique' (*monogenēs*), and in different equivalents to the Hebrew *razon* (Aramaic *raēva*, *raēuth*), namely 'grace', 'will' and 'acceptance'. References to the second sefirah appear in the Prologue as allusions to the personification of Wisdom speaking in Proverbs. 'Voice', 'beginning', and mention of baptism also indicate Hokmah. References to the third sefirah appear in the term 'word' (*logos*), in 'understand' (*katalambanein*), in mention of the Spirit, its form of the dove, in the verbs 'remain or dwell' (*skēnoein* and *menein*), 'turn around' (*strephein*), in the participle 'the coming one' (*ho erchomenos*), and in 'wilderness', which is a homonym of 'word' (*midbar*) in Hebrew. The fact that *logos* has another explanation, since it connotes the planet Mercury, may seem a trite coincidence, but John has a special predilection for finding symbols that perform several functions simultaneously, as will be seen.

Light and darkness, mentioned in the Fourth Gospel's Prologue (i 5-9), often appear in the symbology of the first triad of sefiroth, but their attributions are inconsistently given. Some qabalistic texts make light stand for Ḥokmah and darkness for Binah; in other texts the attribution is reversed; Kether can be symbolised by light, or darkness.[1.22]

> 1.1: Aryeh Kaplan, *Sefer Yetzirah: The Book of Creation* pp. 19, 38; *The Bahir* p. 131-132. Daniel C. Matt, *The Zohar: Pritzker Edition* vol. 1 p. 11 n. 74; ibid p. 116 n. 65; vol. 3 p. 265 n. 39; ibid p. 404 n. 505; vol. 4 p. 264 n. 232; ibid p. 335 n. 484; ibid p. 381 n. 41; vol. 6 p. 350 n. 260.
>
> 1.2: *Zohar* ('*Idra Rabbah Qadisha*) 3:129a (*The Greater Holy Assembly* vv. 87-100); ('*Idra Zuta Qadisha*) 3:288b, 289a (*The Lesser Holy Assembly* vv. 87-111). It is useful to compare translations of '*Idra Rabbah Qadisha* and '*Idra Zuta Qadisha*, by Mathers, Michael Berg, Work of the Chariot, and by Dale and Sassoon.
>
> Qabalists distinguish between the *Zohar* proper and the Greater *Zohar* (*Zohar Gadol*). The former is a verse-by-verse commentary on the Pentateuch. The latter includes in addition to the *Zohar* proper a number of self-contained sections which do not directly deal with the Pentateuch. They stand out from the rest of the text because they bear little or no relationship to what immediately precedes

or follows them. *The Greater Holy Assembly* (*'Idra Rabbah Qadisha*) and *The Lesser Holy Assembly* (*'Idra Zuta Qadisha*) are examples of self-contained works within the codex of the Greater *Zohar*. One also encounters passages that provide a glosses on the *Zohar* proper that are interspersed through the text in piecemeal fashion and partially integrated into it. Several of these supercommentaries exist. See Scholem, Matt, Westcott, Mathers, Waite for an analysis of the *Zohar*'s many components.

1.3: The Aramaic word *raēovuth* or *raēva'*, is noted by Gesenius (*Hebrew Lexicon*) to be equivalent to the Hebrew *razon*, and can be seen in these passages of *The Greater Holy Assembly* and *The Lesser Holy Assembly* to have much the same technical meaning as the Hebrew word, that is, it connotes a function of the first sefirah.

1.4: *Thayer's Lexicon* notes that *thelēma* normally appears in the Greek of the Septuagint for *razon* in the original Hebrew of the Tanakh.

1.5: Aryeh Kaplan, *Sefer Yetzirah: The Book of Creation* pp. 11-13, 39, 45, 70-71.

In qabalistic texts, 'Voice' (*qol*) and 'Word' (*dibur*), 'Utterance' or 'Saying' (*ma'amar*) and 'Speech' (*midbar*) are technical terms. In the *Zohar*, Voice and Word usually serve to denote Tif'areth and Malkuth rather than Hokmah and Binah. However the verb *'amar* sometimes implies silent speech that is verbal thinking. See *Zohar* 1:16b, 234b; 2:25b, 137a, 226b; (*'Idra Rabbah Qadisha*) 3:132b (*The Greater Holy Assembly* vv. 351-356). Daniel C. Matt, *The Zohar: Pritzker Edition* vol. 1 pp. 122-3 nn. 109, 110; vol. 3 p. 420 n. 584;

vol. 4 p. 93 n. 84; vol. 5 p. 263 n. 207; vol. 6 p. 298 n. 103; vol 7 p. 171 n. 7.

1.6: *Zohar* 1:10a-b; 3:205b. Daniel C. Matt, *The Zohar: Pritzker Edition* vol. 1 p. 69 n. 518.

Exodus Rabbah ii 4.

1.7: *Zohar* 1:25a, 50a. Daniel C. Matt, *The Zohar: Pritzker Edition* vol. 1 p. 282 n. 1340. Aryeh Kaplan, *The Bahir* para. 171; ibid p. 200 n. 193.

1.8: Aryeh Kaplan, *The Bahir* pp. 120-121, 173.

1.9: *Zohar* 1:219a; 3:15b, 16a, 75a. Daniel C. Matt, *The Zohar: Pritzker Edition* vol. 1 p. xlviii; vol. 3 p. 323 n. 122; vol. 7 p. 95 n. 290; ibid pp. 97, 98 nn. 296, 297; ibid p. 104 n. 316; ibid p. 505 n. 482. Gershom Scholem, *On the Kabbalah and Its Symbolism* p. 49 n. 1.

1.10: *Zohar* 1:1b. Daniel C. Matt, *The Zohar: Pritzker Edition*, vol. 1 p. 3 n. 17; ibid p. 4 n. 19; ibid pp. 264-265 nn. 1222-4; vol. 4 p. 16 n. 63; ibid p. 130 n. 223.

1.11: The first, third and sixth chapters of the Gospel correspond to paths joining Binah to other sefiroth. The eleventh chapter answers to the letter *lamed*, which serves as a numeral for the number thirty, and can denote Binah for that reason; Binah, moreover, is associated with the Day of Atonement, around which xi largely based; see note 11.3. For *mem* as a symbol of Binah see: Aryeh Kaplan, *The Bahir* pp. 114, 149. Daniel C. Matt, *The Zohar: Pritzker Edition*, vol. 1 p. 216 n. 893; vol. 6 p. 4 n. 11; ibid p. 7 n. 18; ibid p. 439 n. 255.

1.12: *Zohar* 1:31b, 145a. Daniel C. Matt, *The Zohar: Pritzker Edition*, vol. 1 p. 50 n. 352; ibid p. 190 n. 678; vol. 2 p. 310 n. 378; vol. 7 p. 492 n. 439. Athanasius Kircher, *Oedipus Aegyptiacus* pp. 225-226.

1.13: *Zohar* 1:29a-b, 39b, 1:94b. Daniel C. Matt, *The Zohar: Pritzker Edition*, vol. 1 p. 170 n. 502; ibid p. 173 nn. 520, 527, 528; ibid p. 176 n. 554; vol. 2 p. 99 n. 753; vol. 7 p. 530 n. 545. Aryeh Kaplan, *The Bahir*, para. 14, 55; p. 124.

1.14: *Zohar* 1:3b, 7b, 15a-b, 29b, 30b, 31b, 145a; 2:221a; 3:53b. Daniel C. Matt, *The Zohar: Pritzker Edition* vol. 1 p. 17 n. 112; ibid p. 50 n. 352; ibid p. 109 n. 12; ibid p. 111 nn. 27, 28; ibid p. 180 n. 596; ibid p. 185 n. 630; ibid p. 186 n. 639; ibid p. 190 n. 678; vol. 2 p. 310 nn. 378, 386; vol. 6 p. 263 n. 13. Rabbi Isaac the Blind, *Treatise on the Process of Emanation* chapter in *The Early Kabbalah* edited Dan p. 80. Aryeh Kaplan, *The Bahir*, para. 3, 17, 18, 51, 103, 105, 142; ibid pp. 91, 99-100, 120; *Sefer Yetzirah: The Book of Creation* p. 45.

1.15: Gershom Scholem, *On the Origins of the Kabbalah* pp. 131-134. *Zohar* 1:141b.

1.16: Athenagoras, *Plea for Christians* x. Justin Martyr, *Dialogue with Trypho* lxi. Theophilus, *To Autolycus*, book 2 x, xviii, xxii. Origen, *De Principis* book i chapter 2, 1-2. Eusebius, *Eccles. Hist.* I 2:15.

1.17: *Genesis Rabbah* i 1.

1.18: See note intro.9.

1.19: Aryeh Kaplan, *The Bahir* para. 14, 15. *Zohar* 1:3b, 145a; 3:35b, 36a. Daniel C. Matt, *The Zohar: Pritzker Edition* vol. 1 p. 17 n. 118; vol. 2 p. 310 nn. 381, 382, 383, 384; vol. 7 p. 209 n. 6.

1.20: *Zohar* 1:29a, 30a; 3:36a. Daniel C. Matt, *The Zohar: Pritzker Edition* vol. 1 p. 116 n. 61; ibid p. 170 n. 502; ibid p. 173 nn. 520, 528.

1.21: 'Bethabara' occurs in manuscript tradition followed by *Stephanus 1551*; others versions of the Fourth Gospel have 'Bethany' or 'Bethraba' here.

1.22: Qabalistic texts sometimes associate Hokmah with darkness and Binah with light. This is because water and fire, which are important symbols of these two sefiroth, are connected with darkness and light (See *Exodus Rabbah* xv 22; Aryeh Kaplan, *Sefer Yetzirah: The Book of Creation*. p. 77-78, 91-92). The attribution relates to the idea that in darkness things cannot be distinguished from one another (the undifferentiatedness of Hokmah), while in the light they can be (the differentiation of Binah). It is also consistent with the account of Genesis i, in which darkness exists before light, evening precedes morning.

Other texts imply light is a symbol of Hokmah, darkness of Binah. This is congruous with the sinistrophobia of qabalistic symbolism. That fire is actually synonymous with darkness, if counterintuitive, is found in qabalistic texts. Certainly Hesed, below Hokmah on the right, is associated with light and water, while Gevurah, below Binah on the left, is associated with darkness and fire.

As for the idea that darkness preceded light, Qabalists object that light was preexistent), taking Genesis i ('and there was light') to read 'but there had [already] been light'.

See Aryeh Kaplan, *Sefer Yetzirah: The Book of Creation* p. 14; Daniel C. Matt, *The Zohar: Pritzker Edition* vol. 1 p. p. 123 n. 114; ibid 184 n. 622. See also Aryeh Kaplan, *The Bahir* pp. 100, 169; and the same author's *Sefer Yetzirah: The Book of Creation* p. 6 table 2; and Gershom Scholem, *On the Origins of the Kabbalah* pp. 179, 340-341, 449-450.

Kether is paradoxically described both as a lamp that radiates darkness and as the ultimate source of all light in the *Zohar*. See Daniel C. Matt, *The Zohar: Pritzker Edition* vol. 1 p. 107-8 nn. 4, 5; vol. 3 p. 40 n. 281.

The Gospel According to John chapter 2;
gimel, a camel; numerical value 3; the third sefirah, Binah (Understanding);
the path from the first sefirah, Kether (Crown), to the sixth sefirah, Tif'areth (Beauty).

The second chapter of the Gospel corresponds to the path connecting Kether (Crown) to Tif'areth (Beauty), the highest path on the middle pillar of the Tree of sefiroth. Jacob's Ladder, the staircase to heaven upon which angels ascended and descended, which he saw in a dream (Genesis xxviii 11-22), appears as a symbol of the central pillar of the Tree at the end of the first chapter of John's Gospel, where Jesus identifies himself with it:

> 'Amen, amen, I tell you: soon you will see the heavens opened and the angels of God going up and down upon the Son of Man'. i 51.

Jesus' comment comes at the end of i, rather than within ii, however, it seems to be that in the final one or two verses of a chapter the use of a future tense (or what amounts to a future-equivalent) indicates that symbolism there found should be referred to the next chapter. Here 'will see' performs the task. John makes use of this device on several occasions. It can be seen at work in v 47 ('If you do not believe his writings, how will you believe what I say?'), and in xiv 30 ('The Ruler of the World is coming'). So, although thematically connected with ii, Jesus' identification of himself with Jacob's Ladder occurs at the end of i, along with the signal future, 'will see'.

The germaneness of the symbol to ii rests partly on the fact that Jacob is said to be the human embodiment of Tif'areth (Beauty). He is 'the bolt that passes all the way through from one end to the other', bridging the gap between the Lower Shekhinah on earth, and the Upper Shekhinah in heaven.[2.1]

The first words of the second chapter,

> On the third day there was a wedding in Cana ... ii 1

convey the position of the path on the Tree through the shadow language of the Qabalah, in which 'the Third Day' is a common designation for Tif'areth (Beauty).[2.2]

The Bridegroom (ii 9-10) is another common and specific symbol of Tif'areth.[2.3]

'Cana' may have been intended to suggest on the Hebrew word *qanah*, 'to stand vertically upright, be erect', since the path from Kether to Tif'areth is one of the vertical paths on the Tree. *Qan* or *qina*' may also mean 'nest', which occurs in the *Zohar* in the context of the image of a mother-bird and her nestlings, which the *Zohar* interprets to be Binah (Mother) and the six sefiroth from Ḥesed to Yesod with Tif'areth at the focus.[2.4]

Thirteen measures of compassion

In rabbinic texts one finds discussion of Thirteen *Middoth Raḥamim* (Thirteen Measures of Compassion), the divine attributes that were revealed to Moses in Exodus xxxiv 6-7; Micah vii 18-20 is also understood to allude to them[2.5]. The *Zohar* and qabalistic texts closely associated with it describe these Thirteen Measures of Compassion as extending downward from Kether (Crown) to Tif'areth (Beauty). Compassion (Rahamim) is an alternative name for Tif'areth[2.6].

In the Gospel the idea figures in:

> Six stone water-jars, each holding two or three measures, were sitting there, in accordance with the purification customs of the Jews. Jesus says to them, 'Fill the water-jars with water'. And they filled them up to the very top. And he says to them, 'Draw some off now, and take it to the governor of the feast'. ii 6-9.

Six jars containing two or three measures apiece must hold between twelve and eighteen measures in total: this is how John obliquely hints at the Thirteen Measures. There are six stone jars because Tif'areth is the sixth sefirah, and often considered to be focal point of the six sefiroth from Hesed (Mercy) to Yesod (Foundation)[2.7]. The Talmud says a covenant existed with God that the congregation would always obtain forgiveness whenever there is proclamation of these Thirteen *Middoth*[2.8], the last of which is taken to be 'and cleanses'. Hence John adds, 'for the purification customs of the Jews' (ii 6).

The precise significance of the transformation of water into wine is more elusive. Wine, like water, is a symbol of the Torah, which is itself a symbol of the sixth sefirah.[2.9] Qabalists understand the Torah to be the one who speaks of herself as mixing wine in Proverbs ix 2-5.[2.10] The Thirteen *Middoth* of Compassion are occasionally linked with the Thirteen Measures of the Torah.[2.11] The verb *entolasthai*, 'to keep back, to save or preserve' (ii 10) also means 'to observe a rule, to keep a commandment', and is used elsewhere in John's Gospel because the Torah connotes Tif'areth (Beauty).

Sifra De̱zeni'utha, *'Idra Rabba Qadisha*, and *'Idra Zuta Qadisha*, texts found in the codex of the Greater *Zohar*, strongly associate the persona of Kether, known variously as the Long Suffering, the Ancient One, or the Hoary Head, with the colour white; he emanates light, a clear dew in thirteen streams.[2.12] The colour red, on the other hand, is emblematic of the Short Tempered One, who is also called the Bridegroom, the persona of Tif'areth, and whose irascible nature contrasts with the perfect compassion of the Long Suffering or Ancient One.[2.13] The transformation of water into wine may intimate the descent from Kether to Tif'areth, into the world of feeling and emotion.[2.14] Where the Hebrew of the Massoretic has *qana'* and *qanah* the Greek of Septuagint has *zēlos* ('zeal') and *zēloein* ('to be zealous'), as in LXX Psalm lxviii 10 (Mass. Psalm lxix 9) which John quotes in ii 17. 'Cana' (ii 1) may therefore be a pun on *qanah* 'to be zealous, or jealous', literally 'to turn red with passion'.

Higher Shekhinah

Since the letter *gimel* is used as a numeral denote the number three in Jewish writings, it can denote the third sefirah, Binah (Understanding).[2.15] Qabalists frequently represent Binah in the form of a personification, *'Imma*, the Matron or Mother, citing Proverbs ii 3, which they read 'Call Understanding "Mother"'.[2.16] The *Zohar* describes her as the patroness of matrimony and the protector of its sanctity.[2.17] In the Gospel this manifests in the setting of ii and the presence of Mary.

A temple or palace (Hebrew *hekal*) is symbol of Binah (Understanding).[2.18] This explains why, in the latter part of ii, after

Jesus has expelled the merchants, the Temple or House of God becomes the centrepiece of discussion, and Jesus identifies his body as a temple:

> His disciples remembered what is written: 'Zeal for your house devoured me'.
> The Jews replied to him saying, 'Are you signifying something to us that you should do this?'.
> Jesus answered and said to them, 'Tear this temple apart and in three days I shall raise it up'.
> The Jews said, 'This Temple was built [*ōikodomēthē*] over forty-six years and in three days you will raise it up?'. But he was speaking about the temple of his body. ii 17-21.

Qabalists sometimes indicate Binah by punning on the unrelated but similarly sounding verb *banah*, 'to build'.[2.19] John uses the same verb, *oikodomein*, that the Septuagint normally uses for *banah* in the original Hebrew.

Wine is a symbol of Binah in the *Zohar*, sometimes intimating an aspect of Tif'areth that has its ultimate source in Binah.[2.20]

An unexpected feature of the Gospel's organisation

When discussing the way John handles astrological symbolism in Part 1, we saw that a personification could appear one chapter too late, that is, not in the appropriate chapter, but in the chapter which immediately follows it. Such planetary or zodiacal types leave Jesus' presence, often abruptly or dramatically. This evidently is how their being out of place is tagged. It appears that qabalistic symbolism is also sometimes moved about, though in this case, the structure of the Tree of Life determines when and how symbolism is moved from one chapter to another. It is an idiosyncratic feature of the Gospel's organisation of qabalistic symbolism.

Looking at the Tree, one can see that the path connecting Kether (Crown) to Tif'areth (Beauty), continues on vertically downward as the path connecting Tif'areth to Yesod (Foundation), and then as the path connecting Yesod to Malkuth (Kingdom). (see diagram 3, page 182). These three paths that make up the central vertical pillar correspond to three chapters of the Gospel, namely ii, xiv and xxi. Now, it appears chapters that are related in the way ii, xiv and xxi are related can share a certain amount of symbolic material. For when we examine v and x, which correspond to the paths making up the Pillar of Mercy on the right side of the Tree, and vii and xii, which correspond to the paths making up the Pillar of Severity on the on the left side of the Tree, we see that they treated analogously. The relationship between v and x and that between vii and xii are matters to which we shall return in due course. It is perhaps worthwhile to note at this point that when we consider v and x on one hand, and vii and xii on the other, it appears that symbolism related to Jewish festivals has been moved – from x to v, and from xii to vii. For one consequence of the relationship between ii and xiv is that ii contains symbolism derived from a Jewish feast which would be more congenial to xiv.

Among the various correspondences of xiv is the ninth month of the year, Kislev. The most notable event of the month is the beginning of the Feast of Dedication or Ḥanukah. The holiday recalls an important Jewish victory against the Selucid king Antiochus Epiphanes, who had tried to enforce hellenisation upon the Jews. He forbade observance of their religious customs, plundered the Temple, violated the Holy of Holies, and turned the altar over to pagan cults. Mattathias, of a priestly family, sorely grieved over the fate of the Temple and abandonment of the Torah, led a rebellion. As recounted in 1 Maccabees iv 52-59 and 2 Maccabees x 5-8, the Feast of Dedication commemorates the recapture of the Temple by the Maccabees, its repair and reconsecration, three years to the day (Kislev 25) after its profanation.

Nothing related to Hanukah appears in xiv, where one might have expected to find it. Instead, it manifests in ii 14-21, an episode commonly known as 'the Cleansing of the Temple'. 'Zeal for your house has consumed me' (ii 17) is actually a perfect motto for the events recalled at Feast of Dedication and a central theme of the Maccabean apocrypha.[2.21]

Another consequence of the affinity between ii, xiv and xxi is the prominence given to knowing or knowledge in all three chapters. Here we have:

> When the governor of the feast tasted the water that had become wine, he did not know whence it came, although the waiters who had drawn out the water knew, the governor of the feast calls the bridegroom. ii 9.

> But Jesus did not confide in them, because he knew them all, and he did not need anyone to testify about a person for he knew what was in a person. ii 24-25.

The other relevant passages are in xiv 7, 9, 16-17, 20, 23-24, 26, 31, and xxi 4, 12, 15-17, 24.

We can account for mention of knowing in ii since Da'ath (Knowledge, Gnosis), which denotes the union of Hokmah (Wisdom) and Binah (Understanding) as male and female, is spoken of as if it lay on the path between Kether (Crown) and Tif'areth

(Beauty).[2.22] Knowledge appears germane to xiv for another reason: that chapter answers to the sector of the horoscope corresponding to higher knowledge or gnosis. However, the most likely explanation for the repeated references to knowing in xxi is that it was imported, as it were, from ii or xiv or both. In any case, the fact that knowledge is evidently thematic to all three of these chapters hints at their special relationship, and suggests that they are best considered together.

Another manifestation of the relationship between ii and xiv is the word *eklēthē* ('he was called') in ii 2, which is intended to recall the *paraklētos* ('Paraclete', literally 'one called beside') of xiv.

In summary

In summary, references to the sixth sefirah appear in the phrase, 'the third day', and mention of the bridegroom (ii 9). The central pillar of the Tree is often connected with the idea of harmonising the male and female principles and manifests in the wedding that is the setting of the chapter. Details of the miracle of the transformation of water to wine also conceal an oblique reference to the relationship between Kether and Tif'areth. The path The from Kether to Tif'areth is the uppermost part of the middle pillar on the Tree of sefiroth. In the Gospel, Jacob's Ladder becomes a symbol of the middle pillar on the Tree of Life. Jesus identification with Jacob's Ladder takes place at the very end of the first chapter of the Gospel, but the futurity of 'you will see' intimates that the symbol belongs in ii.

As noted, John has two sets of assignments for the letters, that is the chapters. On one hand they represent paths on the Tree of Life. One the other hand, the letters directly connote sefiroth because of their numerical value. The letter *gimel*, to which this chapter is assigned, is used a numeral for three, and in qabalistic texts connotes the third sefirah Binah. A temple, especially Solomon's (First) Temple, is a symbol of Binah in qabalistic texts. Mary's presence is explained by the fact that Binah is referred to as *'Imma*, Mother. The fact that Jesus' mother can be understood either as a lunar type, or as a representative of the third sefirah, the Superior Shekhinah, is no happy coincidence. John's symbols can often be understood in both astrological and qabalistic terms. This happens so frequently it can only be something he deliberately strives for. The filling of the stone waterpots (ii 6-8) also has both astrological and qabalistic connotations.

The second, fourteenth and twenty-first chapters stand in special relationship because they correspond to paths making up the middle pillar of the Tree. An unexpected feature of the Gospel is that chapters like these are evidently allowed to share symbolic material. Jesus' Cleansing of the Temple would be suitable for xiv, since that chapter corresponds to the month Kislev, when the Feast of Dedication is begins, but John places it in ii instead of xiv.

2.1: *Zohar* 1:1b, 2a.

2.2: *Zohar* 1:17a, 18a, 19b, 46a. Daniel C. Matt, *The Zohar: Pritzker Edition*, vol. 1 p. 128 n. 157; ibid p. 134 n. 209; ibid p. 147 n. 313; ibid p. 245 nn. 1080, 1081; vol. 4 p. 439 n. 260; vol. 5 p. 370 n. 511.

2.3: *Zohar* 1:8a, 9a; 2:133b, 137a, 145a-b; 3:148b. Daniel C. Matt, Zohar, *The Zohar: Pritzker Edition*, vol. 1 p. 53 n. 379; vol. 5 p. 241 n. 143.

2.4: *Zohar* 1:219a; 2:8a; 2:85b, 93a. Daniel C. Matt, *The Zohar: Pritzker Edition*, vol. 3 p. 323 n. 120; vol. 4 pp. 26-27 nn.

102, 109; ibid p. 480 n. 413; ibid p. 530 nn. 597-598. Aryeh Kaplan, *The Bahir* p. 162-163.

2.5: *Numbers Rabbah* xxi 16. Daniel C. Matt, *The Zohar: Pritzker Edition* vol. 1 p. 1 n. 4.

2.6: *Zohar (Sifra Dezeni'utha)* 2:177a (*Book of the Mystery* chap. 2); 3:62a; (*'Idra Rabba Qadisha*) 3:131a-b, 134b; (*The Greater Holy Assembly* vv. 213-237, 256-277, 315-316, 474, 483-485); 3:146b, 147a; (*'Idra Zuta Qadisha*) 3:288b, 289b (*The Lesser Holy Assembly* vv. 69, 155). Daniel C. Matt, *The Zohar: Pritzker Edition* vol. 1 p. 153 n. 357; vol. 5 p. 549 n. 10; ibid p. 556 nn. 22, 24; ibid p. 558 n. 29; vol. 7 p. 407 n. 154; ibid p. 438 n. 251.

2.7: Daniel C. Matt, *The Zohar: Pritzker Edition* vol. 1 p. 86 n. 649; vol. 2 p. 188 n. 563; ibid p. 336 n. 129; vol. 4 p. 39 n. 172.

2.8: TB *Rosh ha Shanah* 17b. Daniel C. Matt, *The Zohar: Pritzker Edition* vol. 5 p. 558 n. 30.

2.9: TB *Ta'anith* 7a. *Genesis Rabbah* liv 1; ibid lxxxiv 16. *Deuteronomy Rabbah* vii 3. *Song of Songs Rabbah* i 18-19. *Zohar* 1:12b, 182a; 2:60a, 124b; 3:95a, 270a. Daniel C. Matt, *The Zohar: Pritzker Edition* vol. 1 pp. 86, 87 nn. 655, 664; ibid p. 252 n. 1133; vol. 3 p. 128 n. 274; vol. 4 p. 320 n. 427.

2.10: *Zohar* 1:165a; 3:189b.

2.11: *Zohar* 3:62a. Daniel C. Matt, *The Zohar: Pritzker Edition* vol. 7 p. 408 n. 154.

2.12: *Zohar* (*'Idra Rabba Qadisha*) 3:128b, 129b, 130b, 135a, 137a, 140b (*The Greater Holy Assembly* vv. 51-57, 122-132, 211,

515, 637, 638, 856). Daniel C. Matt, *The Zohar: Pritzker Edition* vol. 5 p. 549 n. 10; ibid p. 550 n. 12.

2.13: *Zohar* (*'Idra Rabba Qadisha*) 3:130a-b, 133a, 135b, 137b, 141a (*The Greater Holy Assembly* vv. 139, 152, 155, 367, 548, 550-551, 665, 890-894); (*'Idra Zuta Qadisha*) 3:293a, 295a (*The Lesser Holy Assembly* vv. 496-498, 637-638).

2.14: Daniel C. Matt, *The Zohar: Pritzker Edition* vol. 5 p. 577 n. 76. For the Ancient of Days likened to fine wine: *Zohar* (*'Idra Rabba Qadisha*) 3:128b, 140b (*The Greater Holy Assembly* vv. 60, 855).

2.15: Aryeh Kaplan, *The Bahir* para. 19, 28; ibid pp. 100, 103.

2.16: Aryeh Kaplan, *The Bahir* para. 104; ibid p. 130. TB *Berakhoth* 57a. *Numbers Rabbah* x 4.

Zohar 2:101a.

2.17: *Zohar* 1:50b. Daniel C. Matt, *The Zohar: Pritzker Edition*, vol. 1 p. 278 n. 1309

2.18: *Zohar* 1:3b, 6b, 13b, 15a-b, 16b, 18a, 20a; 2:9b, 68b, 142b, 143a, 215a, 220b. Daniel C. Matt, *The Zohar: Pritzker Edition*, vol. 1 p. 18 n. 119; ibid p. 39 n. 266; ibid p. 110 nn. 17, 19; ibid p. 137 n. 230; vol. 4 pp. 36 n. 163; ibid pp. 381, 382 nn. 42, 43; vol. 5 p. 310 n. 358; vol. 6 p. 7 n. 18; ibid p. 168 n. 162; ibid p. 227 n. 358; ibid p. 233 n. 380.

2.19: *Zohar* 2:9b. Daniel C. Matt, *The Zohar: Pritzker Edition*, vol. 3 p. 512 n. 924; vol. 4 p. 37 n. 164; ibid p. 127 n. 213. Gershom Scholem, *Major Trends in Jewish Mysticism* p. 219. *Genesis Rabbah* xviii 1.

2.20: *Zohar* 1:88a, 239b-240a; 3:39a, 40a-b, 127a. Daniel C. Matt, *The Zohar: Pritzker Edition*, vol. 3 p. 463 n. 756; vol. 5 p. 335 n. 408; vol. 7 p. 5 n. 13; ibid pp. 72, 73 n. 224, 225; ibid pp. 235, 236 nn. 90, 91; ibid p. 237 nn. 94, 96; ibid p. 243 n. 123; ibid p. 244 n. 125.

2.21: 1 Maccabees ii 21-27.

2.22: *Zohar* 2:123a. Daniel C. Matt, *The Zohar: Pritzker Edition*, vol. 5 p. 155 n. 43; vol. 7 p. 249 n. 137; ibid p. 314 n. 190. Aryeh Kaplan, *The Bahir* pp. 98, 202 n. 220.

The Gospel According to John chapter 3;

daleth, a door; numerical value 4; the fourth sefirah, **H̱esed (Mercy);**
the path from the second sefirah, **H̱okmah (Wisdom),**
to the third sefirah, Binah (Understanding).

The path assigned to the letter *daleth* joins H̱okmah (Wisdom) and Binah (Understanding). Qabalistic writings associate these sefiroth with the *Parẕufim* or Faces called Father and Mother respectively. The remaining sefiroth are likened to the offspring of their mating, to whom Binah figuratively gives birth. This explains why birth dominates the discussion in the opening section of iii, where Nikodemos, the Pharisee, pays Jesus a nocturnal visit during which he instructs him:

> 'Amen, amen, I tell you: unless someone is born from above (or: born again), he can not see the kingdom of God'.
> Nikodemos says to him, 'How can a man who is old be born? Can he enter his mother's womb a second time and be born?'.
> Jesus replied, 'Amen, amen, I tell you: unless he is born of water and spirit, he can not enter the kingdom of God. What is born of flesh is flesh and what is born of spirit is spirit. Do not

be amazed because I told you that you must be born from above (or: born again).' iii 3-7.

Nikodemos' question about entering the womb a second time is another example of compact Johannine wordplay: *deuteron*, 'second' or 'a second time', alludes to Ḥokmah, the second sefirah; the womb is a frequently encountered symbol of Binah as Mother (*'Imma*) or Matrona.[3.1]

Ḥokmah is the highest sefirah on the Pillar of Mercy on the right side of the Tree of Life, and Binah holds an equivalent position on the Pillar of Severity on the left side. These two side pillars of the Tree represent the two complementary poles of existence, and are often symbolised by pairs of opposites. This is why this chapter contains a series of contrasts: heaven and earth, above and below, spirit and flesh, light and darkness, good and evil, increase and decrease, life and death. Curiously, in the *Zohar* we often see these used as symbols of Ḥesed and Gevurah or Tif'areth and Malkuth. The differences between the *Zohar* and According to John are significant, but not all that great. Ḥesed and Gevurah, which sit on the right and left columns of the Tree and are depicted as complementary or diametrically opposed in nature, share several important symbols with Ḥokmah and Binah respectively. And Tif'areth and Malkuth are likened to the Son and Daughter of Ḥokmah and Binah, their Father and Mother, from whom they inherit various attributes.

Heaven and earth, or above and below, are the most important such pair of opposites. In Jesus' conversation with Nikodemos (iii 3-7), the phraseology of dualism overlays the theme of birth. Later in the chapter, the theme, which is foreshadowed in the opening pericope, is developed further, and quite independently of the subject of birth:

> 'If I speak to you about earthly matters and you do not believe me, how will you believe if I speak to you about heavenly matters? For no one went up to heaven except him who came down from heaven: the Son of Man.' iii 12-13.

The contrast between heavenly and earthly returns, and is used to create a comparison between Jesus and John the Baptist – Jesus is of course above, while the Baptist is below:

> 'He must increase and I must decrease. The one coming from above is above everyone. He who comes from the earth is of the earth and speaks from the earth. The one coming from heaven is above all.' iii 30-31.

In the Qabalah, heaven and earth often appear as a male and female pair. However, when heaven and earth are spoken of as a couple in this way in the *Zohar*, it is usually the Bridegroom or Son (Tif'areth) and the Daughter or Bride (Malkuth) who are indicated, rather than Hokmah (Father) and Binah (Mother).[3.2] When discussing the six directions in space, *Sefer Yezirah* relates 'above' and 'below', which in the Gospel are aligned with heaven and earth, to Nezah and Hod.[3.3]

It is true that Binah is occasionally symbolised by earth in qabalistic writings. It is as though two earths existed: a lower earth that is identified with Malkuth (Kingdom), and a higher earth that is Binah (Understanding).[3.4] Malkuth is designated 'the World' or 'this world', while Binah is 'the World to Come'.[3.5] That at the end of the current aeon the Daughter will in some way be elevated to the position of Mother is a recurring subject in qabalistic writings. It is unusual, however, that Heaven should be a symbol for Hokmah, or that the relationship between Hokmah (Father) and

Tif'areth (Son) should be so strongly developed as to parallel the relationship between Binah (Mother) and Malkuth (Daughter).

Light and darkness, and good and evil constitute two further antithetical pairs:

> This is the judgement: the light has come into the world but men love darkness more than light, because their works are wicked. Everyone who does wrong hates the light and does not come to the light lest he be proven guilty of his works. The one who acts true comes to the light so that his works may be shown to have been performed in God." iii 19-21.

Light and darkness often appear in the *Zohar* in the context of left and right sides of the Tree, but when this is so they typically stand for Hesed and Gevurah, though occasionally they stand for Tif'areth and Malkuth, which are more commonly denoted by Day and Night.[3.6] Good and evil are strongly associated with Hesed and Gevurah.[3.7]

Spirit and flesh (iii 6), in the *Zohar*, may represent Tif'areth (the breath or *ruah*) and Malkuth (the physical body)[3.8], although 'the end of spirit' and 'the end of flesh', 'end of right' and 'end of left', are aspects of Shekhinah that derive from Hesed and Gevurah.[3.9]

Increase and decrease generally connote Hesed and Gevurah, though sometimes Tif'areth and Malkuth.[3.10]

Hokmah is associated with beginnings, Binah with endings.[3.11] That is to say, Hokmah and Binah may be represented as past and future. In addition, among the planets, Binah corresponds to Saturn, the 'old man' of astrologer's parlance. In the Gospel, infancy and senility, the beginning and end of life, manifest in the shape of Nikodemos' question about returning to the womb in old age (iii 4).

daleth, H̲esed (Lovingkindness), Abraham

Daleth, the letter assigned this chapter, is used as a numeral for the number four, and may connote the fourth sefirah, H̲esed (Mercy). The fourth sefirah is embodied in Abraham, a paragon of faith, softheartedness, piety, generosity and hospitality.[3.12] One particular episode won him especial fame, proving his perfect faith in and love for God, and thus qualifying him for the grade of H̲esed: he was willing to offer up in sacrifice his only legitimate son. Since Abraham reveals this particular aspect of the divine, his actions foreshadow a similar act by God, and this is the source of:

> For God so loved the world that he gave his only son so that everyone believing in him might not perish but have eternal life. iii 16.

The nobleman or royal official in the fourth chapter of the Gospel is a type of Abraham.[3.13] His son, who never shows his face in the Gospel, because he is at home dying of fever, is a type of Isaac, as explained. Abraham was especially renowned for his great faith, and so the nobleman of iv is placed in the testing position of having to believe that his son is cured without seeing it, just in order to demonstrate his faith. One would expect to find Abraham in iii, not in iv, but as noted, personifications occasionally appear one chapter too late, and when this happens, their being out of place is signalled by their leaving Jesus' presence. Such is the case here: the nobleman leaves Jesus and returns home as soon as his son's cure is pronounced (iv 50). All the other instances of this have involved astrological personifications. In fact, the Samaritan woman who converses with Jesus in the early part of the chapter (iv 7-28) is an such example. The nobleman of iv shows that characters embodying the sefiroth are treated in the same way.

In summary

In summary, the third chapter of According to John contains allusions to Hokmah (Wisdom) and Binah (Understanding). These sefiroth are complementary, and the Gospel portrays them in terms of paired opposites: heaven and earth, above and below, spirit and flesh, water and blood, light and darkness, good and evil, increase and decrease, beginning and end, young and old. A prominent feature of Johannine symbolism is that several of these antithetical pairs are more commonly used to denote Hesed and Gevurah (e.g. good and evil, light and darkness, increase and decrease), or Nezah and Hod (e.g. above and below), or Tif'areth and Malkuth (e.g. heaven and earth, light and darkness, spirit and flesh).

While the rationale for such a transference of symbolism is not completely clear, it is not inordinately difficult to follow. Hesed and Nezah lie below Hokmah on the right side of the Tree, as Gevurah and Hod lie below Binah on the left. Hokmah and Binah have picked up various symbols from the sefiroth below them, or perhaps these symbols are nonspecific, and refer to the whole right and left sides of the Tree respectively. And Hokmah and Binah stand as Father and Mother to Tif'areth and Malkuth, their Son and Daughter. That the parents should inherit symbolic attributes from their children is slightly unusual, but again it may be that some symbolism is common or shared. We have already seen that Voice and Word denote Hokmah and Binah in John's Gospel, rather than Tif'areth and Malkuth as in the *Zohar*. It is possible John is alluding to a transference of symbolism from Son and Daughter to Father and Mother in 'The one who has the bride is the bridegroom' (iii 29).

Birth of children is thematic to iii because these two sefiroth are known as Father and Mother, the lower sefiroth their offspring.

Birth is mentioned in viii and xvi which also correspond to horizontal paths on the Tree of sefiroth.

Daleth, the fourth letter of the Hebrew alphabet, can denote the fourth sefirah, Ḥesed (Mercy). The willingness of Abraham, the human paragon of the sefirah, to sacrifice his only legitimate son is seen the prefigure a similar action by God in iii 16. Abraham appears in the guise of the nobleman in iv 46-50; his departure from Jesus' presence is a way of indicating that he represents one of the correspondences of iii, although he appears in iv.

> 3.1: *Zohar* 1:13b, 29b, 30a, 85b, 237b; 3:65b. Daniel C. Matt, *The Zohar: Pritzker Edition*, vol. 1 p. xlviii; ibid 1 p. 97 nn. 728; ibid p. 17 n. 118; ibid p. 110 n. 17; ibid p. 174 n. 530; ibid p. 176 n. 559; ibid p. 179 n. 590; vol. 2 p. 48 n. 370; vol. 3 p. 445 n. 681; vol. 4 p. 476 n. 395. Aryeh Kaplan, *The Bahir* p. 114, 162. Gershom Scholem *Major Trends in Jewish Mysticism* p. 219-220. *On the Kabbalah and Its Symbolism* p. 103.
>
> 3.2: *Zohar* 1:8a, 9a, 15b, 18a-b, 29b, 31a, 235b; 2:85b. Daniel C. Matt, *The Zohar: Pritzker Edition*, vol. 1 p. 53 nn. 379; ibid p. 112 n. 35; ibid p. 137 n. 233; ibid p. 141 nn. 261, 263; ibid pp. 175, 176 nn. 543, 547, 555; ibid pp. 177, 178 nn. 562, 576; ibid pp. 186, 187 nn. 644, 646, 651; vol. 2 p. 297 n. 281; vol. 3 p. 426 n. 606; vol. 4 p. 481 nn. 415, 416, 417.
>
> 3.3: Aryeh Kaplan, *Sefer Yetzirah, The Book of Creation* pp. 46 (table 8), 84 (table 14), 106 (table 24).
>
> 3.4: Aryeh Kaplan, *The Bahir* p. 159. *Zohar* 1:29b. Daniel C. Matt, *The Zohar: Pritzker Edition*, vol. 1 p. 177 n. 562.
>
> 3.5: See notes 21.16, 21.17.

3.6: *Zohar* 1:11b, 16a-b, 17a-b, 20a; 23a, 31a, 32a, 46a, 141b, 142a, 163a; 2:164b, 167a, 2:220b.

Daniel C. Matt, *The Zohar: Pritzker Edition*, vol. 1 pp. 81 nn. 607, 614; pp. 119, 120, 121 nn. 80, 92, 93, 99; ibid pp. 123, 124 nn. 113, 119, 120, 122, 124; ibid pp. 125, 126 nn. 130, 134, 135; ibid p. 130 n. 176; ibid p. 152 n. 349; ibid p. 184 n. 622; ibid p. 187, 188 nn. 653-658; ibid p. 189 n. 665; ibid p. 192 n. 687; ibid p. 195 nn. 702, 707, 711, 712, 713; ibid p. 196 n. 720; ibid p. 198 n. 737; ibid p. 243 nn. 1068, 1069, 1071, 1074, 1075; vol. 2 p. 12 n. 85; ibid p. 51 n. 393, 394; ibid p. 287, 288 n. 225, 228, 230; ibid p. 409 n. 727; vol. 3 p. 180 nn. 2, 6; ibid pp. 246, 247 nn. 395, 407; vol. 5 p. 452 n. 738; ibid p. 468 n. 793, 794; vol. 6 p. 260 n. 4.

3.7: Daniel C. Matt, *The Zohar: Pritzker Edition*, vol. 1 p. 274 n. 1285; vol. 2 p. 305 n. 340; vol. 3 p. 256 n. 457.

3.8: Daniel C. Matt, *The Zohar: Pritzker Edition*, vol. 1 p. 119 nn. 82, 83; vol. 4 p. 88 n. 65.

3.9: See 7.13, Part 3 12.4.

3.10: *Zohar* 1:20a, 34a; 2:147b, 148a. Daniel C. Matt, *The Zohar: Pritzker Edition*, vol. 1 p. 152 n. 351; ibid p. 212 n. 851.

3.11: Aryeh Kaplan, *Sefer Yetzirah: The Book of Creation* pp. 45, 46 (table 8), 106; *The Bahir* pp. 104, 107, 162, 183.

3.12: Daniel C. Matt, *The Zohar: Pritzker Edition*, vol. 2 p. 12 n. 85; ibid p. 19 n. 134; ibid p. 20 n. 143; ibid. p. 29 n. 206; ibid p. 35 n. 268; ibid p. 36 n. 277; ibid p. 43 n. 331; ibid p. 109 n. 844; ibid p. 119 n. 24; vol. 4 p. 40 n. 174.

3.13: Genesis xxiii 6. TB *Sukkah* 49b; TB *Hagigah* 3a; *Genesis Rabbah* lviii 6-8; *Song of Songs Rabbah* vii 5. Daniel C. Matt *The Zohar: Pritzker Edition* vol. 7 p. 123 n. 370.

The Gospel According to John chapter 4;

heh, window; numerical value 5; the fifth sefirah, Gevurah (Strength);
the path from the second sefirah, Hokmah (Wisdom), to the sixth sefirah, Tif'areth (Beauty).

The letter *heh*, which is coordinate with this chapter, is assigned to the path joining Hokmah (Wisdom) and Tif'areth (Beauty). In qabalistic literature the patriarch Jacob is the chief personification of the sixth sefirah.[4.1] The second sefirah is likened to a wellspring initiating the flow or stream that emanates the remaining sefiroth.[4.2] This forms the basis of the opening scene of the chapter, in which Jesus meets a Samaritan woman at Jacob's Well, and describes to her a spring bubbling up with living water:

> And Jacob's Well was there. Being tired out from his journey, Jesus sat on the well. It was about the sixth hour. There comes a woman of Samaria to draw water.
> Jesus says to her, 'Give me to drink', for his disciples had gone away to the city to buy food.
> Then the Samaritan woman says to him, 'How is it that you, a Jew, can ask drink from me, a Samaritan woman?', for Jews do not share utensils with Samaritans.

> Jesus answered saying, 'If you knew the gift of God and who it is that says to you, "give me to drink", then you would have asked him for living water, and he would have given it to you'. The woman answered him, 'But Sir, you have nothing to draw with, and the well is deep. Where would you get living water from? Are you greater than Jacob, who gave us the well, and himself drank from it along with his children and cattle?'. Jesus answered and said, 'Whoever drinks of this water shall thirst again but whoever drinks of the water I shall give him shall not thirst for eternity. Rather, the water I shall give him will be a spring bubbling up within him for eternal life'. iv 6-14.

The letter *heh* has other associations because it appears twice in the divine name of four letters, a fact which has always fuelled the speculations of qabalists. The *heh* which is the second letter of the Tetragrammaton connotes Binah (Understanding) and the *Parzuf* called Mother; the *heh* which is its fourth letter connotes Malkuth (Kingdom) and the *Parzuf* called Daughter. Both Binah and Malkuth have a well among their symbols.[4.3] Jacob's Well is therefore another example of John's mastery of equivocation.

Tif'areth (Beauty) is sometimes referred to as a throne or seat in qabalistic writings.[4.4] In the Gospel, this manifests as Jesus' sitting down upon the edge of the well (iv 6). However, since a throne may also represent Binah or Malkuth, the symbolism is therefore also polysemous.[4.5]

'Truth' is a common designation of Tif'areth (Beauty).[4.6] In the Gospel, this leads to Jesus' comment,

> 'But the time is coming and is here now, when true worshippers will worship the Father in spirit and truth, and

the Father desires such to worship him. God is spirit and they who worship him ought worship in spirit and truth'. iv 23-24.

'Spirit' (*pneuma*) has various in other places in John's Gospel sometimes connotes Tif'areth (vi 18, 63; xi 33; xiii 21), which corresponds to the *ruaḥ* or breath in man.[4.7]

Oil is a symbol of Ḥokmah (Wisdom).[4.8] Kings, moreover, were ritually anointed with oil upon entry into office, and Nisan is known as the 'month of kings', since regnal years were counted from the first day of that month. This is why Jesus is identified in this chapter as the Anointed One, both the Greek (Christ) and Hebrew (Messiaḥ) terms being supplied for emphasis:

> 'I know the Messiah', which means 'Anointed', 'is coming, and when he comes he will inform us of everything'. iv 25-26.

> 'Come and see a man who told me everything I ever did. Is he perhaps the Anointed?'. iv 29

> And they said to the woman, 'We no longer believe because of your report, but because we have heard him ourselves, and know he really is the Saviour of the World, the Anointed'. iv 42.

The attribution to Ḥokmah (Wisdom) to the letter *beth* leads to a similar mention of Jesus' status in the first chapter:

> First he finds his own brother Simon, and says to him, 'We have found the Messiah', which is translated 'the Anointed'. i 41.

4.1 *Zohar* 1:58a. Daniel C. Matt, *The Zohar: Pritzker Edition*, vol. 1 p. 279 n. 1318; ibid p. 329 n. 1617; vol. 2 p. 59 n. 465;

ibid p. 195 n. 618; ibid p. 344 n. 203; ibid p. 377 n. 467; vol. 3 p. 5 nn. 28, 32; ibid p. 16 n. 116; ibid p. 33 n. 231; ibid p. 426 n. 607; ibid p. 544 n. 1028; vol. 6 p. 395 n. 390. Aryeh Kaplan, *The Bahir* p. 172-173.

4.2: *Zohar* 1:29b, 247b; 2:42b, 90a; 3:6a. Daniel C. Matt, *The Zohar: Pritzker Edition*, vol. 1 p. 340 n. 6; vol. 3 p. 518 n. 945; vol. 4 p. 1 n. 3; ibid p. 41 n. 178; ibid p. 121 n. 193; ibid p. 510 n. 524; vol. 7 p. 56 n. 166. Aryeh Kaplan, *Sefer Yetzirah: The Book of Creation* pp. 12, 73-4, 77-78, 81; *The Bahir* p. 125.

4.3: *Zohar* 1:60a, 141b, 146b, 147b, 148b, 152b; 2:63b; 3:21b, 62a. Daniel C. Matt, *The Zohar: Pritzker Edition*, vol. 1 pp. 345, 346 nn. 49, 50; vol. 2 p. 320 n. 3; ibid p. 321 n. 8; ibid p. 322 n. 19; ibid p. 327 n. 54; ibid p. 348 n. 233; vol. 4 p. 343 n. 512; vol. 7 p. 143 n. 437; ibid p. 334 n. 9; ibid p. 406 n. 146.

4.4: e.g. Aryeh Kaplan, *The Bahir* para. 146; ibid p. 173. *Zohar* 2:241a. Daniel C. Matt, *The Zohar: Pritzker Edition*, vol. 4 p. 395 n. 391; vol. 6 p. 395 nn. 389, 390. Jacob ben Sheshet of Gerona, *Response of Correct Answers* in *The Early Kabbalah*, edited Dan, p. 133ff.

4.5: Daniel C. Matt, *The Zohar: Pritzker Edition*, vol. 4 p. 522 n. 564; vol. 6 p. 239 p. 399; ibid p. 262 nn. 8, 9. Aryeh Kaplan, *The Bahir* pp. 113, 159.

4.6: Gershom Scholem, *Origins of the Kabbalah*, p. 144-148. Aryeh Kaplan, *The Bahir* para. 135, 137, 138, 190. *Zohar* 1:96a; 2:57a. Daniel C. Matt, *The Zohar: Pritzker Edition*, vol. 2 p. 109 n. 842; vol. 3 p. 378 n. 395; vol 4 p. 299 n. 357; vol. 7 p. 69 n. 214.

4.7: See 6.5.

4.8: *Zohar* 1:88a; 3:34a-b, 39a. Daniel C. Matt, *The Zohar: Pritzker Edition*, vol. 3 p. 464 n. 757; vol. 7 p. 175 n. 21; ibid p. 195 n. 92; ibid pp. 235, 236 n 90, 91.

According to John chapter 5;
**vau, a hook or nail; numerical value 6;
the sixth sefirah, Tif'areth (Beauty);
the path from the second sefirah, H̱okmah (Wisdom),
to the fourth sefirah, H̱esed (Mercy).**

The opening scene of the fifth chapter of the Gospel has Jesus performing a miraculous healing at a place called *Bethesda*. Although some dispute exists about the interpretation of the name of the place, most lexica tend towards the view that it is a hellenisation of the Hebrew *Beth-ḥesidah*, 'House of Mercy'.[5.1] The name of the place puns on the path attributed to the letter *vau* on the Tree of Life: *ḥesidah* is merely a feminine form of H̱esed (Mercy); and as we have already noted, *beth*, since it is serves as the numeral two, can stand for the second sefirah, H̱okmah (Wisdom). *Beth-ḥesidah* therefore neatly alludes to both sefiroth relevant to the path denoted by the letter *vau*.

H̱esed, the fourth sefirah, is coordinate with the commandment which prescribes rest on the Sabbath while enjoining work for the rest of the week. The right-hand pillar, moreover, is the dynamic, active pillar of the Tree. This motivates the discussion in this chapter, especially Jesus' instruction to the former invalid to break the Sabbath:

> And it was the Sabbath day. The Jews therefore said to the one who was cured, 'It is the Sabbath day. You are not permitted to carry your bed'. v 8-10.
>
> 'My Father has always been working and I too am working'. v 17.
>
> 'But I have greater testimony than John's. The works that the Father has given me to complete, the works I perform, themselves testify about me that the Father has sent me.' v 36.

As often happens, John can creatively combine astrological and qabalistic ideas – Taurus, like the other earth signs of the zodiac, is associated with labour and enterprise – so that it is impossible to determine the origin of certain motifs.

The sefiroth on the left side of the Tree bring death, while those on the right side of the Tree are vivifying and enlivening.[5.2] This aspect of H̲okmah (Wisdom) and H̲esed (Mercy) is mirrored in the Gospel with:

> 'Just as the Father raises the dead and makes alive, likewise does the Son make alive those whom he wants.' v 21.
>
> 'Amen, amen, I tell you: the one hearing my word and believing in the one who sent me has eternal life, and does not come to judgement but has crossed over from death to life.' v 24.
>
> 'For just as the Father has life within himself, he has granted the Son likewise to have life within himself.' v 26.

H̲okmah (Wisdom) is associated with spontaneity and causelessness; it denotes the subjective knowledge, revelation, and inspiration. The miraculous, the wonderful, the strange, the paradoxical connote this aspect of the second sefirah[5.3], and manifest in this chapter in,

> 'He will show him even greater things than these, so that you will all be amazed.' v 20

> 'Do not be amazed at this, the time is coming...' v 28

and in other chapters corresponding to paths leading to and from Hokmah,

> 'Do not be amazed because I tell you that you must be born from above'. iii 7

> 'After this his disciples came and were greatly amazed that he was talking with the woman...' iv 27.

> 'You will not believe unless you see signs and wonders'. iv 48.

Hokmah is associated with sameness, similarity and equality[5.4], qabalists sometimes deriving the idea from numerological considerations of the number two and the shape of the letter *beth*, which serves as a numeral for two. In the Gospel, the idea appears clearly in:

> ... he also said that God was his own Father, making himself God's equal [*ison tōi theōi*]. v 18.

> '... for whatever he does, the Son does likewise [*homoios*]'. v 19.

> 'For just as [*hōsper*] the Father raises up the dead, and makes them alive, likewise [*houtōs*] does the Son make alive whomever he wishes'. v 21.

> '... in order that all may honour the Son just as [kathōs] they honour the Father'. v 23.
>
> 'For just as [hōsper] the Father has life within himself, he has granted the Son likewise [houtōs] to have life within himself'. v 26.

In the soul, H̱okmah represents the virtue of self-negation or self-nullification (Hebrew, *bitul*). The idea is perfectly conveyed in Jesus' words:

> Then Jesus answered and said to them, 'Amen, amen, I tell you: unless he sees the Father doing something, the Son can do nothing on his own'. v 19.
>
> 'I can do nothing by myself'. v 30.

In According to John, Voice and Utterance are apparently designations of H̱okmah (Wisdom) and Binah (Understanding). Aryeh Kaplan describes similar usage in *Sefer Yeẕirah*. As previously noted, 'Voice' connotes H̱okmah (Wisdom) because it represents thought or creative energy that is too inchoate to be formulated into words.[5.5] This partly motivates the occurrences of 'voice' in this chapter:

> 'Amen, amen, I tell you: the time is coming and is here now when the dead will hear the voice of the Son of God and they who hear will live'. v 25.
>
> 'Do not be amazed that the time is coming when all in their tombs will hear his voice...' v 28.
>
> 'You have never heard His voice nor seen his form'. v 37.

This last verse quoted is meant to recall Deuteronomy iv 12, 16 ('... for you saw no form, but only heard the voice'), which forms part of a warning against idolatry; the prohibition against molten or graven images is the second commandment and therefore coordinate with H̱okmah.

It is also possible however, that the repetition of *phōnē* in v may be due to a special relationship between v and x, for the word plays an important role in x, where it indicates the trumpet blasts of New Year's Day.

The relationship between v and x

The phrase 'upon the Sheep [Gate]' (*epi tēi probatikēi* [*pulēi*]) has more than one layer of hidden meaning, like so much else in According to John. As one can (see diagram 3, page 182), the right-hand pillar of the Tree comprises two paths; the upper joins H̱okmah to H̱esed, the lower joins H̱esed to Neẓah. The former corresponds to v, the latter to x. Because Jesus calls himself 'the Gate for the Sheep' in x 7, 'Sheep Gate' in effect serves as a quasi-title of the tenth chapter itself – for these 'I am' statements, a notable and unique feature of the Gospel are of extreme importance in the economy of its symbolism. The phrase 'upon the Sheep Gate' in v 2 is therefore intended to recall that Jesus becomes the Gate of the Sheep in x 7 – it simply indicates the relative position of the paths denoted by *vau* and *kaf*, which correspond to v and x respectively.

The theme of judgement which appears throughout v looks somewhat out of place since this chapter falls on the Pillar of Mercy while retributive justice characterises the left side of the Tree. One explanation for the appearance of judgement in this chapter is that the letter *vau*, which is used to represent the number six, can denote the sixth sefirah, which is sometimes connected with the decision-making faculty.[5.6]

The more likely explanation, however, is that the theme of judgement has been imported, so to speak, from x because of an idiosyncrasy of John's handling of qabalistic symbolism. That is, since v and x designate the paths forming the right hand pillar of the Tree, John allows them to share material. According to the calendar scheme John uses, the tenth chapter falls to New Year's Day (*Rosh ha Shanah*), a feast having judgement as one of its dominant themes; Judgement Day (*Yom ha Din*), is another name for the holiday. The phrase 'cross over from death to life' (v 24) sounds derived from the liturgical imagery of New Year's Day, and echoes Jesus' statement in x that he lays down his life and takes it back again (x 17-18).

The relationship between v and x is analogous to that between ii and xiv; in the latter case, the Hanukah-derived motif behind the Cleansing of the Temple would have made it suitable for xiv, though John places it in ii. And vii and xii are related in similar fashion, the Feast of Tabernacles having been moved into vii from xii.

These explanations are not exclusive; the *Zohar*, discussing the books opened on New Year's Day, compares Tif'areth to the book of those who are intermediate in terms of vice and virtue, and whose fate hangs in the balance.[5.7]

vau, six

Because *vau* serves as the numeral for six in Hebrew, the letter frequently connotes Tif'areth, the sixth sefirah. Moreover, Tif'areth is taken as focal point of the set of six sefiroth from Hesed to Yesod which together form the *Parzuf* known as Son or

Bridegroom, whom qabalists saw represented in the letter *vau* in the divine name of four letters.[5.8]

In qabalistic texts, one of the most important symbols of Tif'areth is the Written Torah.[5.9] The claim that Jesus is foretold in Mosaic scripture, which is the main point of the closing section, reflects the association:

> 'You search the Scriptures, because you think to have eternal life in them, but they are what testifies about me.' v 39.
>
> 'The one accusing you is Moses, upon whom you have placed your hopes. If you believed him you would believe me too, since he wrote about me. But if you do not believe the words he wrote, how will you the words I say?' v 45-47.

The five gates of Beth-ḥesidah (v 2) represent the five books of the Torah, which are called in English the Pentateuch, from the Greek for 'Five Scrolls', and are sometimes called *Humash*, meaning 'Pentad, Set of Five' in Hebrew. The opening lines of the *Zohar*'s Prologue also mention 'five gates of salvation', though the meaning is less clear; it may refer to the five sefiroth (Ḥesed, Gevurah, Neẓaḥ, Hod, Yesod) converging on Tif'areth.[5.10]

The Hebrew word *halakhah* has two meanings. The literal meaning is 'a walk'. In its extended and commoner sense, *halakhah* means the Mosaic Law, and all vast apparatus for its interpretation. *Halakhah* is not concerned with books of the Tanakh other than the Pentateuch, nor is it concerned with those sections of the Pentateuch that do not contain Mosaic Law or codify ritual. To follow the injunctions Torah is idiomatically described as walking in the Torah in the Bible.[5.11] Of course, to a modern Jew, *halakhah* includes what Jews now call the Oral Law, of which the Talmud is an important part. When John wrote, the Oral Law was still just that – it was largely not set down in writing. The Mishnah was in composition from 70 to 200 CE, but John probably did not move in the same circles as the Mishnah's editors. Precisely how John understood the term *halakhah*, is therefore not clear, but he probably equated it with Mosaic Law and its exegesis. In the Gospel this yields Jesus' exhortation to the invalid to walk, which is quoted and requoted:

> Jesus says to him, 'Arise, take up your bed, and walk'. And immediately the man became healthy, and took up his bed, and walked. v 8-9.
>
> He answered them, 'The one who made me healthy said to me, "Take up your bed and walk"'.
> So they asked him, 'Who is it that said to you, "Take up your bed and walk"?'. v 11-12.

In summary

In summary, references to Ḥokmah appear as voice, sameness or similarity, surprise or amazement, and self-nullification. References to Ḥesed appear in the mention of love, references to the fourth commandment, which forbids work on the Sabbath while enjoining it on the other days. Bethesda, or *bet-ḥesidah* alludes to both second and fourth sefiroth.

The phrase, 'upon the Sheep Gate' alludes to a certain relationship between the fifth and tenth chapters of the Gospel. It is analogous to the relationship between the seventh and twelfth chapters, and to that between the second, fourteenth and twenty-first chapters. This relationship is easy to understand in terms of the structure of the Tree of sefiroth.

The letter *vau*, denoting Tif'areth, motivates mention of scripture toward the end of the chapter, and Jesus' repeated injunction to walk.

- 5.1: *Strong's Exhaustive Concordance of the Bible and Lexicon. Gesenius' Hebrew-Chaldee Lexicon to the Old Testament. Thayer's Greek-English Lexicon of the New Testament.*
- 5.2: *Zohar* 1:22b.
- 5.3: *Zohar* 3:31a. Daniel C. Matt, *The Zohar: Pritzker Edition* vol. 7 p. 179 n. 36.
- 5.4: Aryeh Kaplan, *The Bahir* pp. 97, 104-107, 132. *Sefer Yezirah: The Book of Creation* pp. 11-12, 86.
- 5.5: Aryeh Kaplan, *Sefer Yezirah: The Book of Creation* pp. 39, 70.
- 5.6: See intro.14.
- 5.7: *Zohar* 1:37a-b. Daniel C. Matt, *The Zohar: Pritzker Edition* vol. 1 p. 235 n. 1030. TB *Rosh Ha Shanah* 16b.
- 5.8: Daniel C. Matt, *The Zohar: Pritzker Edition* vol. 1 p. 86 n. 649; ibid p. 161 n. 430; ibid p. 329 n. 1619; vol. 2 p. 188 n. 563; ibid p. 336 n. 129; vol. 3 p. 4 n 27; ibid p. 23 p. n. 160; ibid p. 24 n. 168; ibid p. 183 n. 25; ibid pp. 288, 289 nn. 166, 172; ibid p. 505 n. 906; vol. 4 p. 2 n. 207; ibid p. 29 n. 117; ibid p. 39 n. 172; ibid p. 78 n. 29; ibid pp. 93, 94 nn. 86, 88; vol. 6 p. 1 n. 3; ibid p. 11 n. 28; ibid p. 13 n. 38.
- 5.9: *Zohar* 1:8a, 16a; 2:226b; 3:35a. Daniel C. Matt, *The Zohar: Pritzker Edition* vol. 1 p. 51 nn. 361, 365; ibid p. 118 n. 73; vol. 4 p. 334 n. 482; vol. 6 p. 300 nn. 109, 111; vol. 7 p. 203 n. 114; ibid p. 248 n. 135.

5.10: *Zohar* 1:1a, 2:145b. Daniel C. Matt, *The Zohar: Pritzker Edition* vol. 1 p. 2 n. 8; vol. 4 p. 503 n. 497; vol. 5 pp. 325, 326 n. 380; vol. 6 p. 1 n. 3; ibid p. 300 n. 109.

5.11: e.g. '... to see if they will walk in my Torah' (Exodus xvi 4); 'But Jehu did not take heed to walk in the Torah' (2 Kings x 31); 'If you do not hear me, to walk in my Torah ...' (Jeremiah xxvi 4); 'They did not walk according to his Torah' (Psalm lxxviii 10); 'Happy are those who walk in the Torah' (Psalm cxix 1); 'They took an oath to walk in God's Torah' (Nehemiah x 30); 'so that your children take care to their way, that they walk in my Torah' (2 Chronicles vi 16).

The Gospel According to John chapter 6;
**zayin, a sword or lance; numerical value 7;
the seventh sefirah, Ne_zah_ (Victory);
the path from the third sefirah, Binah (Understanding),
to the sixth sefirah, Tif'areth (Beauty).**

The sixth chapter of John's Gospel corresponds to the letter *zayin* and the path from Binah (Understanding) to Tif'areth (Beauty).

The Feast of Loaves, which lies behind much of the imagery in vi, is called *Shavuēoth*, which means 'Weeks' or 'Sevens' in Hebrew. A ritual prayer, the Counting of the *'Omer*, is a daily religious observance during the seven weeks (i.e. a week of weeks) from Passover to Shavu'oth, which falls on the fiftieth day, whence the holiday's alternative name, *Pentecost*, from the Greek for 'Fiftieth'. In According to John this manifests in the detail that the crowd numbered five thousand, a feature of the story found also in the Synoptic Gospels, where its significance is spelled out more clearly: in Mark vi 39-40, the crowd are seated in 'squares of fifties and hundreds', while in Luke ix 14, Jesus has the disciples sit them down 'in fifties'. However, Binah (Understanding) has its own associations with the number. Binah is often known as the Jubilee or Fiftieth Year; the phrase 'the Fifty gates of Understanding' is frequently encountered in qabalistic texts, and recorded in the Talmud[6.1]; elsewhere fifty is noted to be the value by gematria of the word *mi* ('who?'), which is used to connote Binah for other reasons[6.2]. Sometimes Binah's association with the number links it directly with Pentecost[6.3].

The great wind that arises when Jesus crosses the Sea of Galilee (vi 18) alludes to Tif'areth as *rua<u>h</u>*, the breath or spirit, as much as it does to the airy nature of Gemini.[6.4]

In the *Zohar*, Tif'areth is said to be the source of 'bread from heaven', the manna that fell for the Israelites in the desert[6.5]. In the Gospel, this is just what Jesus keenly denies to be the real heavenly bread:

> 'Our fathers ate manna in the wilderness, as it is written, "He gave them bread from heaven to eat"'.

> Then Jesus said to them, 'Amen, amen, I tell you: Moses did not give you the bread from heaven, but my Father gives you the true bread from heaven.' vi 31-32

> 'Your fathers ate manna in the wilderness, and are dead.' vi 49.

> 'This is the bread that came down from heaven. Unlike what your ancestors ate and died, one who eats this bread shall live for eternity. vi 58.

6.1: *Zohar* 1:3b, 13b, 106a; 2:137b, 175b; 3:262a. Daniel C. Matt, *The Zohar: Pritzker Edition* vol. 1 p. 18 n. 120; ibid p. 97 n. 729; vol. 2 p. 147 n. 242; vol. 4 p. 266 nn. 216, 217; vol. 6 p. 28 n. 72.

TB *Rosh Ha Shanah* 21b. TB *Nedarim* 38a.

6.2: *Zohar* 2:138a. Daniel C. Matt, *The Zohar: Pritzker Edition* vol. 5 p. 273 n. 232.

6.3: *Zohar* 2:46a-b, 83b, 84a, 85b, 183a; 3:262a. Daniel C. Matt, *The Zohar: Pritzker Edition* vol. 4 p. 198 n. 200; ibid p. 215 n. 55; ibid p. 219 nn. 68, 70; ibid p. 466 nn. 358, 359; ibid p. 478 n. 403; vol. 6 pp. 26, 27 nn. 70, 71.

6.4: Daniel C. Matt, *The Zohar: Pritzker Edition* vol. 1 pp. 119-121 nn. 82-84, 96, 100; ibid p. 200 n. 754; vol. 2 p. 31 n. 225; ibid p. 55 n. 425; ibid p. 324 n. 38; vol. 3 p. 262 n. 26; ibid p. 263 nn. 32; vol. 7 p. 469 n. 354.

6.5: *Zohar* 1:157b, 246a; 2:40a, 61b, 62a-b, 183a-b; 3:283b. Daniel C. Matt, *The Zohar: Pritzker Edition* vol. 2 p. 375 n. 454; vol. 3 p. 505 n. 906; vol. 4 p. 197 n. 199; ibid pp. 331, 332 nn. 472, 477; ibid p. 334 n. 481; pp. 337, 338 nn. 493, 496; ibid p. 342 n. 507; vol. 6 p. 28 n. 73; ibid p. 30 n. 78.

The Gospel According to John chapter 7;
<u>h</u>eth, a fenced field; numerical value 8;
the eighth sefirah, Hod (Splendour);
the path from the third sefirah, Binah (Understanding),
to the fifth sefirah, Gevurah (Severity).

As we have already seen, John has made a minor modification to the scheme of *Sefer Ye<u>z</u>irah* which allows him to place an account of Jesus at the Feast of Tabernacles in xii. If not for this, references to the festival would be expected in xi, since xi has the month Tishri among its correspondences. Other examples of the same thing exist: New Year's Day has been moved to x, although it too should belong in xi; references to Tevet 10 should be in xv, but are actually found in xvi; references to Purim have made their way into xix, though they should be in xviii. In every case, a double or mother letter picked up symbolism related to a religious holiday from an adjacent simple letter.

If Tabernacles' appropriateness to xii is understandable, we still need to account for the fact the holiday figures so prominently in the narrative in vii. According to John contains a number of other instances of disagreement between the stated time of events and the Gospel's internal calendar. In vi 4 we are told that it is near Passover, while the symbolism consistently and clearly points to the Feast of Loaves. Again in x 22, we are told that it is near Dedication, which falls in the month Kislev, but the symbolism of the chapter strongly points to New Year's Day in the month Tishri. In xii 1, we are told that it is in the week leading up to Passover, but Passover has absolutely nothing to do with the action of the chapter. In vii, however, the Tabernacles and its themes are hardly peripheral to the events narrated. The holiday has a significant effect on Jesus' acts and words as well as those of others. This is what distinguishes vii from other chapters in which the expressly stated time is completely out of step with the Gospel's internal calendar, which is anchored to the attributions of *Sefer Yezirah*.

The explanation lies in an idiosyncrasy of Johannine Qabalah that we have already met with: symbols, though generally tightly confined to their relevant chapter, are allowed to wander with some freedom between chapters corresponding to Tree's vertical pillars. For instance, ii contains allusions of Dedication (*Hanukah*) in the episode of the Cleansing the Temple. Since Dedication falls in the month Kislev, it would be more appropriate for xiv. The fact that ii and xiv correspond to paths on the same vertical pillar on the Tree, the central Pillar of Compassion or Mildness, is apparently sufficient to allow it to be placed in ii. And similarly, v contains allusions to New Year (*Rosh Ha Shanah*), which would otherwise be fit only for x, because the paths corresponding to v and x together form a vertical pillar of the Tree, the Pillar of Mercy. The phrase 'upon the Sheep Gate' (v 2) is another pointer to the relationship between v and x, for in x 7-9, Jesus assumes the title of 'Gate for the Sheep'.

As one can (see diagram 3, page 182), vii and xii correspond to paths on the Tree that join, respectively, Binah with Gevurah, and Gevurah with Hod. These two paths and the three sefiroth they link compose the vertical left-hand pillar of the Tree, the Pillar of Severity. This is enough to allow John to place the celebration of the Feast of Tabernacles in the narrative of vii.

Curiously, in vii John draws on some of the same associations of Tabernacles he uses in xii to indicate the festival. The solemn processions that were characterise the holiday figure in,

> For some said, 'He is a good man', while others said, 'No. Rather, he leads the crowd astray'. vii 12

> Then the Pharisees answered them, 'Have you been led astray too?' vii 47

as well as,

> The Pharisees therefore said among themselves, 'Do you see that nothing profits you? Look! The world has gone after him'. xii 19.

The prophecy found in the last chapters of Zechariah that in the Messianic Age Gentiles will convert to Judaism en masse at a Feast of Tabernacles appears in,

> Will he go into the Diaspora among the Greeks, and teach the Greeks?' vii 35

as well as,

> And there were certain Greeks among those who came up to worship at the feast. They approached Philip, who was from

Bethsaida in Galilee, and asked him, saying, 'Sir, we want to see Jesus'. xii 20-21.

Bloodshed and the fifth sefirah

The *Zohar* associates Gevurah with the Angel of Death, who inspires bloodshed and murder[7.1]. Evidently John has similar ideas: in all the chapters answering to paths that join Gevurah (Strength) to other sefiroth on the Tree (vii, viii, xi, xii) we encounter references to killing:

> After this Jesus travelled in Galilee, for he would not travel in Judaea, because the Jews were trying to kill him. vii 1.

> 'Did not Moses give you the Law? And yet none of you observes the Law. Why are you trying to kill me?'.

> The crowd answered and said, 'You have a demon. Who is trying to kill you?'. vii 19-20.

> Some of the Jerusalemites said, 'Is he not the one they are trying to kill?' vii 25.

> 'I know you are Abraham's seed, but you are trying to kill me ...' viii 37

> 'But now you trying to kill me, a man who has told you the truth that I heard at God's side.' viii 40.

> 'He was a murderer from the beginning ...' viii 44.

> Therefore from that day on they considered how they might kill him. xi 53.

But the chief priests considered how they might kill Lazarus too, because on his account many Jews were leaving and believing in Jesus.' xii 10-11.

Circumcision

Circumcision is performed on eighth day after birth; no exception is made for the Sabbath. The fact that *ḥeth* serves as a numeral for the number eight partly motivates the mention of circumcision in this chapter (vii 22-23). Another reason is that the seven lower sefiroth are called days of the week, while Binah, immediately before them is associated with the eighth day, the day of circumcision[7.2]. The Solemn Assembly of the Eighth Day, which comes at the end of Tabernacles, is also linked to Binah for the same reason.

Moses (vii 23) often personifies Gevurah in qabalistic texts[7.3].

7.1: *Zohar* 1:35b, 36a-b, 54a; 2:231a-b. Daniel C. Matt, *The Zohar: Pritzker Edition*, vol. 1 p. 226 n. 967; ibid p. 303 nn. 1468, 1469; vol. 6 n. 329 n. 196.

7.2: See 20.6.

7.3: *Zohar* 1:21b. Daniel C. Matt, *The Zohar: Pritzker Edition*, vol. 1 p. 165 n. 458.

The Gospel According to John chapter 8;

**_teth_, a serpent; numerical value 9; the ninth sefirah, Yesod (Foundation);
the path from the fourth sefirah, Hesed (Mercy), to the fifth sefirah, Gevurah (Strength) or Din (Justice).**

The eighth chapter of the Gospel answers to the letter _teth_, and to the path joining Hesed (Mercy) and Din (Justice) or Gevurah (Strength), an assignment which influences the events of the chapter in a predictable way. In the opening scene of viii, the subject of illicit sexual intercourse around which the action revolves derives in part from the fact that complementary sefiroth, like Hesed and Gevurah, are at times symbolised by male and female.[8.1] In the _Zohar_, curiously, they are never described as cohabiting with each other as male and female in the way that Hokmah and Binah, lying above them, are consistently portrayed. It is as though Hesed and Gevurah had to become Tif'areth (Bridegroom) and Malkuth (Bride) in order to properly consummate union. If there were something irregular about Hesed and Gevurah's directly coupling, the metaphor at the heart of this passage would fit even more seamlessly with the astrological correspondences.

Typically, John effortlessly adds another dimension to the scenario: Jesus has to find a compromise in the moral tug-of-war between the diametrically opposed principles of Hesed (Mercy) and Din (Justice). Since Moses sometimes personifies the fifth sefirah, his name is dropped in support of a harsh punishment. Jesus solves the ethical dilemma by permitting the woman's accusers to stone her, thus formally satisfying the requirements of strict justice, but adding a stipulation that leaves them unable to carry out the sentence, so that mercy ultimately prevails:

> The scribes and Pharisees bring a woman who had been caught in adultery, and placing her in the middle, said to him: 'Teacher, this woman was caught in flagrant adultery. In our Law, Moses commanded stoning such women. What then do you say?'.
> They said this, testing him, in order to have reason to accuse him. But Jesus, bending down, wrote on the ground with his finger, pretending not to hear. When they continued asking him, he straightened himself up, and said to them, 'Let the sinless one be first among you to cast a stone at her'. viii 3-7.

North and south are symbols of Gevurah and Hesed respectively[8.2]. The Mount of Olives appears as the setting in viii 1 because of a prophecy in Zechariah xiv 14 that the Mount of Olives will be split in two, and that one half going to the north, the other half to the south.

John also hints at the position of the path denoted by *teth*, the middle of the three horizontal paths with:

> ... placing her in the middle [*en mesōi*] ... viii 3

> ... the woman being in the middle [*en mesōi*] ... viii 9

Jesus went out of the Temple, going through the middle [*dia mesou*] of them. viii 59.

(*Stephanus 1550* contains the phrase, *dia mesou*, in viii 59, which is not in all manuscript traditions.)

Found in some of the oldest Latin and Aramaic versions of the Gospel, but not the oldest Greek papyri, the authenticity of viii 1-11 has been called into question. For some time it was placed in the According to Luke, or at the very end of According to John, taking its current position about 600 AD. If it was not originally part of the Fourth Gospel, whoever decided it should be given its present location evidently knew exactly what they were doing. It is more likely that John composed this pericope, and its current position is precisely the one he intended for it. The blending of astrology, Qabalah and Jewish holiday into a single tableau is inimitable.

Personifications of H̲esed and Gevurah

Abraham frequently appears in qabalistic writings a the human incarnation of all the virtues of H̲esed. The fifth sefirah, Gevurah, is in some mysterious way, the origin of the evil and demonic, in particular, Samael, the chief of demons is associated with the sefirah[8.3]. References to these representative types of H̲esed and Gevurah, one a man, the other an angel, pepper the latter half of viii:

> They answered him, 'We are Abraham's seed, and have never been in servitude to anyone. How can you say we shall become free?'. viii 33.

> 'I know you are Abraham's seed, but you are trying to kill me, because you have no room for my word in you....'

They answered and said to him, 'Abraham is our father'. Jesus says to them, 'If you were Abraham's children, you would perform Abraham's works... Abraham did not do this.' viii 37-40.

'You are of your father the Devil, and you desire to act out the lusts of your father.' viii 44.

Then the Jews answered, and said to him, 'Do we not correctly say that you are a Samaritan, and have a demon?'. Jesus answered, 'I do not have a demon, but rather I honour my Father, though you dishonour me.' viii 48-49.

Then the Jews said to him, 'Now we know you have a demon. Abraham died, along with the prophets, and yet you say, "If anyone observes my word, he shall never experience death for all eternity"? Are you greater than our father Abraham, who died?'. viii 52-53.

'Your father Abraham was delighted to see my day, and he saw it, and rejoiced'.
Then the Jews said to him, 'You have not yet reached fifty years, and you have seen Abraham?'.
Jesus said to them, 'Amen, amen, I tell you: before Abraham was born, I am'. viii 56-58.

It is extremely useful to compare viii with iii and xvi, since these chapters correspond to the three horizontal paths on the Tree of sefiroth. One sees for instance that birth is mentioned in all three chapters. It is likely that above and below are, like male and female, general designations of the right and left sides of the Tree, for the tension between above and below plays a part in all three chapters[8.4]. In viii it manifests in:

And he said to them, 'You are from what lies below, I am from what lies above. You are of this world, I am not of this world. viii 23.

In several places John uses the commandments to indicate the sefiroth. In this chapter we have, 'I honour my father...' (viii 49) because the fifth commandment orders it, and Gevurah (Strength) is the fifth sefirah.

teth

The letter *teth* can serve as a numeral for the number nine, and in qabalistic texts may therefore serve to denote the ninth sefirah, Yesod (Foundation). Qabalists often relate truthfulness to Yesod, because the corresponding commandment forbids falsehood. In the Gospel the idea manifests in the references to truthfulness that occur sporadically through this chapter:

> The Pharisees said to him, 'You are testifying about yourself. Your testimony does not count as true'.
> Jesus answered and said to them, 'Even if I am testifying about myself, my testimony is true'. viii 13-14.

> 'And my judgment is true even if I do judge, because it is not I alone, but I and the Father, who sent me. It is also written in your Law that the testimony of two persons is true.' viii 16-17.

> 'And you will know the truth, and the truth will set you free'. viii 32.

> 'But now you are trying to kill me, a man who has told you the truth that I heard at God's side'. viii 40.

> 'He was a murderer from the beginning, and does not stand in the truth, because the truth is not in him. When he tells a lie, he tells one of his very own, for he is a liar, and the father of such. And because I tell you the truth, you do not believe me. Which of you proves me guilty of sin? And if I am telling the truth, why do you not believe me?'. viii 44-46.

In the human body, the ninth sefirah corresponds to the reproductive organs. Not surprisingly qabalistic texts often use seed, that is semen, as a symbol. In the Gospel the idea takes the form of references to the Jews as Abraham's seed [*sperma*] in viii 33, 37.

Jesus' mention of darkness and his identification with the light in viii 12 is inspired by the fact that Hesed and Gevurah are often symbolised by light and darkness[8.5]. Moreover, the letter *teth* is closely linked with light in qabalistic writings[8.6], for a somewhat convoluted reason: it is the light of Hesed that is reserved for the righteous, because the righteous is termed good (Isaiah iii 10), like the original light of creation (Genesis i 4), and light is sown for the righteous (Psalm xvii 11).

The form of the letter *teth* is the result of its having begun as a pictogram of a coiled serpent; Kircher thought the letter meant 'bending or leaning' (*inclinatio*)[8.7]. The Gospel alludes to the letter's shape by having Jesus bend and straighten, bend and straighten, writing on the ground each time (viii 6-10).

> 8.1: *Zohar* 1:30a, 70a; 3:14a, 43b. Daniel C. : *The Zohar: Pritzker Edition*, vol. 1 p. 179 nn. 582, 583; ibid p. 411 n. 525; vol. 7 p. 83 n. 257; ibid p. 267 n. 34; ibid p. 269 n. 40. *Soncino Zohar, Appendix III – The Designations and The Categories.*

8.2: Aryeh Kaplan, *The Bahir* para 162, 163, 199; ibid pp. 112, 113; *Sefer Yetzirah: Book of Creation* pp. 83-84, 106, 164. Daniel C. Matt, *The Zohar: Pritzker Edition* vol. 1 p. 174 nn. 531, 532; ibid p. 199 nn. 745, 746; ibid. 270 n. 1252; vol. 2 p. 4 n. 27; ibid p. 19 n. 134; ibid pp. 320, 321 n. 6, 7; ibid pp. 402-403 nn. 672-673; vol. 3 p. 41 n. 294; vol. 6 p. 158 n. 145; ibid pp. 311-312 nn. 145, 147.

8.3: See 13.2.

8.4: Daniel C. Matt, *The Zohar: Pritzker Edition* vol. 7 p. 53 n. 156. *Soncino Zohar, Appendix III – The Designations and The Categories.*

8.5: See 3.6.

8.6: *Zohar* 1:1a, 21b, 30b, 32a, 33a, 204a; 2:35a. Daniel C. Matt, *The Zohar: Pritzker Edition*, vol. 1 p. 2 n. 10; ibid p. 162 n. 434; ibid pp. 184, 185 nn. 625, 629, 635, 636; ibid p. 194 n. 699; ibid p. 204 nn. 782, 783; ibid pp. 242 n. 1065; vol. 3 p. 250 n. 424; vol. 4 p. 154 n. 56; vol. 6 pp. 321-322 nn. 172.

8.7: Aryeh Kaplan, *Sefer Yetzirah: Book of Creation* p. 8 table 3. Athanasius Kircher, *Oedipus Aegyptiacus* vol. 2 p. 225.

The Gospel According to John chapter 9;
**yod, hand; numerical value 10;
the tenth sefirah, Malkuth(Kingdom);
the path from the fourth sefirah,
Hesed (Mercy), to the sixth sefirah, Tif'areth (Beauty).**

The ninth chapter of According to John corresponds to the path between Hesed (Mercy) and Tif'areth (Beauty). Mention of light in ix 4-5 is partly inspired by the fact that Hesed is sometimes symbolised by light, especially the primordial light which came into being on the First Day of creation[9.1].

As previously noted, Hesed, the fourth sefirah, situated on the active side of the Tree, is especially connected with work and activity. The fourth commandment, with which it is coordinate, enjoins work for six days a week, only prohibiting it on the Sabbath. In ix, Jesus introduces the subject with:

> Jesus answered, 'Neither this man, nor his parents sinned, rather it was so that the works of God might be demonstrated in him. I must perform the works of the one who sent me while it is still day. Night is coming, when no one can work.' ix 3-4.

It eventually transpires that, just as in v, he has laid himself open to charges of disregarding the fourth commandment, on this occasion by making mud from dirt and spittle on the Sabbath:

> And the day when Jesus made the clay and opened his eyes was the Sabbath. ix 14.

> Then some of the Pharisees said, 'This man is not from God, because he does not observe the Sabbath'. ix 16.

The germaneness of the subject of work can also be perfectly understood in terms of the astrological correspondences of the chapter – earth signs of the zodiac (Capricorn, Taurus, Virgo) are associated with labour and toil, and this is especially true of Virgo. Once again one sees that John gravitates towards symbolism which performs multiple functions simultaneously.

The Fountain of the Virgin, the source of the waters of Pool of Siloam, serves to point toward the astrological correspondences, but it also has qabalistic overtones. *Yod* represents the number ten, and may denote the tenth sefirah, Malkuth which is commonly personified in the Shekhinah, the Virgin Bride[9.2].

As the first letter in the Tetragrammaton, *yod* is also taken as a symbol of the *parzuf* called Father, and symbolised by a fountain or wellspring.

9.1: See 3.6.

9.2: Daniel C. Matt, *The Zohar: Pritzker Edition* vol. 5 p. 554 n. 16; vol. 6 p. 358 n. 283.

The Gospel According to John chapter 10;

**kaf, palm of hand; numerical value 20;
the second sefirah, Hokmah (Wisdom);
the path from the fourth sefirah, Hesed (Mercy)
or Gedulah (Greatness), to the seventh sefirah,
Nezah (Victory).**

The tenth chapter of the Gospel corresponds to the letter *kaf* and the path connecting Hesed (Mercy) and Nezah (Victory). The Good Shepherd's altruism reflects the nature of Hesed, which can be rendered 'Benevolence, Piety, Charity'. Jesus' words, 'I came so that they may have life and have it more abundantly' (x 10), recall that Gedulah (Greatness) is an alternative title of the sefirah, since it manifests in abundance, generosity, expansion, largeness. These aspects of x have already been explained by the fact that Jupiter is the astrological attribution of the letter *kaf*, however, Jupiter is also the planetary correspondence of the fourth sefirah, and shares many of its essential qualities.

There is specifically qabalistic word-play, a tangle of allusions to sefiroth and meanings of letters, in:

> 'I give them eternal life, and they will not perish for eternity, nor will anyone grab them out of my hand. My Father, who

gives to me, is greater than anyone (or: What my father gives me is greater than anything), and no one can grab anything out of my Father's hand.' x 28-29.

Ne<u>z</u>a<u>h</u> (Eternity), the lower of the two sefiroth joined by this path, is here alluded to in the words 'eternal' and 'eternity'. *Kaf* means 'the palm of the hand'; it symbolises the generosity that characterises <u>H</u>esed[10.1].

<u>H</u>esed (Mercy) on the right, active side of the Tree, has a special association with work, because the corresponding commandment enjoins that one work six days a week. As in v and ix, which also correspond on the Tree of sefiroth to paths leading to <u>H</u>esed, this chapter Jesus talks about the importance of performing works:

> Jesus answered them, 'I told you, and you do not believe. The works I do in my Father's name themselves testify about me'. x 25.

> Jesus answered them, 'I have shown you many good works from my Father. On account of which one of these works are you stoning me?'. x 32

> 'If I do not perform the works of my Father, then do not believe me. But if I do, and if you still do not believe me, believe the works, so that you may know and believe that the Father is in me, and I in him'. x 37-38.

10.1: Aryeh Kaplan, *The Bahir* pp. 105, 110, 113, 121.

The Gospel According to John chapter 11;

lamed, an ox-goad; numerical value 30;
the third sefirah, Binah (Understanding);
the path from the fifth sefirah, Gevurah (Severity)
or Din(Justice), to the sixth sefirah,
Tif'areth (Beauty) or Rahamim (Love, Compassion).

Rahamim (Love or Compassion) is an alternative designation of the sixth sefirah, which is the focal point in the world of emotion and feeling. In the Gospel this contributes to the repeated mention of love in the chapter:

> Therefore his sisters sent word to him, saying, 'Master, look, the one you love is sick'. xi 3.

> Jesus loved Martha, and her sister, and Lazarus. xi 5.

> Then the Jews said, 'See how much he loved him!'. xi 36.

Tif'areth also corresponds to the *ruah* or breath-spirit in man[11.1]:

> When Jesus saw her weeping, and the Jews accompanying her weeping, he was deeply moved in the spirit [*tōi pneumati*] and was troubled. xi 33.

Tif'areth with its twelve obliquities or boundaries is symbolised by the day with its the twelve hours, which provides yet another motivation for Jesus' comment in xi 9[11.2].

The theme of judgement underlying the Day of Atonement, which forms a background to the chapter, is agreeable to the position of the path within the ethical or moral triad on the Tree, 'Justice' (Din) being an alternative title of the fifth sefirah.

In the *Zohar* the Day of Atonement is linked with Binah (Understanding)[11.3]. The fact that resurrection is a major theme of xi may also be due to the its association with the third sefirah. The subject first appears if only briefly in ii, which corresponds to the letter *gimel*, and the number 3, when Jesus promises to raise up his bodily temple after it has been torn down (ii 19-21). Here in xi, corresponding to *lamed*, and the number 30, Jesus directly identifies himself with the Resurrection and the Life (xi 25), raising Lazarus to prove it. Jesus' own resurrection takes place in xx, corresponding to the letter *shin*, and the number 300. The parallels between Lazarus' resurrection in xi and that of Jesus in xx – the tomb, a stone that is rolled away, Mary weeping nearby, gravekerchief – make it clear they are cast in the same mould.

In view of the importance of resurrection in xi, and its being termed *anastasis* 'standing up', it is interesting to note that the *'Amidah* (Standing Prayer), the most important prayer in Jewish liturgy, and one of great antiquity, contains a section which is known both as *Teḥiyat ha Meṭim* (Resurrection of the Dead), because it repeatedly mentions God's quickening of the dead, and *Gevurah* or *Gevuroth* (Might or Mighty Deeds)[11.4].

11.1: See 6.5.

11.2: *Zohar* 1:231b. Daniel C. Matt, *The Zohar: Pritzker Edition* vol. 3 p. 400 n. 487.

11.3: *Zohar* 3:15b. Daniel C. Matt, *The Zohar: Pritzker Edition* vol. 4 p. 445 n. 282; vol. 6 p. 39 n. 100; ibid p. 43 n. 113; ibid p. 47 n. 121; vol. 7 p. 95 n. 290; ibid p. 98 n. 297; ibid p. 456 n. 306; ibid p. 462 n. 326.

11.4: *The Standard Prayer Book*, translated by Simeon Singer, 1915.

The Gospel According to John chapter 12;

**mem, water; numerical value 40;
the fourth sefirah, Hesed (Mercy);
the path from the fifth sefirah, Gevurah (Severity),
to the eighth sefirah, Hod (Splendour).**

The twelfth chapter of According to John corresponds to the path connecting the fifth sefirah, Gevurah (Strength), and the eighth sefirah, Hod (Splendour). The letter *mem* represents the number forty, and can therefore denote the fourth sefirah, Hesed (Mercy). The fact that Hesed and Gevurah are strongly associated with light and darkness partly motivates[12.1]:

> Then Jesus said to them, 'The light is with you for a little while longer. Walk while you have the light, lest darkness come upon you, for one walking in darkness does not know where he goes. While you have light, believe in the light so that you may be the children of light'. xii 35-36.

> 'I have come as a light into the world, so that everyone believing in me may not dwell in darkness'. xii 46.

Gevurah (Strength) and the Hod (Splendour) and the path connecting them make up the lower part of the Pillar of Severity. Qabalists term this left-hand pillar on the Tree of sefiroth the Pillar of Fire. The corresponding pillar on the right side of the Tree is the Pillar of Cloud[12.2]. These titles are meant to recall the pillars of cloud and fire that followed the Israelites throughout their desert journey from Egypt to Canaan, the former during the day and the latter at night. The Feast of Tabernacles, which provides the background for events of xii, is said to commemorate how the Israelites were protected by these pillars of cloud and fire during their forty year desert journey. When the Second Temple was in still existence, a huge candelabrum, almost eighty feet high was set up in the courtyard as a part of the holiday's festivities. When the enormous bowls were filled with oil and set ablaze, with old priestly garments to serving as wicks, the flame cast a light bright enough to illuminate much of Jerusalem[12.3]. To the Jews of the era of the Second Temple the huge torch represented the pillar of fire that accompanied the Israelites by night. This may also have influenced xii 35-36, 46.

An allusion to Gevurah (Strength) is seen in:

> Lord, who has believed our report, and to whom has the arm of the Lord been revealed? xii 38.

For Gevurah (Strength) is called the 'left arm' and qabalists understand, on the authority of the Midrash, the adjective 'right' to be used of paired organs whenever the right-sided member is indicated, so that in the absence of any specification, the left-sided organ is always implied[12.4]. Thus, 'arm' means 'left arm'.

Isaiah liii 1, which John cites here, introduces an important passage describing God's suffering servant who pays the price for the sin of others:

> Despised and rejected of men, a man of sorrows and acquainted with suffering... Though he has carried our suffering and borne our sorrows, yet we counted him as one stricken, smitten of God, afflicted. But he was wounded for our transgressions and bruised for our iniquities... it is with his stripes that we are healed. Isaiah liii 3-5.

The left sided Pillar of Severity is strongly connected with sin and guilt, crime and punishment. The theme of this passage is therefore also perfectly harmonious with the position of the path on the qabalistic Tree.

The *Zohar* takes thunder to be a symbol of Gevurah (Strength)[12.5]. Significantly, it uses 'Who can understand the thunder of his mighty deeds [*guvurotov*]' (Job xxvi 14) to expound 'the voice of the Lord is upon the waters; the God of glory thunders; the Lord is upon many waters' (Psalm xxix 3). As both the Septuagint (the Greek translation of the Jewish Scriptures) and Vulgate (the Latin translation) note, Psalm xxix is intended 'for the closing at Tabernacles', so it is appropriate in this chapter. In the Gospel this becomes:

> 'Father, glorify your name'.
> And then a voice came from heaven saying, 'I have glorified it and will glorify it again'.
> And the crowd who were standing there and heard it said that it had thundered. xii 28-29.

Hod, the eighth sefirah, is associated with confession or acknowledgement (*vidui*, *hodah*)[12.6]. In the Gospel:

> Nevertheless many of the rulers believed in him, but because of the Pharisees they did not confess [*hōmolegēsen*] him, lest they be put out of the synagogue. xii 42.

Although the verb 'confess' does not explicitly appear there, the same idea occurs in the nineteenth chapter, in Pilate's confession (xviii 38; xix 4, 6), and in the twentieth chapter in Thomas' confession (xx 24-29), and for the same reason: the nineteenth and twentieth chapters also correspond to one of the paths leading from Hod.

The eighth sefirah, is connected with the eighth commandment, which prohibits stealing. In addition, John lets the sefiroth inherit all the attributes of the planets, which are often those of the GraecoRoman gods. John, in fact, seems to regard the sefiroth and their corresponding planets as equivalent. Mercury, the planetay attribution of Hod, is associated with thievery in astrological tradition, because the classical god had this trait. For these reasons, mention is made of this facet of Judas' character in this chapter:

> Then Judas Iscariot, one of his disciples, the one who was going to betray him, says, 'Why was this ointment not sold for three hundred denarii and given to the poor?'. He did not say this because he cared for the poor, but because he was a thief, and while holding the coin-box used to carry off what was deposited in it. xii 4-6.

Since Gevurah is connected with death, Judas the Iscariot or Assassin, in whose heart dwells the Devil, who doubles as the Angel of Death, is able to personify Gevurah as well as Hod. The *Zohar* notes that the Devil is prone to show up uninvited at festive occasions if the poor are not remembered[12.7].

Hod manifests as references to glory and glorification in:

> His disciples did not understand this at first, but when Jesus had been glorified, they remembered that this had

been written about him, and that they had done these things for him. xii 16

And Jesus answered them, saying, 'The time has come for the Son of man to be glorified.' xii 23

Isaiah said this when he saw his glory, and spoke of him. xii 41.

For they loved the glory of men more than the glory of God. xii 43.

In the Septuagint, the Greek word *doxa* ('glory') may stand for more than a score of different Hebrew words[12.8], some of these have distinct connotations in qabalistic texts. For example, *doxa* in the Septuagint, may represent *tif'areth* in the original Hebrew; but it may also represent *hod* in the Hebrew; often it represents *kavod*, which qabalists take to indicate the Shekhinah; sometimes it stands for *hadar*[12.9].

Doxa, or its cognate verb, *doxazein*, occur more than forty times in According to John. In v 41- 43 *doxa* probably represents 'thought, or supposition'. On every the other occasion the only possible rendering for *doxa* is 'praise, honour, glory' (and 'to praise, to glorify, to give honour' for *doxazein*). In order to explain the pattern of the distribution of these words in the Gospel, we must assume *doxa* and *doxazein* represent different Hebrew words on different occasions, just as they do in the Septuagint. Obviously, it can add no weight to the argument that John had the qabalistic Tree of Life in front of him to propose that in one place 'glory' represents a particular Hebrew word, while in another place it stands for something else; it would be the blatantly circular[12.10]. However, if one does accept that John does use the correspondences of the sefiroth and knows several of them by their common designations – and there does seem to be ample evidence to believe he does – then the extent to which he avoids the mechanical use of keywords with static meanings is illustrated here. Another reason for considering the distribution of 'glory' in the Gospel is that it is a favourite of John's, and the different Hebrew words it may represent are almost invariably significant in qabalistic texts.

Only in the synoptics

If we examine the Synoptic Gospels' accounts of events which John relates in xii, we can see once again that they include a detail that John leaves out, namely Jesus' promise of worldwide fame to Lazarus' sister, Mary:

> Truly I tell you that wherever the gospel is preached in all the world, what this woman has done will also be recounted in memory of her. According to Matthew xxvi 13, and Mark xiv 9 is parallel.

Hod (Glory) connotes fame, reputation, public praise or approbation, which makes this comment germane to xii.

12.1: See 3.6.

12.2: *Zohar* 2:51b. Daniel C. Matt, *The Zohar: Pritzker Edition* vol. 3 p. 67 n. 455; vol. 4 p. 256 n. 210, 211.

12.3: TB *Sukkah* 51a, 52b-53a.

12.4: Gershom Scholem, *Origins of the Kabbalah* p. 149. Daniel C. Matt, *The Zohar: Pritzker Edition* vol. 1 p. 179 n. 582; vol. 3 p. 288 n. 164; vol. 4 p. 317 n. 417. Aryeh Kaplan, *The Bahir* p. 117.

12.5: *Zohar* 1:31a. Daniel C. Matt, *The Zohar: Pritzker Edition* vol. 1 p. 189 n. 662, 663.

12.6: *Zohar* 2:169a. Daniel C. Matt, *The Zohar: Pritzker Edition* vol. 5 p. 480, 482 n. 825, 826, 830.

12.7: *Zohar* 1:10b, 11a. Daniel C. Matt, *The Zohar: Pritzker Edition* vol. 1 p. 72 n. 541.

12.8: Abbott-Smith, *A Manual Greek Lexicon of the New Testament* sv. *doxa*.

12.9: Isaiah lx 7-8, 19; ibid lxiii 12, 14. Jeremiah xiii 18. Job xxxvii 22; xxxix 20. LXX Psalm xxi 6 (Mass. xx 6); cxlix 5. Psalm cxlix 9. Daniel v 18, 23.

12.10: In ii 11 and xiv 13, *kavod* or *tiph'areth* (or *p'ar*); in xvii *kavod*, *hadar* or *nezah*; in xxi 19, *kavod*; in viii 50 and 54, xi 4 and 40, xiii 31, 32, *tiph'areth* (or *p'ar*); in ix 24, xv 8, *hod* or *tiph'areth* (or *p'ar*); in i 14, vii 18 and 38, xii 16, 23, 41 and 43, and xvi 14, *hod*; in v 41, 43 *doxa* represents 'thought, or supposition'. This is a superficial analysis taking into account not only the disposition of the relevant path on the Tee of Life, but also the fact that the numerical value of letters allows them to represent sefiroth (*heth* = 8 = Hod), and the fact that John regards sefiroth and planets interchangeably (Mercury = Hod, Sun = Tiph'areth), and often uses the planetary ruler of a zodiacal sign to stand for the sign (Virgo is ruled by Mercury, Leo by the Sun).

The Gospel According to John chapter 13;
nun, a fish; numerical value 50; the fifth sefirah, Gevurah (Strength);
the path from the sixth sefirah, Tif'areth (Beauty) or Raḥamim (Love), to the seventh sefirah, Neẓaḥ (Victory).

The thirteenth chapter of According to John corresponds to the path connecting Tif'areth (Beauty) and Neẓaḥ (Eternity).

In a human being, the sixth sefirah, Tif'areth (Beauty), represents the heart as the centre of conscious faculties. John turns to the symbol in,

> Supper being over, and the devil having put into the heart of Judas Iscariot, Simon's son, to betray him ... xiii 2.

He employs it again in the next chapter, since this also corresponds to a path from Tif'areth,

> 'Do not let your heart be troubled.' xiv 1

> 'Do not let your heart be troubled, nor let it be afraid.' xiv 27.

An alternative title for Tif'areth is Raḥamim, that is Compassion or Love, an aspect of the sefirah seen in this chapter:

Now before the Feast of Passover, Jesus, knowing that the time had come that he leave this world to go to the Father, having loved those who were his own in the world, loved them to the very end [*eis telos*]. xiii 1.

One of the disciples, whom Jesus loved, was leaning on Jesus' breast. xiii 23.

A new command I give you: that you love one another, and that you love one another just as I have loved you. If you have love for one another everyone will thus know that you are my disciples'. xiii 34-35.

It can also be seen in other chapters that correspond to paths leading to and from Tif'areth, for example:

'If you love me, observe my commandments.' xiv 15.

'The one who has my commandments and observes them is the one who loves me. And the one who loves me will be loved by my Father, and I shall love him and reveal myself to him'. xiv 21.

Jesus answered and said to him, 'If someone loves me, they shall observe my teaching, and my Father will love them, and we shall come to them, and make our dwelling with them. The one who does not love me does not observe my teachings'. xiv 23-24.

'But so that the world may know that I love the Father, I act just as the Father commanded me. xiv 31.

'Just as the Father loved me, so did I love you. Remain in my love. If you observe my commandments, you will remain in my love, just as I have observed my Father's commandments, and remain in his love.' xv 9-10.

'It is my commandment that you love one another, just as I loved you. No one has greater love than someone who lays down their life for their friends. You are my friends, if you do what I command you. xv 12-14.

'This I command you, in order that you may love one another.' xv 17.

Mention of Jesus' commandments and their observance occurs side by side with mention of love, in xiii 34 as in these other instances, because Torah is also a symbol of the sixth sefirah.

As in the fourth, sixth and eleventh chapters, John plays on the fact that Tif'areth represents the *ruaḥ* or breath-spirit in man:

'Having said this, Jesus was troubled in spirit [*tōi pneumati*], and testified, and said, 'Amen, amen, I tell you: one of you shall betray me'. xiii 21.

The phrase *eis telos*, 'to the end' (xiii 2) is a specific pointer to the seventh sefirah. As a noun, Neẓaḥ means 'end or finish; eternal, forever; altogether, completely'. *Eis telos* frequently appears in the Septuagint for *neẓaḥ* or *lmnẓḥ* in the Hebrew[13.1]. It is usually rendered 'forever'; sometimes it has the sense of 'completely, wholly, to the limit'. In xvii 4 and 23, John uses the cognate verb *teleiousthai* 'to complete, to finish, to perfect', in order to connote the seventh sefirah.

The letter *nun*, having a numerical value of fifty, can denote the fifth sefirah, Gevurah, which has Samael, the Angel of Death, among its angelic representatives[13.2]. The Devil is an aspect of this being, and this provides another motivation for his appearances in this chapter (xiii 2, 27) apart from those mentioned in Part 1.

> 13.1: LXX Psalm xii 1 (Mass. xiii 1); LXX Psalm xliii 24 (Mass. xliv 24); LXX Psalm xlviii 10 (Mass. xlix 9); LXX Psalm lxvii 17 (Mass. lxviii 17); LXX Psalm lxxiii 1, 3, 10, 19 (Mass. lxxiv 1, 3, 10, 19); LXX Psalm lxxviii 5 (Mass. lxxix 5); LXX Psalm lxxxviii 47 (Mass. lxxxix 47). Job xiv 20.
>
> *Eis to telos* ('to the end') – almost the same phrase John uses in xiii 2, apart from presence of the definite article – occurs scores of times in the Septuagint's Book of Psalms as part of the title or dedication, where it represents *lmnzh* in the Hebrew. The cognate verb, *nazah* may mean 'to be eminent, to superintend music, to excel, to oversee'. Jewish scholars read it as *la-menezah*, that is 'to one the superintending or conducting (the choir or orchestra), to the chief musician or choirmaster'. Western scholars are more varied. Some take the phrase to read *lamo-nezah*, that is 'to the end' that is, 'for eternity, forever'.
>
> 13.2: *Zohar* 1:46b, 47a, 1:210b; 3:45a. Daniel C. Matt, *The Zohar: Pritzker Edition* vol 1 ibid p. 245 n. 1080; ibid p. 251 n. 1124; ibid p. 253 n. 1146; ibid p. 301 n. 1460; ibid p. 364 n. 165; vol. 3 p. 291 n. 181; vol. 4 p. 142 n. 18; vol. 6 p. 78 n. 65; vol. 7 p. 276 n. 63. Aryeh Kaplan, *The Bahir* para. 162. See Part 3 note 12.4.

The Gospel According to John chapter 14;
samekh, a prop; numerical value 60; the sixth sefirah, Tif'areth (Beauty);
the path from the sixth sefirah, Tif'areth (Beauty), to the ninth sefirah, Yesod (Foundation).

Sixth and ninth sefiroth

The path corresponding to xiv joins Tif'areth (Beauty) and Yesod (Foundation), and forms a part of the central vertical pillar on the Tree of sefiroth.

Extending from Kether at the summit of the Tree to Malkuth at its base, the middle pillar is the way par excellence, and this leads to Jesus' identification with the Way (xiv 6). Moreover, Yesod is occasionally designated a way in qabalistic writings because it is joins Malkuth (Kingdom) to the rest of the central pillar on the Tree of sefiroth[14.1]. Jesus' identification with the Truth and the Life (xiv 6) is also explicable in terms of the sixth and ninth sefiroth, for John's ideas resemble those we encounter in qabalistic texts. Truth (Hebrew *'Emeth*) frequently appears as a title of Tif'areth[14.2]. On the other hand, Yesod (Foundation) is associated with the virtue of truthfulness just because the ninth commandment prohibits falsehood, an idea which John turns to on more than one occasion. 'Life of Worlds' or 'Life of the Universe' is a common title of the ninth sefirah[14.3]. 'I am the Way, the Truth, the Life' is therefore perfectly understandable in terms of common designations Tif'areth (Beauty) and Yesod (Foundation).

Jesus' promise of peace (xiv 27) also conforms to the nature of the six and ninth sefiroth: Tif'areth is called Peace in the *Bahir*[14.4]; Yesod is called a peacemaker or covenant of peace in the *Zohar*[14.5].

The Torah

The fact Jesus, by styling himself as the Way, the Truth and the Life, is identifying himself with the Torah has been noted and explained from an astrological viewpoint. However, the Torah also has specific associations in qabalistic texts that make Jesus' statement even more germane. That the Torah is a path to be walked, or that it shows or even consists of the ways and paths of the Holy One, is a recurring motif of the *Zohar*.[14.6] Truth is a strong association of the Torah, the phrase 'Torah of truth' being sometimes used to cement the connection.[14.7] Life is also part of the Torah's symbolic epiphany.[14.8] Peace is also linked with the Torah, partly because 'All her paths are paths of peace' (Proverbs iii 17) is understood to refer to the Torah.[14.9]

Since qabalistic texts directly identify the Torah with Tif'areth (Beauty), references to the Torah are also thematic to xiv because of the qabalistic correspondences of the chapter. In the *Zohar* it is said that students of the Torah ascend to Tif'areth while prophets attain only to the lower grades of Nezah and Hod. Jacob, the human paragon of the sixth sefirah, is said to embody the Torah, or else has it for his inheritance, spouse, or voice.[14.10] The Torah is routinely symbolised by the Tree of Life, a common specific designation of Tif'areth.[14.11]

In the Gospel references to commandments come in xiii and xv as well as xiv, because all three of these chapters correspond to paths joining Tif'areth to other sefiroth. As already noted, they occur side by side with references to love in xiii 34-35 and xv 9-10, 12-13, 17, as in xiv 15, 21, 31, because Compassion or Love (Raḥamim) is another aspect of the sixth sefirah.

Jesus' identification with the Torah in this chapter is therefore in perfect keeping with the Torah's close connection with Tif'areth (Beauty).

When the Torah is connected with the ninth sefirah, it is usually because it is a type of covenant, and because it provides the world with a stable foundation without which it would dissolve[14.12].

Torah as Paraclete

The Gospel's references to a Paraclete or Advocate or Helper in this chapter (xiv 16, 26) have been explained from an astrological perspective. That some of the Torah's meanings and associations – a journey, a moral code, higher knowledge – are so congruous with many of the correspondences of the ninth house may seem hardly remarkable, merely something of a coincidence. Surprisingly, astrology associates the ninth horoscopic house with legal advocates, while the *Zohar* also portrays the Torah as a mediatrix, intercessor or advocate who protects a man against his accusers.[14.13] Elsewhere the *Zohar* describes the Torah as a defender against the evil prompter and the Angel of Death, whom understands to be different aspects of a single being.[14.14] The *Zohar*, it is interesting to note, uses the term *peqilta* or *peraqlita*, which derives from the Greek *paraklētos*, the same word John uses here.

In the *Zohar*, the letter *samekh* is associated with the idea of helping or assisting since it is cognate with the verb 'to support'.[14.15]

The Shekhinah in xiv

Several of Jesus' in this comments in this chapter allude to the Shekhinah, the Indwelling Presence of the Godhead:

> 'In my Father's house there are many dwellings [*monai*].' xiv 2.
>
> 'The words I speak to you I do not speak on my own accord. Rather, it is the Father, dwelling in me, who performs the works.' xiv 10.
>
> '... the Spirit of Truth, whom the world can not accept because it neither sees nor knows him. However, you know him because he dwells with you and will be within you.' xiv 17.
>
> Jesus replied saying to him, 'If someone loves me, he shall observe my teaching. My Father will love him and we shall come to him and make our dwelling [*mon'*] with him.' xiv 23.

'My Father's house' (xiv 2) another name for the Temple, is also an alias of the Shekhinah, which John uses also in ii 16.[14.16] The word *monai*, translated as 'dwellings' or 'mansions' (xiv 2), has the sense of a rest-house or way-station for travellers, so it contains the idea of journeying from home as well as abiding.

In the *Zohar* the Holy Spirit (xiv 17, 26) is often identified with the Shekhinah.[14.17]

Interestingly, the Shekhinah shares a number of the symbolic associations of the Torah which are directly pertinent to xiv. The Shekhinah is said to function as a paraclete or intercessor.[14.18] She is also described as the guide and patron of travellers with whom one needs to associate on the way whenever journeying from home.[14.19] As the Shekhinah is the Oral Torah in qabalistic writings, she is inextricably linked with the Written Torah in a number of other ways, which, however, do not have much bearing on this chapter of the Gospel.[14.20]

The fact that references to the Shekhinah and Torah can be found side by side in this chapter is at least in part a consequence of the Evangelist's confusing tendency to allow symbolic material to wander between chapters that answer to paths on the same vertical column of the Tree. Jesus' cleansing of the Temple, which comes not in xiv, but in ii, is another example. Similarly, references to the Shekhinah might have been otherwise confined to xxi, but for John's habit of transferring symbolism in this way. Because the Gospel has this confusing feature, it is difficult to know how closely John's Gospel mirrors the *Zohar*'s ideas about the complex relationship between the Torah and the Shekhinah.

14.1: *Zohar* 1:29b. Daniel C. Matt, *The Zohar: Pritzker Edition* vol. 1 p. 176 nn. 560, 561.

14.2: See 4.6.

14.3: Aryeh Kaplan, *The Bahir*, Introduction p. xx, ibid para. 180. *Zohar* 1:4b, 6a, 16b, 18a, 132a, 135b, 167b, 193b; 2:138a, 3:11a. Daniel C. Matt, *The Zohar: Pritzker Edition* vol. 1 p. 25 n. 176; ibid p. 38 n. 260; ibid p. 44 n. 303; ibid p. 135 n. 214; ibid p. 137 n. 231; vol. 2 p. 261 n. 24; vol. 3 p. 14 n. 96; ibid p. 185 n. 35; vol. 5 p. 272 n. 231; vol. 7 p. 58 n. 176.

14.4: Gershom Scholem, *Origins of the Kabbalah* p. 144-148. Aryeh Kaplan, *The Bahir* para. 11, 59, 137, 190, and pp. 98, 139-140.

14.5: *Zohar* 1:6a, 33a, 50a, 59b, 66b, 76b, 193b, 197b; 2:200b, 3:57b. Daniel C. Matt, *The Zohar: Pritzker Edition* vol. 1

p. 34 nn. 233, 234; ibid p. 170 n. 500; ibid p. 276 n. 1298; ibid p. 341 n. 17; ibid p. 391 n. 381; vol. 2 p. 1 n. 5; ibid p. 340 n. 165; vol. 3 p. 183 n. 21; ibid pp. 210, 211 n. 189, 190; vol. 5 p. 195 n. 26; ibid p. 482 n. 831; vol. 6 p. 144 n. 105; vol. 7 p. 180 n. 41; ibid pp. 368, 369 p. 38, 39.

14.6: *Zohar* 1:92a, 124b, 145b, 175b, 201a-b, 204a; 2:62b; 3:8b, 20a-b, 75b, 76a, 113a-b, 269b.

14.8: *Zohar* 1:50b, 151a, 157b-158a, 171a. Daniel C. Matt, *The Zohar: Pritzker Edition* vol. 1 p. 279 n. 1318; vol. 2 p. 344 n. 203; ibid p. 377 nn. 467, 468; vol. 3 p. 16 n. 107; ibid p. 32-33 nn. 230-232; vol. 7 p. 491 n. 432. Aryeh Kaplan, *The Bahir*, para. 137, 138. Gershom Scholem, *Origins of the Kabbalah*, p. 144-5.

14.7: *Zohar* 1:74a, 134b, 168a, 177b, 190a, 201a; 2:96b, 181b, 206a, 239b; 3:148b, 149b. Aryeh Kaplan, *The Bahir*, para. 118, 137, 138, 151.

14.8: *Zohar* 1:92a, 131b, 184b, 199b; 2:86b; 3:268a.

14.9: *Zohar* 1:190a, 197b, 199a; 3:35a, 176b. Daniel C. Matt, *The Zohar: Pritzker Edition* vol. 3 pp. 210, 211 n. 189, 190.

14.10: *Zohar* 1:50b, 151a, 157b-158a, 171a. Daniel C. Matt, *The Zohar: Pritzker Edition* vol. 1 p. 279 n. 1318; vol. 2 p. 344 n. 203; ibid p. 377 nn. 467, 468; vol. 3 p. 16 n. 107; ibid p. 32-33 nn. 230-232; vol. 7 p. 491 n. 432. Aryeh Kaplan, *The Bahir*, para. 137, 138. Gershom Scholem, *Origins of the Kabbalah*, p. 144-5.

14.11: *Zohar* 1:11a, 27b, 63b, 106b, 131b, 151a, 152b, 156b, 168a, 174b, 182a, 193a-b, 199a, 202b; 2:17b, 60b; 3:53b, 260a. Daniel C. Matt, *The Zohar: Pritzker Edition* vol. 1 p. 74 n.

556; ibid p. 370 n. 205; vol. 2 p. 149 n. 255; p. 238 n. 272; ibid p. 344 n. 200; ibid p. 345 n. 204; ibid p. 349 n. 241; ibid p. 371 nn. 421, 423; vol. 3 p. 15 n. 105; ibid p. 53 n. 379; ibid p. 76 n. 510; ibid p. 106 n. 138; vol. 7 p. 338 n. 27.

14.12: *Ruth Rabbah* Prologue i. *Zohar* 1:24b, 25a, 56a, 59b, 89a, 176b, 185a, 197a; 2:94a, 200a; 3:11b, 13b, 14a, 3:73a-b, 91b. Daniel C. Matt, *The Zohar: Pritzker Edition*, vol. 1 pp. 315-6 16 nn. 1545, 1549; vol. 3 p. 68 n. 460; ibid p. 129 n. 277; ibid p. 205 n. 167; vol. 4 p. 536 n. 610; vol. 6 p. 139 n. 92; vol. 7 p. 65 n. 200; ibid p. 80 nn. 246, 247; ibid p. 83 n. 257; ibid p. 491 n. 433; ibid p. 493 nn. 442, 443, 444.

14.13: *Zohar* 1:174b, 175b, 176a, 185a; 2:32b; 3:268b. Daniel C. Matt, *The Zohar: Pritzker Edition* vol. 3 p. 61 n. 426; ibid pp. 127, 128 nn. 266, 270; vol. 4 p. 136 nn. 2, 5.

14.14: *Zohar* 1:152b, 201a-b, 202a. Daniel C. Matt, *The Zohar: Pritzker Edition*, vol. 2 p. 238 n. 273; vol. 3 p. 15 n. 104; vol. 6 p. 33 n. 84.

14.15: *Zohar* 1:34b, 35a. Daniel C. Matt, *The Zohar: Pritzker Edition*, vol. 1 p. 35 n. 248; ibid p. 217 n. 900; ibid p. 219 n. 911.

14.16: Daniel C. Matt, *The Zohar: Pritzker Edition* vol. 2 p. 34 n. 262; ibid p. 338 n. 147, 152; ibid p. 342 n. 183; vol. 3 p. 48 n. 349.

14.17: See 20.4.

14.18: *Zohar* 3:74a. Daniel C. Matt, *The Zohar: Pritzker Edition* vol. 7 p. 500 n. 465.

14.19: *Zohar* 1:49b, 50a, 58b, 59a. Daniel C. Matt, *The Zohar: Pritzker Edition* vol. 1 p. 275 nn. 1292, 1294, 1295; ibid

p. 335 n. 1646; ibid p. 439 nn. 732, 733, 734; vol. 2 p. 34 nn. 256, 260; vol. 6 p. 61 n. 15; ibid p. 224 n. 350; ibid p. 338 n. 225; vol. 7 p. 177 n. 28.

14.20: *Zohar* 1:23a-b, 27b, 230a; 2:188b; 3:25b, 40b. Daniel C. Matt, *The Zohar: Pritzker Edition* vol. 3 p. 161 n. 483; vol. 6 p. 61 n. 15; ibid p. 224 n. 350; ibid p. 338 n. 225; vol. 7 p. 165 n. 512; ibid p. 249 n. 137. Gershom Scholem, *On the Kabbalah and its Symbolism* p 47, 58, 67-68.

A. E. Waite, *The Holy Kabbalah* p 162.

The Gospel According to John chapter 15;
'*ayin*, eye; numerical value 70; the seventh sefirah, Ne<u>z</u>ah (Victory);
the path from the sixth sefirah, Tif'areth (Beauty), to the eighth sefirah, Hod (Splendour).

Esau

The path corresponding to xv connects Tif'areth (Beauty) and Hod (Splendour). On examining such chapters as xii, xvi, and xix, it becomes clear that, for John, Hod, which lies at the bottom of the Pillar of Severity on the left side of the Tree, has a number of negative connotations, such as crime, guilt, and punishment. It is therefore hardly surprising that in the latter half of xv Jesus discourses on the causeless hatred of the world for Christians, their persecution within the world, the world's sin and guilt, and its impending punishment. Moreover, as we have seen, John has chosen the Devil, the Ruler of the World, to be an emblem of the zodiacal sign Capricorn and the tenth horoscopic mansion (xiv 30).

Sefer ha Bahir and the *Zohar* says the Devil, Samael, was spiritual guardian of Jacob's wicked twin brother, Esau, and that he was the angel who wrestled all night with Jacob and rendered him lame by injuring his thigh (Genesis xxxii 25).[15.1] The relevance to xv lies in the fact that Tif'areth (Beauty) is personified in Jacob, and Hod (Splendour) is called 'the Left Thigh'.[15.2]

As the Midrash and *Zohar* note, the word *sa'ir*, 'hairy man', which is used to describe Esau (Genesis xxv 24, lxv 15), and which is related to the Greek *satyr*, is elsewhere in the Bible rendered as 'goat' or even 'goat demon' (e.g. Isaiah xxxiv 14; 2 Chronicles xi 15, xxix 21-23). The *Zohar* remarks that Jacob sent his brother a goat as a peace-offering because he knew that the goat is Esau's totem.[15.3] For this reason, John has another motivation to use the Devil as a symbol for the sign Capricorn.

If Esau the man never came to be Ruler of the World, Esau the nation nevertheless achieved world dominion: in John's time, and for many centuries after, the Romans were always understood in rabbinic literature to be Edomites, the descendants of Esau, or Edom, as he was nicknamed.[15.4]

Rules of the game

When reading the Gospel, one is often led to wonder precisely what rules of composition John feels obliged. He has a formula that determines the action of each chapter, yet on occasion he does not adhere to it. Crucially, for the most part he deviates only under specific conditions and in precise ways. This suggests the existence of certain rules or conventions which can be inferred by observation. For instance, a character who stands for one of the astrological or sefirothic correspondences sometimes does not show up in the chapter expected, but in the immediately following chapter. Importantly, the lateness of such characters, or their being out of place, is regularly signalled by their leaving Jesus' presence, sometimes dramatically, but always explicitly. This happens so often one can safely infer that there is a rule which allows personifications to appear one chapter late, as long as they quit the scene.

Another rule is that the double letters and mother letters sometimes collect from adjacent simple letters symbolism related to Jewish festivals. This too is unexpected, for the only the twelve simple letters, and not double or mother letters, correspond to months of the year. There can be no doubt, however, that x contains symbolism pertaining to New Year's Day, or that xii contains symbolism pertaining to Tabernacles, although this should have been confined to xi. Just as striking is the Purim related imagery, the dice rolling and garment tearing, which is found at the foot of the cross in xix though it should otherwise be confined to xviii.

Yet another rule seems to be that chapters like ii, xiv and xxi, or like v and x, or like vii and xii, or like iii, viii, and xvi, are allowed to share certain material, or that certain motifs can be moved from one chapter to another. Thus, Tabernacles lies behind the action of xii, but it is in vii that John narrates Jesus attendance at the feast.

A question that arises more than once on reading the Gospel is whether a character is allowed to represent the correspondences of two consecutive chapters. Judas seems to embody the correspondences of both xii and xiii, while Pontius Pilate seems to embody the correspondences of both xviii and xix.

With respect to present matters, the opening words of the next chapter contain an allusion to Esau in shape of the verb 'to ensnare' (*skandalizein*), 'to catch in a trap', related to *skandalon*, 'a trap or snare', for Esau hunts with snares and traps.[15.5] The astrological attribution of that chapter is Mars. Esau is associated with Gevurah, the sefirah cognate with the planet. He is said to love violence and bloodshed. The *Zohar* says that Isaac favoured Esau over Jacob, because Isaac also typified Gevurah.[15.6] Esau's other name, 'Edom', means 'Red'[15.7], a colour traditionally associated with Gevurah, and with Mars; in fact, *Adom* (Ruddy) is a modern Hebrew name for the planet. Indications exist elsewhere in the Gospel that John understands the Devil (Samael), the angelic archetype of Esau, to be the angel of Mars, as well as the fifth sefirah, Gevurah.

One reason for thinking that a single character is allowed to embody the correspondences of two consecutive chapters John is that consistently follows certain patterns, and a common feature is present on each of the occasions John seems to do this: the chapters involved denote letters of different types. Thus, with respect to Judas, *mem* (xii) is a mother letter, while *nun* (xiii) is a simple; with respect to Samael or Esau, *'ayin* (xv) is a simple letter, *peh* (xvi) is a double letter; with respect to Pilate, *quf* (xviii) is simple, while *resh* (xix) is double.

> 15.1: Aryeh Kaplan, *The Bahir* para. 200. *Zohar* 1:35b, 138a, 144a-b, 146a, 166a, 170a-b, 171a-b, 203b; 2:163b; 3:45a, 197a, 199b. Daniel C. Matt *The Zohar: Pritzker Edition* vol. 1 p. 162 n. 438; ibid p. 224 nn. 949, 951; vol. 2 p. 269 n. 82; ibid p. 302 n. 320; ibid p. 306 n. 345; ibid p. 315 nn. 419, 421; vol. 3 p. 4 n. 22; ibid p. 28 n. 195; ibid p. 30 n. 210; ibid p. 32 n. 220; ibid p. 38 n. 267; ibid p. 44 n. 315; ibid p. 248 n. 409; vol. 4 p. 48 n. 207; vol. 5 p. 444 n. 716; vol 7 p. 275 n. 59.

> 15.2: The *Zohar* says that it was Jacob's left thigh that was injured, but seems confused as to whether Ne<u>z</u>ah or Hod is the 'Left Thigh'. *Zohar* 1:21b, 26b, 241a. Daniel C. Matt *The Zohar: Pritzker Edition*, vol. 1 p. 164 nn. 452, 454, 456; vol. 5 p. 481 n. 827. *Genesis Rabbah* lxxviii 6.

15.3: *Zohar* 1:65a, 138b, 145b; 2:185a-b; 3:64a. Daniel C. Matt, *The Zohar: Pritzker Edition*, vol. 1 pp. 380-1 nn. 291, 292; vol. 2 p. 271 n. 102; ibid p. 314 n. 412; vol. 6 pp. 41, 42 nn. 105, 107; vol. 7 p. 419 n. 190. *Genesis Rabbah* lxv 15.

15.4: Daniel C. Matt *The Zohar: Pritzker Edition* vol. 2 p. 344 n. 203; vol. 3 p. 30 n. 207; ibid p. 45 n. 327; ibid pp. 70, 71 nn. 471, 480; ibid 214 n. 210; vol. 4 p. 60 n. 264; ibid. p. 126 n. 208; ibid p. 200 n. 207; vol. 6 p. 62 n. 18; vol. 7 p. 140 n. 431.

15.5: *Zohar* 2:167a. Daniel C. Matt *The Zohar: Pritzker Edition*, vol. 2 p. 268 n. 79; vol. 5 p. 468 n. 792; vol. 7 p. 245 n. 129. *Genesis Rabbah* xxxvii 2; ibid lxvii 2.

15.6: *Zohar* 1:137b. Daniel C. Matt, *The Zohar: Pritzker Edition*, vol. 2 p. 268 nn. 77, 78; ibid p. 291 n. 248; ibid p. 314 n. 413; vol. 7 p. 354 nn. 77, 78.

15:7. *Zohar* 1:153a. Daniel C. Matt *The Zohar: Pritzker Edition*, vol. 2 p. 352 n. 263; vol. 3 p. 71 n. 480; vol. 7 p. 322 n. 220. *Genesis Rabbah* lxiii 12.

The Gospel According to John chapter 16;

peh, a mouth; numerical value 80; the eighth sefirah, Hod (Splendour, Glory);
the path from the seventh sefirah, Ne*z*ah (Victory), to the eighth sefirah, Hod (Splendour).

Seventh and eighth sefiroth

The sixteenth chapter of the Gospel corresponds to the path joining Ne*z*ah (Victory) and Hod (Glory, Splendour). *Nikē* ('victory') and *doxa* ('glory') are respectively the nearest Greek equivalents for the Hebrew names of these sefiroth. John hints at their titles with the cognate verbs *nikasthai*, 'to be victorious, to overcome' and *doxazein*, 'to glorify':

> 'He will glorify [*doxasei*] me, for he will take from what is mine, and will proclaim it to you'. xvi 14.

> 'But be confident. I have had victory over [*nenikēka*] the world'. xvi 33.

Nikasthai, which does not occur in any other chapter, is a simple and fairly obvious pointer to the seventh sefirah. Confidence or self-assuredness (Hebrew *bi*t*ahon*) is an aspect of the psyche connected with Ne*z*ah (Victory). Although *doxazein* ('to glorify') and *doxa* ('glory') are, for reasons already given, distributed through the Gospel in such a way that they cannot be specific markers for Hod, it is nevertheless possible and useful to explain their occurrences.

Lying at the bases of their respective pillars, Ne<u>z</u>ah (Victory) and Hod (Glory, Splendour) possess complementary qualities, just like <u>H</u>okmah (Wisdom) and Binah (Understanding), or <u>H</u>esed (Lovingkindness) and Gevurah (Strength). It is natural to conceive of such sefiroth in terms of antithetical pairs, and in iii John employs a litany of antonymous pairs to suggest <u>H</u>okmah and Binah: light and darkness, heaven and earth, spirit and body, even good and evil. In xvi, as in several other chapters, we see Ne<u>z</u>ah and Hod represented in terms of pleasure and pain, happiness and unhappiness, joy and sorrow:

> But because I have told you these things, sorrow has filled your heart. xvi 6.

> 'Amen, amen, I tell you: you will weep and mourn but the world will be happy, you will be sorrowful but your sorrow will turn to happiness. When she is giving birth, a woman feels sorrow because her time has come, but after giving birth she no longer remembers her distress, due to her happiness that a human being has been born into the world. And therefore you have sorrow now, but I shall see you again and your hearts will be full of happiness and no one takes that happiness from you'. xvi 20-22.

> 'Until now you have asked for nothing in my name. Now ask, and you will receive, so that your happiness may be complete.' xvi 24.

> 'In the world you will have distress ...' xvi 33.

It is not too difficult to see how the idea has come about. Qabalists take 'Bliss in your right hand is for Eternity (*nezah*)' (Psalm xvi 11) to indicate the nature of the seventh sefirah. Amongst its several senses Nezah may mean 'what leads one, a goal or objective'; this is why qabalists refer to it a 'primary purpose'. John, moreover, conflates sefiroth and planets, and astrological tradition strongly associates Venus with pleasure and satisfaction. In contrast, Hod, lying at the base of the other, sinister side of the tree, is associated with suffering.

The seventh and eighth sefiroth are also related to specific types of prophetic revelation.[16.1] John alludes to this aspect of their function in:

> 'But I have told you these things, so that when their time comes, you may remember that I told you about them. xvi 4

> 'However when the Spirit of Truth comes, he will lead you into all truth. For he will not speak on his own accord, but he will tell whatever he hears, and he will proclaim to you things to come. He will glorify me, for he will take from what is mine, and will proclaim it to you. All that the Father has is mine. Because of this, I said that he will take from what is mine, and proclaim it to you.' xvi 13-15.

Nezah is the superior type of visionary ability and reveals things to come; Hod is a lower level of prophecy which merely repeats what is heard elsewhere.

Coming and going, like the appearance of lightning

In xvi, Jesus makes a statement in this chapter that so mystifies the disciples they discuss it amongst themselves until Jesus comes to repeat it with explanation:

> 'In a little while you will not see me anymore, and a little while later you will see me again, because I am going to the Father'. Then some of his disciples said among themselves, 'What is it that he is saying to us: "In a little while you will not see me anymore, and a little while later you will see me again"? And: "because I am going to the Father"?'. And they said, 'What is this "little while"? We cannot understand what he is saying'.
> Jesus knew they wanted to ask him, and said to them, 'Are you asking one another about this, because I said, "In a little while you will not see me anymore, and a little while later you will see me again"?'. xvi 16-19.

'A little while' or 'a short time', because Jesus is identifying himself with lightning here.

Several reasons may have led John to consider Jesus' identification with lightning to be appropriate to this chapter.

Mars is the astrological attribution of xvi. Works that deal with planetary angelology list Samael as the angel of Mars; in qabalistic and aggadic texts Samael is the proper name of the Devil, the Evil Inclination, or Tempter. As discussed above, he is qualified to personify of both the fifteenth and sixteenth chapters of John's Gospel. If 'I saw Satan fall from heaven like lightning' (According to Luke x 18) was familiar to John, then it would explain why John might associate the Devil with lightning here. The Talmud[16.2] describes his comings and goings: he descends to earth in order to tempt men to evil, then ascends back to heaven in order to accuse them, the image possibly explaining Jesus' words later in the chapter:

> 'I proceeded from the Father's side, and have come into the world. I leave the world again, and go to the Father.' xvi 28.

The most likely explanation is that lightning is being used to hint at aspects of Ezekiel's vision. Analysis of Ezekiel was the subject of a strand of Jewish esotericsm called 'the Work of the Chariot' (*Ma'aseh Merkabah*). Merkabah-mysticism, as it was known, which seems to have existed alongside and somewhat independently of the Qabalah, had as its goal a vision of the enthroned God of Israel as described in Exodus xxiv, Ezekiel i and x, and Isaiah vi. Qabalists, when analysing these passages, quite naturally attempted to understand different parts of these visions in terms of the sefiroth and Tree of Life. Unfortunately, their explanations are at variance with one another, nor is their thinking easy to follow. All in all, qabalists do not seem to have been very successful in elucidating these passages with their ideas. John's ideas, however, as far as they can be inferred, do not greatly differ from some of the opinions expressed by Jewish qabalists.

Jesus' statement (xvi 16) that he comes from God and returns to him may be due John's having in mind a specific verse: 'And the Living Beings, running and returning, like the appearance of lightning' (Ezekiel i 14). *Sefer Yezirah* alludes to the verse, with 'their vision is like lightning' and 'the word in them is running and returning', and 'running and returning: upon this a covenant was made'.[16.3]

Commentators have suggested that 'running and returning', when it occurs in *Sefer Yezirah*, relates to the oscillation of the mind between Hokmah and Binah, rather than Nezah and Hod.[16.4] However, it is possible that John relates the phrase to the right and left pillars of the Tree generally. The matter is difficult to resolve because iii, viii, xvi, which correspond to the three horizontal paths, are allowed to share symbolic material. We see, for example, that several important symbolic motifs are common to iii, viii, and xvi – childbirth, the relationship between heavenly and earthly.

It is possible that John understands the Holy Living Creatures described by Ezekiel to occupy the level on which Neẓaḥ and Hod and the horizontal path connecting them lie. One reason for thinking this is that the Holy Living Creatures are below the Divine Throne, just as Neẓaḥ and Hod lie together on a level below Tif'areth, which is symbolised by the Divine Throne. With respect to the Living Creatures' running and returning, *Sefer Yeẓirah* remarks that 'upon this a covenant was made', which agrees with Neẓaḥ and Hod being above Yesod, which is symbolised by a covenant.

If 'holy' was a keyword that signalled the seventh sefirah, it would explain why the word *hagios* ('holy') or its cognate verb *hagiazein* ('to make holy, to sanctify') occur four times in the next chapter of the Gospel (xvii 11, 17, 19).

John sometimes strings the correspondences of several consecutive chapters into a single figure. This appears to be the case in,

> 'And upon coming, he will prove the world's error regarding sin, righteousness and judgment. Regarding sin: because they did not believe in me. Regarding righteousness: because I go to my Father, and you see me no more. Regarding judgment: because the Ruler of this World has been judged.'
> xvi 8-11

where sin, righteousness, and judgement signal the correspondences of *nun*, *samekh*, and *'ayin* respectively.

16.1: *Zohar* 1:21b, 23b, 24a; 3:35a. Daniel C. Matt, *The Zohar: Pritzker Edition*, vol. 1 p. 4 n. 20; ibid p. 165 n. 459; vol. 3

p. 32 n. 220; ibid p. 114 n. 190; ibid p. 243 n. 380; ibid p. 450 n. 697; vol. 7 p. 203 n. 115; ibid p. 339 n. 29.

16.2: TB *Baba Bathra* 16a.

16.3: Appendix 3: *Sefer Yetzirah* 1:6-8.

16.4: Aryeh Kaplan, *Sefer Yetzirah: Book of Creation* p. 67.

Daniel C. Matt, *The Zohar: Pritzker Edition*, vol. 5 p. 554 n. 17.

The Gospel According to John chapter 17;

**zaddi, a fish-hook or fish-net; numerical value 90;
the ninth sefirah, Yesod (Foundation);
the path from the seventh sefirah, Nezah (Victory),
to the ninth sefirah, Yesod (Foundation).**

The seventeenth chapter of According to John answers to the letter *zaddi*, and the path from Nezah (Victory) to Yesod (Foundation).

According to the lexicographer, one meaning of the Hebrew verb *nazah* is 'to be perfect or complete'; *nezah*, the cognate noun, may mean 'completeness, perfection'; it can be used adverbially in the sense of 'completely, wholly, altogether'.[17.1] It is easy to see how these senses of the word manifest in the chapter:

> 'I have glorified you on the earth, completing [*teleiōsas*] the work that you gave me to do.' xvii 4.

> 'And now come I to you, and I speak these things in the world, that they may have my happiness perfected in them.' xvii 13.

> 'I in them, and you in me, that they may be completed [*teteleiōmenoi*] in unity ...' xvii 23.

Joy or happiness (xvii 13) is another pointer to Ne<u>z</u>ah (Victory) for reasons already given when discussing xvi. In fact, joy or happiness and completion are mentioned side by side in xvi 24 as they are in xvii 13. A similar comment appears in xv because *'ayin* is used as a numeral for seventy and may therefore denote the seventh sefirah:

> 'I have told you this, so that my happiness may remain in you, and your happiness may be perfected.' xv 11.

Katabolē (foundation) is the Greek equivalent of Yesod (Foundation), the usual name for the ninth sefirah; in fact, 'Foundation of the World' quite often appears in the *Zohar* as the full title of the sefirah. The phrase 'before the foundation [*katabolē*] of the world' (xvii 24) is therefore a straightforward pointer to Yesod.

In the next verse Jesus addresses God as 'Righteous Father' (xvii 25) because <u>z</u>addi, the letter assigned this chapter, is used to pun on the <u>z</u>addik, 'the righteous one', which is another code term for Yesod.[17.2] Sometimes the association is made indirectly, through the person of Joseph, who is described as righteous, and who is the personification of Yesod.[17.3] More often the idea is drawn directly from 'the righteous one is the foundation of the world' (Proverbs x 25), which is frequently cited in this context.[17.4] The proximity of 'righteous' and 'foundation of the world' in xvii 24-25, strongly suggests John has this verse in mind.

'Power' (xvii 2, also xix 10-11) seems to be a code-word for Yesod or Yesod and Malkuth together as a combined grade.[17.5] This is understandable: 'Almighty' or 'Omnipotent' (*Shadai*) is the divine name associated with the ninth sefirah; it is also implied, as non-Jewish commentators have noted, by the common doxology to the Lord's prayer, 'Thine is the Kingdom, the

Power, the Glory, for ever and ever' – with 'Kingdom' standing for Malkuth (Kingdom), 'Power' for Yesod (Foundation), 'Glory' for Hod (Glory), and 'for ever and ever' for Ne<u>z</u>ah (Eternity)'. The Greek of the doxology has *dunamis* ('power') instead of John's *exousia* ('power'), but these words are very close in meaning.

From 1 Chronicles xxix qabalists understood 'all' to be another signal word used to denote the ninth sefirah.[17.6] In this chapter it occurs in xvii 21 and in:

> 'Just as you gave him power over all flesh, so that he might give eternal life to all you have given him.' xvii 2

> 'Now they know that all the things you gave me are from you.' xvii 7

> 'And all that are mine are yours, and yours mine.' xvii 10.

Yesod (Foundation) is spoken of as hub in which the tendencies represented by the preceding five sefiroth are gathered together and amalgamated.[17.7] The unification of the entire spectrum of sefirothic energies in Yesod partly motivates Jesus' prayer for unity and assimilation in:

> 'Holy Father, keep them in your name, which you have given me, so that they may be one just as we are one'. xvii 11

> 'So that they may all be one, just as you, Father, are in me, and I in you, so that they too may be one in us, so that the world may believe that you have sent me. And I have given them the glory you gave me, so that they may be one, just as we are one.' xvii 21-22.

Missing from John's Gospel

Mark xiv 51 records a detail surrounding Jesus' arrest not found in John's Gospel: a young man, 'wearing only a linen cloth on his naked body', follows Jesus and the soldiers who have him in custody. Briefly caught, he runs away naked, having abandoned his linen cloth in his hurry to escape.

If John had described this event, he would have had no choice but to place it in xviii. For xviii begins with Jesus not yet arrested, and finishes with him standing before Pilate. And it would have been an easy matter to explain this episode if it had occurred in xviii. Western (non-Jewish) commentators often list a naked man among the symbols of the ninth sefirah[17.8] This sounds merely a euphemistic way of saying that Yesod (Foundation) denotes the genitalia. However, the idea is also derivable from the nakedness of the original human couple, and their creation on the sixth day, 'the Sixth Day' being a standard designation of Yesod. We can reasonably infer that John is familiar with the symbolism from xix (Jesus naked on the cross) and xxi (Peter naked on the boat). The episode Mark describes, moreover, has been influenced by Genesis xxxix 12-16, where the biblical patriarch Joseph, the foremost human paradigm of Yesod, leaves his garment behind when fleeing from the clutches of Potiphar's wife.

Now, an idiosyncratic feature of John's handling of symbolism has been met with: characters who embody the correspondences of a certain chapter sometimes appear not where they should, but in the following chapter; such characters explicitly depart, often dramatically or hastily, from Jesus' presence. The episode Mark describes, if it occurred in the eighteenth chapter of According to John, would be immediately comprehensible – but only because of this idiomatic feature of John's handling of personifications. The omission of this detail, found only in According to Mark xiv 51, must therefore join the list of things which are inexplicably missing from John's version though tailor made for it, but it is by far the most telling of all. It implies that the source from which Mark borrowed made use of a peculiar trope of John's – something we might have otherwise believed to be as distinctive as a signature or hallmark.

17.1: *Gesenius' Hebrew-Chaldee Lexicon to the Old Testament*, s.v. *nazah*. Jerome's Vulgate (Psalmi Liber Iuxta Hebraicum Translatus) Psalm xii 1 renders *nezah* (Massoretic Psalm xiii 1) as *penitus* ('completely, wholly').

17.2: *Zohar* 1:2b. Aryeh Kaplan, *The Bahir* para. 61; ibid p. 126-127.

17.3: *Zohar* 1:21b, 59b, 71b, 153b, 158a, 168b, 176b, 193b, 194b, 196b, 197a, 203b; 3:14a.

Daniel C. Matt, *The Zohar: Pritzker Edition* vol. 1 p. 166 n. 465; ibid p. 340 n. 4; ibid p. 422 nn. 609, 610; vol. 2 p. 357 n. 300; ibid p. 379 n. 485; vol. 3 p. 19 n. 131; ibid p. 92 nn. 49, 50; ibid p. 110 n. 167; ibid p. 122 n. 233; ibid p. 201 n. 139; ibid 205 n. 166; ibid p. 228 n. 303; ibid p. 232 n. 325; ibid p. 335 n. 191; ibid p. 544 n. 1029; vol. 4 p. 43 n. 185; vol. 6 p. 221 n. 340; ibid p. 291 n. 85; vol. 7 p. 81 n. 249.

17.4: *Zohar* 1:32a-b, 33a, 59b, 82a-b, 93a, 181b, 186a, 193b, 195a, 245b; 2:85b; 3:58a, 69a. Daniel C. Matt, *The Zohar: Pritzker Edition* vol. 1 p. 166 n. 465; ibid p. 194 n. 699; ibid p. 198 n. 735; ibid p. 203 n. 781; vol. 2 p. 24 n. 174; ibid p. 86 n. 657; vol. 3 p. 102 n. 117; ibid p. 185 n. 35; ibid p. 195 n. 105; ibid p. 427 n. 611; ibid p. 503 n. 902;

vol. 4 p. 481 n. 417; vol. 7 p. 460 nn. 319, 320, 321. Aryeh Kaplan, *The Bahir* para. 101-102, 157, 180.

17.5: *Zohar* 1:33b; 3:11b. Daniel C. Matt, *The Zohar: Pritzker Edition* vol. 1 p. 206 n. 800; ibid p. 268 n. 1241; vol. 7 pp. 63, 64 nn. 196, 197.

17.6: Aryeh Kaplan *The Bahir* Introduction p. xx; ibid para. 22, 78; ibid pp. 101, 142. *Zohar* 1:17a, 30b, 87b, 122a; 3:58b. Daniel C. Matt, *The Zohar: Pritzker Edition* vol. 1 p. 185 n. 637; vol. 2 p. 60 n. 472; ibid p. 205 n. 18; ibid p. 226 n. 172; ibid p. 340 n. 164; vol. 7 p. 376 n. 59.

17.7: *Zohar* 1:18a, 33a. Daniel C. Matt, *The Zohar: Pritzker Edition* vol. 1 p. 83 n. 625; ibid p. 138 n. 237; ibid p. 204 n. 786; vol. 2 p. 340 n. 164.

17.8: Dion Fortune, *The Mystical Qabalah*, p. 252. Gareth Knight, *A Practical Guide to Qabalistic Symbolism* p. 175. Israel Regardie, *Foundations of Practical Magic*, p. 77.

The Gospel According to John chapter 18;
quf, an ear or an axe; numerical value 100;
the tenth sefirah, Malkuth (Kingdom);
the path from the seventh sefirah, Ne<u>z</u>a<u>h</u> (Victory),
to the tenth sefirah, Malkuth (Kingdom).

On the Tree of Life the letter *quf* answers to the path between Ne<u>z</u>a<u>h</u> (Victory) and Malkuth (Kingdom).

A garden (xviii 1, 26) is a standard symbol of Malkuth in qabalistic writings.[18.1] The earth or ground (xviii 6) is another.[18.2]

The name of the High Priest's slave, who loses and regains his ear, is Malchos (xviii 10), a simple pun on the tenth sefirah, Malkuth (Kingdom). He is a slave because Malkuth is the lowest sefirah; he is the High Priest's property because the High Priest personifies the right hand pillar of the Tree at whose base Ne<u>z</u>a<u>h</u> lies. For this reason John notes it is his right ear that Peter removes with his sword.

The coal-fire, mentioned in xviii 18, is a symbol of Malkuth (Kingdom).[18.3] Reasons for the association are several. Qabalists understand 'Her coals are coals of fire' (Song of Solomon viii 6) to refer to the Shekhinah, who personifies the tenth sefirah. A *'ishah*, 'fire offering' is a homonym of *'ishah*, 'woman', a common designation of the Shekhinah. Here, the blackness of coal is also relevant, as Malkuth has an association with that colour, sometimes deduced from Song of Solomon i 5: 'I am black but comely'.

The Shekhinah is often symbolised by a sword (xviii 10-11).[18.4] A gate or its guardian (xviii 16-17) is another symbol.[18.5]

'I am' (Hebrew *'ani* or *'anokhi*) appears as a name of the Shekhinah.[18.6] The idea is reflected in this chapter (xviii 5-8) in Jesus' reply, *egō eimi* ('I am'), to the soldiers searching for him. Such 'I am' statements of Jesus, a conspicuous and unique feature of John's Gospel, usually relate directly to the correspondences of the chapter in which they occur.

Question about a king, answer about a kingdom

The concluding section of xviii contains some word-play based on various astrological and qabalistic attributions of xviii and xix:

> Then Pilate entered into the Praetorium again, and called Jesus, and said to him, 'Are you the King of the Jews?'. xviii 33

> Jesus answered him, 'Do you say this of your own accord or did others tell you about me?'. xviii 34

> Pilate answered, 'Am I a Jew? Your own people and the chief priests have handed you over to me. What have you done?'. xviii 35

> Jesus answered, 'My kingdom is not of this world. If my kingdom were of this world, then my soldiers would fight so that I might not be handed over to the Jews. But my kingdom is not from here'. xviii 36

> Pilate therefore said to him, 'So then, you are you a king?'. Jesus answered, 'You say that I am a king. For this was I born, and for this did I come into the world: to testify to the truth. Everyone who comes from the truth hears my voice'. xviii 37
>
> Pilate says to him, 'What is truth?'. And after saying this, he went out again to the Jews, and says to them, 'I do not find any fault in him. xviii 38
>
> But it is your custom that I release someone for you at Passover. So then, do you want me to release the King of the Jews to you?'. xviii 39
>
> Then they all cried again, saying, 'Not this man, but Barabbas'. And Barabbas was a robber. xviii 40.

Asked whether he is a king in xviii 33, Jesus first avoids the question altogether, just because the John has decided to make Jesus' portrayal as king thematic to the next chapter. For the nineteenth chapter has the Sun as its astrological correspondence, and the king is a traditional and highly specific solar symbol, and as we shall see in Part 3, John has other reasons to represent Jesus as king – and indeed xix is replete with clear references to Jesus as king. Dodging the issue, Jesus admits instead to possessing a kingdom, not once but three times in xviii 36. It is because xviii corresponds to the path ending in Malkuth (Kingdom), that mention of a kingdom is suitable for the chapter.

Pilate, despite being repeatedly told Jesus has a kingdom, quite sensibly fears some doublespeak, and needs to check: 'So then, you are a king?' (xviii 37). Finally, Jesus admits to being a king, and talks about the truth, Pilate admits Jesus' faultlessness, and offers Barabbas the robber as a substitute. It is precisely at this point – xviii 37 – that xix actually begins, for a king (xviii 37 and 39), truth (xviii 37), faultlessness (xviii 38), admission or confession (xviii 38), stealing (xviii 40), all belong one way or another to the network of correspondences specific to xix. Langton, who was responsible for the division of the Gospel into chapters as we know it, made a minor error here: the eighteenth chapter ends at xviii 36, and xviii 37-41 should properly be counted as belonging to xix.

Only in the synoptics

The physical body is a symbol of the tenth sefirah. Jesus' comment that 'the spirit is willing but the flesh is weak', which he makes just before his arrest (According to Matthew xvi 41, Mark xiv 38), refers to this aspect of the tenth sefirah. The word has the same connotation in the phrase 'power over all flesh' in xvii 2.

The ground as a symbol for Malkuth appears in According to Mark xiv 35 and Matthew xxvi 39 where Jesus falls face down on the ground during his despondent prayer.

Jesus' assurance that he could summon more than twelve legions of angels to his defence if he wished (According to Matthew xxvi 53), which has no analogue in John's Gospel, is a pointer to the Shekhinah, who is typically accompanied by an escort of angels arranged in twelve armies or tribes.[18.7]

The Shekhinah is often represented by a field in qabalistic writings.[18.8] Blood[18.9] and death[18.10] are emblematic of her dark side. The symbolism appears in the Field of Blood, the Potter's Field, which was purchased with the money given to Judas for Jesus' betrayal, and which became a cemetery for foreigners (According to Matthew xvii 7-10).

Jesus prophesies in the Synoptic accounts of his trial that his accusers will see him 'seated at the right side of Power [*dunameōs*]' (According to Matthew xxvi 64, Mark xiv 62, Luke xxii 69) because Power, as already explained, is a designation of Yesod or Yesod and Malkuth as a combined grade. The statement also alludes to Nezaḥ's association with prophecy, which manifests also in the soldiers' taunt, 'Prophesy! Who is it that hit you?' (According to Matthew xxvi 67, Mark xiv 65, Luke xxii 64).

In summary, allusions to the tenth sefirah appear in xviii in mention of a garden, the ground, the name Malchos, a coal-fire, a sword, Jesus' possession of a kingdom; 'I am' as a divine name is also associated with Malkuth. The Synoptic Gospels allude to Nezaḥ's role in prophecy. They also contain various symbols related to Malkuth not found in John's Gospel: the Field of Blood, and mention of twelve legions of angels.

18.1: See 20.1.

18.2: *Zohar* 1:13b, 18b; 2:222a. Daniel C. Matt, *The Zohar: Pritzker Edition*, vol. 1 pp. 92, 93 nn. 698, 703; ibid p. 114 n. 48; ibid p. 141 n. 261; ibid p. 143 n. 271; ibid p. 183 n. 620; ibid p. 186 n. 646; ibid p. 218 n. 906; ibid pp. 270, 271 n. 1256, 1265; vol. 3 p. 261 n. 23.

18.3: *Zohar* 1:48b, 49a, 50b, 51a, 1:70a, 245a, 166a; 2:14a, 50b, 114a; 2:126b; 3:27b, 59b, 110b, 191a, 197a. Daniel C. Matt, *The Zohar: Pritzker Edition*, vol. 1 p. 105 n. 774; ibid p. 142 n. 267; ibid p. 158 n. 400; ibid p. 268 n. 1242; ibid p. 282 nn. 1341, 1342; ibid pp. 410-412 nn. 519, 524, 527; vol. 3 p. 2 n. 11; vol. 4 p. 249 n. 185; vol. 5 p. 138 n. 392; ibid p. 185 n. 4; vol 6 p. 185 n. 229; ibid 215 n. 321. Aryeh Kaplan, *Sefer Yetzirah: The Book of Creation*, p. 63.

18.4: *Zohar* 1:237a, 240b. Daniel C. Matt, *The Zohar: Pritzker Edition*, vol. 1 p. 299 n. 1446; vol. 3 p. 442 nn. 665, 667; ibid p. 468 nn. 774, 775; vol. 4 p. 95 n. 93; ibid p. 249 n. 185; ibid p. 360 n. 566; vol. 7 p. 72 n. 223; ibid p. 122 n. 367; ibid p. 332 n. 4; ibid p. 409 n. 158.

18.5: *Zohar* 1:7b, 8a, 21a, 36, 37a, 47b, 54b, 75b, 96b, 98a-b 103a-, 106b, 219a; 2:51a, 220a; 3:14a, 95a. Daniel C. Matt, *The Zohar: Pritzker Edition*, vol. 1 p. 50 n. 350; ibid p. 51 n. 357; ibid p. 261 nn. 1196, 1199; ibid p. 443 n. 767; vol. 2 p. 112 n. 869; ibid 119 n. 22; ibid p. 131 n. 117; ibid p. 148 n. 251; vol. 6 p. 255 n. 452; vol. 7 p. 83 n. 255.

18.6: *Zohar* 6a-b, 150a; 2:85a, 236b. Daniel C. Matt, *The Zohar: Pritzker Edition*, vol. 1 p. 35 n. 242; ibid p. 39 n. 269; vol. 2 p. 67 n. 518; ibid p. 337 nn. 137, 138, 140; vol. 3 p. 253 n. 436; vol. 4 p. 477 nn. 398, 400; vol. 7 p. 311 n. 180.

18.7: *Zohar* 1:61a, 101a, 102b, 113a, 120b, 159b, 165b, 166a, 231b, 241a, 247a; 2:5a, 9b, 126b, 147a, 197b, 229b, 230a; 3:118b. Daniel C. Matt, *The Zohar: Pritzker Edition* vol. 1 p. 142 n. 268; vol. 2 p. 125 n. 64; ibid p. 168 n. 405; ibid p. 201 n. 654; ibid p. 390 n. 575; vol. 3 p. 2 n. 11; ibid pp. 398-399 nn. 480, 485, 486; ibid p. 470-471 nn. 782, 784, 785; ibid pp. 513-514 nn. 926, 927; vol. 4 p. 2 n. 9; ibid p. 38 n. 167, 169; ibid p. 253 n. 201; vol. 5 pp. 185-186 n. 5; ibid p. 337 n. 413; vol. 6 pp. 125, 126 nn. 50, 52; ibid pp. 319, 320 nn. 165, 166, 169. A.E. Waite, *The Holy Kabbalah* p 197. See Part 4 note 14.2.

18.8: *Zohar* 1:122b; 2:60b. Daniel C. Matt, *The Zohar: Pritzker Edition* vol. 1 p. 218 n. 904; ibid p. 305 n. 1482; vol. 2 p. 206 nn. 20, 22; ibid p. 225 n. 162; ibid pp. 294, 295 nn. 262,

269; vol. 3 p. 372 n. 368; ibid p. 535 n. 1003; vol. 4 p. 188 n. 172; ibid p. 190 n. 180; ibid p. 321 n. 432; vol. 6 p. 392 n. 379; vol. 7 p. 392 n. 108.

18.9: *Zohar* 3:54a. Daniel C. Matt, *The Zohar: Pritzker Edition* vol. 7 p. 343 nn. 42, 43, 44. See also 18.4.

18.10: *Zohar* 1:35b, 152b; 3:113b, 153b, 155b, 176b, 261b. Daniel C. Matt, *The Zohar: Pritzker Edition* vol. 1 pp. 222, 223 nn. 936, 223 n. 943; vol. 2 p. 349 n. 241; vol. 3 p. 161 n. 483; vol. 6 p. 103 n. 128.

The Gospel According to John chapter 19;

resh, head; numerical value 200; the second sefirah, **H**okmah (Wisdom);
the path from the eighth sefirah, Hod (Splendour), to the ninth sefirah, Yesod (Foundation).

The path corresponding to the nineteenth chapter of the Gospel joins Hod (Splendour) and Yesod (Foundation), the eighth and ninth sefiroth on the Tree of Life.

Hod is usually translated 'Glory, Splendour or Magnificence', but also means 'Reputation, Fame, Renown'. Some of the symbolism of xix, in particular Jesus' being lifted on high beneath a sign stating his crime, relates to this aspect of the eighth sefirah. It also points to the Sun, which is the astrological attribution of the chapter, and which is connected with fame and celebrity – John delights in such polyvalent images.

The eighth commandment forbids stealing. And the planet Mercury, the planetary correspondence of Hod (Splendour), is connected with theft – Hermes counted *Pheletēs*, 'Thief', and *Archōn Pheletōn*, 'Leader of Thieves' among his cult titles. So in this chapter the crowd have to chose between Jesus and Barabbas, a notorious robber. The sefiroth on the left side of the Tree are associated with sin or crime and its negative consequences in the qabalistic tradition, which manifests in this chapter as the capital sentence passed on Jesus. When Jesus is executed, it is between two thieves ('in their midst' xix 18); elsewhere he is said to be 'counted with the criminals'.

Hod is associated with admission, acknowledgement or confession (Hebrew *vidui* or *hodaah*).[19.1] Although the word 'confess' does not appear in xix (the Greek verb is *homolegein*), Pilate's repeated admissions of Jesus' perfect faultlessness and innocence is used to convey the idea:

> And after saying this, he went out again to the Jews, and says to them, 'I find no fault in him'. xviii 38

> Pilate went out again, and says to them, 'Behold, I bring him out to you, so that you may know I find no fault in him'. xix 4 Pilate says to them, 'You take him and crucify him, for I find no fault in him'. xix 6.

Curiously, 1 Timothy vi 13, describing this episode, speaks of Jesus' having made a good confession before Pilate, not the other way around. The next chapter likewise corresponds to one of the paths leading from Hod, which there motivates Thomas' confession:

> And Thomas answered and said to him, 'My Lord and my God!'. xx 28.

One of the ninth sefirah's correspondences is truth, because the ninth commandment prohibits falsehood. In the Gospel this manifests as:

> '... For this was I born, and for this did I come into the world: to testify to the truth. Everyone who comes from the truth hears my voice'.

Pilate says to him, 'What is truth?'. xviii 37-38

... and his testimony is true, and he knows he speaks true, in order that you too may believe. xix 35.

Joseph of Arimathea and Nikodemus, who collect and inter Jesus' body (xix 38-40), represent two the sefiroth joined by the path of the letter *resh*. The former is Joseph the patriarch, the commonest personification of the ninth sefirah, while the latter is Samuel the prophet, who can personify the eighth sefirah as well as the seventh.[19.2]

Resh, the Hebrew letter assigned this chapter, means 'head'. In the Gospel, this manifests, firstly, when Jesus bows his head in xix 30, and secondly, more obviously, in the place *Golgotha*, 'Skull'. Gesenius notes that *gulgoleth* means 'a head' as well as 'a skull'.

Mysticism of the divine throne

In Exodus xxiv 10, the Israelite elders see a vision of the enthroned God of Israel, and under his feet something like a pavement or tiling or brickwork of sapphire. In one the texts found incorporated within the codex of the *Zohar*, this part of the vision is explained as a symbol of the ninth sefirah.[19.3] In the John's Gospel, the *Lithostrōtos*, 'Paved with Stone', or 'Tessellated Pavement', is therefore mentioned as the location of Jesus' trial before the governor.

John immediately adds that the Tessellated Pavement is called in Hebrew, *Gabbatha*, which means 'Elevated Place'. It is related to Hebrew words *gab*, meaning 'elevation, vault, arch, rim or felly of a wheel', *gabbatha*, 'to be high' and the cognate adjective *gabboah*, high, and noun, *gobbah*, height. *Gab* and *gobbah* occur in Ezekiel's vision, 'And their rims were so high [*gabbahen gobbah*] they were fearful, and their rims [*gabbotham*] were full of eyes ...' (Ezekiel i 18). Ezekiel i, like Exodus xxiv, was one of the few times when human beings had a vision of God on his throne. If John associates Ne<u>za</u>h with the Holy Living Creatures of Ezekiel's vision, it is likely he associates Hod with the Wheels (*'Ofanim* or *Gilgalim*) who are paired with them. Alternatively, John may have had in mind the fact that Yesod is associated with elevation or height, often because <u>Z</u>ion, the Temple Mount, which is the location of Jesus' appearance before Pilate, is a symbol of the sefirah.[19.4]

Only in the synoptics

A homonym of the Hebrew word *resh* means 'gall or wormwood or poison, possibly poppy juice'. In According to Matthew xvii 34, Jesus is offered a drink mixed with gall or wormwood immediately before crucifixion. Mark talks instead of wine mixed with myrrh, but the significance is the same: myrrh is bitter.

In the Gospel nakedness serves to signal Yesod. In xix it manifests as Jesus' nakedness on the cross. Qabalistic sources especially relate circumcision to Yesod.[19.5] The Synoptics contain indirect references to details of the rite. A widespread Jewish legend tells how God was displeased when Elijah the prophet falsely accused the Israelites of having 'forsaken the covenant', that is of having abandoned the rite of circumcision. After his translation to heaven, it was decreed Elijah should personally attend in spirit every circumcision that would ever be performed, just so that he could testify that the rite was not being neglected. To this day, a place at the table is always set aside for Elijah whenever a circumcision is performed.[19.6] His mandatory presence at the rite is known to both Matthew and Mark:

> Some of those standing by heard him and said, 'He is calling out for Elijah!'.
> One of them immediately running up, taking a sponge, soaking it in cheap wine, and putting it around a stick, offered it to him to drink.
> But others said, 'Wait! Let us see whether Elijah comes saving him!'. According to Matthew xxvii 47-49, and Mark xv 35-36 is parallel.

Placing a wine-soaked cloth in the baby's mouth, in order to relieve the pain of circumcision, remains a prevalent Jewish custom even today. In xix 29, it has become a vinegar-soaked sponge.

'Good' and 'righteous' are signal words connoting Yesod.[19.7] Joseph the patriarch, the commonest personification of the sefirah's qualities, appears in the person of Joseph of Arimathea, who is described when he approaches Pilate to collect Jesus' body for burial:

> And behold, there was a man by the name of Joseph, a member of the Sanhedrin, a man good and righteous. According to Luke xxiii 50.

In summary

In summary, Hod (Splendour) manifests as references to celebrity, crime, particularly that of theft, and the punishment it entails, and confession or acknowledgement. Yesod (Foundation) appears in references to the truth, in Jesus' nakedness on the cross, the vinegar soaked sponge, and in the word 'power'. Gabbatha and the Tessellated Pavement relate to qabalistic interpretations of Ezekiel i and x, and Numbers xxiv. Golgotha, 'Skull', suggests the letter *resh*, a head. The Synoptics record details not found in the Fourth Gospel: the bitter drink given to Jesus on the cross, the calls for Elijah, and the wine-soaked sponge placed in Jesus' mouth.

19.1: See 12.6.

19.2: See Part 1 note 3.3.

19.3: Michael Berg, *The Zohar by Simeon bar Yochai with the Sulam Commentary by Rabbi Yehuda Ashlag* vol. 2, chapter 2, Bereshit B, section 27; vol. 13, Pequde, chapter 26, section 46. Daniel C. Matt, *The Zohar: Pritzker Edition*, vol. 4 p. 367 n. 589.

19.4: *Zohar* 1:206; 2:83a, 222b; 3:65b, 66a. Daniel C. Matt, *The Zohar: Pritzker Edition*, vol. 3 p. 266 n. 45; vol. 4 p. 458 n. 331; vol. 6 p. 273 n. 31; vol. 7 p. 433 nn. 233, 234.

19.5: Daniel C. Matt, *The Zohar: Pritzker Edition*, vol. 2 pp. 74, 75 nn. 576, 577, 578; ibid pp. 103, 104 nn. 785, 795; ibid p. 404 n. 692; vol. 7 p. 82 nn. 253, 254.

19.6: *Zohar* 1:13a, 93a, 209a-b; 2:169a, 190a. Daniel C. Matt, *The Zohar: Pritzker Edition*, vol. 1 pp. 90, 91 nn. 687, 688; vol. 2 pp. 88, 89 nn. 678, 679; vol. 3 p. 284 n. 144; vol. 5 p. 484 n. 834; vol. 6 p. 73 n. 54. *Pirqe Rabbi Eliezer* chap. xxix.

19.7: *Zohar* 1:30b, 33a, 60a, 82b; 2:11b. Daniel C. Matt, *The Zohar: Pritzker Edition*, vol. 1 p. 204 n. 782; ibid p. 340 n. 4; vol. 2 pp. 24, 25 nn. 174, 176; vol. 7 p. 135 n. 416.

The Gospel According to John chapter 20;
**shin, a tooth; numerical value 300;
the third sefirah, Binah (Understanding);
the path from the eighth sefirah, Hod (Splendour),
to the tenth sefirah, Malkuth (Kingdom).**

The twentieth chapter of According to John, which describes the events surrounding Jesus' resurrection, corresponds to the path from Hod (Splendour) to Malkuth (Kingdom). The significance of the tenth sefirah in the context of resurrection is easy to understand: Malkuth refers to the material world; in a human being it is just the physical body. That the dead do not remain as vaporous beings in paradise but will ultimately obtain a type of body is a very fundamental aspect of Christian theology. In According to Luke xxiv Jesus explicitly denies being a ghost, then eats a meal in front of the disciples just to prove he is truly corporeal. This is the reason for Jesus' eating in John's Gospel, though it is not spelled out so clearly.

It also lies behind Thomas' insistence on examining the hard evidence with his own senses:

> Thomas said, 'Unless I see the imprint of the nails in his hands and put my finger in the imprint of the nails, and put my hand in his side, I shall not believe'. xx 25.
> Then he says to Thomas, 'Stretch your finger out, here are my hands. Stretch your hand out and put it into my side. And do not be an unbeliever, but a believer'.
> And Thomas answered and said to him, 'My Lord and my God!'.
> Jesus says to him, 'Thomas, have you believed because you have seen me? Happy are they who have not seen, and yet believe'. xx 27-29.

Whether the eighth sefirah is connected with the concept of resurrection, and if so, precisely how it is relevant, is less clear. Since the path extending from Ne<u>z</u>ah to Malkuth, which is denoted by the letter *quf*, has sleep as one of its associations, it is possible that the path from Hod to Malkuth, its mirror image on the Tree, came to intimate awakening, which is a metaphor for resurrection. In any case, the resurrection body is often spoken of as the body of glory in the New Testament, and the Evangelist himself talks of Jesus as having been raised to glory, and his resurrection a glorification:

> For at that time there was no Holy Spirit, because Jesus had not been glorified [*edoxasthē*]. vii 39.

> But when Jesus was glorified [*edoxasthē*] they remembered that this had been written about him... xii 16.

The commandment coordinate with Hod (Splendour), the eighth, is the prohibition against stealing. The thief, moreover, is one of the chief guises of Mercury, the planetary counterpart of Hod. In the Gospel the idea manifests in several different ways.

Since Malkuth denotes the physical frame, and Hod is associated with theft, John combines the two into a single symbolic motif: the stolen corpse. In xx, when Mary goes to the tomb while it is 'early and still dark', only to discover the tomb has already been disturbed, evidently burgled, and the body of Jesus stolen. Of course, it is the thief who is awake and on the job when everyone else is still asleep; he is the one for whom one must proverbially be ever vigilant in the New Testament. After telling the disciples that the body has been stolen, she says the same thing to the angels, and to the newly resurrected Jesus, whom she accuses of having purloined the body (xx 15):

> 'They have taken the Master from the tomb and we do not know where they placed him'. xx 2.
>
> She says to them, 'Because they have taken my master, and I do not know where they placed him'. xx 13.
>
> Thinking him to be the gardener, she says to him, 'Sir, if you carried him off, tell me where you placed him, and I shall take him'. xx 15.

It is the nature of a thief to penetrate locked doors, which manifests in the Gospel in Jesus' ability to come and go unimpeded though the disciples have cloistered themselves away:

> At evening on the same day, the first day of the week, although the doors had been shut where the disciples were gathered on account of fear of the Jews, Jesus came and stood in their midst, and says to them, 'Peace to you'. xx 19.
>
> And after eight days again his disciples were indoors, and Thomas with them. Jesus came, although the doors had

been shut, and stood in their midst, and said, 'Peace to you'. xx 26.

A garden is frequently used as a symbol of Malkuth in Qabalah.[20.1] Sometimes it is derived from 'A locked garden is my sister, my bride' (Song of Solomon iv 12). John uses the symbol in xviii since that chapter also corresponds to a path ending in Malkuth. Jesus' tomb, which is situated within a garden, is evidently partially submerged in the earth, since Peter and Mary have to stoop down to look into it (xx 5, 11). The tomb is also a symbol of Malkuth, the lowest sefirah on the Tree, which is often represented by earth, and sometimes connected with death in various ways.[20.2]

In the *Zohar*, tomb and garden occur together in a single symbol: the cave of the field of Mahpelah (Genesis xxiii 9ff), legendary burial place of Adam and Eve and the patriarchs, but also the secret entrance to the Garden of Eden, the odour of whose spices initially attracted Abraham to the place. There Adam, Abraham, Isaac and Jacob along with their respective wives are resurrected to physical life three times a day, when Elijah comes to visit them. Adam is the gardener for whom Mary mistakes Jesus (xx 15), for with resurrection Jesus has regained Adam's original unfallen form. Mahpelah is needless to say itself a symbol of Malkuth (Kingdom) in the *Zohar*. The name means 'doubled' and is said to suggest the fact that Binah and Malkuth parallel each other in many ways.[20.3]

Jesus' tomb and the garden in which it lies form the setting of the opening of pericope of xx. The first mention of these important and specific symbols of Malkuth occurs in the final verses of xix:

> Now in the neighbourhood [*en tōi topōi*] where he was crucified there was a garden, and in the garden a new tomb, in which no one had yet been placed. There they placed Jesus because of the Jewish Day of Preparation, since the tomb was close by. xix 41-42.

Although xix has no connection with Malkuth, we have seen that in the final one or two verses of a chapter, John sometimes has symbolism which is apposite to the immediately following chapter. In other cases, a future or future-equivalent provide a clue that a symbol to be considered part of the next chapter. In this instance, the garden's being 'in the vicinity or in the neighbourhood' (*en tōi topōi*) (xix 41) – the phrase is completely superfluous in the sentence – and the tomb's being 'close or nearby' (xix 42) intimate that garden and tomb are part of the network of symbolic associations of xx, rather than xix. Or perhaps John intended xx to commence at xix 41.

In qabalistic writings the Shekhinah, the personification of the tenth sefirah, is identified with the Holy Spirit, whom Jesus breathes onto the disciples in xx 22.[20.4] She often takes the form of elemental fire[20.5], and as noted, when the disciples receive the Holy Spirit in Acts ii 2-4, it descends like tongues of fire, as foretold in According to Matthew iii 11 and Luke iii 16. 'Woman' (xx 13-15) is used to denote the Lower Shekhinah, the Daughter, the *parzuf* or face of Malkuth (Kingdom). The *Zohar* plays on the fact that *'ishah* means both 'fire' and 'woman'.

The letter *shin* (300), like *gimel* (3) and *lamed* (30), may connote the third sefirah, Binah (Understanding). Qabalistic texts often relate the sefirah to the idea of turning around or turning back (Hebrew *teshuvah*). In the Gospel this manifests in this chapter in:

> On saying this, she turned around and saw Jesus standing there, but she did not know it was Jesus. xx 14.
>
> Turning around, she says to him in Hebrew, 'Rabboni', which is to say, 'Teacher'. xx 16.

Perhaps John associates Binah with resurrection, since it is a theme common to ii, xi and xx (*gimel, lamed, shin*).

The seven sefiroth from Ḥesed (Mercy) to Malkuth (Kingdom) are denoted by the seven days of the week. Binah (Understanding), immediately preceding them, is sometimes termed the 'eighth day', an aspect of the sefirah alluded to by having the initial action take place on the first day of the week, then 'eight days later' (xx 1, 19, 26). However sometimes 'the eighth day' represents Malkuth.[20.6]

Only in the synoptics

The synoptics' accounts of Jesus' entombment and the subsequent discovery of the empty sepulchre contain details missing from According to John, although they would have been perfectly at home there:

> And taking the body, he wrapped it in clean linen. And he took the body and placed it in his new tomb, which he had hewn in the rock, and after rolling a great stone across the door, he went away. According to Matthew xvii 59-60
>
> And suddenly there was a great earthquake. For an angel of the Lord having come down from heaven, went and rolled away the stone, and sat down upon it. ibid. xxviii 2

> Having purchased some linen, Joseph, after taking him down, wrapped him in linen, and placed him in the tomb, which had been hewn in the rock, and rolled a stone across the door of the tomb. According to Mark xv 46.

> And they said to one another, 'Who will roll the stone away from the door of the tomb for us?'. And looking up, they saw that the stone had already been rolled away, although it was a very large stone. ibid. xvi 3-4.

'Hewn in the rock' is a perfect description of the tenth sefirah, which is routinely symbolised by a stone or rock in the *Zohar*. The Shekhinah, who represents the tenth sefirah in the world of divinity, is said to be the stone (*galuth*) that Israel rolls along in exile (*galuth*) or appears in connection with the stone that must be rolled away to release the wellwaters so that the shepherd may water his sheep. *Galuth* means 'a large stone, one that must be rolled rather than carried'.

The motif of the stolen corpse that occurs in xx can be found also in Matthew's account of events surrounding Jesus' resurrection, but it has been reworked into a different form, with a mysterious reversal of roles – now it is the disciples rather than the authorities who are involved in making off with the body:

> The chief priests and Pharisees approached Pilate together, saying, 'Sir, we remember that while he was alive, the deceiver said, "After three days I shall rise again". Therefore command that the tomb be secured until the third day, lest his disciples, coming by night, steal him, and tell the people, "He rose from the dead". Then the final error would be worse than the first'. According to Matthew xxvii 62-64.

'Say, "His disciples came by night and stole him while we slept"'. ibid xxviii 13-15.

In summary

In summary, Malkuth (Kingdom) manifests as the tomb in which Jesus was buried, the stone rolled away from the tomb's entrance, the garden in which the tomb is located, and in the idea of bodily resurrection. The motif of the stolen corpse fuses the correspondences of Hod and Malkuth. Jesus' ability to gain entry to the disciples' hiding place despite the locked doors derives from the eighth sefirah's association with thievery.

> 20.1: Aryeh Kaplan, *The Bahir* p. 108. *Zohar* 1:7a, 32b, 35b, 82b; 2:11a; 3:43b. Daniel C. Matt, *The Zohar: Pritzker Edition*, vol. 1 p. 45 n. 311; ibid p. 186 n. 641; ibid p. 191 n. 679; ibid pp. 223, 224 n. 942, 945; ibid p. 326 n. 1601; vol. 2 p. 25 n. 177; vol. 4 p. 2 n. 5; ibid pp. 49, 50 nn. 211, 219; ibid p. 168 n. 100; vol. 7 p. 266 n. 32.
>
> 20.2: See note 18.9.
>
> 20.3: *Zohar* 1:57b, 127a-b, 128a-b, 129a, 219a, 225b, 248b; 2:39b. Daniel C. Matt, *The Zohar: Pritzker Edition* vol. 1 p. 327 n. 1603; vol. 2 p. 221 n. 141, 142; ibid pp. 224, 225 nn. 161, 163, 165; vol. 3 p. 321 n. 108; ibid p. 356 nn. 291, 293; ibid p. 525 n. 967; vol. 4 p. 190 n. 180. *Pirqe Rabbi Eliezar* xx. TB *Eiruvin* 53a.
>
> 20.4: *Zohar* 1:67b-68b, 228a; 2:140a-b, 236b, 239b, 269a. Daniel C. Matt *The Zohar: Pritzker Edition* vol. 1 p. 168 n. 483; ibid p. 378 n. 268; vol. 2 p. 42 n. 326; ibid p. 210 n. 55; vol. 3 pp. 373-374 nn. 372, 375; vol. 5 p. 288 nn. 271,

272; vol. 6 pp. 364, 365 n. 301, 302. A.E. Waite *The Holy Kabbalah* p. 362-369.

20.5: See note 18.3.

20.6: Aryeh Kaplan, *The Bahir* pp. 159, 177-178. Daniel C. Matt, *The Zohar: Pritzker Edition*, vol. 7 p. 219 n. 43; ibid p. 226 n. 63; ibid p. 231 n. 74.

The Gospel According to John chapter 21;
tau, cross or mark; numerical value 400;
the fourth sefirah, Hesed (Mercy);
the path from the ninth sefirah, Yesod (Foundation),
to the tenth sefirah, Malkuth (Kingdom).

The rock and the shepherd

The twenty-first chapter of According to John corresponds to the path from Yesod (Foundation) to Malkuth (Kingdom), which forms the lowest part of the central pillar on the Tree of sefiroth.

Malkuth, the tenth sefirah, is often symbolised by a stone or rock in the *Zohar*. It is the foundation stone of the Temple, the stone upon which Jacob rested his head at Bethel (Genesis xxviii 18), the nucleus around which the cosmos crystallised (Job xxxviii 6), the stone the builders rejected (Psalm cxviii 22), the stone hewn from the mountain without hands (Daniel ii 34, 45), the precious corner stone (Isaiah xxviii 16), the seven eyed stone (Zechariah iv 10), the rock in whose clefts Moses hid when the Divine Glory was revealed to him (Exodus xxxiii 22), the stone that Moses struck with his rod to obtain water for the Israelites in the desert (Numbers xx 11).[21.1]

David, the shepherd boy who rose to become king over Israel, is put forward in qabalistic texts as a human paradigm of the specific virtues of the tenth sefirah.[21.2] Joseph the biblical patriarch is the commonest personification of Yesod (Foundation). When explaining the relationship between Yesod and Malkuth, qabalistic texts sometimes cite Genesis xlix 24 ('thence comes the Shepherd, the Rock of Israel' or 'thence nourishes the Rock of Israel'), a verse from Joseph's blessing by his dying father.[21.3] The idea is simply that Malkuth, the tenth sefirah (David, Shepherd, Rock), comes from, or depends on Yesod, the ninth sefirah (Joseph), for its existence or ability to nourish the lower worlds. It is very likely that John has Genesis xlix 24 in mind in this chapter, for here we find Simon, alias Peter or Kephas, 'the Rock', taking on the role of Shepherd, charged with the duty of feeding the flock. In the *Zohar*, the Shekhinah, the divine *Parzuf* of the tenth sefirah is typically represented by the Community of Israel or the aggregate of the souls of the elect.[21.4] And as noted, the image of a shepherd rolling away a stone from a well in order to water his sheep occurs in the *Zohar* in connection with the tenth sefirah.[21.5] A similar thread of symbolism permeates xxi, though the Shekhinah has come to denote the Community of Christians, rather than the Jews:

> When they had eaten, Jesus says to Simon Peter, 'Simon son of Jonah, do you love me more than they do?'.
> He says to him, 'Yes, Master, you know I love you'.
> Jesus says to him, 'Feed my lambs'. A second time he says to him, 'Simon son of Jonah, do you love me?'.
> He says to him, 'Yes, Master, you know I love you'.

> Jesus says to him, 'Be shepherd to my sheep'. Then he says to him a third time, 'Simon son of Jonah, do you love me?'. Peter was saddened because he asked him a third time, 'Do you love me?', so he says to him, 'Master, you know everything: you know I love you'.
> Jesus says to him, 'Feed my sheep'. xxi 15-17.

In qabalistic texts, the Shekhinah is called the Bride. Her Bridegroom to be is the King's Son, who in the Gospel exists in the person of Jesus. In this passage the idea manifests as Jesus' repeated questioning of Peter about his love for him. It may have been suggested also by the fact that David, the human embodiment of the tenth sefirah, means 'Beloved'.

In qabalistic writings, the genitalia commonly denote Yesod (Foundation). Western, that is non-Jewish, commentators, perhaps not merely euphemistically, list a naked man among the traditional associations of the sefirah. In xxi, the symbolism manifests as Peter's nakedness in the boat.

'One place' (Hebrew *maqom*) is a technical term indicating Yesod, or sometimes Malkuth, or both together as a combined grade.[21.6] In the Gospel this appears in the form of the Greek word *homou*, 'together in one place' in xxi 2.

Burning coals (xxi 9) are a symbol of Malkuth (Kingdom), as has been noted discussed in the context of the coal-fire of xviii 18.

The Sea of Galilee (xxi 1) is below sea level, the second lowest fresh water lake on earth, certainly lower than any other body of water in the area. Since Malkuth is the lowest sefirah on the Tree, and often referred to as the sea into which all others ultimately flow, it is not surprising that in the *Zohar*, Lake Galilee (also called Lake Tiberias, Lake Genaresset or Kineret) is a symbol for Malkuth.[21.7]

Taste of the world to come

According rabbinic legend, after the dead have been resurrected and judged, history as we know it will end, and a new aeon, the World to Come, will begin. To inaugurate the new age, the elect will be hosted to a dinner whose main course will consist of Leviathan, the mythical great fish or sea-serpent, and his mate.[21.8] The monster banquet at the end of time is the inspiration for the opening scene xxi 1-12, in which the disciples go fishing in their boat and come back with full nets to enjoy a fish meal with Jesus on the sea shore.

In the *Zohar*, Leviathan appears as a symbol of Yesod.[21.9] It cites Psalm civ 26 ('There go the ships, and Leviathan, this one whom you made to play in it'), which contains two words (*sham*, 'there', and *zeh*, 'this') that qabalists construe to indicate Yesod.[21.10] Ships are symbols of Yesod or Malkuth.[21.11]

For reasons given below, it is probably relevant that the world is said to balance on one fin of Leviathan.[21.12]

In one version of the legend, only the female Leviathan will be served up.[21.13] The number of great fish drawn up in the net, one hundred and fifty-three (xxi 11), is probably derived by gematria to the word *nequba* (*nun-quf-beth-'alef* =50+100+2+1=153), which means female, pierced or perforated. It may relate to the blow hole of cetaceans which is explained in the *Zohar* by 'You broke the heads of the sea serpents upon the waters' (Psalm lxxiv 13).[21.14]

The Leviathan-feast at the end of time is a fitting motif for the Gospel's final chapter, though the World to Come or Future World usually connotes Binah (Understanding). Symbolism related to Binah appears in xxi because the astrological attribution of the chapter is Saturn, the planet cognate with Binah. In other places we have seen John the planets take on symbolism proper to the sefiroth as though interchangeable. Also, a special relationship exists between the second, fourteenth and twenty-first chapters. As we have seen, this results in symbolism proper to the Lower Shekhinah, which might be confined to xxi, being found in ii and xiv. The corollary is also true: symbolism proper to the Superior Shekhinah, which might be confined to ii, can be found in xxi.

In addition, there is an important tradition that Malkuth, the Lower Shekhinah, the Daughter or Bride, will be elevated to the level of Binah, the Mother, or Superior Shekhinah to unite with her, and this will take place or be revealed at the end of this aeon. The close relationship between Binah (Mother, Superior Shekhinah) and Malkuth (Daughter, Lower Shekhinah) seems partly inspired by the fact that the second and fourth letters of the Tetragrammaton, which qabalists associate with Binah and Malkuth respectively, are the same letter (*heh*). 'Like mother like daughter' (Ezekiel xvi 44) is cited in the *Zohar*.[21.15]

Malkuth (Kingdom) is often termed 'this world' or 'the present world', while Binah (Understanding) very frequently designated 'the World to Come' or 'Ultimate Future'. Or Binah is the Upper World, Malkuth the Lower World.[21.16] The phrase 'from world to world' is often appears in this connection.[21.17]

Binah's association in qabalistic writings with the idea of *teshuvah*, that is 'turning around or turning back', of which John is evidently aware, since he himself plays on the idea in i 38 and xx 14-16, leads in this chapter of the Gospel to:

> Turning around, Peter saw the disciple whom Jesus loved, the one who had been leaning on his chest at the supper, ... xxi 20.

Yesod, or Yesod and Malkuth considered together as a combined grade, is referred to as the Recording Book or Book of Remembrance in the *Zohar*.[21.18] This symbol explains the final verses of xx, which John may have originally intended to be the first two verses of xxi:

> And Jesus performed many other signs in the disciples' presence that are not written down in this book. But these things have been written down, so that you may believe that Jesus is the Anointed, the Son of God, and by believing you may have life through his name. xx 30-31.

And together with the fact that 'the World' is a designation for Malkuth (Kingdom), the symbolism motivates the content of the last verse of the Gospel:

> There are many other things that Jesus did, and if they were written down one by one, I think the world itself would not contain the books written. xxi 25.

In summary

In summary, the final chapter of the Gospel contains references to the tenth sefirah in the words 'book' and 'world', in the Sea of Galilee, which is the location of the story, in the charcoal fire, and in the person of Peter, 'the Rock', who is appointed to shepherd over the community of Christians. The Shekhinah, as Bride, is alluded to in Jesus' questions about Peter's love. The ninth sefirah, Yesod (Foundation), shows itself in the word *homou*, in Peter's nakedness, the disciples' boat, and the fish they catch. The opening scene of this chapter is inspired by a legend that elect the future world will feast on the great sea serpent, Leviathan, who is another symbol of the ninth sefirah.

21.1: *Zohar* 1:71b, 72a-b, 146b, 151a, 231a-b; 2:184b, 222a-b, 229b, 230a, 232b. Daniel C. Matt, *The Zohar: Pritzker Edition*, vol. 1 p. 423 n. 619; ibid p. 426 n. 641; vol. 2 p. 34 nn. 259, 262, 263; ibid pp. 72-73 nn. 558-563; ibid p. 318 nn. 440, 442; ibid p. 338 nn. 147, 152; ibid p. 342 nn. 178, 179, 182, 183; vol. 3 p. 48 n. 349; ibid pp. 396-397 nn. 470-472; vol. 4 p. 14 n. 58; vol. 6 p. 36 n. 89; ibid p. 339 n. 227. Louis Ginzberg, *Legends of the Jews* chap. vi.

21.2: *Zohar* 3:21a, 23b. Daniel C. Matt, *The Zohar: Pritzker Edition* vol. 4 p. 113 n. 161; vol. 6 p. 262 n. 9; vol. 7 p. 135 n. 415; ibid p. 148 n. 456; ibid p. 189 n. 71; ibid p. 349 n. 64.

21.3: Aryeh Kaplan, *The Bahir* para. 193. *Zohar* 1:146b, 231b, 247a; 2:230a. Daniel C. Matt, *The Zohar: Pritzker Edition* vol. 3 p. 270 n. 67; ibid p. 397 n. 472; p. 399 n. 483; ibid p. 510 n. 918; ibid p. 516 n. 933; vol. 6 p. 320 n. 167.

21.4: Daniel C. Matt, *The Zohar: Pritzker Edition* vol. 1 p. 1 n. 2; ibid p. 33 n. 230; ibid p. 219 n. 917; vol. 3 p. 21 n. 147; ibid p. 169 n. 528; ibid p. 276 n. 99; ibid p. 454 n. 716; vol. 7 p. 3 nn. 5, 6.

21.5: *Zohar* 1:152a; 2:13a, 230a; 3:62a, 270a. Daniel C. Matt, *The Zohar: Pritzker Edition* vol. 2 p. 347 nn. 219, 224; vol. 4 p. 63 n. 281; vol. 6 p. 320 n. 168; vol. 7 pp. 406, 407 nn. 146-150.

21.6: *Zohar* 1:12a, 18a-b, 33a, 147a, 148a-b, 150b; 2:28b, 207a. Daniel C. Matt, *The Zohar: Pritzker Edition* vol. 1 p. 83 n. 625; ibid p. 141 nn. 260, 263; ibid p. 203 n. 775; ibid p. 272 n. 1273; vol. 2 p. 320 n. 5; ibid p. 323 n. 24; ibid p. 338 nn.

142-145; vol. 3 p. 399 n. 485; vol. 4 p. 112 n. 157; vol. 6 p. 180 nn. 214, 216, 217. *Bereshith Rabbah* lxviii 9. *Pirqe de Rabbi Eliezer* xxxv.

21.7: *Zohar* 2:23a, 149b. Daniel C. Matt, *The Zohar: Pritzker Edition*, vol. 4 pp. 76-77 nn. 24, 25; ibid p. 236 n. 137; vol. 5 p. 369 nn. 507, 508; vol. 6 p. 298 n. 104.

21.8: TB *Baba Bathra* 74b-75a. *Leviticus Rabbah* xiii 3; ibid xxii 10. *Pirqe Rabbi Eliezer* x. Louis Ginzberg, *Legends of the Jews* chap. i. Daniel C. Matt, *The Zohar: Pritzker Edition*, vol. 7 p. 293 n. 119.

21.9: *Zohar* 1:13a; 2:11b, 48b, 50b; 3:58a. Daniel C. Matt, *The Zohar: Pritzker Edition*, vol. 1 p. 91 n. 688; vol. 3 p. 514 n. 927; vol. 4 p. 54 n. 238; ibid p. 235 n. 133; vol. 7 p. 373 n. 50.

21.10: Aryeh Kaplan, *The Bahir*, para. 193. *Zohar* 2:70b. Daniel C. Matt, *The Zohar: Pritzker Edition*, vol. 2 p. 93 nn. 707, 709, 710; vol. 4 p. 235 n. 133; ibid p. 251 n. 194; ibid p. 390 n. 71.

21.11: *Zohar* 1:124a; 2:48b, 50b, 56a. Daniel C. Matt, *The Zohar: Pritzker Edition*, vol. 1 p. 214 n. 867; ibid p. 249 n. 1109; vol 2 p. 211 n. 62; vol. 4 pp. 234, 235 nn. 131, 132; ibid p. 249 n. 186; ibid p. 293 n. 337.

21.12: *Zohar* 2:34b, 108b. Daniel C. Matt, *The Zohar: Pritzker Edition*, vol. 1 p. 183 n. 614; vol. 4 p. 153 n. 53; vol. 5 p. 107 n. 306. *Pirqe Rabbi Eliezer* ix.

21.13: TB *Baba Bathra* 74b. Daniel C. Matt, *The Zohar: Pritzker Edition* vol. 1 p. 213 n. 863; ibid p. 251 n. 1128; vol. 4 pp. 150-151 n. 45.

21.14: Daniel C. Matt, *The Zohar: Pritzker Edition* vol. 4 p. 152 n. 51; vol. 6 p. 358 n. 282.

21.15: *Zohar* 1:2a, 10b, 50a-b, 173b, 183b; 2:126b. Daniel C. Matt, *The Zohar: Pritzker Edition* vol. 1 p. 9 n. 64; ibid p. 10 n. 70; ibid p. 68 nn. 512, 513, 516; ibid p. 98 n. 737; ibid pp. 264, 265 nn. 1222-4; ibid p. 282 n. 1340; vol. 3 p. 48 n. 349; ibid p. 120 n. 226; vol. 5 p. 186 n. 7.

21.16: *Zohar* 1:1b, 2b, 3b, 37a; 2:185a. Daniel C. Matt, *The Zohar: Pritzker Edition* vol. 1 p. 3 n. 17; ibid p. 4 n. 19; ibid p. 10 n. 70; ibid p. 11 n. 75; ibid p. 16 n. 111; ibid p. 176 nn. 554, 555; ibid pp. 234-235 nn. 1023, 1028; vol. 2 p. 377 n. 465; vol. 7 p. 135 n. 415.

21.17: Gershom Scholem, *Origins of the Kabbalah* p. 219. *Zohar* 1:34a, 153b, 158b, 210a, 248b; 2:22a, 53b, 144a; 3:145b. Daniel C. Matt, *The Zohar: Pritzker Edition* vol. 1 p. 210 nn. 837, 839; vol. 2 p. 356 nn. 297, 298; ibid pp. 381, 382 nn. 499-502; vol. 3 p. 289 n. 170; ibid p. 528 n. 978; vol. 4 p. 71 n. 6; ibid p. 274 n. 263; vol. 5 p. 316 n 355.

21.18: *Zohar* 1:8a-b, 37b; 2:70a, 200a. Daniel C. Matt, *The Zohar: Pritzker Edition* vol. 1 p. 53 n. 373; ibid p. 236 n. 1033; vol. 4 p. 390 n. 71; vol. 6 p. 140 n. 94.

Part 3:
Genesis and John's Gospel

T he Gospel According to John is not the only book of its kind within the Christian canon of scripture. The First Letter from John was composed by someone within John's circle who was familiar with the scheme of correspondences that underpins John's Gospel. While differing from John's Gospel in that it deals with the astrological and qabalistic attributions of only a handful of letters rather than those of the whole alphabet, it is nevertheless useful in confirming some tentative ideas about Johannine symbolism. Also written by someone within the same circle, the Revelation of John, while promising much at first sight because of the wealth of evocative symbolic imagery it contains, is ultimately not greatly helpful in unravelling John's Gospel. On the other hand, the Synoptic Gospels, as we have noted, contain a score of details which are the product of John's conceptual framework, many of which are not even to be found in John's Gospel.

It remains possible to talk about According to John without touching upon any of these books, since John's Gospel sheds far more light on them than they shed on it. Nor is there any reason to believe John was directly influenced by the content of these works. One book exists within the Bible, however, deserves special attention when thinking about the Fourth Gospel, namely the book of Genesis. Its significance to the Evangelist consists in the fact that he regards it, or one section of it at least, as something very akin to his own composition. That is to say, John understands Genesis vi to xix to contain a series of coded references to the very same system

TABLE 1: Genesis vi to xix and its relationship to According to John

letter	chapter of According to John	Section of Genesis	subject matter
mem	xii	Genesis vi 13 to vii 20	Noah builds the Ark
nun	xiii	Genesis vii 21 to viii 14	Deluge and extinction of terrestrial life
samekh	xiv	Genesis viii 15 to ix 19	covenant with Noah; Noahide Law
'ayin	xv	Genesis ix 20 to x 32	Noah's vine; Ham's curse; Nimrod
peh	xvi	Genesis xi 1 to xiv 24	Tower of Babel; Abram at war
zaddi	xvii	Genesis xv 1 to xv 8	Abram's promise of descendants
quf	xviii	Genesis xv 9 to xvi 16	Abram's sleep and horror of darkness
resh	xix	Genesis xvii 1 to xvii 27	circumcision of Abraham
shin	xx	Genesis xviii 1 to xix 28	incineration of Sodom and Gomorrah

of attributions upon which his Gospel is based. And he in turn weaves allusions to this section of Genesis into the Gospel.

It is difficult to define where each section in Genesis begins and ends. Only nine chapters of the Gospel, namely xii to xx, are involved. A rough outline to the scheme is set out in table.

While the Hebrew text of Genesis supplies most of the material John takes for granted, many pertinent details are found only in apocryphal legends that amplify stories in the Old Testament. Though not set down in writing until fairly late, many of these do undoubtedly reflect ancient traditions. The *Book of Jubilees*, a retelling of the history of the world from creation to the giving of the Law on Sinai, was composed in the 2nd century BCE. The Babylonian Talmud was set down between the end of 2nd century to the middle of the 6th century. While primarily concerned with legal interpretations of the Pentateuch relevant to conduct, its peripatetic style leads it to expound and enlarge upon many events told in Genesis. The *Midrash Rabbah*, a homiletic discourse covering ten books of the Old Testament, was written between the 6th and 12th centuries; the part dealing with Genesis was written in the 6th century. The *Targum PseudoJonathan*, an Aramaic paraphrase of sections of the Pentateuch, shows additions dating from the end of the 7th century. *Pirqe Rabbi Eliezer* did not exist in its present form before the 8th century. Apart from *Jubilees*, the author of the *Zohar* is well acquainted with all these works and freely borrows from them. Many of the relevant stories are to be found in Ginzberg's *The Legends of the Jews*.[intro.1]

As far as I am aware, John's insight into this section of Genesis is unique. Although *Sefer Yezirah* was intimated to be part of a larger tradition called *Ma'seh Bereshith* (*Work of Genesis* or *Business of Genesis*), and although qabalists certainly made an intensive study of the early chapters of Genesis, one will not find anything remotely like John's interpretation of this passage in the literature. One reason for this is the fact that the precise scheme of correspondences John employs seems never to have been widely adopted. John's assignment of the seven double letters to the seven planets is not followed by the common versions of *Sefer Yezirah*. The assignment of letters to paths on the Tree of Life that John operates with, though known to Kircher, is of uncertain provenance, and also seems to have been unknown among Jewish qabalists. Since the complete scheme of attributions of the Hebrew letters that underpins John's Gospel was never familiar to Jewish qabalists, it is not surprising that John's ideas about Genesis are without precedent in their writings.

Whether these allusions are actually present in the text of Genesis is a difficult matter, but fortunately it suffices for our immediate purposes to know why John may have believed them to be there, and how he adapted the material for his own ends. However, if John is correct, there are profound implications for the history of certain ideas. For one thing, John assumes that the author of Genesis possesses astrological knowledge that appears quite anachronistic – the connection between Scorpio (or the eighth house) and death, Sagittarius (or the ninth house) and laws and legal codes, Capricorn (or the tenth house) and governmental authority and rulers, Aquarius (or the eleventh house) and hopes and wishes, Pisces (or the twelfth house) and sleep, anxieties and fears, captivity – none of these associations should have existed at the time Genesis was written, even allowing the latest possible date for the composition of Genesis and the earliest possible date for the emergence of horoscopic astrology.

intro.1: Louis Ginzberg, *The Legends of the Jews* (translated by Henrietta Szold).

The Gospel According to John chapter 12;

mem, **water; 40
(or 600 when final); the fourth sefirah, Ḥesed (Mercy);
the path from the fifth sefirah, Gevurah (Strength),
to the eighth sefirah, Hod (Glory);
Water;
Genesis vi 13 to vii 20: Noah builds the Ark.**

The sixth and first half of the seventh chapters of Genesis describe events leading up to the Deluge of Noah, including the construction of the Ark. The immediate question to answer is why John may have imagined that the various correspondences relevant to the letter *mem* appear in this passage of Genesis.

First, the original signification of *mem* is water, and water is also the attribution of *mem* in *Sefer Yeẓirah*, while the Deluge is directly concerned with water's power of destruction.

Second, the letter *mem* serves as a numeral to represent either forty or six hundred, taking the former value in the middle of a word, and the latter when falling in final position. Both numbers appear explicitly in the text, forty being the number of days the rains fell (Genesis vii 4, 17), while six hundred is Noah's age in years when he entered the ark (Genesis vii 6, 11).

Lastly, the Hebrew text of Genesis vii 18-19 points to the fifth sefirah with the repetition of the verb *gabar* ('prevail, overpower'), which is cognate with *geburah*, and of the word *ma'ad* ('very, exceedingly'), which is one of the *Zohar*'s shadow terms connected with Geburah (Strength), and with the Angel of Death in particular.[12.1] 'The end of all flesh' (Genesis vi 13) is a common designation of the Angel of Death who derives from Gevurah.[12.2]

The next matter to consider is how references to this passage appear in the Gospel.

First, it is significant John has chosen to connect xii with the Feast of Tabernacles, whose liturgy is largely concerned with the beneficial power of rain, although rain on the holiday itself was inauspicious.[12.3] The Talmud calls Tabernacles the time when the world is judged with respect to or through rain.[12.4] The anniversary of the beginning of the Deluge, the first rain ever to fall on the earth, falls in the next month, Marḥeshvan, which commences only about a week after Tabernacles ends. References to Noah are entirely missing from the liturgy, for the Deluge was an expression of divine wrath, while Tabernacles' prayers are for 'rains of blessing'. Tabernacles is the most joyous of all holidays, and commemoration of the Deluge would hardly be in keeping with its mood. Nevertheless, the fact that the major themes of Tabernacles are water and rain make it harmonious with events related in Genesis vi and vii.

Second, in the Gospel, Jesus likens himself to the ark, borne up by the waters of the Flood in 'When I am lifted up from the earth...' (xii 32), which is an echo of, 'and the waters lifted up the ark above the earth' (Genesis vii 17). John uses the same verb, *hupsoein* ('to lift up'), that appears in the Septuagint in this passage. 'I shall gather all men to me' (xii 32) may refer to the detail recorded in the *Targum PseudoJonathan* and *Book of Jasher* that when the rains began to fall all the doomed people on earth crowded around the Ark begging to enter.

Third, Judas, Jesus' foil in this chapter, is said to be in charge of the money chest, *glōssokomon* (xii 6). The Greek word literally means 'tongue-box'. According to the lexicon, the temple musicians kept the reed tongues of their wind instruments within the wooden box whose rigid walls protected them from injury in a way that a soft leather bag could not.

In the Septuagint, *glōssokomon* appears in place of the Hebrew *'aron* (2 Chronicles xxiv 8-11), the same Hebrew word that is used for the Ark of the Covenant, and later also for the Ark of the Torah, both important symbols in Tabernacles. For the Ark of Noah and Moses' ark of bulrushes, and initially for the Torah Ark, the Hebrew term was *tebet* ('coffin, chest'); the Greek equivalent is *kibōtos*. However, since the measurements of Noah's Ark given in Genesis (three hundred by thirty by fifty cubits) can be taken to be related by gematria to the Hebrew word for 'tongue', *lashon* (*lamed* = 30, *shin* = 300, *nun* = 50), Noah's Ark was figuratively a type of *glōssokomon* or 'tongue-box' by virtue of its dimensions.

It must be suspected John also intends *glōssokomon* to intimate the form of the letter *mem*: a square or box with a small tongue projecting from the top left corner.

It is interesting to note that in *Sefer Yezirah*, the three mother letters are compared to a set of scales: one letter is a pan of credit or merit, one letter is a pan of blame or guilt, and one letter is the tongue (*lashon*) or pointer of the balance that inclines one way or the other in order to indicate the outcome. Since *'alef* falls at the beginning of the alphabet, *shin* near the end, and *mem* near the middle, it may be that John considered *mem* to be the tongue of the balance. *Glōssokomon* would then be explicable in terms of this idea. A problem with this explanation is that commentators are unanimous that *mem* is the pan of credit, *shin* the pan of blame, and *'alef* is the pointer or tongue. Nor is it is hard to understand why: fire (*shin*) and water (*mem*) are archetypal opposites; one is hot and dry, and its nature is to ascend, the other is cold and moist, and its nature is to fall. Air (*'alef*) is neutral, so to speak. *Sefer Yezirah* itself leads to this interpretation. Nonetheless, it remains possible that John, who is quite original in many respects, had his own ideas on the matter, and was influenced by the fact that *mem* falls in near the middle of the alphabet.

Rabbinic writings read Genesis vi 16 after the fashion of *Targum PseudoJonathan*, 'you shall make a light [*zohar*] for the Ark', taking it that Noah should take a shining jewel and suspend it from the Ark's ceiling to illuminate everything within.[12.5] This idea may have contributed to Jesus' mention of light in xii 46.

This in summary is how John may have perceived the correspondences to the letter *mem* in Genesis vi-vii, and how he alludes to the passage in xii.

> 12.1: *Zohar* 1:14a, 47a, 144b; 2:68b, 98a, 103a; 2:149b, 150a, 163a. Daniel C. Matt, *The Zohar: Pritzker Edition*, vol. 1 p. 100 n. 748; ibid p. 254 n. 1147; vol. 2 p. 307 n. 354; vol. 4 p. 380 n. 38; vol. 5 p. 27 n. 77; ibid p. 60 n. 175; ibid p. 372 n. 516. *Genesis Rabbah* ix 10ff.

12.2: *Zohar* 1:58a, 62b, 63a, 64b, 65a-b, 152b, 153a; 2:33a-b, 134a-b. Daniel C. Matt, *The Zohar: Pritzker Edition* vol. 1 ibid p. 329 n. 1622; ibid pp. 363, 364 nn. 160, 162, 164, 165; vol. 2 p. 351 nn. 253, 254; vol. 4 p. 142 n. 18; vol. 5 p. 244 n. 150.

12.3: TB *Sukkah* 28b.

12.4: TB *Ta'anith* 2a. TB *Rosh ha Shanah* 16a.

12.5: *Pirke Rabbi Eliezer* chapter xxiii. *Genesis Rabbah* xxxi 11. TB *Sanhedrin* 108b.

The Gospel According to John chapter 13;

nun, fish; 50 (or 700 when final);
the fifth sefirah Gevurah (Might);
the path from the sixth sefirah, Tif'areth (Beauty),
to the seventh sefirah, Ne<u>z</u>a<u>h</u> (Victory);
Scorpio (and the eighth house);
the eighth month, Mar<u>h</u>eshvan;
Genesis vii 21 to viii 14: Deluge and extinction
of terrestrial life.

The thirteenth chapter of According to John is assigned the sign Scorpio, and the eighth house of the horoscope. Among other things, this sector of the sky rules over death, and all matters connected with it. In the Gospel this manifests partly in the figure of Judas, the son of Iscariot, that is to say the Assassin's son. The section of Genesis relevant to xiii extends from about Genesis vii 21-viii 14. It begins:

> And all flesh moving upon the earth died: the birds, cattle, beasts, every creeping thing that creeps on the earth, and every man. Everything on dry land in whose nostrils was the

spirit of the breath of life died. Every living thing was wiped off the face of the earth, from man to cattle, creeping things and the birds of heaven ... Genesis vii 21-23.

The waters of the Flood are, the *Zohar* says, the form that the Angel of Death, 'End of All Flesh', assumes when he manifests physically.[13.1] The Angel of Death, or Samael, appears in the Gospel as the Devil who enters Judas' heart in xiii 1, for, as noted, the Devil is an alterego of the Angel of Death.

Marḥeshvan, the month to which *Sefer Yeẓirah* assigns to the letter *nun*, is particularly associated with the Deluge story: Noah entered the Ark on the 17th of the month, and emerged on the 27th of the month the following year (Genesis vii 11-13 and viii 14).

In the Gospel, the Deluge has been transformed into Jesus' washing of the disciples' feet (xiii 5-12).

13.1: *Zohar* 1:63a, 65b; 2:227a. Daniel C. Matt, *The Zohar: Pritzker Edition*, vol. 1 p. 366 n. 176; vol. 6 p. 303 n. 119.

13.2: A Jewish (lunar) year of twelve months is 354 days, about ten days short of a full solar year. Noah is in the Ark for a lunar year plus ten days, that is a full solar year.

The Gospel According to John chapter 14;

samekh, a prop; numerical value 60;
the sixth sefirah, Tif'areth (Beauty);
the path from the sixth sefirah,
Tif'areth (Beauty), to the ninth sefirah,
Yesod (Foundation);
Sagittarius (and the ninth house);
the ninth month, Kislev;
Genesis viii 15 to ix 19: the rainbow as a token of the covenant with Noah, Noahide Code of Law.

The portion of the Genesis narrative related to the letter *samekh*, and thus to xiv, is Genesis viii 22-ix 17.

Since Noah emerges from the ark on the twenty-seventh day of Marḥeshvan, a month of twenty-nine or thirty days, it is reasonable to infer the events of this passage to have taken place early in the next month, Kislev, which is the calendar assignment of the letter *samekh*, and corresponds to the sun's passage through Sagittarius in the zodiac.

The rainbow is given as the specific token of the covenant between God and man (Genesis ix 13, 14, 16). Since the Hebrew word for 'rainbow', *qesheth*, also means 'bowman' or 'archer', and is the normal Hebrew name for Sagittarius, 'When I see my bow in the clouds' (Genesis ix 16) can be read as 'When I see my Archer in the clouds' or even 'When I see my Sagittarius in the clouds'. The bow also symbolises Yesod.[14.1]

A sign or token, which is repeatedly mentioned in this passage (Genesis ix 12, 13, 17), is also a symbol of Yesod.[14.2] A covenant is another (Genesis ix 9, 11, 12, 13, 15, 16, 17).[14.3] 'Were it not for my covenant [with] day and night, it is as though I had not made ordinances for heaven and earth' (Jeremiah xxxiii 25), to which the *Zohar* often appeals in order to suggest a relationship between the Torah and the ninth sefirah, recalls:

> 'As long as there is an earth, seed-time and harvest, cold and hot, summer and winter, day and night shall not cease'. Genesis viii 22.

Another important feature of this passage is that it contains the Laws of Noah (Genesis ix 4ff.). This conforms to the astrological attribution, since the ninth mansion of the heavens rules over ethics and morality including their codification as laws of the land. The Laws of Noah are sometimes compared to the Torah, as though they constitute, so to speak, a sort of Torah for Gentiles.[14.4] The Fourth Gospel mirrors aspects of this passage with the multiple allusions to the Torah, which has its own associations with Tif'areth and Yesod, as explained.

14.1: *Zohar* 1:57b, 71b, 247a; 2:66b. Daniel C. Matt, *The Zohar: Pritzker Edition*, vol. 1 p. 4 n. 22; ibid p. 139 n. 245; ibid p. 328 n. 1610; ibid p. 422 n. 610; vol. 3 p. 330 n. 163; ibid p. 515 n. 930; vol. 4 p. 365 n. 584. Aryeh Kaplan, *The Bahir* p. 117. *Genesis Rabbah* lxxxvii 7. TB *Sotah* 36b.

14.2: *Zohar* 1:47b, 72b, 94a, 222b; 2:66b. Daniel C. Matt, *The Zohar: Pritzker Edition*, vol. 1 p. 91 nn. 690, 691; ibid p. 259 n. 1185; ibid p. 428 n. 654, 655; vol. 2 p. 95 nn. 724, 725, 726; vol. 4 p. 363 n. 580.

14.3: *Zohar* 1:32a-b, 59b, 89a, 91b, 96b. Daniel C. Matt, *The Zohar: Pritzker Edition*, vol. 1 p. 91 n. 690; ibid p. 196 nn. 718, 719, 720; ibid pp. 339-341 nn. 3, 4 10, 12, 17; vol. 2 p. 53 n. 406; ibid p. 66 nn. 514, 515, 516; ibid pp. 74, 75 nn. 576, 577, 578; ibid p. 113 n. 872.

14.4: *Zohar* 1:71b. Daniel C. Matt, *The Zohar: Pritzker Edition*, vol. 1 p. 420 n. 591.

The Gospel According to John chapter 15;

'*ayin*, an eye; numerical value 70;
the seventh sefirah, Ne<u>z</u>a<u>h</u> (Victory);
the path from the sixth sefirah, Tif'areth (Beauty),
to the eighth sefirah, Hod (Glory);
Capricorn and the tenth house;
the tenth month, Tevet;
Genesis ix 20 to x 32: Noah plants a vine;
curse of slavery falls on Ham;
Nimrod the tyrant.

The gardener and his vine

The portion of the Genesis narrative related to the letter '*ayin*, and thus to xv, is Genesis ix 20-x 32. The first section in this passage relates how Noah began to till the soil and planted a vineyard, pressed the grapes, and became intoxicated on wine. As he lay drunk and uncovered in his tent, his youngest son Ham saw him, and informed his brothers, Shem and Japheth. They promptly came in, walking backwards with averted faces so as not to look upon the shameful spectacle, and respectfully covered him up. Afterwards, guessing what had happened, Noah decided to curse Ham for having maliciously reported his shameful behaviour. Since Noah knew better than to wish evil upon someone whom God had already blessed, he cursed Ham's son, Canaan, rather than Ham himself. The malediction was one of perpetual slavery.

In the Gospel, Noah's vine-planting is transformed into Jesus' identification with the Vine (xv 1ff). The Septuagint describes Noah as a *geōrgos* (gardener), the same word Jesus uses in xv 2. The numerical value of the Hebrew word for wine (*yayin*) is seventy, as qabalistic texts sometimes note, relating it to the seventy faces of the Torah, or seventy languages of the gentile nations.[15.1]

The servitude with which Ham's descendants were cursed for all generations is alluded to in:

> 'From now on I do not call you slaves, for a slave does not know what his master does'. xv 15

> 'Remember the saying that I told you, "The slave is not greater than his master"'. xv 20.

Nimrod

The latter portion of this passage in Genesis relates the story of Nimrod, the first man on earth to become a tyrant, the prototype of human despots. In the *Zohar* Nimrod is said to style himself Ruler of the World.[15.2] He embodies Capricorn's autocratic or dictatorial tendencies and the tenth house's association with powers of government control and people in authority. This is what qualifies him to be the earthly counterpart of the Devil, the Ruler of the World (*archōn tou kosmou*), whose imminent coming is announced at the close of xiv.

Like Esau, Nimrod is renowned for his hunting prowess, and for his employment of snares and traps. In fact, Nimrod and Esau are often compared or linked to each other in rabbinic and qabalistic literature. Sometimes it is explained that Nimrod was in possession of the skins that God gave Adam (Genesis iii 21), which gave their wearer extraordinary powers. They were made from the skin of the serpent that tempted Eve, which had been killed and skinned at God's order, or which had shed its skin as serpents do. These garments gave their owner not only a praeternatural skill in hunting animals, but also the ability to ensnare and enslave people.[15.3]

The Book of Jasher relates how they passed from Adam to Enoch, to Methuselah, to Noah.[15.4] Ham stole them from Noah, and gave them to his son Cush, who passed them to Nimrod. But Esau murdered Nimrod, and robbed him of these garments, which granted him the same irresistible skill in hunting man and beast. They are the same hides Jacob borrowed in order to deceive Isaac into thinking he was Esau. Esau is said to have the Devil as his angelic guardian; if this is not explicitly said of Nimrod, his wickedness and the meaning of his name, 'rebel', imply as much.[15.5] Both Nimrod and Esau are known for being proponents of idolatry.[15.6]

An apocryphal legend tells how Abram smashes the idols belonging to Terah, his father, who drags him before Nimrod for suitable punishment.[15.7] Unable to entice Abram into idolatrous worship of fire, Nimrod catapults him into a blazing furnace, but he emerges completely unharmed. However, Abram's faithless brother, Haran, is immediately burned up when Nimrod throws him into the flames. This is the source of:

> 'If someone does not remain in me, he is cast off as a branch, and is withered, and they gather them up, and throw them into the fire, and they are burned.' xv 6.

And of:

> I have told you these things lest you be ensnared. They will expel you from the synagogue. The time will come when whoever kills you will think he is offering worship to God.
> xvi 1-2

which also refers to Nimrod's characteristic method of hunting. Like Esau, Nimrod is able to personify the correspondences of both xv and xvi.

A world of enemies

This section of Genesis ends with an enumeration of the seventy (the numerical value of *'ayin*) ethnic groups of the Gentiles.[15.8] It is a common theme of rabbinic literature that the seventy nations which encompass Israel are all inimical to it. In the Gospel this translates into the hatred of the world towards Christians, the closing theme of xv.

This in summary is how John would have perceived the correspondences to the letter *'ayin* in *Genesis* ix-x, and how they appear in the Gospel.

> 15.1: *Numbers Rabbah* xiii 16. Daniel C. Matt, *The Zohar: Pritzker Edition* vol. 1 p. 25 n. 174; ibid p. 257 n. 1167; ibid p. 301 n. 1458; vol. 7 p. 26 n. 81.
>
> 15.2: *Zohar* 1:73b, 74a.
>
> 15.3: *Genesis Rabbah* xxxvii 2-3, lxiii 13, lxv 16. *Targum PseudoJonathan* Genesis xxv 27, xxvii 15.
>
> *Pirqe Rab Eliezer* xxiv. *Zohar* 1:137b, 139a, 142b; 2:39a. Daniel C. Matt, *The Zohar: Pritzker Edition* vol. 1 p. 437 n.

724; vol. 2 p. 268 n. 79; ibid p. 292 n. 253; vol. 4 pp. 188-190 nn. 173, 176-179; vol. 6 p. 189 n. 238.

15.4: *The Book of Jasher*, chap. vii 24-30.

15.5: TB *Pesaḥim* 94b; TB *Ḥagigah* 13a; TB *Ḥullin* 89a; TB *Eiruvin* 53a. *Genesis Rabbah* xliv 2. Daniel C. Matt, *The Zohar: Pritzker Edition* vol. 2 p. 12 n. 83.

15.6: *Genesis Rabbah* lxiii 6, 10; *Exodus Rabbah* xlii 7. *Zohar* 1:139a.

15.7: *Genesis Rabbah* xxxviii 13, xxxix 3, xliv 7, xlix 11. *Song of Songs Rabbah* viii 10. TB *Avodah Zara* 3a. TB *Pesaḥim* 118a. *Book of Jasher* chaps. xi, xii. Louis Ginzberg *Legends of the Jews* chap v. Daniel C. Matt, *The Zohar: Pritzker Edition* vol. 2 p. 5 n. 34.

15.8: *Targum PseudoJonathan* Genesis xi 8ff. *Pirqe Rabbi Eliezer* chaps. xxiv, xxx. *Book of Jasher* ix 32; ibid xlviii 45-47. Daniel C. Matt, *The Zohar: Pritzker Edition* vol. 1 p. 67 n. 502; ibid p. 251 n. 1129; vol. 3 p. 48 n. 350; vol. 6 p. 40 n. 104; ibid p. 156 n. 142.

The Gospel According to John chapter 16;

peh, mouth; numerical value 80
(or 800 when final); the eighth sefirah, Hod (Glory);
the path from the seventh sefirah, Ne<u>z</u>ah (Victory),
to the eighth sefirah, Hod (Glory);
Mars;
Genesis xi 1 to xiv 24: building of the Tower of Babel, and the confusion of tongues; Abram's war.

Heaven and earth at war

The portion of the Genesis narrative related to the letter *peh* tells of the construction of the Tower of Babel, the confusion of tongues, and subsequent dispersion of humanity over the face of the earth. The section ends with Abram's embroilment in the war between the kings of Siddim Valley after his kinsman, Lot, is taken hostage, in Genesis xiv. Abram's participation in the war, the first war recorded in the Bible, is the passage's most obvious nod to the nature of Mars, the planet of battle and strife, the astrological correspondence of the letter *peh*.

Of equal relevance are the fascinating aggadic legends of the Tower of Babel that vividly portray a war between heaven and earth, where the builders want to cleave the firmament open with axes and take heaven by main force.¹⁶·¹ The reasons for their brazen and violent attack are variously given. Josephus says Nimrod wanted to avenge the deaths of his ancestors in the flood.¹⁶·² In the Midrash it is said that the people of the Babel were peeved at having been relegated to the terrestrial world, while the angels enjoyed the freedom of the heavenly spheres.¹⁶·³ In *Targum PeudoJonathan* it is said that they feared God would scatter them over the earth. Both *Genesis Rabbah* and the *Targum* state that the people placed at the very summit of the Tower an idolatrous image holding a sword in its hand to signify that they were openly engaged in battle with the celestials. According to the *Book of Jasher*, when the builders launched arrows into the sky, the angels let them fall back to earth covered in blood just to encourage them in their folly.

The *Targum PeudoJonathan* and *Book of Jasher* add that when God confused the language of the builders so that they could not understand one another, quarrels immediately broke out. These escalated into a general slaughter. The construction of the Tower of Babel was abandoned because the builders killed one another off until too few remained for the job.

Above and below are among the primary symbols of Nezah (Victory) and Hod (Glory), which are complementary in nature.¹⁶·⁴ War between heaven and earth therefore conforms to the path joining these sefiroth.

One legendary gloss records that women engaged in building of the Tower of Babel were forced to lay bricks throughout pregnancy, stopping only long enough to give birth, after which they summarily resumed work.¹⁶·⁵ This may have inspired:

> 'When she is giving birth, a woman feels sorrow because her time has come, but after giving birth, she no longer

remembers her distress, because of her happiness that a human being has come into the world.' xvi 21.

Language

Aggadic legends about Nimrod's Tower say its builders spoke Hebrew. The confusion of tongues was necessary to prevent them gaining control over the angels, who understand only Hebrew, and are thoroughly baffled even by Aramaic, which is closely related. God had to teach Hebrew to Abraham, since the language had been forgotten after Babel. Several things suggest that the construction of the edifice involved operating with a magical language, and in particular that 'let us make a name for ourselves' intimates that the builders of the tower were manipulating divine names to attain their ends.[16.6]

Robert Graves records a tradition in an Irish legend, *In the Hearings of the Scholars*, where the construction of the Tower of Babel is said to be 'linguistic researches' undertaken by one Fenuisa Farsa, whose name Graves interprets as a corruption of *Foeneus ho Farsas*, 'The-Vine-Man-Who-Binds'.[16.7] The various materials of which the Tower was built (clay, water, lime, bitumen ...) are just the various parts of speech (noun, pronoun, adjective, verb ...).

If we compare Genesis xi and According to John side by side, several parallels may be seen. In Genesis, on one hand,

> 'Let us make a name for ourselves...' Genesis xi 4

> 'One people, and one language for them all. This is how they begin to act. Soon nothing which their imagination conceives of doing will be impossible for them.' Genesis xi 6.

and in the Gospel, on the other:

> 'Amen, amen, I tell you: if you ask the Father for anything in my name, he will give it to you.' xvi 23

> 'In that day you will ask the Father in my name...' xvi 26.

The implicit comparison is not hard to see: the attempt to storm heaven by those who literally 'make a name' for themselves is contrasted with praying in Jesus' name. The builders of the Tower were are on the verge of getting all their imagination conceives, while those who pray in Jesus' name actually do get anything the ask for.

And:

> "Come on, let us go down, and there confuse their speech so that no one may understand the speech of his neighbour." Genesis xi 7

leads to:

> So they said, 'What does he mean, "a little while"? We do not understand what he is saying'. xvi 18

> 'I have told you these things in figures of speech. The time is coming when I shall no more speak to you in figures ...' xvi 25

> 'Now see, you are speaking to us plainly, not in a figure of speech ...' xvi 29.

And:

> And from there God scattered them far and wide over the earth. Genesis xi 9

to:

> 'Behold, the time is coming, indeed is now come, when you will be scattered ...' xvi 29.

This in summary is how John perceived the correspondences to the letter *peh* in Genesis xi-xii, and how he used them in the sixteenth chapter of the gospel.

16.1: TB *Sanhedrin* 109a.

16.2: Josephus, *Jewish Antiquities* i 113.

16.3: *Genesis Rabbah* xxxviii 6. *Book of Jasher* ix 29.

16.4: Aryeh Kaplan, *Sefer Yetzirah: Book of Creation* pp. 83-4, 106, 164.

16.5: *3 Baruch*. Louis Ginzberg *Legends of the Jews* chap. iv.

16.6: *Targum PseudoJonathan* Genesis xi; *Jerusalem (Fragment) Targum* Genesis xi. *Book of Jubilees* xii 25. *Genesis Rabbah* xxiii 7; ibid xxxviii 8. *Zohar* 1:75a-b, 76a-b. Daniel C. Matt, *The Zohar:Pritzker Edition* vol. 1 p. 442 n. 760; ibid p. 445 n. 780.

16.7: Robert Graves, *The White Goddess* p. 121.

The Gospel According to John chapter 17;

**zaddi, fish-hook; numerical value 90
(or 900 when final); the ninth sefirah,
Yesod (Foundation);
the path from the seventh sefirah,
Nezah (Victory), to the ninth sefirah,
Yesod (Foundation);
Aquarius, and the eleventh house;
the eleventh month, Shevat;
Genesis xv 1 to xv 8: Abraham receives a promise
of innumerable descendants.**

The section of the Genesis narrative related to the letter *zaddi*, and thus to xvii, is Genesis xii 1-v 8. The most significant verse in the passage is:

> He brought him outside and said to him, 'Look up to the heavens and number the stars if you can count them – just so shall your seed be.' Genesis xv 5.

Rabbinic literature renders this verse more poignant with the gloss that both Abram and Sarah were destined to die childless by their horoscopes, and Abram, who was well versed in these matters, despaired of ever becoming a father.[17.1] In the Midrash 'he brought him outside' is explained to mean God took him outside the celestial spheres, reminding him he was a prophet, not an astrologer. Rabbinic commentaries often see a double meaning in the fact that God led Abram from his home in Ur of the Chaldees (Genesis xv 7). Since *Hasdim* ('Chaldees') can mean 'astrologer' and Ur means 'light', the implication is that God led away from worship of the host of heaven.

But why would John think this passage contains some references to the system of correspondences he is using? First, Nezah (Victory) is strongly associated with prophetic revelation. Second, this verse explicitly likens stars to seed. Nezah has celestial objects as one of its correspondences because the host of heaven came into existence on the Fourth Day of creation, 'the Fourth Day' being one of Nezah's designations. The ninth sefirah, Yesod (Foundation), is associated with the organs of reproduction; and seed appears as a specific symbol for the sefirah[17.2]; John resorts to the symbol himself (viii 33, 37). Genesis xv 5 thus likens stars, symbol of Nezah, to seed, a symbol of Yesod.

The eleventh house of the horoscope, moreover, is said to chart the hopes and wishes of the native, favours done by benefactors, and fertility. These themes are mirrored in this passage, as God granting Abram's great dream of descendants from his own body.

In the Gospel, xvii opens with Jesus praying by night:

> Jesus lifted up his eyes to heaven. xvii 1.

The verse is meant to recall Genesis xv 5.

Jesus' remark that he lost none of those that had been given to him (xvii 12) it may derive from Genesis xiv 16, where Abram liberates his kinsmen and household servants, who had been abducted;

he is said to have saved them all to a man. The son of perdition, whom Jesus mentions here as the only exception (xvii 12), ostensibly referring to Judas, would be represented in Genesis by the King of Sodom, whom he also rescues, but who is soon to be destroyed.

- 17.1: *Genesis Rabbah* xliv 10-12. *Numbers Rabbah* ii 12. *Exodus Rabbah* xxxviii 6. TB *Nedarim* 32a. TB *Shabbath* 156a-b. *Zohar* 1:90a-b; 3:148a. Daniel C. Matt, *The Zohar: Pritzker Edition* vol. 2 p. 10 n. 64; ibid pp. 67, 68 nn. 524, 525.
- 17.2: *Zohar* 1:1a, 13a, 19a, 162a-b; 2:166b. Daniel C. Matt, *The Zohar: Pritzker Edition* vol. 1 p. 90 n. 686; ibid p. 146 n. 301, 302; vol. 2 p. 406 n. 705; vol. 5 p. 465 n. 783.

The Gospel According to John chapter 18;

quf, ear; numerical value 100;
the tenth sefirah, Malkuth (Kingdom);
the path from the seventh sefirah,
Ne<u>z</u>a<u>h</u> (Victory), to the tenth sefirah,
Malkuth (Kingdom);
Pisces and the twelfth house;
the twelfth month, Adar;
Genesis xv 9 to xvi 16: Abraham's sleep and horror of darkness, foreshadowing of Egypt, birth of Ishmael.

The portion of the Genesis narrative related to the letter *quf*, and thus to xviii, is Genesis xv 9-xvi 16, where Abram has a prophetic revelation of his descendants' affliction during their Captivity in Egypt:

> And as the sun was going down, a deep sleep fell upon Abram, and then a horror of great darkness fell on him. Genesis xv 12.

Ne<u>z</u>a<u>h</u>'s association with prophecy has already been noted. In the Gospels this manifests when Jesus prophesies in response to the soldiers' demands, a detail only found in the Synoptic Gospels.

Abram's horror great darkness reflects the twelfth house's connection with fears and anxieties. In the Synoptic Gospels takes the form of Jesus' anguished prayer and bloody sweat just prior to his arrest. Captivity is also a traditional association of the twelfth house. It appears in Jesus' arrest by the soldiers accompanying Judas. As already noted, some versions of *Sefer Yezirah* give sleep as the bodily function denoted by *quf*; in astrology, the twelfth house, which is cognate with Pisces, is connected with sleep and unconsciousness; all three Synoptic Evangelists (According to Matthew xxvi 36-44, Mark xiv 36-42, Luke xxii 42-46) report that immediately prior to his arrest Jesus finds the disciples fast asleep.

John has the soldiers and accompanying mob who come to arrest Jesus carry torches and lamps (xviii 3), a detail partly due to:

> ... and it was dark and behold: a smoking furnace and a fiery lamp, which went between the pieces. Genesis xv 17.

The association of Malkuth with fire has been noted.[18.1]

18.1: See Part 2 note 18.3.

The Gospel According to John chapter 19;
resh, head; numerical value 200;
the second sefirah (Hokmah);
the path from the eighth sefirah, Hod (Glory),
to the ninth sefirah, Yesod (Foundation);
the Sun;
Genesis xvii 1 to xvii 27:
the circumcision of Abraham's household.

Genesis xvii 1-xvii 27, which is the section of the narrative relating to the letter *resh*, and thus to xix, describes how Abraham received the covenant of circumcision, which was to be imposed upon his seed for all generations. It is easy to see why John thought this passage significant. Prophetic revelation is associated with the eighth sefirah, Hod. The ninth sefirah, Yesod (Foundation) is strongly associated with the covenant of circumcision (Genesis xvii 2, 9-14, 19, 21, 23-27). As explained, the Synoptic Gospels allude to Jewish customs surrounding the rite when they describe how a wine-soaked sponge was thrust into Jesus' mouth to the crowd's jeers of 'Let's see if Elijah comes saving him'.

Seed, which is repeatedly mentioned here (Genesis xvii 8-9, 12, 19), is also a symbol Yesod.

God promises Abraham and Sarah individually that they would have kings among their descendants if the injunction to circumcise their offspring was adhered to (Genesis xvii 6, 16). In the Gospel this manifests in the presentation of Jesus as the King of the Jews, a central theme of xix, where it also serves to indicate the Sun, the yeziratic assignment of the letter *resh*.

The Gospel According to John chapter 20;
shin, tooth; 300; the third sefirah, Binah (Understanding);
the path from the eighth sefirah, Hod (Glory), to the tenth sefirah, Malkuth (Kingdom);
Fire;
Genesis xviii 1 to xix 28;
incineration of Sodom and Gomorrah.

Genesis xviii 1 to xix 28, the section of the narrative relating to the letter *shin*, and thus to xx, describes God's intention to bring judgement upon Sodom and Gomorrah, Abraham's plea that they be spared, and the precipitous escape of Lot and his family. It ends with the plain cities' fiery destruction:

> Then the Lord rained down upon Sodom and Gomorrah brimstone and fire from himself out of heaven. And he overturned the cities and the whole plain, all the inhabitants of the cities, and what grew from the ground. But his wife looked back behind her and became a pillar of salt.
>
> And early in the morning Abraham went up to the place where he had stood before the Lord. And he looked toward Sodom

and Gomorrah, and the whole land of the plain, and he saw it: the smoke of the land was going up just like the smoke of a furnace. Genesis xix 24-28.

It is not difficult to see how John perceived the correspondences here: fire is the yeẓiratic attribution of the letter *shin*. Moreover, the tenth sefirah is often represented by elemental fire.[20.1]

When asking God to spare the city for the sake of the righteous men within it, Abraham begins with the possibility of fifty, which is associated with Binah, and ends with the possibility of ten, which is associated with Malkuth (Genesis xviii 26-32). The door of the tent (Genesis xviii 1), dust and ashes (Genesis xviii 27), the ground (Genesis xviii 2, xix 25), and judgement (Genesis xviii 25) are standard symbols of the tenth sefirah.[20.2]

The twentieth chapter of John's Gospel contains several echoes of this passage. Not all of these are traceable back to the chapter's correspondences, but John evidently believed them to be thematic:

- Two angels save Lot (Genesis xix 1). Two angels meet Mary at the tomb (xx 12).
- Lot shuts the door behind him when he goes out to talk to the gathered men of Sodom, then the angels shut the door as they threaten to break in (Genesis xix 6, 10). The disciples hide behind shut the doors for fear of the authorities (xx 19, 26).
- Lot's family takes flight early in the morning (Genesis xix 10). Mary makes an early morning visit to the tomb (xx 1).
- Abraham runs to meet the angels, then to Sarah (Genesis xix 2, 6); the angels urge Lot's family flee with all haste

(Genesis xix 15, 22). Mary runs to tell of the empty tomb (xx 2); Peter and John run there to check (xx 4).

– Lot's wife turns around to look behind her (Genesis xix 26). Mary turns around to face Jesus (xx 16).

20.1: See Part 2 note 18.3.

20.2: *Zohar* 1:21a, 49a, 98a, 103a, 106b; 2:24a-b, 36a, 186b, 227b; 3:14a. Daniel C. Matt, *The Zohar: Pritzker Edition* vol. 1 p. 162 n. 435; ibid pp. 270, 271 nn. 1255, 1265; vol. 2 p. 119 n. 22; ibid p. 147 nn. 237, 242, 243; vol. 3 p. 28 n. 189; ibid p. 303 n. 5; vol. 4 p. 84, 85 nn. 51, 54; ibid p. 88 n. 63; ibid p. 164 n. 86; vol. 6 p. 48 n. 124; ibid p. 49 n. 128; ibid pp. 306-307 nn. 125-128; vol. 7 p. 58 n. 177; ibid p. 64 n. 197; ibid p. 84 nn. 258, 259; ibid p. 199 nn. 102, 103.

Part 4:
A Pictorial Guide to John's Gospel

The Tarot is a deck of seventy-eight cards, the forerunner of modern playing-cards. We know little about the time and place of the Tarot's origins except that it was circulating in Italy by the fifteenth century. Although it has been said that the meaning of the cards is a mystery, this is not true: we can say with confidence the Tarot was intended as a pictorial summary of the ideas that make up the Fourth Gospel's symbolic framework.

That the trump cards of the Tarot are somehow connected with the Qabalah seems to have been first seriously proposed by a Frenchman, Alphonse Louis Constant, who wrote in the latter half of the nineteenth century under the pseudonym of Eliphaz Levi. A century earlier, two of his countrymen, Antoine Court de Gebelin and Comte de Mellet, had suggested that the cards were a relic of the arcane wisdom of the ancients, but Levi understood more clearly than they that the trumps were intimately related to the letters of the Hebrew alphabet, and specifically to the qabalistic letter mysticism of *Sefer Yezirah*. His opinions were popularised by another Frenchman, Gerard Encausse, a more successful author, who wrote under the name Papus.

In 1909, Aleister Crowley, the notorious occultist, published a brief work called *Liber 777*, a compilation of correspondences based on a version of *Sefer Yezirah* and the qabalistic Tree of Life, which took the form of a table with thirty-two rows (because there are ten sefiroth plus twenty-two letters) and almost two hundred columns. Crowley did not claim to have invented any part of the system of correspondences. This had been passed to him under a strict oath of secrecy upon his reaching a certain grade within the Golden Dawn, and he made enemies for himself by revealing it. Significantly, it is identical to the system of attributions we have been using throughout Parts 1 and 2 of this book.

Liber 777 was privately published by Crowley, only two hundred copies being initially printed. Most modern readers who are familiar with the notion that the Tarot is a pictorial version of *Sefer Yezirah* will have met with it because Crowley later designed a Tarot deck, and wrote his own commentary to the cards and their relationship to the attributions of *Sefer Yezirah* and the qabalistic Tree, titled *The Book of Thoth*.

What was new in *Liber 777* and what was old? The attributions of the Hebrew letters to the qabalistic Tree (column xiii) first came to light in Kircher's *Oedipus Aegyptiacus*; his tables and diagram of the Tree were reprinted hundreds of times in the following centuries. Crowley added nothing to Kircher's scheme.

As for the astrological attributions of the letters (column vii), it is obvious these are based on a version of *Sefer Yezirah*. However, the precise system by which the seven double letters ae assigned to the planets (that is, *beth* to Mercury, *gimel* to the moon, *daleth* to Venus, *kaf* to Jupiter, *peh* to Mars, *resh* to the Sun, *tau* to Saturn) differs

TABLE 1: Correspondences of the Tarot after Crowley's *Liber 777*

letter	element	from sefirah	to sefirah	English title of trump
'alef	Air	1 Kether	2 Ḥokmah	0. The Fool
beth	Mercury	1 Kether	3 Binah	I. The Magician
gimel	Moon	1 Kether	6 Tif'areth	II. The High Priestess
daleth	Venus	2 Ḥokmah	3 Binah	III. The Empress
heh	Aries	2 Ḥokmah	6 Tif'areth	IV. The Emperor
vau	Taurus	2 Ḥokmah	4 Ḥesed	V. The High Priest
zayin	Gemini	3 Binah	6 Tif'areth	VI. The Lovers
ḥeth	Cancer	3 Binah	5 Gevurah	VII. The Chariot
teth	Leo	4 Ḥesed	5 Gevurah	VIII. Fortitude
yod	Virgo	4 Ḥesed	6 Tif'areth	IX. The Hermit
kaf	Jupiter	4 Ḥesed	7 Nezah	X. Wheel of Fortune
lamed	Libra	5 Gevurah	6 Tif'areth	XI. Justice
mem	Water	5 Gevurah	8 Hod	XII. The Hanged Man
nun	Scorpio	6 Tif'areth	7 Nezah	XIII. Death
samekh	Sagittarius	6 Tif'areth	9 Yesod	XIV. Temperance
'ayin	Capricorn	6 Tif'areth	8 Hod	XV. The Devil
peh	Mars	7 Nezah	8 Hod	XVI. The Tower
ẓaddi	Aquarius	7 Nezah	9 Yesod	XVII. The Star
quf	Pisces	7 Nezah	10 Malkuth	XVIII. The Moon
resh	Sun	8 Hod	9 Yesod	XIX. The Sun
shin	Fire	8 Hod	10 Malkuth	XX. Judgement
tau	Saturn	9 Yesod	10 Malkuth	XXI. The World

from what is found in the manuscript tradition. This is the first thing that is completely new. The attributions of the other fifteen letters of the alphabet are the same in any version of *Sefer Yezirah*.

Where do these correspondences of the seven double letters come from? Though the matter is never directly addressed in the Golden Dawn teaching materials, most of which have been published, the answer is they were deduced from the Tarot. These correspondences of the Tarot trumps had never been published before. This is the second thing that is new.

It is true that Eliphaz Levi and Papus had given a set of correspondences of the Tarot trumps, but they differ from those which Crowley published. Crowley asserted that Levi knew the correct attributions, but felt bound by an oath of secrecy not to reveal them. A story has it that they came to early Golden Dawn members in the form of a manuscript in Levi's own hand that provided the correct correspondences, not the absurd ones Levi published in *Dogme et Rituel de la Haute Magie* and other works. Levi never met any members of the Golden Dawn face to face, though he was influential with members of Societas Rosicruciana in Anglia, an organisation with links to the Golden Dawn.

Another innovation is that two of the trumps, *Fortitude* and *Justice* have swapped positions. In 1909, the same year that Crowley published *Liber 777*, Arthur Edward Waite, who was also a member of the Golden Dawn, released a Tarot deck executed by Pamela Coleman-Smith which followed the orders teachings: it has *VIII. Fortitude* and *XI. Justice*, just as in Crowley's *Liber 777*. This became a very popular deck in English speaking countries.

The reasons for supposing a relationship between the Marseilles Tarot and *Sefer Yezirah* are not difficult to see, though it is necessary to examine them in some detail.

First, there are twenty-two trumps cards in the Tarot. This is a rather strange number to choose – twenty, twenty-one, twenty-four or twenty-five would seem more suited to practically any purpose whatsoever. Even twenty-three might have been better because then we would have room for the full tetrad of Aristotlean elements, along with seven planets, and twelve signs. As things stand, the element earth has to be omitted from the scheme. But twenty-two is of course just the number of the letters in the Hebrew alphabet. In addition, the remainder of the deck consists of four suits, each containing ten 'pip' cards and four 'court' cards, which is also held to derive from qabalistic ideas.

Second, many of the cards seem to have astrological symbolism as their basis. It is here the core of the argument lies. Since it is somewhat technical and is crucially dependent upon the order of the trumps, I shall take the order of trumps as they appear in the Marseilles Tarot as given, and briefly return to the problem of the existence of other Tarots.

According to *Sefer Yezirah*, the twelve simple letters are the fifth (*heh*), sixth (*vau*), seventh (*zayin*), eighth (*heth*), ninth (*teth*), tenth (*yod*), twelfth (*lamed*), fourteenth (*nun*), fifteenth (*samekh*), sixteenth (*'ayin*), eighteenth (*zaddi*), and nineteenth (*quf*). These correspond to the twelve zodiac signs and twelve months of the calendar year in their standard order. No pattern is discernible to this sequence. It begins at the fifth letter and ends at the nineteenth, and there are three places where the continuous run of simple letters is broken up, namely in the eleventh (*kaf*), thirteenth (*mem*) and seventeenth (*peh*) positions. Of course, the randomness of the sequence is only to be expected because it was not constructed mathematically.

Having placed the Tarot trumps in the order, with the unnumbered Fool at the head, we can assign to each trump a letter. If we then extract from it the trumps answering to simple letters – the fifth (*IV. The Emperor*), sixth (*V. The Hierophant*), seventh (*VI. The Lovers*), and so on – it is fairly obvious that there exists a certain affinity between the trumps and zodiacal signs in many instances. Even with no knowledge of astrology other than the names of the signs and the animals they denote, it is probably easy to see that at least six are good matches. In short, *Sefer Yezirah* appears to predict which trumps are related to the zodiacal signs, and more often than not even the precise sign that a given trump represents.

Is there a way to quantify the relationship between the Tarot and *Sefer Yezirah*? Suppose one believes that within the twenty-two trumps of the Tarot there exists a subset of twelve that connote the signs of the zodiac. (What the other ten trumps may represent is for the moment not relevant.) What is the chance that *Sefer Yezirah* would correctly predict which trumps represent zodiacal signs, rather than planets or elements?

If one takes twenty-two objects, there are 646,646 ways of dividing them into a set of twelve and a set of ten; this is the number of unordered selections of twelve elements from twenty-two (22!/10!12!). This means there exists 646,646 ways of choosing a set of twelve trumps – namely those that represent signs of the zodiac – out of the full complement of twenty-two. If *Sefer Yezirah* was unrelated to the Tarot, the chance of its correctly dividing the trumps into two groups, namely those that correspond to signs of the zodiac and those which do not, is 1 in 646,646.

If the Tarot could do even more than this, and predict accurately in every case the correct sign, it might be argued that the chances are less than 1 in 300 million (22!/10!), the number of ordered selections of a subset of twelve from a larger set of twenty-two. There are, however, several problems with this. First, two of

TABLE 2: Simple letters and the corresponding twelve signs of the zodiac after *Sefer Yezirah*, and trumps falling in position of simple letters (*'alef* = *0. The Fool; beth* = *I. The Magician;* etc.) after the Marseilles Tarot (and the Waite Tarot).

Simple letter	Zodiacal sign	Marseilles Tarot	(Waite Tarot/ Crowley 777)
heh	Aries	*IV. The Emperor*	
vau	Taurus	*V. The High Priest*	
zayin	Gemini	*VI. The Lovers*	
ḥeth	Cancer	*VII. Chariot*	
ṭeth	Leo	*VIII. Justice*	*(VIII. Strength)*
yod	Virgo	*IX. The Hermit*	
lamed	Libra	*XI. Strength*	*(XI. Justice)*
nun	Scorpio	*XIII. Death*	
samekh	Sagittarius	*XIV. Temperance*	
'ayin	Capricorn	*XV. The Devil*	
ẓaddi	Aquarius	*XVI. The Star*	
quf	Pisces	*XVIII. The Moon*	

the trumps in the Marseilles Tarot, namely *VIII. Justice* and *XI. Fortitude*, have to swap position in order for the signs of the zodiac and trumps to agree. It can be seen in the table above that in the Golden Dawn material, which Crowley published in *Liber 777*, this change had already been made. (Curiously, Crowley in his Tarot, produced many years after *Liber 777*, left the trumps ordered as in the Marseilles. Possibly he feared people might say he had copied Waite's lead, something his overgrown ego could not allow.) Second, the order of signs that is implied in Waite's Tarot is just the order that any astrologer would normally use – there is nothing special or unusual about it.

Even allowing for the fact that *Fortitude* and *Justice* are interchanged, and that a few of the trumps may not at first sight bear compelling resemblance to the signs of the zodiac, the unusual way certain trumps are distributed within the larger sequence of twenty-two makes it clear that the Marseilles Tarot and *Sefer Yezirah* are connected.

Throughout this book, unless specifically indicated to the contrary, the Tarot is taken to be synonymous with either the Marseilles-type Tarot, or the modified Marseilles deck, like the one designed by Waite and executed by Pamela Coleman-Smith. Since a certain circularity of argument can be avoided simply by taking the Marseilles Tarot as given, this is the approach I have adopted. As long as one confines oneself to the question whether anyone has ever understood the true nature of According to John, the priority of the Marseilles Tarot is not relevant. The mere existence of the Marseilles Tarot answers the question in the affirmative, whatever its antecedents or history may be. While getting lost in the maze of variations serves little purpose, it would be pleasing to know who may have understood the true nature of the Fourth Gospel, and how and when they came to know about it.

Varieties of Tarot

The earliest Tarot trumps, both hand-painted and printed, lacked titles and an explicit order. By the time the cards were mass produced, manufacturers of cards had found it expedient to give the trumps titles as well as numbers. Tarocchi, for centuries the most popular game played with the Tarot, requires the trumps be numbered.

Three main Tarot lineages appear to exist, representing the cities of Ferrara, Bologna, and Milan. They differ chiefly in order of the trumps rather than in their designs or titles. Although the matter is complicated by the existence of variants within each group, at least it can be said all three orderings of the trumps are similar, so that one need postulate few changes to go from one to the others. Some cards are consistently found near to one another; there are clusters and runs; some cards always come near the beginning of the series, some near the middle, others always near the end. It is only the placement of half a dozen cards that is problematic.

The oldest record that deals with the names and ordering of the trumps is found in *Sermones de Ludo cum Aliis* (the Steele Manuscript), the preaching of a fifteenth-century Dominican or Franciscan from Ferrara, who warns against their use in card games. Not only does it list the trumps in a sequence, it is the earliest record of their titles. The trumps are twenty-two, and from their titles it is clear that they are Tarot cards.

The second way of ordering the trumps is seen in decks from Bologna. It is well attested to in literature only from the seventeenth century onwards. However, the highly conservative nature of local customs lead many to believe it had not changed in the preceding two centuries during which it is known to have enjoyed unbroken popularity.

The third way of ordering the trumps is seen in the Marseilles Tarot. It may have originated in the Piedmont region of northern Italy and been taken back to Marseille when the French conquered Milan in the last decade of the fifteenth century. The earliest extant example of a Marseilles Tarot is a very incomplete mid-sixteenth century deck by Catelin de Geofroy, of which only a dozen trumps survive. The earliest complete Marseilles-type decks date from the early seventeenth century.

Political forces, quality of materials, attractiveness of designs, and cost, conspired together so that rival versions of the Tarot did not vanish, but the Marseilles Tarot eclipsed its competitors and eventually came to dominate the highly lucrative market.

Golden Dawn view of the Tarot, and what the Tarot is

In the Golden Dawn literature, the Tarot trumps are understood to have two aspects. On one hand the trumps symbolise the seven astrological planets, twelve signs of the zodiac, and three elements (air, water, fire); the order of the trumps is determined by a version of *Sefer Yezirah*. On the other hand, the trumps are also assigned to the paths on the qabalistic Tree of sefiroth. The symbolism behind the trumps is therefore basically astrological, but it has been altered to make it more compatible with ideas derived from the qabalistic Tree and its system of paths, or with teachings from unnamed arcane sources.

However, when we look at According to John and the Marseilles Tarot (or better still, the deck designed by Waite) side by side, it becomes obvious that the Tarot was actually meant to provide a graphic summary of the ideas John had in mind when writing his Gospel. And it really is a most excellent key to Johannine symbolism.

How could a pictorial version of According to John be mistaken for a pictorial version of *Sefer Yezirah*? I should hope this question has been answered in Part 1. If the Tarot draws upon astrological iconography, it is just because According to John makes extensive use of astrological symbolism. If the Tarot sometimes seems otherwise, it is because John also makes use of symbolism that is not astrological: Jewish feasts, the qabalistic Tree of Life, a large section of Genesis, all play an important role in the Fourth Gospel.

It is impossible to ignore the Tarot, since it does such an outstanding job of illuminating the Fourth Gospel's inner workings. The Tarot points to the threads of symbolism which actually appear in the Gospel or else constitute important parts of symbolic matrix underlying the text. Its author seems very well informed about every aspect of the Fourth Gospel: the astrological and calendar symbolism, the sefirothic symbolism, the relationship to Genesis.

More than that, The Tarot alone supplies a highly important piece of information. Different recensions of *Sefer Yezirah* have been noted to exist, and although these are in complete agreement in the way they assign twelve simple and the three mother letters, they disagree with respect to the way the seven double letters are allotted the seven planets. But the system of attributions John uses is the one implicit to the Tarot.

With respect to the order of the trumps in the different varieties of Tarot, it is clear that the original order of the trumps must have been the one that appears in Waite's Tarot and Crowley's *Liber 777*, knowledge which came to them both through their membership of the Golden Dawn. Once the trumps are ordered thus, the Tarot points to the symbolism present in According to John with such uncanny precision that it is impossible to conceive of any other purpose lying behind its creation. But the Marseilles deck differs from what I am calling the correct order only in position of two cards, *Justice* and *Fortitude*; to get the correct order of trumps from the Ferrarese or Bolognese Tarot likewise requires only a few changes; in this respect, they are all extremely similar. If, merely by swapping a few cards, we get something that is undeniably meant to illustrate what John's Gospel is all about, it can only be that the Tarot was geared to this purpose from the very outset. It could not have been designed for something else, and later taken over for this purpose.

In the end, it is not necessary to take the Tarot too seriously. It merely shows a set of ideas that someone who lived in northern Italy in the fifteenth century had about the Fourth Gospel. Just as it takes a certain amount of time to get used to John's style, so too does it take time to get used to the style of the Tarot, which is permeated by a unique aesthetic and sense of humour. Often a Tarot trump will have multiple explanations. The author of the Tarot has a mind as eclectic as John's, just as familiar with astrological, calendar, and qabalistic symbolism employed in the Gospel, as with images from classical myth, the Bible, or Christian iconography.

In what follows I have tried to address the most important questions: What are the reasons for believing that the author of the Tarot understood According to John in the fashion I have outlined in Parts 1, 2, 3? How probable is it that commentators, such as Crowley and Waite, were aware of this aspect of the Tarot?

0. The Fool;
The Gospel According to John has no corresponding chapter;
'*alef*, an ox; numerical value 1;
the first sefirah, Kether (Crown);
the path from the first sefirah,
Kether (Crown) to second sefirah,
Hokmah (Wisdom);
Air.

In the Marseilles Tarot, the name of the trump is *Le Mat* or *Le Fol* (*The Fool*); in Italian decks, *Il Matto* (*The Fool or Madman*). It depicts a man dressed in motley rags strolling along while an animal bites at his legs. Over his shoulder he carries a bag on a long pole, possibly an air-filled bladder that a medieval clown might brandish. Commentators describe the Fool of the Tarot as a vagrant misfit, an embodiment of chaos and disorder. Some relate his proverbial vacuity or emptiness to the element air. In divination the trump represents the influence of something new and unexpected; foolish errors or reckless behaviour.

In the Ferrarese and Bolognese decks it generally comes at the first place of the sequence. It was usually not accorded a number in the Marseilles Tarot, and there were conflicting views about its placement by those who took the Marseilles Tarot as their standard. Eliphaz Levi, for instance, put it between *XX. Judgement* and *XXI the World*. Waite correctly indicated the relationship of *The Fool* to the other trumps by giving it a value of zero.

The absence of a chapter corresponding to *'alef* and the fact that *The Fool* was not assigned a number in the Marseilles Tarot is not coincidental. Importantly, because John assigned no chapter to *'alef*, the letters of the alphabet and chapters of the Gospel are all out of step by one. Thus the first chapter of According to John answers to the second letter of the alphabet; the second chapter answers to the third letter of the alphabet; and so on. But because the creators of the Marseilles Tarot left *The Fool* unnumbered, and began numbering with the next trump, each trump now bears the Roman numeral of the chapter of the Gospel it is intended to illustrate. Thus the first chapter of the Gospel corresponds to *I. The Magician*; the second chapter corresponds to *II. The High Priestess*; and so on. The fact that *The Fool* was left unnumbered is one of the many features of Marseilles Tarot that suggest it was primarily intended as a pictorial commentary on the Gospel According to John rather than *Sefer Yeẓirah*.

I. The Magician;
According to John chapter 1;
beth, house; numerical value 2;
the second sefirah, Hokmah (Wisdom);
path from the first sefirah, Kether (Crown)
to third sefirah, Binah (Understanding);
Mercury.

El Bagatello or *Il Bagatella* means Cobbler or Artisan; *Il Bagatto* probably means Innkeeper or Taverner; *Le Bateleur*, the Conjurer, Trickster, or Juggler. The oldest versions of the trump show a man wearing a broad-brimmed hat and standing before a table littered with dice, coins and various other paraphernalia of his trade.

Traditional interpretations of the card include: wisdom, skill, adroitness, adaptability, versatility, charlatanism, craft, cunning, deceit, theft, business transactions, strength of will. All are perfectly compatible with the trump's attribution to Mercury. The first-century Christian apologist Aristides lists the god's guises: thief, interpreter, athlete, magician.[1.1]

The true source of the image is probably the money-changers and dove-sellers of the Temple at their tables which Jesus, brandishing a whip, overturns.

Crowley and knowledge of the esoteric aspects of According to John

In *The Book of Thoth* in his essay on *I. The Magician*, Aleister Crowley offers some personal insights into the card[1.2]:

> This card represents the Wisdom, the Will, the Word, the Logos by whom the worlds were created. (See the Gospel according to St. John, chapter I.) *Book of Thoth* p 69. Brackets are Crowley's.

And in a supplementary essay on the card called *De Mercurio* he quotes from another of his works:

> In the Beginning was the Word, the Logos, who is Mercury; and is therefore to be identified with Christ. ibid p. 128.

Later in the same essay he says Jesus' identity with Mercury is shown by his dealings with money-changers.

Whenever discussing relationship of the Tarot to the Tree of sefiroth and the letter mysticism of *Sefer Yezirah*, there is an excellent chance one will unwittingly cross paths with the Fourth Gospel. If the Fourth Gospel was fabricated around *Sefer Yezirah*, and if the Tarot was meant to illustrate it, then this is almost inevitable. It hardly necessitates any knowledge of the Fourth Gospel's true nature on the part of the writer. However, Crowley's writings contain a number of similar comments. It is hard to dismiss them all as accidental. The remarks concerning *I. The Magician* must be among the most blatant examples of Crowley's advertising knowledge of the esoteric aspects of According to John.

1.1: Aristides *Apology* x.
1.2: Aleister Crowley *Book of Thoth* pp 69, 128.

II. *The Papess;*
The Gospel According to John chapter 2;
gimel, camel; numerical value 3;
the third sefirah, Binah (Understanding)
the path from the first sefirah, Kether (Crown) to
the sixth sefirah, Tif'areth (Beauty);
Moon.

II. *The Papess* or *High Priestess* shows a woman dressed in ecclesiastical garb with papal triple tiara, seated, with a book or scroll on her lap. In the Marseilles Tarot there is a suggestion of two pillars in the background. The Italian trump's name is *La Papessa* or *Papissa*; in French, *La Papesse*. A Latin title of the card was *Flaminica*, the wife a Roman priest. Traditional meanings include: mystery, wisdom, knowledge, science, fluctuation, change, intuition.

Waite's Tarot has the High Priestess in flowing robes of Marian blue, seated between the pillars of Solomon's Temple, B(oaz) and J(akin). In *A Pictorial Guide to the Tarot*, he puts down some of his thoughts on the trump[2.1]:

> The scroll in her hands is inscribed with the word Tora, signifying the Greater Law, the Secret Law, and the second sense of the Word. ...

> [She] is really the Secret Church, the House which is of God and man. She represents the Second Marriage of the Prince who is no longer of this world. ...
> In a manner she is the Supernal Mother herself – that is to say she is the bright reflection. It is in the sense of reflection that her truest and highest name in symbolism is *Shekinah* – the cohabiting glory. A.E. Waite, *A Pictorial Guide to the Tarot*, pp. 76-79.

So excellent a summary of the precise ideas that form the basis of second chapter of John's Gospel makes it difficult to doubt that Waite knew of the relationship between According to John and the Tarot.

2.1: A. E. Waite, *A Pictorial Guide to the Tarot* pp. 76-79.

III. The Empress;
The Gospel According to John chapter 3;
daleth, door; numerical value 4;
the fourth sefirah (**H**esed);
the path from the second sefirah,
Hokmah (Wisdom) to the third sefirah, Binah
(Understanding); Venus.

The trump shows a woman equipped with imperial crown and sceptre reclining on a couch. Following ideas of Papus, Waite models his Empress after Revelation xii 1-14, which describes a woman clothed in the sun, with the moon at her feet and a crown of twelve stars on her head; she is suffering the pangs of childbirth; after she delivers she is given the wings of an eagle to escape the dragon pursuing her. The identification is probably correct, explaining why in the older Marseilles Tarot, the Empress is depicted with eagle's wings growing from her back.[3.1] In later decks she is reduced to having an eagle emblazoned on her shield.

Traditional divinatory significations of the *III. The Empress* fruitfulness, fertility, motherhood, love, pleasure, happiness, material comfort. All perfectly compatible with qabalistic and astrological assignments of the chapter and found in the third chapter of John's Gospel.

   3.1: Gareth Knight, *A Practical Guide to Qabalistic Symbolism* vol. 2 p. 192.

IV. The Emperor;
The Gospel According to John chapter 4;
**heh, a window; numerical value 5;
the fifth sefirah, Gevurah (Might);
the path from second sefirah, Hokmah (Wisdom) to
the sixth sefirah, Tif'areth (Beauty);
Aries, the first house (ascendant);
the first month, Nisan or Abib.**

The trump shows a man, enthroned, holding tokens of imperial power. In divination the card implies leadership, authority, government, energy, originality, war, conquest, pride, ambition. It is possible to understand the Emperor in astrological terms, that is, as an embodiment of the Aries, the first sign of the zodiac. The bellicose Lamb of Revelation, the first-born male child who rules over the nations with an iron rod from his throne, is a perfect example of the type. The form and title of trump recalls Jesus' identification with the Anointed One in iv 25-26, 29, 42, partly because Nisan is the month of kings.

V. The High Priest;
According to John chapter 5;
path from the second sefirah, **H**okmah (Wisdom) to the fourth sefirah, **H**esed (Mercy);
vau, nail; numerical value 6;
the sixth sefirah, Tif'areth (Beauty);
Taurus, the second house;
second month Iyar.

The fifth numbered trump in the sequence was initially called *The Pope*; but it was later changed to *The High Priest*, or *The Hierophant*. It shows a man in ecclesiastical garb, often holding a pair of keys, with two attendants kneeling before his throne. Divinatory meanings include good counsel, sound advice, revelation, inspiration, benevolence, superstition, prejudice.

The form of the trump may have been influenced by the nature of corresponding path on the Tree, which joins Hokmah (Wisdom) and Hesed (Mercy). The second sefirah is connected with mystical revelation. The fourth sefirah is associated with priesthood.[5.1] Among the planets Hesed (Mercy) corresponds to Jupiter, which is said to lead to philosophical or religious interests and priestly vocations when emphasised in the horoscope. *The High Priest* recalls a magical talisman to attract the influence of Jupiter – a man in episcopal garb, enthroned, one hand raised in benediction. Alternatively, the form of trump may have been inspired by the mention of Moses and the scriptures in v 45-46.

5.1: *Zohar* 1:47b, 87a; 2:49b, 67b, 225a, 231a, 232b; 3:145b, 146a, 151b. Daniel C. Matt, *The Zohar: Pritzker Edition*, vol. 1 p. 259 n. 1180; vol. 2 p. 56 nn. 436, 437; vol. 4 p. 243 n. 166; p. 372 n. 11; vol. 6 p. 289 n. 78.

VI. The Lovers;
The Gospel According to John chapter 6;
zayin, a weapon; numerical value 7;
the seventh sefirah, Ne*zah* (Victory);
the path from the third sefirah, Binah (Understanding)
to the sixth sefirah, Tif'areth (Beauty);
Gemini, and the third house;
the third month, Sivan.

Italian titles include *Cupido* (Cupid or Eros), *L'Amore* (Love), *Gli Amanti* and *Gli Innamorati* (The Lovers) and *L'Innamorato* (The Lover); French titles include *L'Amoreux* (The Lover) and *Les Amoreux* (The Lovers). The card is a representation of the sign Gemini, though oddly, the oldest examples typically show three human figures rather than two: a man flanked by two women. Commentators have interpreted the trump as a scene from classical mythology, the Judgement of Paris. It is more likely that it was intended to suggest Jacob and his two wives, the sisters Leah and Rachel.

Waite's *Lovers* is based on an idea found in the *Zohar*: the first human being had the form of a man and woman joined together. Because they were back to back, the male and female halves were ignorant of each other, and were unable to mate.[6.1] So God divided them into two. This idea, without the qabalistic elaborations, is found in the Talmud and Midrash.[6.2] Similar ideas can be found in Greek mythology, and the *Brihadaranyaka Upanishad*.

Divinatory meanings include decision, choice, temptation, trial.

- 6.1: *Zohar* 1:2b; 2:231a; 3:44b, 83b. Daniel C. Matt, *The Zohar: Pritzker Edition* vol. 1 p. 13 n. 90.
- 6.2: TB *Berakhot* 61a. TB *Erubin* 18a-b. *Genesis Rabbah* viii 1. *Leviticus Rabbah* xiv 1.

VII. The Chariot;
The Gospel According to John chapter 7;
<u>h</u>eth, **field; numerical value 8;**
the eighth sefirah, Hod (Glory);
the path from the third sefirah, Binah (Understanding), to the fifth sefirah, Gevurah (Might);
***Cancer*, and the fourth house;**
the fourth month, Tammuz.

In the Marseilles deck the seventh numbered trump shows a man armed, dressed in armour, and riding in a chariot. In earlier versions, the vehicle is a simple cubical box within or upon which the charioteer stands; in later depictions it has acquired an ornate canopy.

The design of the trump points to the astrological attribution of the card, the sign Cancer, the Crab, an animal with a soft body in a hard shell. Another significant factor in the choice of the trump's design may be the fact that Ezekiel's vision (Ezekiel i 1ff.) of the divine *merkhabah* (chariot) took place in the month of Tammuz.

Il Carro Triomphale or *Triomphante* (The Triumphal Chariot), or *Il Triompho* (The Triumph) is one of the early titles of the card. The original meaning of 'triumph' was a festive procession. The Feast of Tabernacles, which figures explicitly and so prominently in vii, was celebrated with a series of triumphal processions, one on each of the seven days of the feast. The image of a fixed course or track or curriculum of the triumphal procession probably lies behind:

> ... others said, 'No, but he leads the people astray.' vii 12

> The Pharisees replied to them, 'Have you been lead astray by him too?' vii 47.

Jewish synagogue art in the Diaspora in the first and second centuries depicted Tabernacles in a manner recognisable enough today: a victory procession lead by the Ark of the Torah. This was a conventional and unambiguous way of portraying the feast. Artists depicted the Torah Ark borne up like a palanquin on wooden staves running along its length in the same way that the Ark of the Covenant was carried so that it is not always clear which ark is meant, or even anachronistically showed the celebrants at the Feast of Tabernacles carrying the Ark of the Covenant long after it had been lost.[7.1] The original name for the Torah's receptacle, *tebah* ('coffin'), was later replaced by the word *'adon* ('chest or ark'), used regularly for the ancient prototype. On the last day of Tabernacles the congregation made seven circuits around the altar in commemoration of the seven times the Ark of the Covenant circled around Jericho (Joshua vi 11-16). On occasion the Ark of the Covenant was depicted in a cart drawn by oxen after the episode described in 1 Samuel vi 7-12 and 1 Chronicles xv.

For these reasons, the Torah Ark, carried around at the head of the festive procession of Tabernacles, may have been a prototype for the trump.

In divination, meanings of this trump include: authority under authority, a hierarchical chain of command, faithfulness and obedience in transmission of orders, ruthlessness.

7.1: Erwin Goodenough, *Jewish Symbols in the Greco-Roman Period (abridged)* p. 234ff. ibid p 257.

VIII. Fortitude;
The Gospel According to John chapter 8;
teth, a coiling serpent; numerical value 9;
the ninth sefirah, Yesod (Foundation);
the path from the fourth sefirah, Hesed (Mercy) to
the fifth sefirah, Gevurah (Might);
Leo, and the fifth house; the fifth month, Av.

Waite's big change to the Marseilles Tarot was to swap the positions of *Justice* and *Fortitude*. As noted, in *Liber 777*, Crowley has *VIII. Fortitude* and *XI. Justice*, which was evidently part of the Golden Dawn teachings. Not only is the change defensible the grounds that *Fortitude* represents Leo, the fifth sign, and *Justice* Libra, the seventh sign, it is also in excellent agreement with According to John.

Form of the Tarot trump

The trump called *VIII. Strength* or *Fortitude* most usually depicts a woman fearlessly grasping a lion's jaws, as if forcing them shut, or holding them open. The presence of the lion on the card follows immediately from the attribution of the letter *teth* to sign of the Lion in the zodiac. The presence of the woman points towards particular aspects of the corresponding house of the heavens, and the festivities of Ab 15, which figure in the pericope of the adulterous woman, which opens viii. The Golden Dawn called this trump *Lust*.

Like several other trumps, *Fortitude* recalls well known mythological and biblical motifs. The title and form of the trump was probably meant to suggest the story of Samson, recounted in Judges xiii-xvi. Graves suggests the existence of 'a primitive icon showing a naked woman tussling amorously with a lion, while a bee hovers over the carcass of another lion', which he says is the inspiration for the story of Samson.[8.1] Samson embodies aspects of the fifth house of the heavens as well as the cognate zodiacal sign, Leo. He had a lion as his totem, having killed one with his bare hands. His hair, the secret of his strength, was like the lion's mane. His name is just the name of the sun (*Shamash*), ruler of the sign Leo, with a 'n' (*nun*) suffixed. His life is marked by a series of love affairs with women of questionable virtue: his Philistine bride runs off with the best man on the wedding night; the second is a prostitute; the third betrays him. Samson's fondness of gambling and his death 'making sport' also suggest the fifth house. Some Tarot decks show no lion, only a woman and a pair of broken pillars, another way of pointing towards the legend of Samson.

Crowley suggested an additional referent for this trump can be found in Revelation xvii. His comment that the author of Revelation is too immature to understand that the woman clothed with the sun and the Whore of Babylon are related is an example of his mendacious humour.[8.2]

Some divinatory meanings of the card are courage, fortitude, strength, action.

8.1: Robert Graves, *The Greek Myths* 82.4.
8.2: Aleister Crowley, *Magick: In Theory and Practice*, p. 343.

IX. The Hermit;
The Gospel According to John chapter 9;
yod, hand; numerical value 10;
the tenth sefirah, Malkuth (Kingdom);
the path from the fourth sefirah, Hesed (Mercy) to
the sixth sefirah, Tif'areth (Beauty);
Virgo, and the sixth house;
the sixth month, Elul.

Astrological and calendar symbolism of the ninth chapter

The Italian title of the trump is *El Gobbo* (The Hunchback), *Il Vecchio* (The Old Man), or *L'Heremita* (*The Hermit*); in French decks the trump became *L'Hermite*. As a hermit is one who lives a solitary life, the title hints at the sign of the Virgin. Commentators note that title of the card may be a pun on Hermes, since Mercury is ruler of the sign Virgo, even though the etymology is false, for 'hermit' is related to *herēmitos*, 'a desert dweller, a monastic', not to Hermes.

The trump depicts an old man, staff in one hand. Sometimes he carries an hour-glass, possibly suggested by Jesus comments about time running out (ix 4-5); sometimes he carries a lantern, recalling Jesus' claim to be the light of the world (ix 4-5), his miraculous giving of sight to one born blind, and the theme of searching that runs through the chapter.

In divination the trump indicates the need for prudence, circumspection and caution, virtues of the Virgo persona.

X. The Wheel of Fortune;
The Gospel According to John chapter 10;
**kaf, the palm of the hand; numerical value 20;
the second sefirah, Hokmah (Wisdom);
the path from the fourth sefirah, Hesed (Mercy) to
the seventh sefirah, Nezah (Victory);
Jupiter.**

Fortune's Wheel is a common symbol of classical paganism. Fortuna was a calendar goddess, 'Turner-of-the-Wheel-of-the-Year' (from roots *vort*, 'turn' and *ann*, 'year'); she is often depicted as standing on or throwing a wheel or ball. She was known also as Cardea (related to a word denoting 'a hinge'), and Jana, for she was the female counterpart of Janus, god of doors – and also god of the new year, who lent his name to January on that account. Sometimes she is depicted with two faces, like him, representing the going (*Postvorta*) and coming (*Antevorta*) year.

X. *The Wheel of Fortune* is an emblem of New Year's Day (*Rosh ha Shanah*), which forms the background of the tenth chapter of According to John. It represents the end of a cycle becoming a new beginning. It is a Jewish custom at *Rosh ha Shanah*, to eat bread baked in the shape of a circle to recall the revolution of the year. John himself puns on the fact that the year is a wheel with the

Greek verb *kukloein*, 'to encircle or surround' from *kuklos*, 'wheel' in 'they made a circle [*ekuklōsan*] around him' (x 24). Jesus' repeated statement that he lays down his life to take it up again (x 17, 18) probably has a similar origin.

While the Wheel of Fortune, which God spins to the right or left to bring good or bad to the world, is a fairly common symbol in rabbinic literature, there is not a lot to connect it directly with *Rosh ha Shanah*, New Year's Day.[10.1] However, even exoteric religious treatises on *Rosh ha Shanah* commonly refer to the time as one of rapidly changing fortunes. This is why an important part of the day's liturgy is the Song of Hannah (1 Samuel ii 1-10), where she expresses wonder at the sudden turns of destiny – the strong become weak and the weak become strong, the rich lose their wealth while the poor become rich, the barren bear children while those with many lose them, the lowly are elevated and the proud debased, the living die and the dead are resurrected. The Wheel of Fortune is a perfect symbol of New Year's Day.

Traditional meanings in divination: destiny, chance, change in fortune.

Crowley, in his *X. Wheel of Fortune*, shows a wolf, a lamb, and a raven, a radical departure from tradition, which he claimed came from a visionary experience. He may have been influenced by the story of the hired man who abandons his sheep and flees from the approaching wolf in the tenth chapter of John's Gospel.

10.1: *Exodus Rabbah* xxxi 3, 14. *Leviticus Rabbah* xxxiv 3. *Zohar* 1:109a-b, 110a.

XI. *Justice;*
The Gospel According to John chapter 11;
lamed, an ox goad; numerical value 30;
the third sefirah, Binah (Understanding);
the path from the fifth sefirah, Gevurah (Might) to
the sixth sefirah, Tif'areth (Beauty);
Libra, the seventh house (descendant);
the seventh month, Tishri or Ethanim.

The eleventh numbered trump, which shows a seated woman holding an upright sword in one hand and a set of scales in the other, looks like a conventional representation of *Iustitia Aequatrix*, Justice the Equaliser, the personification of the impartiality and dispassionate nature of judicial proceedings, but also retribution, the necessity of satisfaction and redress, and compensation. In the *Tibetan Book of the Dead*, Evans-Wentz remarks on the widespread nature of similar images. In Greek mythology, the archetype appears as the minor goddess Nemesis, a restraint on her whimsical sister and alterego, Fortune (Tyche). Nemesis personified 'due enactment', later on, divine vengeance. He records a Buddhist version: good and evil deeds being weighed against each other, like white and black pebbles, in the pans of the balance of Yamaraja, King of the Dead.[11.1] He notes the angel

Michael weighing souls in a set of scales on the Last Day was common in Christian iconography of the Middle Ages. From an early time, the Egyptians associated the constellation Libra with the balance in which the Maati goddesses weighed a man's heart when his soul was judged after death. The *Psychostasia* (the Weighing of the Soul) is a well known vignette of *The Egyptian Book of the Dead*. According to the *Zohar*, the idea was known to the author of Psalm xxxii 1 who wrote: 'Happy is he whose transgression is lifted up' – lifted up because the pan of merit is heavier.[11.2]

The Day of Atonement, which forms an important part of the background of the eleventh chapter of According to John, is portrayed in rabbinic writings as a time when the world is judged as a whole – the merits of all the good people are placed on one side of the scales, and weighed against the offences of the wicked on the other side, the fate of the entire world literally hanging in the balance.[11.3]

Traditional divinatory meanings include arbitration, negotiation, justice, balance, law suits and legal matters, court trials, suspension of action pending decision; these are compatible with areas of rulership of the seventh horoscopic house and with themes surrounding the Day of Atonement (*Yom Kippur*).

11.1: Evans-Wentz, *Tibetan Book of the Dead*, p. 35, 165, 238.
11.2: *Zohar* 1:71a. Daniel C. Matt, *The Zohar: Pritzker Edition* vol. 1 p. 419 n. 584.
11.3: TB *Rosh ha Shanah* 17a.

XII. The Hanged Man;
The Gospel According to John chapter 12;
mem, water; numerical value 40; the fourth sefirah, Hesed (Mercy);
the path from the fifth sefirah, Gevurah (Might) to the eighth sefirah, Hod (Glory);
the element Water;
Genesis vi 13 to vii 20:
Noah builds the Ark.

The twelfth numbered trump of the Tarot shows a man suspended upside down from a horizontal wooden crossbeam resting on two vertical stakes. Italian title *Il Appeso* or *L'Impiccato* (*The Hanged Man*); the French title is *Le Pendu* (*The Hanged Man*).

The design of *XII. The Hanged Man* seems inspired by a comment of Jesus, who, having just spoken of the suffering he is about to endure, says:

> 'When I am lifted up from the earth I shall draw all men to me.' xii 32.

At the time the Tarot was conceived, thieves and traitors suffered the punishment of being hung upside down, 'baffling' as it was known. In some of the older decks, the name given to the trump is *Il Tadditore* (*The Traitor*), and the card's subject is shown with coins spilling from his bulging pockets, or from a money-bag attached to his belt. The title and form of the trump recalls that Judas is named a traitor (xii 4) and a thief who stole from the group's funds (xii 6).

The design of *XII. The Hanged Man* points to the fact that Jesus and Judas are being set side by side in xii, for Judas' mode of suicide qualifies him to be a type of Hanged Man. And like the figure of the Tarot, he somehow manages to fall headfirst (Acts i 18).

The inverted posture of this trump's subject may have been suggested also by the phrase 'lifting the heel', a biblical idiom for betrayal, in response to a question about his betrayer's identity in the next chapter:

> "He who eats bread with me lifted up his heel against
> me." xiii 32.

Psalm xli, from which Jesus is quoting here, begins with 'Happy is he who concerns himself with the poor', recalling Judas' words in xii 5 in an extremely ironic way.

The two upright posts and crossbeam suggest the form of the *sukkah*.

Commenting on this trump in his *Book of Thoth*, Aleister Crowley advertises his knowledge of the relationship between Genesis vi 13ff. and the other correspondences, remarking *The Hanged Man* had previously been known as the Drowned Man, and by referring to Noah's Ark and the Flood when discussing the form of the trump.[12.1]

Traditional meanings of the card in divination: enforced sacrifice, punishment, loss, voluntary or not, suffering, defeat, failure; ability to adapt to changing circumstances, flexibility of mind, willingness to submit oneself, passivity, pliancy; redemption through sacrifice. All are quite compatible with the position of the relevant path on the Tree of Life.

12.1: Aleister Crowley, *Book of Thoth* pp. 96-98.

XIII. Death;
The Gospel According to John chapter 13;
**nun, a fish; numerical value 50
(or 700 when final); the fifth sefirah, Gevurah (Might);
the path from the sixth sefirah, Tif'areth (Beauty)
to the seventh sefirah, Nezah (Victory);
Scorpio, the eighth house; the eighth month,
Heshivan or Marheshvan or Bul;
Genesis vii 21 to viii 14: the Deluge and extinction
of terrestrial life.**

The thirteenth trump of the Tarot is called *Death*. It corresponds to Scorpio, a sign with a long traditional association with death.

The section of Genesis relevant to xiii extends from about Genesis vii 21 to viii 14, and includes the story of extinction of all life by the waters of the Flood, which are, the *Zohar* says, the form the Angel of Death takes on when he manifests physically.[13.1]

In According to John, the theme manifests in xiii in the person of Judas, Son of the Assassin, into whose heart enters Samael, who is both Devil and Angel of Death.

In divination: transformation, change on a fundamental level, possibly death.

13.1: *Zohar* 1:63a, 65b.

XIV. Temperance;
The Gospel According to John chapter 14;

samekh, a prop; numerical value 60; the sixth sefirah, Tif'areth (Beauty);
the path from the sixth sefirah, Tif'areth (Beauty) to the ninth sefirah, Yesod (Foundation);
Sagittarius, and the ninth house;
the ninth month, Kislev;
Genesis viii 15 to ix 19: the covenant with Noah, the Noahide Law.

In older decks the subject of the fourteenth numbered trump is a seated woman pouring liquid from one vase into another. In the Marseilles Tarot, she is a winged angel standing.

Like many other trumps, classical mythology, provides one possible referent for the card: Iris, a minor Greek divinity, winged in form, who carried a pitcher of water, filled from the underworld river Styx, which she poured out when solemn agreements and promises are made between two parties. In particular, she presided over peace treaties, reconciliation of disputes, resolution of conflict. She lent her name to the coloured part of the eye because the rainbow was one of her chief symbolic attributes. *Iris* means 'rainbow' in Greek.

In his resumé of the trump, Crowley again adumbrates the relationship between Genesis and John's Gospel by centring the discussion around the symbol of the rainbow and the Hebrew word *qesheth* ('archer or bowman, Sagittarius, bow, rainbow').[14.1]

At first sight, the design of *XIV. Temperance* seems far removed from the figure of sign of Sagittarius, however, its form recalls people born under the sign are said to be skilled conciliators, referees, mediators, chaperones, matchmakers.

Traditional divinatory meanings of the trump include: conciliation, agreement, synthesis, harmonious combination of forces, success after elaborate manoeuvres.

From ii

John makes use of the qabalistic Tree of Life in an interesting way. Chapters like ii, xiv, and xxi which correspond to paths making up one of the pillars on the qabalistic Tree of Life share symbolic material, so that motifs that should be confined to one of these chapters may show up in the others.

The authors of the Tarot may have given *XIV. Temperance* the form it has in order to show that they understood this feature of According to John. For *XIV. Temperance* shows fluid being transferred from one vessel to another, recalling the miraculous transformation of water into wine that is the subject of ii. Moreover, the waiters play a significant role in the events of ii. They help to perform the miracle. They know what others at the wedding do not. The figure depicted in the trump is actually interpreted by some commentators as Hebe or Ganymede, Zeus' cupbearers. The relationship between the paths answering to *II. The High Priestess* and *XIV. Temperance* may have been meant to suggest the interaction between Mary and the waiters in ii.

In qabalistic writings the Shekhinah is frequently called Angel of the Presence, Angel of the Covenant, or Angel of the Lord.[14.2]

14.1: Aleister Crowley, *The Book of Thoth* pp. 101-104.

14.2: *Zohar* 1:135b, 166a, 230a, 232a; 2:51a; 3:187a-b. Daniel C. Matt, *The Zohar: Pritzker Edition* vol. 1 p. 351 n. 82; vol. 2 p. 129 n. 102; ibid p. 168 n. 405; ibid p. 170 nn. 419, 421; ibid p. 201 n. 654, 655, 656; ibid p. 260 n. 19; ibid p. 391 n. 581; vol. 3 p. 167 n. 516; ibid p. 193 n. 92; ibid p. 260 n. 15; ibid pp. 378, 379 nn. 396, 398; ibid p. 389 n. 438; vol. 4 p. 253 n. 201; ibid p. 255 n. 205; ibid p. 257 n. 212. See also Part 2 notes 2.27, 18.5.

XV. The Devil;
The Gospel According to John chapter 15;
'*ayin*, eye; numerical value 70;
the seventh sefirah, Ne<u>z</u>ah (Victory);
the path from the sixth sefirah,
Tif'areth (Beauty) to the eighth sefirah, Hod (Glory);
Capricorn, the tenth house;
the tenth month, Tevet;
Genesis ix 20 to x 32: Noah plants a vine;
the curse of Canaan; Nimrod,
the first tyrant, the mighty hunter;
the seventy Gentile nations.

The fifteenth numbered trump of the Tarot is called *Il Diavolo* (*The Devil*), *Il Demonio* (*The Demon*) or *I Demoni* (*The Demons*) in Italian decks; *Le Diable* (*The Devil*) is the French title. Modern decks depict a horned, goat-headed, bat-winged monster, shaggy legs and taloned feet, squatting on a stone block to which a man and woman are tied by chains or ropes about their necks. They seem to have his satyr-like features. It is easy enough to understand the idea behind the trump: Christian iconography often represents the archfiend as a goat-like figure. The link between the Devil and goats is precisely the train of thought behind xiv 30.

XV. The Devil of some older Tarot decks is rather more human than monstrous; his horns do not sprout directly from his head, but he sports a headband to which horns are affixed. He wears a hairy tunic of animal hides. The trump shows Nimrod, who is sometimes depicted with antlers or horns in Jewish and Christian iconology, dressed up in his magical hunting attire, and a couple of those whom he has cunningly ensnared in one of his traps.

In divination, the card implies: inescapable fate, blind impulse, temptation, materiality.

XVI. The Tower;
The Gospel According to John chapter 16;
peh, a mouth; numerical value 80 (or 800 when final);
the eighth sefirah, Hod (Glory);
the path from the seventh sefirah, Ne<u>z</u>a<u>h</u> (Victory) to the eighth sefirah, Hod (Glory);
Mars;
Genesis xi 1 to xi 32: the Tower of Babel and confusion of tongues; wars of Abram.

The sixteenth trump of the Tarot possesses diverse titles: *La Torre* (*The Tower*), *Il Fulmine* (*Lightning*), *Il Fuoco* (*Fire*), *La Sagitta* or *Saetta* (*The Arrow*), *L'Inferno* (*Hell*), *La Casa del Diavolo* (*The House of the Devil*), *L'Hôpital* (*The Hostel*), *La Maison de Dieu* (*House of God*), *La Foudre* (*Lightning*). It depicts a lightning-blasted tower from whose shattered wreck people hurtle headlong earthward. Flames erupt from the edifice and also from deep fissures in the ground at its base.

Eliphaz Levi understands the trump to depict the Tower of Babel, and the crowned figure falling from its summit to be Nimrod.[16.1] And quite correct too: the sixteenth chapter of John's Gospel contains allusions to Genesis xi 1ff, which describes the

Tower of Babel. At the same time, the form of the trump is suggested in the opening verse of xvi:

> '... they will throw you out of the synagogues.' xvi 1.

The trump also recalls Jesus' identification with lightning in xvi. Divinatory meanings include: fall from height, release of tension, quarrels, strife, warfare.

16.1: Eliphaz Levi, *Transcendental Magic* (translated by A.E. Waite) p. 391.

XVII. The Star;
The Gospel According to John chapter 17;
zaddi, fish-hook; numerical value 90 (or 900 when final); the ninth sefirah, Yesod (Foundation); the path from the seventh sefirah, Nezah (Victory) to the ninth sefirah, Yesod (Foundation); Aquarius, and the eleventh house; the eleventh month, Shevat; Genesis xii 1 to xv 8: promise of innumerable descendants to Abraham.

XVII. *The Star* shows a naked female figure pouring water from an urn onto the ground, while a number of stars shine brightly in the night sky above her. In divination: hope, help, insight, fantasy, dreaminess.

While it is not hard to see that while the trump points to the sign Aquarius, it has obviously been influenced also by the opening verse of the seventeenth chapter,

> Jesus lifted up his eyes to heaven. xvii 1,

which has in turn been influenced by Genesis xv 5,

> He brought him outside and said to him, 'Look to the heavens and see whether you can count the stars – just so shall your seed be.'

A bird sitting in a tree in the background of the card recalls that the 'Sabbath of Birds' falls early in Shevat, with 'New Year of Trees' in the middle of the month.

XVIII. The Moon;
The Gospel According to John chapter 18;
**quf, ear; numerical value 100;
the tenth sefirah, Malkuth (Kingdom);
the path from the seventh sefirah, Nezah (Victory)
to the tenth sefirah, Malkuth (Kingdom);
Pisces, and the twelfth house;
the twelfth month, Adar;
Genesis xv 9 to xvi 16:
Abraham's horror of deep darkness.**

XVIII. *The Moon* shows, in the foreground, a pool with some kind of crawling creature at its bottom. A path leads up towards a pylon in the distance. A dog and a wolf howl at a crescent moon, which is drawn with female face, shining alone in the starless night.

The form of the card recalls a peculiar fact about the night of Jesus' betrayal: it is so dark so that the soldiers coming to arrest Jesus need lamps and torches (xviii 3), even though the moon must be full on the night before midmonth feast of Passover. The towers forming a pylon or gateway in the background of the card may be drawn from the gate mentioned in xviii 16.

Crowley's description of the trump in *Book of Thoth* recalls the dark and dirty Qidron and the drops of Jesus' sweat falling like drops of blood just before his arrest. Once again flaunting his knowledge about the relationship between Genesis and the correspondences underpinning John's Gospel, he cites 'And a horror of deep darkness came upon him' (Genesis xv 9).[18.1]

Traditional divinatory meanings of the card include hidden enemies, danger, darkness, terror, deception, illusion, intoxication, error, and silence. All are easily explicable as aspects of the twelfth house, or of the Feast of Purim, and manifest in xviii in various ways.

18.1: Aleister Crowley, *Book of Thoth* pp. 112-113.

XIX. The Sun;
The Gospel According to John chapter 19;
resh, head; numerical value 200;
the second sefirah, Hokmah (Wisdom);
the path from the eighth sefirah,
Hod (Glory) to the ninth sefirah, Yesod (Foundation);
Sun;
Genesis xvii 1 to xvii 27:
circumcision of Abraham and his household.

The nineteenth numbered trump, *The Sun*, usually depicts two children playing in a walled garden beneath a full-face sun. This trump is the only one whose title actually matches the astrological correspondence of *Sefer Yezirah*. The Tarot's authors perhaps wished to bring to mind the most remarkable feature of John's treatment of the crucifixion: he fails to mention the extinction of the sun's light for several hours (According to Luke xxiii 45).

Waite departs from tradition, depicting a child riding a horse, drawing from Revelation xix 11, where John sees the King of Kings and Lord of Lords mounted on a white horse.

In his discussion of this trump, Crowley expounds some of his observations about the symbol of the Rosy Cross.[19.1] No doubt he wished merely to advertise he understands the cross to be an important solar emblem in John's symbolic lexicon, as one may deduce from xix.

Traditional divinatory meanings of the trump include truth, frankness, shamelessness, fame, celebrity, arrogance, vain display. These are of course just the ideas from which xix is woven.

19.1: Aleister Crowley, *The Book of Thoth* p. 114.

XX. Judgement;
The Gospel According to John chapter 20;
shin, a tooth; numerical value 300;
the third sefirah, Binah (Understanding);
the path from the eighth sefirah,
Hod (Glory) to the tenth sefirah, Malkuth (Kingdom);
the element Fire;
Genesis xviii 1 to xix 8:
incineration of Sodom and Gomorrah.

The twentieth numbered trump of the Tarot is called *L'Angelo* (*The Angel*), *Giudizio* (*Judgement*), *Il Paradiso* (*Paradise*), *La Tromba* (*The Trumpet*). It shows the dead rising newly quickened and emerging from their graves and tombs as an angel blasts a trumpet in the sky overhead. It is conventional depiction of the event said to take place at Jesus' Second Coming, which is known in orthodox Christian belief as the Last Day, the Day of Judgement, the Day of the Lord, or the Day of Resurrection.

The twentieth chapter of the Gospel According to John relates the discovery of Jesus' empty tomb, Mary's encounter with angels, and the resurrected Jesus' subsequent appearances to the disciples. Curiously, many aspects of the corresponding path and its yeziratic attribution are far more comprehensible in the context of the Resurrection of the Dead than in that of resurrection of Jesus.

The Tarot trump points toward the element fire, which is the yeziratic attribution of the letter *shin*, since Christian art, liturgy and scripture make fire an prominent feature of Judgement Day, which is described as a conflagration in which the very heavens catch alight and the primordial elements vanish in intense heat:

> But heaven and earth, which are preserved by the same word, are saved for fire for the day of judgment and destruction of ungodly men...

> But the day of the Lord will come as a thief in the night. It is a day in which the heavens will pass away with a loud noise, and the elements, set ablaze, will dissolve, and the earth and the works that are in it will be burned up. Therefore, since all present things are dissolving like this, you should be the sort of people who conduct holy and pious lives, looking forward to and hastening the coming of the day of God, on account of which the heavens will be dissolved, burning with fire, and the elements, set ablaze, will melt. 2 Peter iii 7-12.

Paul (1 Corinthians iii 13) speaks of fire and 'the Day' in such a way that the connection is taken for granted.

XX. Judgement also recalls Abraham that addresses God as Judge of the Earth (Genesis xviii 25) when he pleads for the plain cities.

Theft is an important theme of xx, deriving, as already explained, from the fact that the eighth sefirah, Hod, is associated with the eighth commandment, and also from the fact that Hod is cognate with Mercury. It appears in xx in the motif of the purloined corpse, and Jesus' ability to penetrate the locked the doors of the disciples' house, and then make off again. However, Jesus-qua-thief is also an important theme related to 'the Day of the Lord'. And not only is his coming like that of a thief, is day, too, is itself said to come, as Peter notes (2 Peter iii 10) 'as a thief at night'. Similar symbolism occurs elsewhere in the context of Jesus' coming:

> For you yourselves know quite well that the Day of the Lord comes as a thief in the night. ... But you, brothers, are not in darkness, that the day should come upon you like a thief. 1 Thessalonians v 2-4.

> At that time two will be in the field, one will be taken away, the other left behind. Two women grinding in the mill, one will be taken, the other left behind. Watch out then, because you do not know the day the Master comes. You will understand that if the man of the house had known on which watch the thief would come, he would have stayed awake and not have let his house be burgled. Because of this, be ready, because the Son of Man comes at the very time you do not suppose. According to Matthew xxiv 40-44.

Resurrection of the Dead marks the end of the current cosmic order. As 'Last Day' implies, it is the end of time. The trump also points to the fact that xxi contains a motif drawn from an apocryphal legend concerning the post-Resurrection world, namely the feasting upon Leviathan by the righteous in the World to Come.

Traditional divinatory meanings include final determination, sentence without subject to appeal.

XXI. The World;
The Gospel According to John chapter 21;
**tau, a cross; numerical value 400;
the fourth sefirah, Hesed (Mercy);
the path from the ninth sefirah, Yesod (Foundation)
to the tenth sefirah, Malkuth (Kingdom); Saturn.**

XXI. *The World* shows a figure of a woman, naked apart from a veil or scarf, dancing or floating in space. A wreath encircles her. The trump portrays the Shekhinah as the *Anima Mundi* or World-Soul. The title is suggested by the last words of John's Gospel,

> There are many other things which Jesus did, and if they were written down one by one, I think the world [*ton kosmon*] could not hold the books written. xxi 25

and the last words of the Matthew's Gospel,

> And behold, I am with you every day, until the end of the world [*tou aiōnos*]. According to Matthew xxviii 20.

In the four corners of the card sit a lion, man, bull, and eagle, before each an open book, standard Christian iconographic representations of the Four Evangelists, recalling the final words of John's Gospel as well as the Longer Ending of Mark's:

> Travelling through the entire world [*eis ton kosmon apanta*], announce the gospel to every creature. According to Mark xvi 15.

Quatro Santi Evangelisti (*The Four Holy Evangelists*) is another title of the trump.

Probably drawing on the first chapter of *Sifra De Zeni'utha*, where Leviathan is described as an *ouroboros*, Crowley shows 'the Virgin Universe' dancing in the coils of a serpent.[21.1] Crowley's interpretation correctly points to the ideas presented in the Fourth Gospel.

Some versions (Visconti-Sforza) of *XXI. The World* portray a seascape with boats sailing along the shore, recalling the disciples' fishing trip in the opening scene of xxi.

21.1: *Zohar* (*Sifra De Zeni'utha*) 2:176b (*Book of Concealment* i 26), see translations by Daniel C. Matt, Work of the Chariot, Dale and Sassoon, or G. L. Mathers.

Daniel C. Matt, *The Zohar: Pritzker Edition* vol. 5 p. 551 n. 13.

Part 5:
Epilogue

The big picture

According to John was originally intended to be divided into twenty-one chapters or sections after the manner set out by Stephen Langton in the thirteenth century. The Gospel is organised in this way because every chapter corresponds to one letter of the Hebrew alphabet. For a handful of reasons the first letter, *'alef*, is not included in the scheme, so that there come to be only twenty-one chapters rather than twenty-two. A chapter's correspondence to a letter of the alphabet entails its being invested with an extensive network of symbolic associations. One set of these, which comes from a version of *Sefer Yezirah*, links each chapter to a cosmic element, a planet, or a sign of the zodiac and month of the year. Another set relates each chapter to a single sefirah, while yet another assigns it to a path connecting a pair of sefiroth on the qabalistic Tree. A section of Genesis, which is understood to contain references to the very same scheme of correspondences that underlies his Gospel, provides an additional assortment of symbolism. The Fourth Gospel is in consequence no ordinary narrative. Largely allegorical, it is built around and out of the correspondences, from the places and times that form the background of events, to the words and deeds of the characters, many of whom are little more than types or personifications.

The Fourth Gospel's author seems not to have made any serious attempt to hide its true nature. While hardly lacking in subtlety, he is often astoundingly simple and direct. He devotes one entire chapter to each letter and its correspondences, and is consistent in his treatment from chapter to chapter. If some chapters are loaded with more symbolic material than others, the variation is not great. John, moreover, largely avoids esoterica. With respect to astrology, he demands little more than a dilettante's acquaintance of the subject. The range of things associated with any house of the heavens, or any planet, is necessarily large, but each has certain primary or chief designations, and it is to these that John regularly turns. An astrologer would hardly find anything difficult or recherché in the elementary knowledge John assumes. Similar observations might be made about John's approach to Jewish religious festivals or Qabalah as sources. Even the basics will take one a long way.

John's Gospel is packed with a wealth of technical data. The sheer density of allusion produces some strange and beautiful effects. Ideas drawn from astrology, the calendar of Jewish feasts, Qabalah, and the shape or meaning of a Hebrew letter sit together in the same passage, often within the same verse. Even a single phrase or word may perform a bewildering variety of functions. For John takes great pains to integrate the different types of symbolism accidentally brought together by the different systems of correspondences. This happens with such regularity it becomes easy to take for granted. Almost every chapter in the Gospel strives to combine qabalistic and astrological symbolism in novel ways. A forced marriage between two independent schemes of correspondences such as Qabalah and astrology sounds like a recipe for confusion, yet John not only carries it off, he makes it look easy. Everything neatly fits together in a natural way, so that he appears to have it all figured out. One is left wondering whether the Fourth Gospel is primarily a book about Jesus or an apologetic for the system of correspondences that make up John's metaphysical picture of the universe.

Although more than half of John's Gospel is very tightly constructed, with each chapter largely devoted to its prescribed themes, it nevertheless contains a few surprises in terms of its organisation. In a number of instances John places symbols in what are, at first sight at least, inappropriate locations. On closer inspection, however, one can perceive the existence of certain patterns John follows when doing this.

(1) The last few verses of a chapter may contain an image or symbol which properly belongs to the immediately following chapter. When marked with a future tense or a construction is equivalent to a future, it is quite conspicuous. Example: 'You will see the heavens opened and the angels of heaven ascending and descending on the Son of Man' (i 51). Another is 'the ruler of this world is coming' (xiv 30). Sometimes John has a roundabout way of indicating a symbol belongs to the next chapter, as 'There was a garden close by the place where Jesus was crucified' (xix 41).

(2) A personification sometimes appears one chapter too late. The merchants and money-changers appear in ii, rather than i; the Samaritan woman in iv, rather than iii; the nobleman with the feverish son in iv, rather than iii; Jesus' brothers in vii, rather than vi; the hired man in x, rather

than ix: all exemplify the phenomenon. John signals their lateness, or the fact that they are out of place, in the same way on each occasion: such characters leave the scene, sometimes dramatically, but always with an explicit statement to the effect.

(3) Symbolism may migrate along one of the vertical pillars on the Tree of sefiroth. Example: Tabernacles is the background of vii, when material connected to that feast should be in xii. Another example is Jesus' Cleansing of the Temple in ii, which has features that are modelled on the Feast of Dedication, and would therefore be more appropriate to xiv. Similarly, v contains allusions to New Year's Day that would be more suitable for x.

(4) Sometimes one of the double or mother letters will pick up symbolism related to Jewish feasts from an adjacent simple letter. Example: references to New Year in x rather than xi. Another: references to Tabernacles in xii rather than xi. Another example is seen in the motifs related to Purim, which are found in xix as well as xviii.

(5) Sometimes a single character may represent the correspondences of two consecutive chapters. Example: Judas in xii and xiii. Nimrod and Esau in xv and xvi. Pontius Pilate in xviii and xix. A common feature is that the relevant letters are of different types: *mem* (xii) is a mother letter, *nun* (xiii) a simple; *'ayin* (xv) is a simple letter, *peh* (xvi) double; *quf* (xviii) is simple, *resh* (xix) double.

It is fortunate that whenever John deviates from the simplest course he regularly observes conventions such as these from which we can infer certain rules of Gospel composition. The very fact that

John does colour outside the lines at all says something important about his style and approach. One effect of John's idiosyncrasies should not be overlooked: we can be quite confident that no meddling with the order of chapters has occurred. We can, for example, be sure that the second chapter really was meant to immediately follow upon the first because of Jesus' identification with Jacob's ladder in i, and the expulsion of the merchants from the Temple in ii. If the second chapter had swapped place with some other, the tampering would be obvious and unaesthetic.

Another striking feature of John's writing is his fondness for using word or phrase in a context specific way. One can see how greatly the significance of a word varies fluidly from place to place by considering the appearance of 'light' (*phōs*) in seven chapters: i 4-9, iii 19-21, v 35, viii 12, ix 4-5, xi 10, xii 46. Far from being fixed, a symbol's meaning depends on the attributions of the chapter in which it lies. The *Zohar* abounds in instances where the meaning of a symbol varies like this. It is the chief reason the book has been charged with self-contradiction and inconsistency. But the *Zohar* is a hundred times longer than the Fourth Gospel, so the Gospel's reader is more liable to suffer confusion due to a symbol's changing significance. It is much more difficult for a writer to use words in this way than it is to write mechanically, that is to ascribe to certain keywords a static meaning. Although John's motivations for are unclear, the fact that he took some effort in this respect should not be overlooked. It may have been done as a sort of blind, to conceal the nature of the Gospel or some of the attributions.

Inconsistencies

While the regimen of correspondences for the most part determines the subject matter of each chapter, with major breaks in the scheme falling into one of the five classes listed above, one also encounters what appear to be a host of minor incongruities, where John apparently chooses not to follow his own formula. We see words that are imbued with technical meaning in one place make sporadic appearances in other places that are inexplicable in terms of the system of correspondences. They cannot be dismissed as instances of context specificity, though some may ultimately turn out to be such. Nor can they seem to fall into any well defined pattern. We have to ask: Why does the title 'Lamb of God' appear in i, when it would be more suited to iv, the chapter assigned Aires, and the Passover month, Nisan? If the term 'only' (*monogenēs*) points to the first sefirah, Kether (Crown) in i, why does it appear in iii? If Jesus' brothers are used to indicate Gemini and the third house of the horoscope, why are they mentioned in ii? Why does Philip appear in vi, rather than Thomas the Twin, who has an obvious affinity with the sign of Gemini? If the Sea of Galilee represents the sefirah Malkuth, why does it play a part in the narrative of vi? If John uses the verb 'seize' in to suggest the sign Cancer in vii, then why does it appear in vi, viii and x? Why does the word 'beginning', which is used in i to indicate Ḥokmah, appear in xiii and xvi? Why does he talk about prayers being answered in xiv? Why does Jesus talk about obeying his commandments in xvi? Why talk about journeying in xvi? If the word 'heart' connotes Tif'areth (Beauty), why mention it twice in xvi, which has no contact with that sefirah? Why does Jesus' mother appear at the foot of the cross in xix?

This is hardly an exhaustive list, but it includes some of the more obvious representative cases. It is important to realise that although such inconsistencies exist, and are too many to ignore, they are relatively few in comparison to mass of symbolic material that is dictated by the scheme of correspondences. John adheres to his formula far more often than he abandons it. More than half the Gospel, based on a verse count, is occupied by symbolism that is determined by the chapter's specific correspondences. John's habit of bringing together astrological and qabalistic motifs results in a unique brand of symbolism whose special features make it hard to mistake for something else. Minor breaks in the Gospel's structure therefore do not cause difficulty in distinguishing the central theme of a chapter from subsidiary matters. In fact, it is only because the Gospel is so tightly constructed that any incongruities immediately stand out.

Why John, who is skilful and meticulous in his choice of words, would fail to remove what could be regarded as imperfections in the text remains a riddle. It cannot be due to carelessness or a lack of ability on his part. However, when we examine a symbol or image that is obviously out of place, and ask where it would properly be expected, it becomes clear that the aberrant placement of symbolic material is often a consequence of relationships between chapters. The most obvious relationship between chapters consists in their sequential order. Astrology provides yet another set of relationships between chapters, the structure of the qabalistic Tree of Life still another.

Some symbolism looks out of place because John occasionally links together themes from several chapters, elaborating a complex figure. In viii 35, for example, we see an image that involves the correspondences of three consecutive chapters. Similar is xvi 8-11. In such cases, the fact that the chapters are consecutive makes it easy to recognise the nature of the construction. However, the reasons for juxtaposing certain symbols are not always so clear.

Cosmic man and historical figure

As a literary composition, the Gospel is outstanding, but the allegorical layer of meaning is irreconcilable with historical accuracy. The book's technical brilliance and flamboyance destroy all semblance of veracity. According to John appears an exquisitely contrived fable in which there is no room for any historical Jesus – he has been entirely pushed out by the mythological figure. The only Jesus that John knows is an entirely synthetic creation. John moreover does not even make an effort to create the illusion of fact. One can barely imagine what more he could have done to make it clear that the story looks to be a complete invention.

If we had absolutely no knowledge at all of first century Judea, but were somehow still left with According to John and the wherewithal to understand it, we should conclude that Jerusalem along with its Sheep Gate and its Pool of Siloam was a mythical place. Real personages like John the Baptist, Pilate, and Peter would be regarded as fictional characters. The obvious error of such conclusion should make us wary of saying that Jesus never existed. It does, however, illustrate how serious the problem is – the best eyewitness account of Jesus' existence is so artificial that it makes Jerusalem seem like a city in the sky inhabited by planetary and zodiacal archons and personifications of the sefiroth.

It goes without saying, if Jesus were a historical figure, and one for whom one felt love and respect, to treat Jesus in the way John does, replacing biographical details with a blatantly forged life story built up from outlandish elements, would be a remarkable thing to do. Overall, one must say that John went to great deal of trouble to make it obvious that his whole story from start to finish is a fable. The veneer of factuality is thin, and once breached, rapidly falls away. For these reasons one must wonder whether John is turning a historical person into the Cosmic Man, or grounding a cosmic figure, who properly lives and moves in a world of celestial archetypes, within a historical setting. The Gospel's Jesus looks not to have originally inhabited the same world we do, but some sort of supramundane sphere.

In his commentary to *Sefer Yezirah*, Aryeh Kaplan, discussing theories about its origins, mentions a tradition that the Essenes were the original custodians of *Sefer Yezirah*, and that Menahem, vice president of the Sanhedrin, and the teacher of Nehunia ben haQana, author of *Sefer ha Bahir*, was Menahem the Essene, famous for having predicted Herod's ascension to the throne, as mentioned by Josephus.[epi.1] This is just a possibility, but an intriguing one, for it has been suggested the Essenes had beliefs which have uncanny similarities to John's.

In *The White Goddess*, Robert Graves discusses a medieval Welsh poetic tradition whose central characters make a series of riddling 'I was' or 'I have been' statements.[epi.2] The sequence of things with which the hero of each poem identifies himself ultimately points back, he says, to the letters of an ancient ogham alphabet, called Boibel-Loth from the names of its first two letters. The letters, which are intimately connected to the calendar, have names sounding like strange corruptions of biblical personages and places: Boibel, Loth, Cailep, Nehushtan, and so on. Graves' interpretation of these poems is astonishing. They are, he says, a lost relic of the inner teaching of the Essenes, to whom each letter of the alphabet represented a ruling power of the universe or fundamental cosmic element. Taken all together in sequence, they compose a name of God. Using the correspondences of the letters of the alphabet, the Essenes, he says, were putting together a story of the life and death of Moses, who had become 'a demigod' mediating between God and man. And not only the Essenes: first century Christians of Jewish background had reverted, Graves says, to worshipping these universal letter-powers, which entailed slavish observance of the calendar. The series of 'I have been' and 'I was' of Gwion's *Hanes Taliesin* point to a set of mystical titles derived from the Boibel-Loth alphabet: the last vestige of a secret of the Essenes.

One could hardly imagine a better summary of the basic concept underlying Fourth Gospel than Graves' description of the Essenes' ideas. Substitute Jesus for Moses, Johannine for Essene, According to John for *Hanes Taliesin* – everything continues to make perfect sense. Even the 'I was' and 'I have been' sayings of Gwion's hero, which Graves mentions here, find a parallel in Jesus' 'I am' statements, a unique feature of the Fourth Gospel. Why Graves thought the Essenes conceived of the letters of an alphabet as the ruling powers of the cosmos and how they used them to compose a story about the life and death of Moses is not easy to understand. But if the Essenes did possess a version of *Sefer Yezirah* and were composing stories based on its alphabet correspondences, then According to John has a clear precedent.

If the goal of the Fourth Gospel had been to rigorously demonstrate from Jesus' life story that he is a type of Cosmic Man, John, being as intelligent as he was, would have certainly realised the Gospel just does not succeed. For one thing, the blatantly fictional nature of the story stands in the way of this conclusion. John is sometimes too gaudy or artificial to take seriously. Much of the symbolism is gratuitous. John often seems to be making facile allusions just for the sake of it, and the results are sometimes glib and fatuous, not profound. John could hardly have been blind to this. He must have known the reader would interpret his work as pure myth.

Apart from this, even if the Gospel were literal history, the letter mysticism underlying it is never used in such a way as to offer convincing proof of this important idea.

For one thing, the many characters of the Gospel who are personifications of astrological abstractions and sefiroth are never unambiguously presented as the ruling powers of the cosmos, merely flesh and blood reflections of their nature. The boy and his father of iv can never really become Isaac and Abraham; nor is the Samaritan woman at the well the goddess Venus; nor Barabbas an incarnation of Mercury. Of course, the allegorical nature of the story invites the reader to make the necessary leap, and understand the story is about Jesus' encounters with the archons though dressed in human form.

The presence of two systems of time, one explicit, one symbolic, running side by side, also makes it difficult to argue that Jesus' life was ordained by divine providence according to a qabalistic yardstick. Why does Jesus become the Good Shepherd of New Year when it is close to Feast of Dedication? Why, after the leisurely pace of the early part of the story, is John forced to have five full months of the year, from Marḥeshvan to Adar, rush by in a single night. If Jesus somehow embodies in himself the mystical significance behind the calendar, then such contortions with time should hardly be necessary.

From an artistic viewpoint it makes good sense not to have Jesus perform a miracle in each chapter in order to demonstrate his mastery over a particular cosmic power. For the same reason, there is no need for an explicit 'I am' statement in every chapter. Undoubtedly, John could trust the reader to make certain extrapolations. It often suffices that Jesus merely discourse about the theme at hand. However, if Jesus' life had been divinely prescribed according to a qabalistic recipe, then it should have been necessary as a formality that Jesus prove himself with signs in every single chapter. Why now signs and wonders, and now only speeches? Ultimately, John gives an informal, poetic statement of faith that Jesus is the Cosmic Man but never goes beyond that to prove it from his life story.

John's statement that he wrote 'in order that you might believe that Jesus is the Son of God' (xx 31) is not too far from the truth. But the Gospel looks primarily geared to inform what the Son of God should be like. It sets forth John's own definition of the Son of God: he is one who unites in himself the complete panoply of cosmic powers, someone who can go the full twenty-one rounds with the archons, and win every round.

Canonised qabalah

It is irony of fate that Christians have always had a form of the qabalistic and yeziratic correspondences of the Hebrew letters intrinsic to their sacred writings. Jesus is said to have fulfilled a variety of prophecies of Jewish scriptures, but it is astrology and Qabalah that play the truly pivotal role in the revelation of Jesus' Christhood. Most importantly, it is not only trivial details of Jesus life that emanate from the philosophical machine. All the major events of the Gospel story are built out of the correspondences. Jesus is never presented in any other way. He always appears in the context of the system of correspondences, never apart from them. If Jesus came to overthrow the archons, to bring an end to their wicked rule, in the end we see his death and resurrection seem to have changed nothing. Astrological and qabalistic correspondences dominate the Gospel's last chapter as completely as they do the rest. Even at the very close of the book, the order of the cosmos has not perceptibly changed. It's business as usual.

The highly unusual nature of John's perspective poses difficulty for modern Christianity, one which will be felt all the more acutely for John's being the theologian among the Evangelists. Many ideas of vital importance to Christian theology are unique to the Fourth Gospel, which provides a missing link between the too human Jesus of the Synoptics and the more divine than human Jesus of Paul. Since the true Christology of the Gospel is transmitted through the medium of astrological and qabalistic language, John blurs all boundaries between theology and murkier subjects like theosophy and metaphysics. Some of the issues the Fourth Gospel raises are of a fundamental theological nature, and cannot be dismissed as merely metaphysical or mystical. For example, According to John raises questions concerning the Evangelist's ideas about what it means that Jesus is 'Son of God', even that he enjoyed historical existence. His beliefs about the number of Persons in the Godhead, another important aspect of Christian dogma, are also unclear. For it seems inescapable the Christian doctrine of the Trinity came out of the qabalistic doctrine of *Parzufin*, or Faces or Personae, even if there are profound and irreconcilable differences.

The presence of Qabalah and astrology in the Gospel opens a terrible Pandora's box of unorthodox ideas. Curiously, although nascent Christianity was surrounded by pagan and Gnostic sects and plagued by internal divisions, Christians never resorted to esoteric interpretations of According to John in their disputes with each other or with their opponents. Nor could the people with whom they argued have had any inkling of these matters. A million and one heresies might be supported, or annihilated, with the Fourth Gospel. In fact, According to John was at one time eyed suspiciously just because Gnostic sects held it in high regard, adopting several words from the Prologue – *Archē*, *Logos*, *Zoē*, *Anthrōpos*, *Monogenēs*, *Charis*, *Plērōma* – and incorporating them into their speculations as technical terms. There is, however, no sign that According to John was ever used by Christians in their diatribes against the Gnostics, nor does it appear that embarrassed Christians had to explain the presence of qabalistic motifs in their scripture. While refuting Gnosticism and other heresies the early Christian apologists often enjoy ridiculing astrology as an absurd superstition at the same time. Their tone is incompatible with the spirit of the Fourth Gospel, whose author ostensibly believes either that the power of heavenly bodies, once real enough, has now been broken, or else that while humanity in general lives in thrall to astral influences, Christians alone are exempt from their rule.

Infinitely more controversy surrounding the status of the Fourth Gospel would have arisen when the New Testament canon was put together if its true nature had been appreciated. The silence is inexplicable unless important knowledge vanished from open sight almost immediately. One can see what John's perspective is – it is that of someone who is thoroughly steeped in qabalistic and astrological notions. John had no qualms about portraying a Jesus whose speech is a mixture of qabalistic double-talk and astrological puns, whose very life history is regulated by the yardstick of astrology and the Qabalah. But after this, total silence on the subject. Modern normative Christianity appears strangely isolated from its origins. If Christians ever did accept the Fourth Gospel on its own terms, they would in effect be following a new religion. The Fourth Gospel is embedded within an extensive symbolic matrix now so utterly alien to Christianity that it can barely even be spoken about. Christians attempting to approach the Fourth

Gospel on its own terms can only do so through systems of knowledge now forbidden, whose very vocabulary is completely foreign to them.

St. Irenaeus, second century bishop of Lyons, asks how it could be that the apostles did not impart any secret wisdom teachings they might have possessed to the bishops, their own hand-picked successors, the ones to whom they entrusted their churches.[epi.3] He argues that this could not have happened, and that what the bishops in apostolic succession do not talk or know about does not exist. In reality, Christianity was very much a religion of secrets, of knowers and know-nots.

Although there never was a time when Christians placed any value on the esoteric knowledge within the Fourth Gospel, someone living in medieval Italy with great insight into its true nature turned it into a set of cards used for fortune-telling and gaming.

The priority of John's Gospel

Every chapter of John's Gospel is constructed out of a mishmash of astrological and qabalistic symbolism which John ambitiously tries to combine. And yet the resultant narrative comes out in good agreement with the account given by the Synoptics. This really is an astonishing feat: operating under so many constraints, John is able to tell a story which largely conforms to that of his Coevangelists. A lot has been made about the differences between John's Gospel and the others, and not without reason. However, the vast gulf between the Fourth Gospel and the others is partly an illusion due to the extraordinary similarity of the Synoptic Gospels to one another. John actually follows the Synoptic storyline closely. Had he not done so, his Gospel would hardly have been included in the Christian corpus of scripture.

Since the Fourth Gospel is almost pure allegory, merely by describing the same events as John, the Synoptic Evangelists inevitably made use of allegorical material. John has certain prerequisites, but despite his choosiness, many episodes from the Synoptic Gospels are found in his work. John's made-to-measure Jesus is already there in the Synoptic Gospels. The most puzzling aspect of the relationship between the Synoptic Gospels and John's, however, is not that they share material in common. Rather, it lies the fact that Matthew, Mark, and Luke include things of relevance to John's secret that John himself leaves out. Some of these scream out to be in John's Gospel, and their failure to appear there is as perplexing as their inclusion within the Synoptic accounts. They constitute the strongest evidence the Synoptics drew from someone familiar with the mysticism of *Sefer Yezirah* and Tree of sefiroth. About a score of such omissions exist:

(1) In the episode of the expulsion of the merchants from the Temple, Jesus' the speaks of the place having been turned into a 'den of thieves' in According to Matthew xxi 13, Mark xi 17, Luke xix 46. If this had appeared in John's Gospel, it would have a natural explanation in Mercury's association with theft, an idea John seems to be fond of.

(2) In According to Matthew iii 11, John the Baptist confesses his unworthiness to lift up Jesus' sandals. If this had occurred in John's Gospel (at i 27) it would be easily understandable as a reference to Mercury's winged sandals.

(3) When discussing the miraculous multiplication of loaves in According to Matthew xvi 12 and Mark viii 14-21, Jesus explains that 'the yeast of the Pharisees' refers to their teaching. If this comment occurred in John's Gospel (in vi),

it would be perfectly understandable as a reference to the fact that Gemini and the third house are especially associated with teaching and education.

(4) Jesus feeds a multitude with miraculously multiplied loaves on two separate occasions in the Synoptic Gospels (According to Matthew xiv and xv, Mark vi and viii). If there were such a duplication in John's Gospel, it would be explicable as a reference to the sign of the Twins.

(5) Jesus promises Mary worldwide fame in gratitude for his anointing in According to Matthew xxvi 9 and Mark xiv 13. If this had happened in John's Gospel (in xii), it would be explainable as a reference to the eighth sefirah, Hod (Glory, Renown, Fame).

(6) In According to Matthew xvi 26-28, Mark xiv 22-24, and Luke xii 19-20, Jesus at the Last Supper, pronounces the memorable words: 'This is my body, which is given up for you... this is cup of the new testament in my blood'. If this had happened in John's Gospel (in xiii), it would be explainable in the association Scorpio and the eighth house have with death and the disposal of the property of the deceased.

(7) According to Mark xiv 51-52 tells how a young man wearing nothing but a linen cloth follows Jesus, who is in the custody of a cohort of soldiers. He is caught briefly, but breaks free, dropping his garment, and flees naked. If this detail had appeared in the eighteenth chapter of John's Gospel, the young man would be explainable as a personification of the ninth sefirah. The episode borrows from Joseph's encounter with Potiphar's wife (Genesis xxxix 12), where he runs away leaving her holding his garment. John actually uses a nakedness to indicate the ninth sefirah in

other places. However, if this episode had been included in John's Gospel, its presence would be explainable because of a rather strange reason: in John's Gospel, we sometimes find that a personification of one of the planets or sefiroth appears one chapter too late, that is, not in the chapter where it would otherwise be expected, but in the very next chapter. When such things occur, fleeing from Jesus' presence seems to be the regular way of signalling it. To see Mark use this device is surprising.

(8) Jesus' anguished prayer and bloody sweat just before his arrest (According to Matthew xxvi 39-46, Mark xiv 36-41, Luke xxii 42-46), if they had been recorded in John's Gospel, would be understandable as reference to the fact that the twelfth house is connected with fears and anxieties. His falling on the ground in this episode, an allusion to the tenth sefirah, which is reworked in John's Gospel into everyone else falling on the ground (xviii 6).

(9) Jesus finds the disciples asleep while he prays just before his arrest in According to Matthew xxvi 39-46, Mark xiv 36-41, Luke xxii 42-46. If this had been recorded in John's account (in xviii), it would be explainable as a reference to the fact that the twelfth house is connected with sleep and unconsciousness, as is Purim, the main observance of the corresponding month, Adar. His comment that 'the spirit is willing but the flesh is weak' reflects the tenth sefirah's association with the physical frame.

(10) If Jesus assurance to Peter that he has recourse to 'more than twelve legions of angels' had occurred in John's Gospel (in xviii), it would explainable as a reference to the Shekhinah's escort of twelve armies of angels.

(11) If the High Priest's rending of his clothes, and the soldiers' violent treatment of Jesus at his trial (According to Matthew xxvi 65-68, Mark xiv 63-65, Luke xxiii 63-64) appeared in John's account (in xviii), they would be understandable as a reference to customs of Purim.

(12) At his trial (According to Matthew xxvi 64, Mark xiv 62, Luke xxii 69) Jesus makes a prophetic declaration. The soldiers who strike him demand he prophesy for them (According to Matthew xxvi 67, Mark xiv 65, Luke xxii 64). If these details had been related in John's Gospel (in xviii), they would be understandable in terms of Nezah's association with prophecy. The prophecy that Jesus makes itself contains symbolism related to the tenth sefirah, which would have been appropriate for xviii.

(13) When Judas tries to return the money he got for betraying Jesus to the Jewish authorities, it ends up going to buy Potter's Field, which becomes a foreigners' graveyard called 'Field of Blood' (According to Matthew xvii 7-10). Had this been recorded in John's Gospel (in xviii), the Field of Blood would be easily understood as a symbol of the tenth sefirah.

(14) Jesus' appearance before King Herod (According to Luke xxiii 8-11), if it had occurred in John's Gospel (in xix), would be explicable as a reference to the sun's association with royalty.

(15) In According to Matthew xxvii 34, Jesus is offered a drink of vinegar mixed with gall or wormwood just before crucifixion; in Mark xv 23, it is wine mixed with myrrh. If this were included in John's account (in xix), it would be

understandable as an allusion to the fact that *resh* is a homonym of a word meaning 'gall or wormwood'.

(16) Extinction of the sun's light during Jesus' crucifixion is told in According to Mark xv 33. If this detail were in John's Gospel (in xix), it would be understandable as a reference to the sun, the astrological attribution of the chapter.

(17) The crowd's jibes about a visit from Elijah, which accompany the thrusting of a wine-sponge into Jesus' mouth during the crucifixion (According to Matthew xvii 47-49, Mark xv 35-36), if they had appeared in John's Gospel, would be understandable as references to circumcision, one of the primary associations of Yesod (Foundation), and related to John's understanding of Genesis xvii.

(18) Jesus promise to the repentant thief that he will soon be with him in Paradise in According to Luke xxiii 43, if it had appeared in John's Gospel, would be explicable as a reference to the fact that garden is a symbol of Malkuth. However it would only be explicable in John's Gospel because he sometimes uses a future tense to indicate that a symbol really belongs in the following chapter.

(19) Joseph of Arimathea is described as 'good and righteous' in According to Luke xxiii 51. If this were recorded in John's Gospel (in xix) it would have been understandable as a reference to Joseph the patriarch as a personification of Yesod, for whom both 'good' and 'righteous' are standard epithets.

(20) The theme of theft which surrounds Jesus' resurrection in the twentieth chapter of John's Gospel is reworked into the Jewish elders' warning to Pilate that the disciples will try to steal Jesus' dead body, and their subsequent resort to that story in According to Matthew xvii 62-64, xviii 13-15.

We see here the full gamut: astrological symbolism, symbolism related to Jewish religious festivals, qabalistic symbolism, and possibly even motifs connected with John's interpretation of Genesis. Again, this is not a catalogue of Johannine symbolism in the Synoptic Gospels: these are just some of the things that can be found only in the Synoptics, things John fails to mention at all. Most telling is (7), According to Mark xiv 51-52. That the Synoptic Evangelists employ astrological and qabalistic symbolism is one thing, but it is another thing altogether if they also follow some of John's quirky conventions of composition, which we might well have expected to be unique to him.

Although the Synoptic Gospels superficially appear to be quite different from the Fourth Gospel, it is inevitable that their story of Jesus borrowed from someone who was using correspondences from *Sefer Yezirah* and the qabalistic Tree of sefiroth. There must have existed a repository of tales about Jesus that cast him in the same mould as John and upon which his Coevangelists could draw.

The simplest explanation for the relationship between the Synoptic Gospels and John's is that the Synoptic Evangelists had access to an early and unfinished version of John's Gospel. For According to John was not written overnight; it must have required many years of labour to put together. It would make sense to begin by first composing the latter portions of the story and work backwards from there. It may be that when the Synoptic Gospels were written, only Jesus' arrest, trial, crucifixion, and resurrection were completed. A few of the earlier events, like his encounter with the Baptist, the Miracle of Loaves, the Triumphal Entry into Jerusalem, the Last Supper, and the Cleansing of the Temple were taking shape. But for the most part, the story of Jesus' ministry before his Triumphal Entry into Jerusalem was still to be filled in when the

Synoptic Gospels were completed. If their accounts contain details that seem tailor-made for the Fourth Gospel that John does not know about, it may simply be that John dropped them from the final recension of his work. If the Synoptic Gospels were circulating by the time his own work was finished, John could afford to omit certain things, knowing his Coevangelists had already made up for any deficiency.

If conventional wisdom is true, and John possessed the Synoptic Gospels when he wrote, then he must have been aware he was exposing their nature. For John extinguishes all hope of finding historical truth within the other three canonical Gospels. He demonstrates elements within the Synoptics are myths by showing just how the story was composed. Eusebius, it is interesting to note, says that John wrote a spiritual gospel intended to illuminate the meaning of external facts recorded by the Synoptic Gospels, with which he was familiar.[epi.4]

Purpose

A multitude of tantalising questions remain unanswered.

It is evident doctrines of Qabalah which surfaced a thousand years later in Europe had already reached a high level of sophistication at the time Fourth Gospel was composed, yet we do not even know what qabalists of the first and second century called themselves or their teachings. John's ability to locate the yeziratic correspondences in Genesis suggests that many of the ideas upon which the Gospel is based have a long history. They may have been part of the original doctrines of Work of Creation (*Ma'asseh Bereshith*). If these correspondences are in fact there, then the traditions of Qabalah really are as old as this section of Genesis.

We can only speculate how John, a Galilean, a member of a heretical sect, obtained his knowledge. The Gospel's very existence implies that qabalistic teachings were not confined to closely knit circles. Apart from anything else, it must be unlikely that John would write as he has done for his own amusement. He surely felt someone would understand his message. A qabalistic worldview may have been quite prevalent in some sections of the Jewish community. If we only knew who possessed and most valued it, we might have a clearer ideas about the audience for whom John wrote. It was never meant for everyone who called themselves Christian.

Nor can we know how readers of the Fourth Gospel was meant to arrive at comprehension its secrets. To approach the Gospel one must possess knowledge about the astrological and qabalistic correspondences. If qabalistic knowledge was widespread, John may have expected that his readers would understand him without the assistance of any teacher or guide. His intended audience may have been small Jewish sect, like the disciples of the Baptist. The problem is that people who were not yet Christians would know about very weighty matters that many Christians themselves did not know about, a dangerous situation. On the other hand, if the true nature of the Gospel was unveiled to selected individuals sitting at the feet of a teacher, at the same time they were taught Qabalah, then they may have come from any background whatsoever.

In any case, Christianity once possessed a hidden side replete with strange doctrines of a type usually associated with occult beliefs or practices and more preoccupied with theosophy than theology. The gulf which separates the beliefs of today's Christians from that of its founders is so vast, their ideas were so different from those professed by Christians today, it would almost be correct to say that the authors of the Gospels were followers of another religion.

What purpose the Fourth Gospel may have been intended to serve is far from clear, only that it was never intended to be taken as a historical document. It may be that its narrative form is a ruse, its true purpose being merely to ensure that details of John's mystic philosophy, his system of occult metaphysics, were faithfully preserved and transmitted. It may even have been written as a reaction against the pious deception that Jesus had already enjoyed incarnate existence on this earth. For after reading According to John, the Jesus of the Synoptic Gospels never looks the same.

Behind rustic style lies concealed extraordinary genius. The Fourth Gospel is one of the most mysterious and unfathomable books written, easy to underestimate in every way conceivable. Its author was highly intelligent, erudite, adept at wordplay, and a master symbolist. It must rank as one of the greatest works of ancient literature. The panoramic vistas into first-and second-century thought that it opens offer invaluable insights into the history of ideas that have dominated Western culture for millennia. It raises new questions of fundamental importance about the origins of Christianity that are all the more acute because of its pivotal place within the New Testament canon of scripture.

epi.1: *Jewish Antiquities* book 15 chapter 10 section 5.

epi.2: Robert Graves In *The White Goddess*, pp. 148-150.

epi.3: St. Irenaeus *Contra Hereses* v.

epi.4: *Ecclesiasticae Historiae* iii 24:7, ibid vi 14:7.

Appendix 1:
Notes on the Jewish Calendar

In the Jewish calendar, the months are determined by the lunar cycle. At the time of the First and Second Temple, several reliable eyewitnesses were required to report the sighting of the crescent of the new moon. Later, the Metonic cycle (after Meton, a 5th century BCE Athenian astronomer) was employed in order to calculate the months. This cycle has 235 lunations in nineteen years. In each nineteen-year cycle, twelve years are ordinary years while seven years are leap years, in which an extra month is intercalated. In a leap year, First Adar, a month of thirty days, is followed by Second Adar, a month of twenty-nine days.

The Jewish calendar is quite accurate in keeping Nisan closely tied to the vernal equinox. The approximation upon which the Metonic cycle is based – 19 years actually contains 234.997 lunations – causes an inevitable drift, so that 1 Nisan gradually falls later with respect to the equinox. If we examine a nineteen year period not too far from the time John was composing, say 100 CE to 118 CE, we see that 1 Nisan could be not more than eighteen days before the vernal equinox (e.g. 1 Nisan 3873 is 5 March 113 CE (Julian), the equinox falling on 22 March 113 CE (Julian)), nor more than thirteen days after the equinox (e.g. 1 Nisan 3865 is 3 April 105 CE (Julian), the equinox falling on 22 March 105 CE (Julian)). Today, nineteen centuries later (say 2000 to 2018 CE), 1 Nisan can be not more than nine days before the vernal equinox (e.g. 1 Nisan 5773 is 12 March 2013, the equinox falling on 20 March 2013), nor more twenty-two days after the equinox (e.g. 1 Nisan is 5765 is 10 April 2005, the equinox falling on 20 March 2005).

Nisan

First month of the Jewish religious calendar, and the seventh of the civil year. It is also called Abib. It always contains thirty days.

Passover or *Pesaḥ* falls on Nisan 14 to 21. It commemorates the liberation of the Israelites from slavery in Egypt to the accompaniment of divine miracles under the guidance of Moses. Passover especially recalls how the Israelites were spared from loss of their firstborn sons by the ritual slaying of a lamb, and painting of their door lintels with its blood. The lamb was roasted and eaten, with bitter herbs and unleavened bread. Only unleavened bread, *mazaḥ*, is eaten during the entire holiday; leaven was scrupulously removed from the household in the days leading up to the feast.

On Nisan 15, a Lifted or Wave Offering of new barley, the first of the year was brought to the Temple. At the time of the Second Temple there was some dispute as to whether the *'omer* should be offered on Nisan 15 or on the first Sabbat after Nisan 14. The former view was that of the Pharisees, who accepted the tradition of the Oral Law. The latter view was popularised by various others, especially the followers of Boethus or Baytus, who accepted only the authority of Pentateuch, which they interpreted literally. (Since the counting of the *'omer* began with this rite, the date of

Shavu'ot might fall up to a week later for those who rejected the oral tradition.)

Nisan is remembered as the month in which the biblical patriarchs were born, and the month in which, according to some traditions, Isaac was bound for sacrifice by his father, Abraham, on Mount Moriah.

Nisan is called 'the New Year for Kings' because kings calculated the years of their reign from the first of the month; even if a king ascended the throne only a few days before, on 1 Nisan he was deemed to have completed the first year of his rule.

Iyar

Second month of the Jewish religious calendar, and the eighth of the civil year. It is also called Ziv. The month always consists of twenty-nine days.

No major festivals fell during this month at the time of the Fourth Gospel. On Iyar 18 modern Jews recall how a plague killing the students of Rab Akiba (2nd century qabalist and supporter of failed Messianic hopeful, Bar Kokhbar) suddenly ceased.

Sivan

Third month of the Jewish religious calendar, and the ninth of the civil year. The month always contains thirty days.

Leviticus xxiii 15-16 orders a count of seven weeks starting from the day of the Wave Offering of the year's new barley crop on Nisan 15. These seven weeks are the 49 Days of the *'Omer*. The Festival of *Shavu'ot* falls on Sivan 6, the fiftieth day, hence its Greek name, Pentecost ('Fiftieth'). The holiday falls on the anniversary of the giving of the Torah on Mount Sinai. During the time of the Second Temple, families offered twin loaves made from the newly cut wheat. This bread, unlike that eaten at Passover, had to be made with leaven; *mazoh* was not suitable.

Tammuz

Fourth month of the religious calendar, and tenth of the civil year. The month always consists of twenty-nine days.

Tammuz 9 is remembered as the day Moses descended from Sinai to find the Israelites worshipping their golden calf, and smashed the original tablets given by God. On Tammuz 9 in 586 BCE, the armies of Nebuchanezar breached the walls of Jerusalem, and subsequently captured the city. After the Babylonian exile, the day was set aside as a one of fasting and mourning. In the second century, Jerusalem's walls were breached on the Tammuz 17 by the armies of Rome. Since that time, the Fast of Tammuz 17 was performed in memory of both events.

Av

Fifth month of the Jewish religious calendar, the eleventh of the civil year. It is also called Menahem. The month always contains thirty days.

Av 9 is remembered as the day spies sent by the Israelites into Canaan came back with a bad report on the land, the indiscretion resulting in the Israelites having to spend thirty-eight more years in the desert than would have otherwise been the case.

The destruction of both First Temple and Second Temple occurred on Av 9.

Elul

Sixth month of the Jewish religious calendar, and the twelfth of the civil year. The month always consists of twenty-nine days.

The month Elul is a chance to prepare for *Rosh ha Shanah* (aka Day of Judgement) and *Yom Kippur* (Day of Atonement) which fall in the next month. It is a time to repent. Special penitential prayers or *selihot* are said daily throughout the month. Psalm xxvii is also recited

Tishri

Seventh month of the Jewish religious calendar, and first of the civil year. It is also called Ethanim. The month always consists of thirty days.

Rosh ha Shanah (New Year's Day) falls on Tishri 1. The day is also called *Yom Ha Din* (Judgement Day), and *Yom Teru'ah* (Day of Blowing [Trumpets]). On New Year's Day, as the Talmud envisions it, all the people of the world pass before God like sheep before a shepherd to be judged, and their fates are recorded in a Book of Life, a Book of Death, and a third book for the intermediate. Those who were in the indeterminate category could hope to make it into the Book of Life during the Ten Days of Repentance or Days of Awe. A central observance of the feat is the repeated blowing of a ram's horn trumpet.

Yom Kippur (Day of Atonement) falls on Tishri 10. It is the most solemn of all the festivals; eating, drinking, washing or anointing the body, wearing leather shoes, and marital relations are all forbidden. When the Temple existed, the major observance of the day involved ritual transference of the sins of the people to a goat, the scapegoat, which was sent into the wilderness, 'to Azazel'. The High Priest entered the Holy of Holies, where the Ark of the Covenant rested, and atoned for the sins of the people. A shofar is blown at the end of the fast.

Sukkoth (Feast of Tabernacles) falls Tishri 15-22. It is also called The Feast of Ingathering. For seven days one was expected to dwell in a hut, outside of one's normal house. After leaving Egypt, during their forty year sojourn in the desert, the Israelites dwelt in such huts or tents. The Talmud and qabalistic sources say that Tabernacles commemorates the fact that the Divine Glory (Shekhinah) formed a protective canopy over the Israelites in the wilderness. At the time of the Second Temple, a number of large candelabra were set up nightly, to recall the pillar of fire that travelled with the Israelites at night. An important observance of the feast is the daily waving of a lulav, a type of festive wreath made from a palm, citron, myrtle and willow branches woven together.

In the Temple period, water was drawn each day from the Pool of Siloam, public rejoicing, and poured out upon the altar as a libation. During the time of the Second Temple, the people carrying their lulavs would make a single circuit of the altar, shouting 'Hoshanah' 'Save us!'. On the seventh day of the feast (Tishri 21), called Hoshana Rabbah ('Great Hosanah'), they circumambulated the altar seven times to the chorus of Hoshana. During the time of the First Temple, they carried the Ark of the Covenant around the altar; in Second Temple they carried the Torah Ark.

Shemini A<u>z</u>eret (Assembly of the Eighth Day) fell on Tishri 22, and closed Sukkoth. It coincided with and was incorporated into another festival, Sim<u>h</u>at Torah (Rejoicing in the Torah), which marked the beginning of a new cycle of Torah readings.

<u>H</u>eshivan

Eighth month of the Jewish religious calendar, and second in the civil year. It is sometimes called Mar<u>h</u>eshvan or Bul. The month sometimes had twenty-nine days, sometimes thirty. It is the beginning of the rainy season. It contains no important religious festivals.

Kislev

Ninth month of the Jewish religious year, and third of the civil year. The month may have twenty-nine or thirty days.

The Festival of Dedication or *Hanukkah* runs for eight days, from Kislev 25 until the second or third day in the next month. Hanukkah celebrates the victory of the Maccabees over the Syrian general Nicanor in 165 BCE. Compulsory hellenisation of the populace ended, and the Torah, which was death had been punishable by death, again became the legal code. Specifically, *Hanukkah* recalls a miracle that occurred when the Temple was recaptured from heathen hands, and was to be rededicated to the God of Israel: although only enough ritually pure oil to burn for one day was found, it lasted for eight days, just long enough to prepare more consecrated oil for the perpetual flame. The central observance of the holiday is the lighting of the candles in commemoration of the event. For this reason it is also called the Feast of Lights.

Tevet

Tenth month of the Jewish religious calendar, and the fourth in the Jewish civil year. The month always consists of twenty-nine days.

Hanukkah finishes on Tevet 2 or 3 (as the preceding month, Kislev, may have twenty-nine or thirty days).

Tevet 10 is a day of fasting and mourning that commemorates the beginning of the siege of Jerusalem by the Babylonian King Nebuchanezar, which led to the breaching of the city walls and destruction of the First Temple and the mass deportation of Jerusalem's population.

Shevat

Eleventh month of the Jewish calendar, though the fifth from the beginning of the Hebraic civil year. The month always consists of thirty days.

Shevat 15 is called the New Year for Trees – if a vine or tree took root before Shevat 15, it was considered a year old on that day. This was important for determining annual tithe, and because the fruit of a tree less than four years old was considered unclean.

Adar

Twelfth month of the Jewish religious calendar, and the sixth in the civil year. Adar always contains twenty-nine days.

In the fifth century BCE, Haman, wicked minister to the Persian king Ahasuerus (Xerxes), and sworn enemy of the Jewish people, cast lots to determine an auspicious day to kill all Jews in the land – Adar 13 being chosen by lot. Thanks to Esther, secretly Jewish wife of Ahasuerus, and her uncle, Mordechai, the plan was thwarted, Haman ended hanging on the gallows he built for Mordechai, and the Jews won a general victory over their enemies. Fast of Esther (Adar 13) commemorates the fasts undertaken by Mordechai, Esther, and the Jews of Shushan in response to the plan to exterminate them, as told in the biblical book of Esther. Purim (Adar 14) recalls the death of Haman and the defeat of the Jews' enemies. The feast is celebrated in a carnival type atmosphere.

In leap years, First Adar, a month of thirty days is intercalated between Shevat and Adar, which then called Second Adar.

Appendix 2:
Notes on Planets, Signs and Houses in Astrology

Aries (Hebrew *Teli*, the Lamb), the first sign of the zodiac is the cardinal sign of the fire triad.

Aries is ruled by the planet Mars.

Natives of the sign are described as abrupt, active, adventurous, aggressive, arrogant, assertive, audacious, brash, brave, competitive, combative, courageous, daring, eager, energetic, enthusiastic, enterprising, frank, forceful, headstrong, impatient, impetuous, impulsive, independent, militant, original, pioneering, rash, reckless, spontaneous, straightforward, surprising, tactless, vigorous, violent, wilful.

Aries governs the head.

Natives are suited to work in the military service, to work as inventors and innovators, to occupations involving fire such as metallurgy. They tend to be leaders.

The sun enters the sign at the vernal equinox, passing through Aries from about March 20 or 21 until April 19 or 20. As explained, this corresponds to the first month of the Jewish year, Nisan.

Vita **(Life)** is the traditional name for the first mansion, which begins at the ascendant or eastern horizon.

It is concerned with the vitality and health of the native. The first house affects the physical appearance, the first impression that we give to others, the immediately obvious aspects of personality. Planets in the first house are said to affect the native's complexion, facial appearance, and speech. It also charts beginnings, or commencement of new cycle, and things which are inborn or innate, rather than acquired by experience.

Taurus (Hebrew *Shor*, the Bull), the second sign of the zodiac, is the fixed sign of the earth triad.

Taurus is ruled by the planet Venus.

Natives of the sign are described as acquisitive, affectionate, artistic, cautious, comfortable, conservative, constructive, dependable, earthy, enterprising, fertile, hard-working, immoveable, indulgent, inflexible, loyal, materialistic, money-wise, musical, obstinate, patient, placid, possessive, persevering, practical, productive, realistic, reliable, resourceful, responsible, rigid, thorough, stable, sensual, steady, slow, solid, stolid, strong, stubborn.

Taurus governs the throat, neck and shoulders.

Occupations suited to Taurus natives include those connected with art and music, gardening and horticulture, or involving banking or management of finances. Hard physical labour also appeals to them. The sun passes through Taurus from April 19 or 20 until May 20 or 21, that is, more or less, during the second month of the Jewish year, Iyar.

Lucrum (**Wealth**) is the traditional name for the second mansion of the heavens.

It charts profit and loss, income and expenditure; how one makes money, and how one spends it; personal, readily disposable wealth, as opposed to frozen assets; material resources that are dependable and useful; what can be converted to money; moveable possessions and belongings, that is property that one normally carries on one's person; material acquisitiveness; what we value or desire; luxury items. It indicates natural abilities and raw talents, capacity for work that can be realised as money. It also shows help or assistance from others.

Gemini (Hebrew *Theomim*, the Twins) is the mutable sign of the air triad. Gemini is ruled by the planet Mercury.

Natives of the sign are described as adaptable, alert, ambivalent, ambiguous, articulate, active, capricious, changeable, communicative, curious, cursory, fickle, flexible, fluent, glib, inconsistent, inconstant, ingenious, inquisitive, gossipy, imitative, independent, lively, mercurial, nervous, nimble, quick, rash, resourceful, restless, sociable, shallow, superficial, talkative, two-faced, versatile, whimsical, witty.

Gemini governs the hands and lungs.

Natives are suited to occupations involving communication, journalism, translation, information processing, basic or lower education, especially teaching children, advertising, oratory, publishing and distribution of literature, travel over short distances. The sun passes through Gemini from about May 20 or 21 until June 20 or 21, that is, approximately during Sivan, the third month of the Jewish year.

Fratres **(Siblings)** is the traditional name for the third horoscopic mansion.

It rules relationships with siblings, neighbours and peers; people whose existence parallels one's own; communication; news, messages, rumours. It charts sharpness and quickness of mental and sensory faculties; early schooling or childhood education; the immediate environment; short journeys and modes of transportation.

Cancer (Hebrew *Sarṯan*, The Crab), the fourth sign of the zodiac, is the cardinal sign of the water triad. Cancer is ruled by the Moon.

Natives of the sign are described as charming, clingy, conservative, defensive, emotional, empathetic, compassionate, defensive, family minded, home-loving, impressionable, introverted, grasping, maternal, moody, mysterious, nurturing, passionate, possessive, private, protective, receptive, retentive, secretive, sensitive, sympathetic, sentimental, tenacious, territorial, touchy, traditional, warm.

Occupations include midwives, hoteliers, publicans, hospitality industry workers, real estate agents, occupations connected with fluids especially water.

Cancer governs the breasts and pectoral region, and stomach.

The sun enters Cancer at the summer solstice, passing through the sign from about June 20 or 21 until July 22 or 23, that is, more or less during Tammuz, the fourth month of the Jewish year.

Genitor or ***Patres*** **(Parent or Ancestors)** is the traditional name for the fourth mansion, which begins at the nadir.

It denotes parents of the native, but also the ultimate ancestral roots; family heritage or traditions; the family home as place of safety and security; retirement from public affairs; rest and repose; domestic affairs and home life generally; the village, town or city where one resides. Secret or concealed things, especially things which are literally buried out of site, are charted here too.

Opinion is divided as to whether it primarily indicates the mother as the caretaker of the household, or father as representative of the paternal lineage or family name.

Leo (Hebrew *'Aryeh*, The Lion), the fifth sign of the zodiac, is the fixed sign of the fire triad. Leo is ruled by the Sun.

Natives of the sign are described as affectionate, ardent, ambitious, attention-seeking, arrogant, boastful, bossy, charismatic, creative, confident, dramatic, dignified, egotistical, expressive, extravagant, flamboyant, fun-loving, generous, grandiose, histrionic, independent, magnanimous, noble, proud, passionate, patronising, playful, pretentious, promiscuous, regal, self-assured, self-conscious, self-important, theatrical, vain, warm.

Leo governs the heart and thoracic spine.

Occupations include those in performing arts, especially theatre, entertainment industry, gambling, recreation, sex industry. Natives of the sign like to exercise their ability to lead by example.

The sun passes through Leo from about July 22 or 23 until August 22 or 23, that is, more or less during the fifth month of the Jewish year, Ab or Menaḥem.

Nati **(Children)** is the traditional name of the fifth mansion.

It denotes pleasure and recreation; leisure and entertainment; play and games; risk taking and gambling; romance, courtship, sexual liaisons outside formal partnership of marriage; procreation; children and offspring; artistic creativity; uninhibited self-expression; public performance.

Virgo (Hebrew *Betulah*, The Virgin), the sixth sign of the zodiac, is the mutable sign of the earth triad. Mercury is the ruler.

Natives of the sign are described as adaptable, analytical, anxious, attentive, conscientious, clean, critical, detail-oriented, discreet, efficient, exacting, fastidious, flexible, fussy, hair-splitting, health conscious, intelligent, industrious, methodical, modest, neat, observant, organised, nervous, painstaking, pedantic, perfectionistic, petty, pragmatic, practical, precise, punctilious, retiring, self-effacing, shy, solitary, thorough, tidy, watchful.

Natives are suited to become teachers, inspectors, analysts, accountants, custodians; they are attracted to professions connected with health and healing especially through medicines; like other earth signs the sign is connected with agriculture.

Virgo governs the intestines and digestion.

The sun passes through Virgo from about August 22 or 23 until September 22 or 23, that is, more or less during Elul, the sixth month of the Jewish year.

Valetudo **(Health)** is the traditional name for the sixth mansion.

It denotes minor sickness and disease; health and hygiene; healing with pharmaceuticals; dietary matters; clothing and grooming; day to day routines, menial chores; ability to adapt to minor inconveniences; refinement of professional skills; apprenticeship;

paid work and services requiring personal face to face contact; household pets and small domesticated animals; employees and servants generally; relationships with dependents, those fallen into miserable or beggarly condition.

Libra (Hebrew *Moznayim*, The Scales), the seventh sign of the zodiac, is the cardinal sign of the air triad. Libra is ruled by the planet Venus.
Natives of the sign are described as aesthetic, affectionate, amiable, artistic, balanced, charming, compromising, congenial, co-operative, diplomatic, egalitarian, elegant, engaging, even-handed, fair, friendly, genteel, gentle, graceful, harmonious, hesitant, helpful, idealistic, impartial, indecisive, just, lazy, moderate, persuasive, popular, reactive, refined, responsive, sociable, tactful, unbiased, urbane, vacillating.
Natives of the sign are suited to work as artists, musicians, poets, cosmeticians or beauticians, diplomats, social workers, arbitrators, members of judiciary.
Libra rules the kidneys.
The sun enters Libra at the autumn equinox, passing through the sign from about September 22 or 23 until October 22 or 23, that is, during the seventh month of the year, Tishri.

Uxor **(Wife or Spouse)** is the traditional name for the seventh mansion, which begins at the descendant (or western horizon).
It denotes one's marriage partner; partnerships based on equality; intimate one-on-one friendships; personal relationships based upon some sort of formal or contractual agreement, legal contracts; one's complement or counterpart or 'opposite number'; a competitor or adversary; one's opponent in a legal dispute.

Scorpio (Hebrew *'Aqrav*, The Scorpion), the eighth sign of the zodiac, is the fixed sign of the water triad. Scorpio is ruled by the planet Mars.

Natives of the sign are described as aggressive, analytical, committed, complex, cunning, compelling, compulsive, dedicated, deep, determined, hypnotic, imaginative, infatuating, insightful, insinuating, intense, intoxicating, inquisitive, irresistible, jealous, magnetic, mysterious, passionate, perceptive, penetrating, perspicacious, purposeful, resolute, resourceful, seductive, shrewd, secretive, sensitive, suspicious, transforming, vengeful.

Natives are suited to become morticians or mortuary workers, or occupations connected with animal slaughter and butchering, to work involving research into forbidden or secret subjects, disposal or recycling of waste, sewerage or toxic material, demolition, and surgery. Like other water signs, they are said to favour occupations involving water.

Scorpio governs the genitalia in both their excretory and reproductive functions.

The sun passes through Scorpio from about October 22 or 23 until November 21 or 22, that is, during the eighth month of the year, Marḥeshvan.

Mors (**Death**) is the traditional name for the eighth mansion.

It denotes death and all connected matters; regeneration and transformation; disposal and recycling of waste; inheritance, especially bequests from deceased relatives; shared or common property, joint funds, group finances; compulsions, obsessions and addictions; deep or hidden feelings, emotional or psychological sensitivities; forbidden or secret matters, and the probing into them.

Sagittarius (Hebrew *Qesheth*, The Archer), the ninth sign of the zodiac, is the mutable sign of the fire triad. Sagittarius is ruled by the planet Jupiter.

Natives of the sign are described as affable, athletic, adventurous, benevolent, blundering, broad-minded, careless, cordial, direct, easy going, exaggerating, expansive, extravagant, extrovert, fanatical, fun-loving, frank, freedom-loving, honest, hospitable, humorous, jovial, knowledgeable, liberal, optimistic, philosophical, proselytising, sincere, straightforward, tactless, truthful.

Natives are suited to follow religious vocations, or work as lawyers, judges, philosophers, teachers, instructors, politicians, explorers.

Sagittarius governs the hips and thighs.

The sun passes through Sagittarius from about November 21 or 22 until December 21 or 22, that is, more or less during the ninth month of the Hebrew year, Kislev.

Iter or *Sapientia* (**Journey or Wisdom**) is the traditional name for the ninth mansion.

It denotes higher education and acquisition of advanced knowledge, especially philosophy and metaphysics or religion; law, morality or ethics; cultural attitudes; conscience; personal code of conduct, way of life; adventure in foreign places, long distance travel; broadening of horizons; personal freedom.

Capricorn (Hebrew *Gedi*, The Goat), the tenth sign of the zodiac, is the cardinal sign of the earth triad. Capricorn is ruled by Saturn.

Natives of the sign are described as ambitious, authoritarian, businesslike, career-minded, cautious, cold, conventional, conscientious, conservative, controlling, constructive, conservative, demanding, despotic, disciplined, economising, enterprising, exacting, formal, hard-working, inflexible, inhibited, insensitive, methodical, miserly, orthodox, overbearing, patient, persevering, prudent, realistic, responsible, restricting, rigid, self-reliant, serious, structured, suspicious, status-seeking, taciturn, traditional, totalitarian, tyrannical.

Natives are suited to work as architects, builders, engineers, managers, civil servants, mathematicians, farmers, builder, politicians, directors, supervisors.

Capricorn rules the knees.

The sun enters Capricorn at the winter solstice, passing through the sign from about December 21 or 22 until January 19 or 20, that is, more or less during tenth month of the year, Tevet.

Regnum **(Government)** is the traditional name for the tenth mansion, which begins at the zenith or midheaven.

It denotes fame and infamy, reputation, social standing, public honour and recognition; personal authority; place in the hierarchy of society; level of achievement in career; nature of vocation followed; ambitions; matters of government; relationships with superiors or rulers or people in high authority.

Aquarius (Hebrew *Deli*, The Bucket or Urn), the eleventh sign of the zodiac, is the fixed sign of the air triad. Aquarius is ruled by the planet Saturn.

Natives of the sign are described as abstract, aloof, altruistic, bizarre, cooperative, detached, dogmatic, eccentric, elitist, friendly, futuristic, helpful, humanitarian, idealistic, imaginative, impractical, individualistic, inventive, intellectual, modern, objective, opinionated, progressive, rebellious, remote, social, sophisticated, surprising, tolerant, thoughtful, unconventional, unorthodox, unpredictable, unrealistic.

Natives are suited to be scientists, inventors, innovators, theoreticians, politicians.

Aquarius governs the blood vessels, and the ankles.

The sun passes through Aquarius from about January 19 or 20 until February 18 or 19, that is, during the eleventh month of the year, Shevat.

Benefacta (**Friendship**) is the traditional name for the eleventh mansion.

It denotes one's larger circle of friends and acquaintances; companionship and fellowship in fraternal clubs and associations; the common aims and objectives that unite their members; affairs involving the community or humanity at large; help and cooperation from others; favours of patrons and benefactors; hopes, wishes, fantasies and dreams; ideals; intellectual or theoretical matters; imagination and mental life generally; political beliefs and partisanship; new trends, fads and fashions; assimilation to a group.

Pisces (Hebrew *Dagim*, The Fishes), the twelfth sign of the zodiac, is the mutable sign of the water triad. Pisces is ruled by the planet Jupiter.

Natives of the sign are described as absorbed, accepting, accommodating, altruistic, charitable, compassionate, complacent, deep, distracted, dreamy, easy-going, empathetic, escapist, gullible, holistic, imaginative, immoderate, impressionable, indiscriminate, inclusive, indirect, inspirational, intuitive, lazy, mystical, neglectful, passive, pious, placid, profound, receptive, reflective, reverent, sensitive, self-effacing, spiritual, subjective, suggestible, tolerant, trusting, unassuming, undiscriminating, unfocused, visionary.

Pisces governs the feet.

Natives are suited to religious vocations, occupations connected with the sea, or with confinement or isolation.

The sun passes through Pisces from about February 18 or 19 until March 21 or 22, that is during the twelfth month of the year, Adar.

Carcer (**Prison**) is the traditional name for the twelfth mansion.

It denotes anxieties; clandestine, secret matters, intrigues, espionage, hidden enemies; deception; self-undoing or self-sacrifice; isolation or seclusion or refuge; concealment; imprisonment; intoxication; illusory or purely subjective experiences; rest, sleep, unconsciousness, coma, delirium; spirituality and mysticism; services performed behind the scenes or without face to face contact; charity; contact with cosmic or supernatural forces; untamed or wild animals, forces of nature; the rabble, the vulgar mob; cessation, finality.

Planets of Astrology

Moon

(Greek *Selene*; Latin *Luna*; Hebrew *Levanah* or *Sihara*). The Moon is the ruling planet of Cancer. It is exalted in Taurus.

Because of its size when viewed from earth – its orb is equal to that of the sun – the Moon is obviously different from the five lesser planets. Its other distinctive features are that it shines by reflected light, and that its appearance changes from day to day as it waxes and wanes. It moves more quickly than any other body in the heavens. It is associated with fluctuation, oscillation, instability, inconstancy or changeableness. Because menstruation occurs on a monthly cycle, the phenomenon was associated with the lunar cycle. It is said to govern feelings and sentiments, moods, unconscious or instinctive habits. It may indicate important females in the life of the native; in a nocturnal the mother. The ancients understood that the Moon was largely responsible for the regular ebb and flow of the tides; it is associated with occupations involving water.

Mercury

Before the planet Mercury was identified with the god Hermes-Mercury, its Greek name was *Stilbōn*, (Latin: *Stilbōn*); Shining; Hebrew *Kokab*, Star.

Mercury is the ruling planet of Gemini and Virgo. It is exalted in Virgo.

Mercury moves more rapidly than any other satellite of the sun. Never more than twenty-eight degrees from the sun, it is often lost to sight within the sun's glare.

Hermes-Mercury was the messenger and herald of the gods. His cult titles include: *Agoraios* (Of the Market Place), *Hermēneutēs* (Interpreter, Translator), *Angelos Markarōn*, *Angelos Athanatōn* (Messenger of the Immortals), *Pheletēs* (Thief, Robber), *Archōn Pheletōn* (Chief of Robbers), *Polutropos* (Shapeshifting). The god's paraphernalia included his caduceus staff, his winged sandals, and the winged hat that formed the basis of the planet's astrological symbol.

As a general significator, Mercury governs basic schooling and childhood education; the immediate environment; the senses; siblings and neighbours; short distance journeys; rapid travel; messages and forms of communication from speaking to writing; translation; reporting of news, spread of rumour; logical disputation and argument; analysis, calculation, reasoning, record keeping, manual dexterity, professional skills, adaptability, obedience, service, pharmacologic remedies, banking, buying and selling, commercial transactions.

Venus

Aphrodite seems to have been identified with the planet Venus from an early time, long before the other Olympian gods were associated with planets. The planet Venus was otherwise known in Greek as *Eosphoros* and *Hesperos* (Latin: *Eosphorus* and *Hesperus*), Morning Star and Evening Star; Hebrew *Nogah*, Shining, or *Kokabeth*, Star. After the Sun and Moon, Venus is by far the brightest object in the heavens.

Venus is the ruling planet of Taurus and Libra. It is exalted in Pisces.

Venus, was the goddess of love and beauty, attractiveness, fertility of nature. She is concerned with the feelings and affections, pleasure, sensuality, physical appetites, sexual attraction. Aphrodite had a strong association with the sea, having been born of foam that arose when Saturn, having castrated his own father, Uranus, dropped his genitals into the ocean. Her cult titles include *Ourania* (Heavenly). *Pandēmos* (Common to All People), *Genetullis* (Protectress of Childbirth), *Nikēphoros* (Bringer of Victory), *Androphonos* (Man-slayer), *Aphrogenēs* (Foam Born), *Pontia* (Marine). Her paraphernalia included her magic girdle, which rendered her irresistibly attractive, and a looking glass, which became the basis of her astrological symbol.

Venus is associated with the principles of harmony, aesthetics, beauty, refinement, culture, intimacy in social relationships, the desire to form close friendships, partnerships especially marriage, comfort and ease, contentment, material wealth, sensuality, the desire for personal possessions, luxuries of life, fertility. In a man's horoscope it may indicate women who are significant. In a diurnal horoscope it may indicate the native's mother. She is called the Lesser Benefic – that is, she is a lucky planet since she indicates that things will come effortlessly.

Sun

Greek: *Helios*; Latin: *Sol*; Hebrew: *Hamah* or *Shamash*. The Sun is the planetary ruler of Leo. It is exalted in Aries.

The Sun is the brightest and most important heavenly body; our daily routines follow its rising and setting; our survival depends directly on the heat and light it produces. It is associated with health and vitality, the life force. It is connected with fame and celebrity, ostentatiousness, personal charisma, heroism, authority. It is personified in the ruler, especially in the king. It represents the personal identity, individual sense of selfhood. It indicates the focus of conscious attention.

The Sun may represent important males in the life of the native. In a diurnal chart it may indicate the father.

Because of it connection with the fifth house, the Sun shows personal creativity, children and offspring – literal and figurative; recreation and entertainment, gambling, performing arts especially theatre; independence.

Mars

Before the gods became established as planetary deities, the planet Mars was called in Greek *Puroeis*; (Latin *Puroeis*) Fiery Red; Hebrew *Madim*, Excessively Strong, or *'Adom*, Ruddy.

Mars is the ruling planet of Aries and Scorpio. It is exalted in Capricorn.

Ares-Mars was the god of warfare and bloodshed. His astrological symbol represents his shield and spear.

As a general significator, Mars governs aggression, accidents, ambition, antipathy, arguments, assertiveness, bellicosity, bravado, daring, drive, death, destruction, discord, disease, emotional intensity, energy, fevers, impulsiveness, initiative, irascibility, jealousy, machismo, masculinity, passion, poisons, rashness, quarrels, sexuality, surgery, suddenness, violence, virility, warfare. In a woman's horoscope it may indicate qualities she finds attractive in a man. Being generally unlucky, it is called the Lesser Malefic.

Jupiter

Before the planet Jupiter was identified with the god Zeus-Jupiter, the Greek name for the planet was *Phaethon* (Latin *Phaethon*), Blazing; Hebrew *Zedek*, Righteous.

Jupiter is the ruling planet of Sagittarius and Pisces. It is exalted in Cancer.

In mythology Zeus-Jupiter became the ruler of the Olympian gods having overthrown his cruel father, Kronos-Saturn. He was father of Ares-Mars, Apollo, Artemis-Diana, Hermes-Mercury, and adoptive father of Aphrodite-Venus – every Olympian god who became associated a planet. He was the guardian of cosmic order, and also protector of moral law and right. He rewarded men for piety and punished them for breaking oaths and for violating sacred customs such as hospitality to strangers, or respect for the gods. While his brothers, Poisedon-Neptune and Hades-Pluto, took over rule of the sea and underworld respectively, Zeus-Jupiter was god of the sky and meteorological phenomena: rain, clouds, storms, lightning, winds; his astrological symbol is a stylised thunderbolt.

As a general significator Jupiter is concerned with philosophy and religion, morality and ethics, remote exploration, distant travel, sport, jokes and humour, altruism, self-sacrifice, compassion, sympathy, conformity to societal norms, tolerance. Jupiter is associated with the principles of growth, expansion, increase, freedom, optimism, enthusiasm, activity, progress, extravagance and excess. He is called the Greater Benefic, since he brings good fortune to the area of the heaven where he is situated.

Saturn

The Greek name for the planet was originally *Phainōn* (Latin: *Phaenon*), Shining One; Hebrew *Shabtai*, Rest or Repose.

Saturn is the planetary ruler of Capricorn and Aquarius. It is exalted in Libra.

In mythology, Kronos-Saturn was not one of the Olympian gods, but belonged to an older race of immortals, that of the Titans. They ruled the universe in a Golden Age, after Kronos-Saturn had overthrown his father, Uranus. But god Kronos-Saturn acted as monstrously as his father, and devoured his children until he was deposed by his son, Zeus-Jupiter.

Saturn had a certain connection with agriculture, his name being thought to be derived from *sator* (sower of seed). His astrological symbol is the sickle with which he castrated his father, Uranus.

Since its orbit was understood in Ptolemy's time to encompass the other planets, Saturn is associated with limitation, restrictions and boundaries, and with finality and termination. Saturn is the most slowly moving of the planets known to the ancients. He presages long delays and retarding influences, but also permanence. Saturn is also connected with planning the future, with old age, and long periods of time, Kronos being sometimes deliberately conflated with Chronos, Time.

As ruler of the tenth house Saturn governs career, authority, and place in hierarchy of society, power of the government to dictate. As ruler of the eleventh houses, he represents coldly logical and dispassionate intelligence. Saturn is called the Greater Malefic. He has a melancholy or morose nature, depressingly serious and solemn. Black is emblematic of his nature. He presages difficulty, loss and privation, bereavement, misfortune and unhappiness, hindrances and obstacles, death. He is described as a strict disciplinarian and controlling taskmaster, stern teacher or testing examiner. He symbolises bondage, imprisonment, compulsion and necessity, the inexorable and mechanical workings of fate.

In a nocturnal chart, he represents the native's father.

Fixed Stars

Greek *Ouranos*; Hebrew *Mazal* or *Mazloth*. In Greek mythology Ouranos was the personification of the heavens and the night sky.

The ancients knew no planets beyond Saturn, beyond whose orbit, in the Ptolemaic cosmos, lay the sphere of fixed stars or constellations. This was thought to provide the impetus or motive force that caused the lower spheres to revolve. Because the proper antegrade motion of the planets is west to east against the background of the fixed stars, and because the celestial equator is inclined to the ecliptic, the zone of fixed stars was linked with originality, unexpectedness, eccentricity. When Uranus was discovered it inherited from the sphere of fixed stars its association with new and unconventional, bizarre, surprising.

Appendix 3:
Order of the Trumps in Different Tarots

The Florentine Minchiate (16th century) has the trumps minus *La Papessa* and *La Stella*, but adds twelve signs of the zodiac, four elements, and four cardinal virtues, bringing the total number of trumps up to forty. The Sicilian Tarot (18th century) is a late arrival. It omits *Il Papa* entirely, and *La Papessa* appears as a female figure of uncertain provenance, censorial changes due to political and religious sensibilities. It replaces *Il Diavolo* with *La Nave* (The Boat), for superstitious reasons or to avoid accusation of dark practices. The number of trumps is brought up to twenty-two with the addition of *La Miseria*. Both the Florentine Minchiate and Sicilian Tarot are believed to be derivative since they contain features not present in the hand-painted or early printed cards.

Features of Ferrara-type order:
- *The Fool* is often the first trump;
- the order *The Empress, The Emperor, The Papess, The Pope* is usual;
- *Temperance* appears early, after *The Pope*, and before *The Lovers* and *The Chariot*;
- *The Hermit* appears between *The Wheel* and *Hanged Man*;
- *Fortitude* appears early, close to *The Lovers* and *The Chariot*;

– *Justice* appears in paenultimate position, between *Judgement* and *The World*.

Features of Bolognese-type:
– *The Fool* is often the first trump;
– *The Empress, The Emperor, The Papess, The Pope* were replaced by the *Quattro Moretti* (Four Little Moors) probably to avoid offending political or religious sensibilities;
– *Temperance* appears early, following *The Pope, The Lovers, The Chariot*;
– *The Hermit* appears between *The Wheel* and *The Hanged Man*;
– *Justice* appears early close to *The Lovers, The Chariot*, Fortitude and *Temperance*;
– *The World* is in paenultimate position, and *Judgement* is last.

Features of Marseilles-type:
– *The Fool Fool* comes first or has no place;
– the usual order is *The Papess, The Empress, The Emperor, The Pope*;
– *Temperance* appears between *Death* and *The Devil*;
– *The Hermit* appears before *The Wheel*;
– *Justice* appears early, close to *The Lovers* and *The Chariot*;
– *Fortitude* appears between *The Wheel* and *The Hanged Man*;
– *Judgement* is in paenultimate position, and *The World* is last.

Imperiali does not number the trumps, merely their order. He does not say where *Il Traditor* falls. He does not give Temperance a name, but describes the trump: 'she who holds two vases, one high, one low'. Citolini, Garzoni and Aldovrandi give the trumps in reverse order. All are typical of the Ferrara-type order. The Latin

TABLE: Names of the trumps and their order in: *Sermones de Ludo cum Aliis* (~1470); Alberto Lollio *Invettiva contra il Giuoco del Tarocco* & Vicenzo Imperiali *Risposta all'Invettiva* (Ferrara ~1550); Alessandro Citolini *Tipocosmia* (Venice 1561)

de Ludo cum Aliis ~1470	Lollio & Imperiali ~1550	Citolini 1561
	Il Matto	Il Matto
I. El Bagatella	Il Bagatella	Il Gabbatella
II. Imperatrix	L'Imperatrix	L'Imperatrice
III. Imperator	L'Imperatore	La Papessa
IV. La Papessa	La Papessa	L'Imperator
V. El Papa	Il Papa	Il Papa
VI. La Temperantia	[La Temperanza]	Temperanza
VII. L'Amore	Il Carro	Il Carro
VIII. Lo Caro Triomphale	L'Amor	L'Amore
IX. La Forteza	La Fortezza	Fortezza
X. La Rotta	La Ruota, La Fortuna	La Ruota
XI. El Gobbo	Il Vecchio Saggio, Il Gobbo	Il Vecchio
XII. Lo Impichato	[Il Traditor]	L'Impiccato
XIII. La Morte	La Morte	La Morte
XIV. El Diavolo	Il Demonio	Il Diavolo
XV. La Sagitta	L'Inferno	Il Fuoco
XVI. La Stella	La Stella	La Stella
XVII. La Luna	La Luna	La Luna
XVIII. El Sole	Il Sol	Il Sole
XIX. Lo Angelo	L'Angel del Ciel	L'Angel
XX. La Iusticia	La Giustitia	La Giustizia
XXI. El Mondo	Il Mondo	Il Mondo
El Matto		

TABLE: Names of the trumps and their order in: Tommaso Garzoni *Piazza Universale* (Venice 1585); Ulisse Aldovrandi MS. (Bologna d. 1602).

Garzoni 1585	Aldovrandi ~1600
Stultus	Stultus
Minimus	Mimo
Imperatrix	Imperatrix
Imperator	Imperator
Papissa	Papissa
Summus Pontifex	Papa
Temperantia	Temperantia
Carrus	Currus
Amor	Amor
Propugnaculum	Fortitudo
Rota Fortunae	Rota
Senex	Senex
Patibulum	Laqueo Suspensus
Mors	Mors
Diabolus	Diabolus
Fulmen	Ignis
Stella	Astrum
Luna	Luna
Sol	Sol
Angelus	Ange
Justitia	Iustitia
Mundus	Mundus
El Matto	

TABLE: Names of the trumps and their order in:
Bolognese *Appropriati* 17th century; Anrea Alciato *Parergon Juris libri vii posteriores* (Lyons 1561); Francesco Piscina *Discorso sopra l'Ordine delle Figure Tarocchi* (Monte Regale 1565).

Bolognese *Appropriati*	Alciato 1543	Piscina ~1567
El Matto	Stultus	Il Matto
Il Bagatella	Caupo	Il Bagatto
Little Moor / Pope	Flaminica	L'Imperatrice
Little Moor / Pope	Regina	L'Imperatore
Little Moor / Pope	Rex	La Papessa
Little Moor / Pope	Sacerdos	Il Papa
Amor	Justus	Il Cupido, Dio d'Amore
Carro	Fortis	Giustitia
Tempra	Amor	Il Carro Triomphante
Giusta	Quadriga	Fortezza
Forza	Fortuna	Fortuna
Ruota	Senex	Il Vecchio Gobbo
Vecchio	Crux	L'Impiccato
Traditore	Nex	La Morte
Morte	Fama	La Temperanza
Diavolo	Daemon	I Demoni
Saetta	Fulmen	Il Fuoco
Stella	Stella	La Stella, Le Stelle
Luna	Luna	La Luna
Sole	Phoebus	Il Sol
Mondo	Angelus	Quattro Santi Evangelisti
Angelo	Mundus	L'Angelo, Il Paradiso

names given by Garzoni and Aldovrandi, like those of Alciato below, are not the trumps' original titles but were translated from Italian.

Appropriati were short ex tempore poems which compare people to Tarot trumps as part of a parlour game played in Bologna in the seventeenth century. They typically list the trumps in reverse order.

Alciato is basically Marseilles, but with Bolognese features (*Fortitude* early; *The Hermit* between *The Wheel* and *The Hanged Man*). He lists the trumps in reverse order. Piscina is Bolognese except *Temperance* lies between *Death* and *The Devil* as in Marseilles-type Tarots.

Tarot of Milan	Tarot of Marseilles
Il Matto	Le Mat
Il Bagatto, Il Bagatello	Le Bateleur
La Papessa	La Papesse
L'Imperatrice	L'Impératrice
L'Imperatore	L'Empereur
Il Papa	Le Pape
Gli Amanti	Les Amoreux
Il Caro Triomphale	Le Chariot
La Iustizia	La Justice
Il Gobbo, L'Eremita	L'Ermite
La Rotta	Roue de Fortune
La Fortezza	La Force
L'Impiccato, L'Appesso	Le Pendu
La Morte	La Morte

Tarot of Milan	Tarot of Marseilles
La Temperanza	La Temperance
Il Diavolo	Le Diable
La Sagitta, La Torre	La Maison de Dieu, L'Hôpital
La Stella	L'Étoile
La Luna	La Lune
Il Sole	Le Soleil
L'Angelo, Il Giudizio	Le Jugement
El Mondo	Le Monde

Bibliography

The New Jerusalem Bible
Darton, Longman & Todd, London, 1990

Biblia Sacra Vulgata
Deutsche Bibelgesellschaft, Stuttgart, 1983

Dov Ben Abba
The Signet Hebrew-English / English-Hebrew Dictionary
New American Library Inc, New Jersey, 1978

Kurt Aland et al. (editor)
The Greek New Testament and Dictionary; 3rd corrected edition
United Bible Societies, 1983
printed in the FDR by Biblia –Druck Gmbh, Stuttgart

The Soncino Books of the Bible
Rev. Dr. A. Cohen MA. PhD. DHL. (editor)
The Soncino Press, London and New York, 1984

G. Abbott-Smith
A Manual Greek Lexicon of the New Testament
T. & T. Clark Ltd, Edinburgh, 1986

Cornelius Agrippa
Three Books of Occult Philosophy
Cthonios Books, Sussex England, 1986

Cornelius Agrippa
The Fourth Book of Occult Philosophy
edited and translated Robert Turner
Heptangle Books, Guillette New Jersey, 1985

Frances Barrett
The Magus
The Citadel Press, Seacausus, New Jersey, 1967

Michael Berg (editor)
The Zohar by Shimon Bar Yochai, with the Sulam Commentary by Rabbi Yehuda Ashlag
Kabbalah Centre International, Sydney, 2000

R. H. Charles (translator)
The Book of Enoch (I Enoch)
Clarendon Press, Oxford, 1912

R.H. Charles (translator)
Book of Jubilees
Clarendon Press, Oxford, 1913

Aleister Crowley
The Holy Books of Thelema
Samuel Weiser, York Beach Maine, 1988

Aleister Crowley
Gems from the Equinox
Falcon Press Phoenix Arizona, 1986

Aleister Crowley
Magick
Samuel Weiser, York Beach Maine, 1984

Aleister Crowley
The Complete Astrological Writings (edited John Symonds and Kenneth Grant)
W.H. Allen & Co., London, 1987

Aleister Crowley
Liber 777 and Other Qabalistic Writings
Samuel Weiser, York Beach Maine, 1988

Aleister Crowley
The Book of Thoth
Samuel Weiser, York Beach Maine, 1988

Alfred Douglas
The Tarot: The Origins, Meaning and Uses of the Cards
Penguin Books Ltd., Harmondsworth Middlesex, 1972

Benjamin Dykes
Using Medieval Astrology, Part 1: Universal Astrology
Minneapolis Minnesota, 2005

Sir William Drummond
Oedipus Judaicus
Thorsons Publishing Group Ltd., Wellingborough Northamptonshire, 1986

Gerard Encausse (Papus)
The Qabalah
The Aquarian Press, Wellingborough Northhamptonshire, 1977

Joseph Enthoffer
Origin of Our Alphabet
B. Westermann Washington 1875

Rabbi Dr I Epstein (editor)
The Soncino Talmud
The Soncino Press, London and New York, 1984

J. W. Etheridge, M.A.
The Targums of Onkelos and Jonathan Ben Uzziel On the Pentateuch, With The Fragments of the Jerusalem Targum From the Chaldee
Longman Green, Longman and Rberts, London, First Published 1862

Colin Evans
(Revised by Brian Gardener)
The New Waite's Compendium of Natal Astrology
Routledge and Kegan Paul, London, 1971

Rabbi Dr. H. Freeman BA. PhD. et al. (translator and editor)
The Midrash Rabbah
The Soncino Press, London and New York, 1984

Gerald Friedlander (translator)
The Chapters of Rabbi Eliezer the Great

Pirqe Rabbi Eliezer
Kegan Paul, Trench, Trubner & Co. Ltd., London, 1916

Dr Karl Feyerabend
Langenscheidt's Pocket Greek Dictionary
Hodder and Stoughton Ltd., Kent.

Dion Fortune
The Mystical Qabalah
Samuel Weiser, York Beach Maine, 1984

Adolphe Franck
The Kabbalah
Bell Publishing Company, New York, 1940

J.G. Frazer
The Golden Bough
Papermac, London ,1988

H. W. F. Gesenius
(translated by Samuel Prideaux Tregellis LLD)
Hebrew-Chaldee Lexicon to the Old Testament
Baker Book House, Grand Rapids Michigan, 1979

Louis Ginzberg
translated by Henrietta Szold
The Legends of the Jews
The Jewish Publication Society of America, Philadelphia, 1909

Erwin R. Goodenough
(edited and abridged by Jacob Neusner)
Jewish Symbols in the GraecoRoman Period
Princeton University Press, Princeton, New Jersey, 1968

Lance Knight Green
The Astrologer's Manual
Arco Publishing Co, 1988

Paul Hudson
The Devil's Picturebook
Abacus, Great Britain, 1972

Z'ev ben Shimon Hallevi
Kabbalah and Exodus
Gateway Books, Bath, 1980

Z'ev ben Shimon Hallevi
The Work of the Kabbalist
Gateway Books, Bath, 1984

Z'ev ben Shimon Hallevi
Kabbalah and Psychology
Gateway Books, Bath, 1986

Z'ev ben Shimon Hallevi
School of Kabbalah
Gateway Books, Bath, 1985

A.C. Highfield
The Book of Celestial Images
The Aquarian Press, Wellingborough Northamptonshire, 1984

Hugh Llyod Jones
Myths of the Zodiac
Duckworth, 1978

Marc Edmund Jones
Astrology, How and Why It Works
Penguin Books Middlesex 1969

C.G. Jung
The Collected Works
Routledge & Kegan Paul, 1986

Isidore Kalisch (translator and editor)
The Sepher Yetzirah
Heptangle Books, Gilette New Jersey, 1982

Aryeh Kaplan
Sefer Yetzirah: the Book of Creation (Revised Edition)
Red Wheel/Weiser LLC, San Francisco 1997

Aryeh Kaplan
The Bahir
Samuel Weiser, York Beach Maine 1989

Aryeh Kaplan
Meditation and Kabbalah
Samuel Weiser, York Beach Maine, 1982

Aryeh Kaplan
Meditation and Bible
Samuel Weiser, New York, 1978

Athanasius Kircher
Oedipus Aegyptiacus
Rome, 1653

Gareth Knight
A Practical Guide to Qabalistic Symbolism
Samuel Weiser, York Beach Maine, 1978

Gareth Knight
The Treasure House of Images: magical dynamics of the Tarot
The Aquarian Press, Wellingborough Northamptonshire, 1986

Theodor Laurence
The Foundation Book of Astrology
University Books, Secaucus New Jersey, 1973

Eliphaz Levi
The Book of Splendours
Samuel Weiser, York Beach Maine, 1973

Eliphaz Levi
Transcedendental Magic, Its Dogma and Ritual
(translated A. E. Waite)
Rider and Co, 1968
Samuel Weiser, New York

Liddell & Scott
Greek-English Lexicon
Oxford University Press, 1989

Rabbi Isaac Luria
A Study of the Ten Luminous Emanations

compiled and edited by R Levi Krakovsky vol I and Dr Philip S Berg vol II
Research Centre of Kabbalah, Jerusalem, 1984

Rabbi Moses Luzatto
General Principles of Kabbalah
(translated Dr Phillip S. Berg)
Research Centre of Kabbalah Jerusalem, New York, 1969

Edward Lyndoe
Complete Practical Astrology
Putnam, London, 1938

Fermicius Maternus
Ancient Astrology, Theory and Practice Matheseos Libri VIII
Jean Rhys Bram (translator)
Noyes Press, Park Ridge, New Jersey, 1975

S.L. MacGregor-Mathers (translator)
The Grimoire of Armadel
Routledge & Kegan Paul, London, 1980

Daniel C. Matt (translator and editor)
The Zohar: Pritzker Edition, vol 1 to 7
Stanford University Press, Stanford California, 2007

W. A. Morfill (translator), R. H. Charles (editor)
The Book of the Secrets of Enoch
Clarendon Press, Oxford, 1896

Bernhard Pick
The Cabala: Its Influence on Judaism and Christianity
The Open Court Publishing Company, Chicago, London, 1913

Claudius Ptolemy (trans J.M. Ashmand)
Tetrabiblos or the Quadripartite Mathematical Treatise
Davis and Dickson, London, 1822

Alfred Rahlfs (editor)
Septuaginta: Vetus Testamentum Graece iuxta LXX Interpretes
Deutsche Bibelgesellschaft, Stuttgart, 1979

Israel Regardie
The Complete Golden Dawn System of Magic
Falcon Press, Phoenix Arizona, 1984

Israel Regardie
The Middle Pillar
Llewellyn Publications, St. Paul Minnesota, 1985

Israel Regardie
The Golden Dawn
Llewellyn Publications St. Paul Minnesota 1984

Israel Regardie
A Garden of Pomergranates
Llewellyn Publications, St. Paul Minnesota 1985

Israel Regardie
The Tree of Life
Samuel Weiser, York Beach Maine, 1983

Joseph E. Rigor
The Power of Fixed Stars
Astrology and Spiritual Publishers Inc., Hammond Indiana, 1979

Vivian Robson
The Fixed Stars and Constellations in Astrology
The Aquarian Press, Wellingsborough Northamptonshire 1969

The Greek New Testament in the Original Greek
Byzantine Textform
compiled and arranged by Maurice A. Robinson and William G. Pierpont
Chilton Book Publishing, Massachsetts, 2005

Dane Rudyar
The Astrological Houses
Doubleday, Garden City New York, 1972

George Sassoon and Rodney Dale
The Kabbalah Decoded
Gerald Duckworth & Co, London, 1978

Gershom Scholem
On the Kabbalah and Its Symbolism
translated by Ralph Manheim
Schoken Books, New York, 1969

Gershom Scholem, R. J. Z. Werblowski (editor), Allan Arkush (translator)
Origins of the Kabbalah
Jewish Publication Society, Princeton University Press, 1987.

Gershom Scholem
Major Trends in Jewish Mysticism
Schoken Books Inc., New York, 1954

Juliet Sharman-Burke
The Complete Book of Tarot
Pan Books, London, 1985

Harry Sperling and Maurice Simon (translators)
The Soncino Zohar
The Soncino Press, London and New York, 1984

The Standard Prayer Book
(Simeon Singer translator)
Bloch, New York 1915.

To Kata Iohannem Hagion Evangelion
Robert Stephanus 1550
www.bibles-online.net/1550/NewTestament/John-4

Richard Sterling
The Complete Book of Astrology
Australian Consolidated Press, Sydney 1980

Richard Sterling
Astrology The Richard Sterling Way
Australian Consolidated Press, Sydney 1992

James Strong
Strong's Exhaustive Concordance of the Bible with Hebrew, Chaldee and Greek Dictionaries
Riverside Book and Bible House, 1980

Moses Stuart
A Grammar of the Hebrew Language
Flagg and Gould Publishers, Codman Press, Oxford, 1831

Carlo Suarez
The Qabalah Trilogy
Shambalah, Boston & London, 1985

Joseph H. Thayer
Thayer's Greek-English Lexicon of the New Testament
Baker Book House, Grand Rapids Michigan, 1988

Joshua Trachtenberg
Jewish Magic and Superstion
Atheneum, New York, 1987

Vettius Valens
Anthologies
Mark Riley translator and editor 2010
www.csus.edu/indiv/rileymt/Vettius20%Valens20%entire.pdf

A.E. Waite
The Pictorial Key to the Tarot
Citadel Press, Seacausus New Jersey, 1959

A.E. Waite (trans and ed)
The Hermetic Museum – restored and enlarged
Samuel Weiser Inc., York Beach Maine, 1990

Robert Wang
The Golden Dawn Tarot
US Games Systems Inc., New York, 1978

James Wasserman
Instructions for Aleister Crowley's Thoth Tarot Deck
Samuel Weiser Inc., New York, 1978

J. Weingreen MA. PhD.
A Practical Grammar for the Clasical Hebrew
Clarendon Press, Oxford, 1959

William Wynn Westcott
Sepher Yetzirah, the Book of Formation with the Fifty Gates of Intelligence and the Thirty-two Paths of Wisdom
J.M. Watkins, London, 1911

William Wynn Westcott
An Introduction to the Study of the Kabalah, with Sepher Yetzirah
Metaphysical Research Group, Hastings Sussex UK, 1978

Work of the Chariot
Idra Rabba Qadusha
www.workofthechariot.com/TextFiles/Translations-IdraRabba.html

Work of the Chariot
Idra Zuta Qadusha
www.workofthechariot.com/TextFiles/Translations-IdraZuta.html

Work of the Chariot
Sifra Detzniyutha
www.workofthechariot.com/TextFiles/Translations-SifraDetzniyutha.html

Patrick Zalewski
Secret Inner Order Rituals of the Golden Dawn
Falcon Press, Phoenix Arizona 1988

Instructions for Use with Rider Tarot Cards
Rider & Co, London, 1960

Jewels of the Wise
Epiphany Press, San Francisco, 1979

Keystone of Tarot Symbols
Epiphany Press, San Francisco, 1979

Book of Jasher, Faithfully Translated from the Original Hebrew into English
J.H. Parry & Co., Salt Lake City, 1887

Index

A

Ab see Av
Abib see Nisan
Abraham or Abram 12, 14, 31, 52-54, 169, 185, 228, 257, 353, 356, 358, 361-362, 364-365, 366-367, 368
Adam Qadmon 173-174
Adar 15, 24, 127-133
aggadah 65, 296, 339, 356, 358
Akiba bar Yosef, Rabbi 14, 146-147
'ain 157, 193-194
air 15, 16, 17, 19, 24, 161, 194, 344, 373, 383
Alciato, Anrea 486-487
Aldovrandi, Ulisse 483, 485, 487
'alef 15, 19, 23, 24, 167, 177, 181, 190-195, 373, 377, 383
angels 109, 171-172, 253, 272, 278, 288, 291, 324, 342, 347, 411, 413, 415, 426
Aphrodite see Venus
Aquarius 15, 24, 30, 125-126, 361-362, 373, 377, 420, 472-473
Ares see Mars
Aries 15, 19, 24, 29, 31, 34, 52-57, 373-377, 391

Aristides 39, 41, 385
Athenagoras 203
Ark of Noah 341-344, 347
Ark of Torah 397, 408, 460
Av or Menahem 15, 24, 77-78, 458
'ayin 15, 24, 34, 119-122, 124, 177, 181, 288-291, 298, 301, 338, 351-354

B

Babel 338, 356-358
Bahir 13-14, 145ff.
baptism 203-205
Baptist, John the 40, 43, 46, 204, 226, 446, 453
Bar Yohai, Rab Simeon 147-149
beauty and ugliness 17, 33
beginning 157, 191-192, 202, 227
Benefacta or Friendship see eleventh house
beth 15, 16, 19, 21, 24, 37, 167, 177, 181, 183, 184, 191-192, 194-195, 197-205, 234, 237, 239
Bethesda 237
Bethabara 204-205
bloodshed 123, 253, 290, 478
bitahon 168, 293
bitul 168

Binah 156, 158, 159, 164ff., 197-205, 212-220, 224-230, 232-236, 240, 247-248, 250-254, 255, 266-267, 294, 297, 323-324, 331-332
Boethus or Baytus 56, 456
Boibel-Loth alphabet 439-440
Bolognese Tarot 381, 383, 483, 486-487

C

Cancer 15, 24, 30, 34, 69-74, 373, 377, 396, 466, 475
Capricorn 15, 24, 30, 34, 119-122, 288-289, 351-352, 373, 377, 416, 471
Carcer or Prison see twelfth house
childbirth 48-49, 258, 298, 357, 389, 480
Citolini, Alessandro 483-484
circumcision 163, 254, 316-317, 366-367
coal-fire 306, 330
cockcrow 128
commandments 116, 169, 170, 184, 215, 237, 241, 259, 262-263, 265, 272, 277, 280, 282, 313, 314, 320, 427
coupling 17, 34
Crowley, Aleister 21-23, 372-374, 377, 381, 382, 386, 399-400, 405, 409, 414, 423, 424, 430
crucifixion 28, 136, 139, 424

D

Daʿath 158-160, 218-219
daleth 15, 16, 19, 21, 24, 48-50, 54, 167, 177, 181, 224-230, 373, 389
daghesh 16
darkness 128, 191, 206, 210-211, 224-230, 260, 269, 294, 364-365
David 169, 328-330

day 96-97, 171, 213, 227, 262, 267, 303, 324, 349, 362
de Ludo cum Aliis 379, 384
Deluge 338, 341-342, 346-347, 411
Devil 66, 108-109, 119-120, 122, 130, 258, 272, 276, 288-291, 296, 347, 352-353, 373, 377, 411, 416-417
Dionysus 121-122
Din see Gevurah
divine names 170, 307
dominion and servitude 17, 33
Donash ibn Tamim 18ff., 179-180
door 86, 90-91, 94, 129, 146, 321, 325, 369, 404, 428
Donnolo, Shabtai 18ff.
double letters 16-22, 49, 88-89, 123-124, 138, 176, 250, 290-291, 340, 362, 372, 374, 381
doxa and *doxazein* 273-274

E

eighth commandment 184, 272, 313, 320, 427
eighth day 74, 254
eighth house 107-110, 470
eleventh house 125-126, 361-362, 473
Elijah 316-317
Eliahu Gaon of Vilna, Rabbi 18ff.
Elul 15, 24, 34, 82-87, 89, 96, 458
Encausse, Gerard 372
Ephraim 100
errant or misplaced symbolism 41-42, 50, 68, 86-87, 216, 228, 303
Esau or Edom 288-291, 352-354
Essenes 439-440
Ethanim see Tishri
Eusebius 203
Ezekiel 297-298, 315-316, 396

F

Father ('Abba) 174-176, 186, 224-230, 263
Ferarese Tarot 379-383, 484
fertility and sterility 17, 33, 49
fever 55
fifth commandment 170, 259
fifth house 26, 34, 75-81, 468
fire 15, 24, 140-141
First Day 262
first house 52-57, 464
First Letter of John 337
Fountain of the Virgin 85, 263
Fourth Day 171, 362
fourth house 34, 69-74, 76, 396, 467
fourth commandment 184, 237-238, 262-263
Fratres or Siblings see third house
future tense 120, 212

G

Garzoni, Tomaso 483-487
Gedulah see Hesed
gematria 151, 167, 248, 331 343
Gemini 15, 24, 29, 34, 63-68, 248, 373, 377, 394, 465
Genitor or *Patres*, Ancestors see fourth house
Gerizim 53-54
Gevurah 32, 53, 160, 164ff., 224-230, 250-254, 255-260, 266-267, 269-274, 341-344
Gevuroth 271
gimel 15, 16, 21, 24, 45-46, 167, 177, 179, 181, 212-219, 267,323-324, 372, 387
Golgotha 315, 317
glory 272-274, 293, 320
glÇssokomon 343-344
Good Shepherd 91-94, 264
Gra Version 18, 21, 33-35, 49, 57, 61, 67, 84, 100, 132, 176
Graves, Robert 121,358, 400, 439-440

H

Halakah 117, 243-244
Haman 130-132, 138-139, 462
Hanes Taliesin 440
Hannukah 31, 72, 94, 117-118, 122, 138, 217-218, 220, 242, 251, 461
happiness 162, 294-295, 301
hearing 17, 34, 79-81
heart 161, 167, 276
heh 15, 24, 34, 52-57, 167, 175, 177, 181, 183, 232-236, 332, 373, 377
Hesed 31, 160, 164ff., 224-230, 237-244, 255-260, 262-263, 264-265
Heshvan 15, 24, 34, 72, 109-110, 342, 346-347, 411, 460
heth 15, 24, 34, 69-74, 76, 177, 181, 183, 186, 250-254, 373, 375, 377
Hermes see Mercury
Hod 32, 162, 164ff., 224-230, 269-274, 288-291, 293-298, 313-318, 319-326, 351-354, 356-360, 368-370, 373, 396, 408, 416, 418, 424, 427
Hokmah 157-158, 164ff., 190-195, 197-205, 224-230, 232-236, 237-244, 264-265, 294, 383, 385, 389, 391, 392, 404
holiness 298
Holy Spirit 140-141, 175-176
hours 29-30, 55, 84, 96, 128, 267
Houses 29-34, 463, 474
Hulda 124
hup'retai 'underrowers' 71, 129

I

Isaac 32, 52-57, 169, 228, 290, 457
Iter or Journey see ninth house
Iyar 15, 24, 59-62, 72, 392, 457

J

Jacob 32, 53, 169, 212-213, 219, 232-233, 281, 288-290, 322, 328, 353, 394
Janus 90-91, 94-95, 128, 404
Joseph 32, 45, 169, 185, 301, 303, 315, 317, 329, 447, 450
Jubilees, Book of 339
Judas 104, 107-110, 127, 129, 272, 290-291, 309, 343, 346-347, 363-365, 409, 411
Jupiter 15, 17, 21, 24, 30-31, 88-95, 128-129, 132-133, 165-166, 172, 264, 372-373, 392, 404, 471, 473, 479
Justin Martyr 38-39, 203

K

kaf 15, 16, 19, 21, 24, 88-95, 124, 177, 180-181, 241, 264-265, 372-373, 375, 404
Kalisch, Isidore 21, 194
Kether 155-159, 164ff., 190-195, 197-205, 212-219, 280, 373, 383, 385, 387
Kaiaphas 100-131, 128
Kircher, Athanasius 21-22, 166, 177ff., 260, 340, 372
Kislev 15, 24, 34, 72, 114-118, 122, 217-220, 251, 348, 413, 461
Kronos see Saturn

L

Lake of Galilee 330
Lambert, Meyer 21
lamed 15, 24, 34, 88-89, 96-102, 124, 177, 181, 266-267, 323-324, 343, 373, 375, 377, 406
Langton, Stephen 22-23, 134, 190, 309
laughing 17, 34, 132-133
Lazarus 97
left 155-156, 161-162, 185, 210, 217, 224-230, 238, 241, 252, 258, 270-271, 288-289, 297, 313
Levi, Eliphaz 22, 371-374, 384, 418
Liber 777 23, 372-374, 377, 381, 399
Libra 15, 24, 30, 34, 88, 96-112, 373, 377, 399, 406-407, 466-467, 477
Loaves see Shav'uot
life and death 17, 33
light 84, 97, 137, 163, 166, 171, 191, 206, 210, 224-230, 260, 262, 269, 294, 344, 402
Leo 15, 24, 26, 30, 34, 75-81, 373, 377, 399-400, 467, 477
Logos 37-38, 199, 203, 205, 386
Lollio and Imperiali 484
love affairs 26, 50, 75, 400
Luke 40, 67, 111, 128, 131, 132, 133, 137, 139, 141, 247, 257, 296, 310, 317, 319, 323, 365, 446-450

M

Malkuth (Kingdom) 155-156, 161, 164ff., 202, 217, 224-230, 233, 255, 263, 280, 302, 306-310, 313-318, 319-326, 328-333, 364-365, 368-370, 373, 422, 426, 429
Marheshvan see Heshvan

Mary 45-46, 97, 184, 215, 220, 267, 274, 321-322, 369-370, 414, 426
Mark 43, 65, 68, 105, 111, 128, 131-133, 137, 139, 247, 274, 303-304, 309-310, 316-317, 325, 365, 430, 446-451
Marseilles Tarot 374ff., 483ff.
Mars 15, 17, 21, 24, 32, 54-55, 107, 109, 123-124, 165-166, 172, 290-291, 296, 356, 372-373, 418, 463, 470, 478
Matthew 40, 43, 65-68, 105, 111, 120, 128-133, 137, 139, 141, 155, 176, 274, 309-310, 316-317, 323-325, 365, 428, 429, 446-450
Menahem see Av
mem 15, 24, 88-89, 103-106, 124, 177, 181, 269-274, 291, 338, 341-344, 373, 375, 408
Mercury 15, 21, 24, 32, 37-44, 85-86, 165-166, 172, 199, 272, 313, 320, 372, 385-386, 404, 427, 465, 468, 475
merkarbah 297, 315-316, 396
Messiah 39, 151, 234
middle pillar 156, 161, 212, 280
Midrash Rabbah 339
Minhah or Afternoon Prayer 55
Moon 15, 17, 21, 24, 32, 45-46, 48, 165-166, 172, 373, 387, 422, 466, 475
monogenes 197-198
months 15, 17, 24, 34, 72, 89-90, 103, 123-124, 138, 290, 375, 441, 455-462
Moriah 52-54
Moses 31, 78, 169, 254, 256, 393, 440
Mother ('*Imma*) 45, 48-49, 159, 174-176, 184, 186, 213, 215, 220, 224-227, 233, 332, 388, 389, 475, 477

mother letters 16-18, 88-89, 103, 123-124, 138, 176, 250, 290-291, 343, 381, 434
Mount of Olives 256

N

nakedness 303, 316-317, 330
Nati or *Filii* Offspring see fifth house
nefesh 162, 174
neshmah 174
Nehunia ben HaQana 14, 146, 439
Nezah 32, 49-50, 155, 162, 164ff., 226, 241, 247-248, 264-265, 276-278, 281, 293-298, 300-304, 306-310, 316, 356-360, 361-362, 364-365, 373
New Year's Day 53, 72, 83, 88-95, 98, 241-242, 250-251, 290, 404-405
New Year for Trees 421
Nikodemos 49-50, 224-225, 227, 315
Nimrod 338, 351-354, 357-358, 416-417, 418, 434
ninth house 34, 114-118, 282, 340, 348-349, 413, 471
Nisan 15, 19, 24, 52-57, 89, 139, 234, 391, 455-456
Noah 338, 341-344, 347, 348, 349, 351-353, 408
notariqon 151
nun 15, 24, 34, 89, 107-110, 177, 181, 276-278, 291, 298, 338, 343, 346-347, 373, 377, 434

O

Oedipus Aegyptiacus 21-22, 166, 177, 179ff., 372
old age 142, 227, 480
omissions from According to John 40, 42-43, 65-68, 105, 111, 120,

128-133, 137, 139, 141, 155, 176, 247, 257, 274, 296, 303-304, 309-310, 316-317, 319, 323-325, 365, 428-430, 446-450
Origen 8, 203

P

Papus 372, 374, 389
Pan 121-122
Paraclete 115-116, 219, 282-283
Parzuf 174-176, 184, 186, 193, 199, 224, 233, 242, 263, 323, 329, 443
Passover or Pesah 31, 52-57, 72, 89, 138-139, 251, 422, 456
peace and strife 17, 33
Pehad see Gevurah
Pentecost see Loaves
peh 15, 16, 21, 24, 123-124, 177, 181, 291, 293-298, 338, 356-360, 372, 373, 418
personification representing correspondences of two consecutive chapters 129-130, 289-291, 434
Peter
Pillars of Tree 156, 185, 216-218, 237, 241-242, 251-252
Pirqe Rabbi Eliezer 109, 339
Pisces 15, 24, 30, 31, 34, 127-133, 340, 364-365, 373, 377, 422, 473-474, 479
Piscina, Francesco 486-487
planets 31-32, 164-166,
pneuma 174, 227, 234, 248, 266, 278
Pontius Pilate 128-129, 134, 272, 290-291, 308, 314, 316, 434
Power 155, 301-302, 304, 309-310
prayer 55, 73, 84, 98, 124, 125, 132, 147, 155, 168, 267, 301, 302, 309, 342, 359, 365

prophecy 100, 169, 281, 295, 310, 362, 364-365, 366
Purim 130-133, 138-139, 250, 290, 462
psyche 92, 164, 168

Q

Qidron 128, 423
quf 15, 24, 34, 124, 127-133, 138, 177, 181, 291, 306-310, 338, 365, 373, 377, 422

R

raging 17, 34, 120, 354
Rahamim see Tif'areth
razon 168, 198
Regnum or Government see tenth house
resh 15, 16, 19, 21, 24, 124, 134-139, 177, 181, 291, 313-318, 338, 366-367
Resurrection 99, 267, 319-325, 331, 426-428
Revelation of John 337, 389, 391, 400, 424
right 155-156, 160-162, 166, 185, 217, 224-230, 237-238, 241-242, 258, 265, 270, 295, 297, 306, 310
ruah 174, 227, 234, 248, 266, 278
Ruler of the World 119, 288-289, 352

S

Saadia Gaon 18ff., 133
Sabbath of the Birds 421
Sadducee 101
Sagittarius 15, 24, 30, 34, 94, 114-118, 133, 340, 348-349, 373 377, 413-414, 471, 479
Samael 109, 172, 257, 272, 278, 288, 291, 296, 342, 346-347, 411

Samuel 32, 49-50, 169, 315
samekh 15, 24 , 34, 114-118, 177, 181, 280-284, 298, 338, 348-349, 373, 377, 413
Sapientia see ninth house
Saturn 15, 17, 21, 24, 32, 142-143, 165-166, 172, 227, 331, 373, 471-472, 479
Scholem, Gershom 16, 149, 185, 194
Scorpio 15, 24, 30, 34, 107-111, 340, 346-347, 373, 377, 411, 470, 478
second commandment 170, 241
second house 29, 34, 59-62, 392, 465
seeing 17, 34
Sefer Yezirah 12ff., 339-340
sefiroth 13, 152ff.
selihot 84, 459
Septuagint 56, 139, 191, 215-216, 271, 273, 278, 343, 352
seven conditions of being 17, 33
seventh house 34, 96-97, 406, 469
seventy nations 354
Shav'uot 25, 63-67, 72, 247-248, 251, 457
Shekhinah 174-175, 186, 199, 213, 215, 220, 227, 263, 273, 283-284, 306-308, 309, 323, 325, 329-332, 388, 415, 429, 460
Shevat 15, 24, 34, 124, 125-126, 361-363, 420-421, 462
shin 15, 19, 24, 140-141, 177, 181, 267, 319-326, 338, 368-370, 373, 426-427
simple letters 16-17, 19, 34, 61, 79, 88-89, 103, 123-124, 138, 176, 290, 375-377
Sivan 15, 24 -25, 34, 63-68, 457
Sixth Day 96, 171, 303
sixth house 34, 76, 82-87, 402, 468
slavery 55, 120, 183, 36, 351-353

sleeping 17, 34-35, 101, 132-133, 338, 340, 364-365, 474
smelling 17, 34
sorrow 271, 288, 294-295
speaking 17, 34, 57
snares 290, 352, 417
Son 175-176, 186, 213, 215, 225-227, 229, 242,
Stephanus 81, 210, 257
stoicheion, stoicheia 14, 16
Sukkoth 72-74, 88-89, 103-106, 242, 250-254, 270-271, 342-343, 396-397, 460
Sun 15, 17, 19, 21, 24 , 27-28, 32, 77, 129, 134-139, 165-166, 308, 373, 424 467, 477
Sychar 50

T

Tabernacles see Sukkoth
Tarot 371ff., 482-488
Targum 109, 147, 202, 339, 343-344, 357
Talmud 13, 14, 73, 91, 98-101, 105, 109, 123, 124, 147,149, 214, 243, 248, 296, 339, 342, 395, 459-460
Tammuz 15, 24, 34, 69-74, 396,458
tasting 17, 34
Taurus 15, 24, 29, 34, 59-62, 238, 263, 373, 377, 464
tau 15, 16, 19, 21, 24, 142-143, 177, 181, 328-333, 373, 429
temurah 151
tenth house 34, 119-122, 340, 351-352, 416, 472
Terah 12, 353
teshuvah 200, 324, 332
teth 15, 24, 34, 75-81, 167, 177, 181, 183, 255-260, 373, 377, 399

Teveth 15, 24, 34, 119-122, 124, 351-354, 416, 461
Theophilus 203
thieves 43, 86-87, 184, 272, 313-314, 320-321, 385, 408-409, 428, 476
thinking 17, 34, 61-62
Third Day 171, 184, 213
Third House 34, 63-68, 466
Thirteen Measures 213-215
Torah 65, 116-118, 151-152, 169, 192, 202, 214-215, 243, 246, 278, 281-284, 349, 352, 397
Tif'areth 32, 161, 164ff., 212-219, 224-230, 232-236, 237-244, 247-248, 262-263, 266-267, 280-284, 288-291, 348-349, 351-354, 373
Tishri 15, 24, 34, 53, 83, 88-89, 90, 96-102, 103, 124, 138, 459-460
Tree of Life 152ff.
truth 77, 115-117, 136, 161, 168, 184, 233, 259, 280-281, 314, 425
twelve basic activities 17, 19, 33-35, 61, 79
twelfth house 34, 127-133, 340, 364-365, 422-423, 474
Trumpets, Feast of see New Year's Day

U

Unleavened Bread, Feast of 55-56, 456
Utterance 154, 186-187, 199, 207

V

vau 15, 24, 34, 59-62, 167, 175, 177, 181, 183, 237-244, 373, 377, 392
Venus 15, 17, 21, 24, 32, 42, 48-50, 60, 165, 166, 295, 373, 389, 464, 469, 476-477

vidui or *hodah* 32, 85-86, 168, 271-272, 314
Virgo 15, 24, 30, 34, 39, 82-87, 263, 373, 377, 402-403, 468, 475
Voice 91-92, 186-187, 199, 207, 229, 240-241

W

Waite, A. E. 176, 374, 377-382, 384, 387-388, 389, 394, 399, 424
water 15-19, 24, 46, 71-73, 103, 107-110, 129, 158, 161, 203-204, 214-215, 232, 263, 271, 341-344, 373
Wave or Lifted Offering 55-56, 456
walking 17, 34, 67
Westcott, Wynn 20-22
wealth and poverty 17, 33
wine 139, 214-218, 317, 351-352, 414
wisdom and folly 17, 33
womb 204, 225
world 200, 226, 331-333, 354, 373, 459
Worlds, Four 156, 160, 162, 173-175
working 17, 34, 83-84, 265

Y

Yesod 32, 163, 164ff., 255-260, 280-284, 298, 300-304, 310, 313-318, 328-333, 348-349, 360-361, 366-367, 373
yod 15, 24, 34, 76, 82-87, 89, 167, 175, 177, 181, 183, 262-263, 373, 377
Yom Kippur 31, 83, 88, 89-90, 96-102, 131, 267, 407, 459
Yom Teru'ah see New Year's Day

Z

zaddi 15, 24, 34, 124, 125-126, 177, 181, 300-304, 338, 361-362, 373, 377, 420

zayin 15, 24, 34, 63-68, 167, 177, 181, 183, 247-248, 373, 377

Zeus see Jupiter

ziruf 151

zodiac 15-20, 24, 29, 31, 35, 41, 463-474

Zohar 13, 145ff.

www.ingramcontent.com/pod-product-compliance
Lightning Source LLC
Chambersburg PA
CBHW071114080526
44587CB00013B/1335